Amazing Agent Jennifer

VOLUME 1

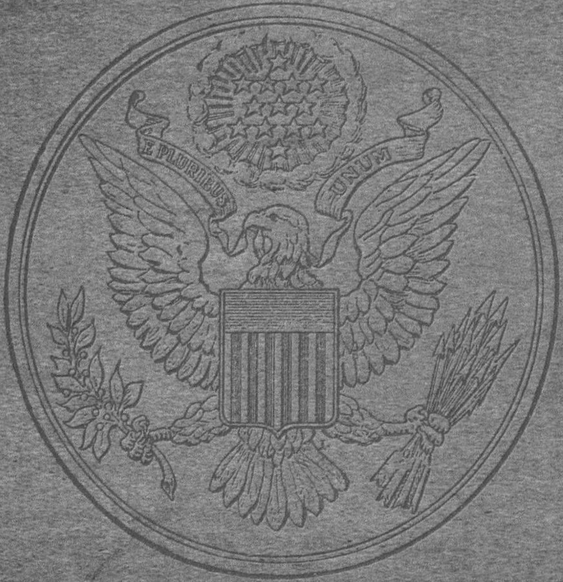
E PLURIBUS UNUM

art by
Kriss Sison

story by
nzio DeFilippis
Christina Weir

Amazing Agent JENNIFER

VOLUME 1

art by **Kriss Sison**

story by **Nunzio DeFilippis & Christina Weir**

STAFF CREDITS

lettering	**Nicky Lim**
toning	**Groundbreakers Studios**
layout	**Adam Arnold**
design	**Nicky Lim**
copy editor	**Shanti Whitesides**
editor	**Adam Arnold**
publisher	**Jason DeAngelis** **Seven Seas Entertainment**

ISBN: 978-1-934876-85-5

Printed in Canada

First Printing: August 2011

10 9 8 7 6 5 4 3 2 1

FOLLOW US ONLINE: **www.gomanga.com**

READING DIRECTIONS

This book reads from *right to left*, Japanese style. If this is your first time reading manga, you start reading from the top right panel on each page and take it from there. If you get lost, just follow the numbered diagram here. It may seem backwards at first, but you'll get the hang of it! Have fun!!

Amazing Agent Jennifer

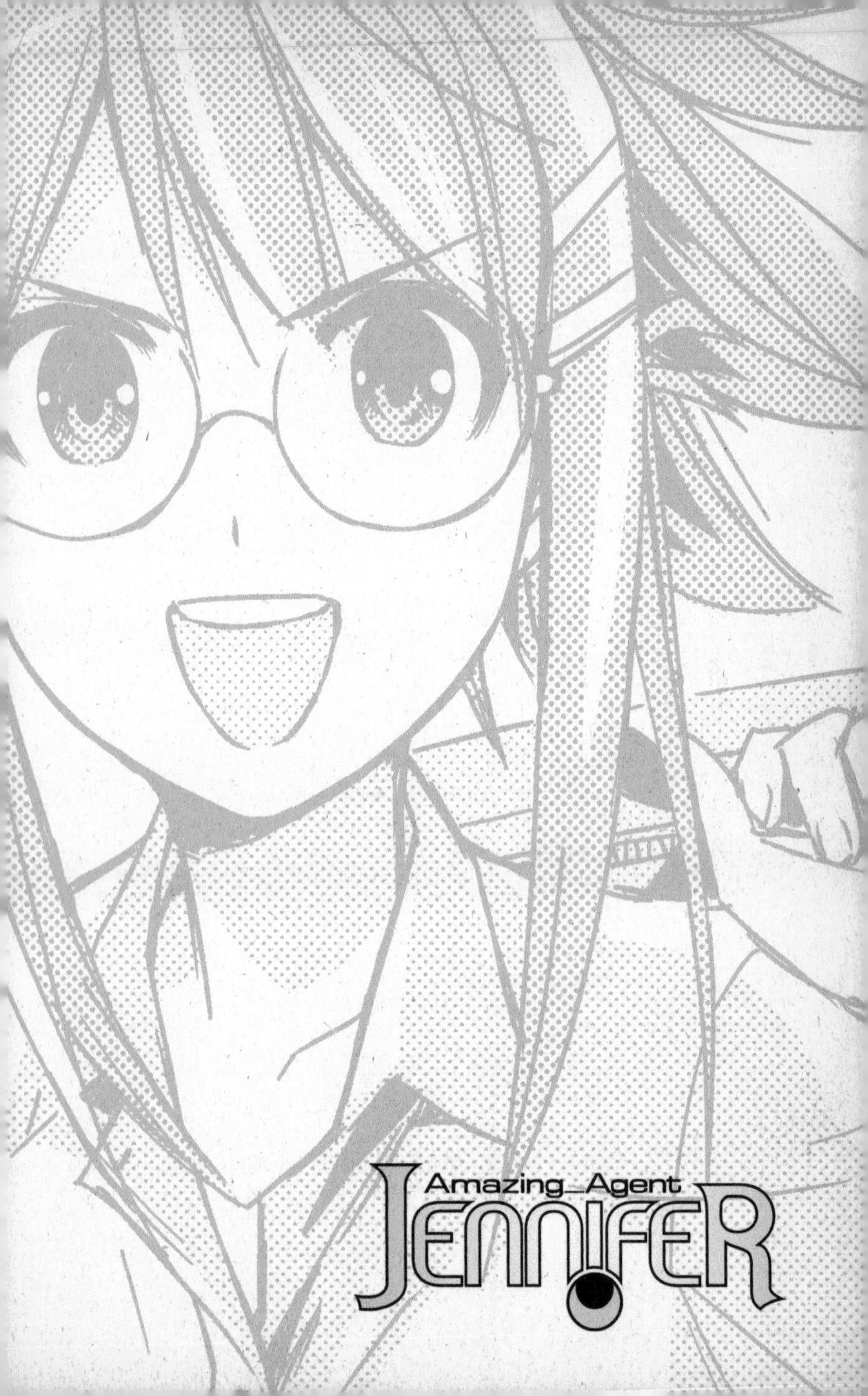
Amazing Agent
JENNIFER

FILE 1:
MISUNDERESTIMATED

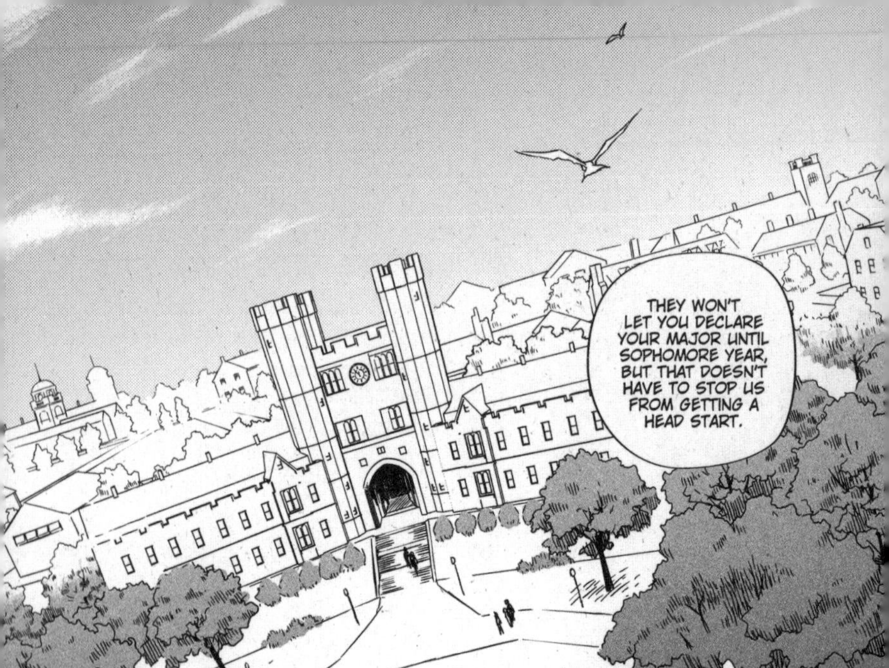
THEY WON'T LET YOU DECLARE YOUR MAJOR UNTIL SOPHOMORE YEAR, BUT THAT DOESN'T HAVE TO STOP US FROM GETTING A HEAD START.
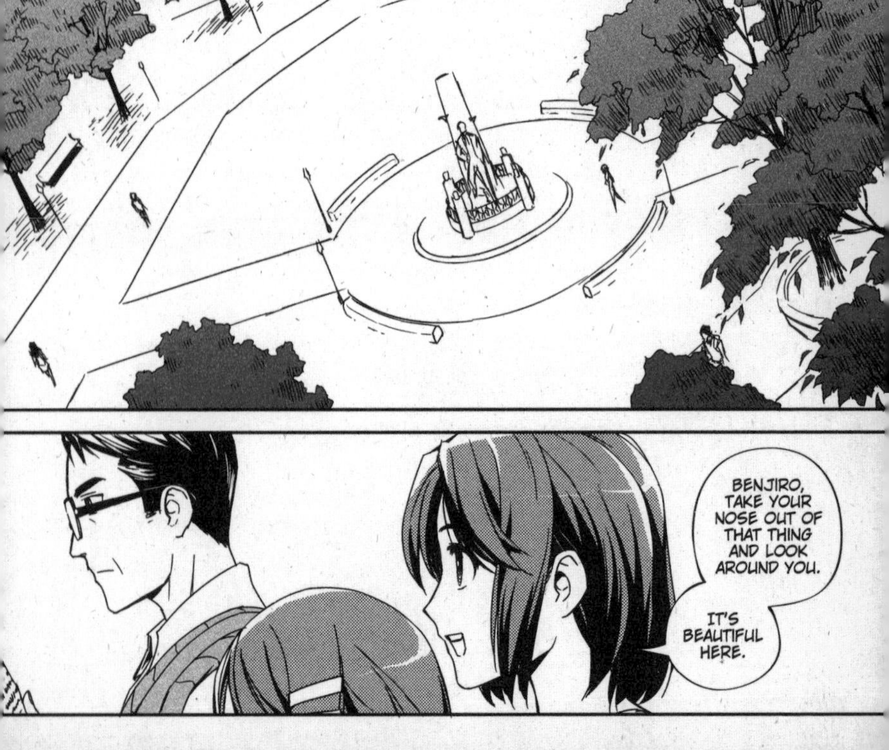
BENJIRO, TAKE YOUR NOSE OUT OF THAT THING AND LOOK AROUND YOU.
IT'S BEAUTIFUL HERE.

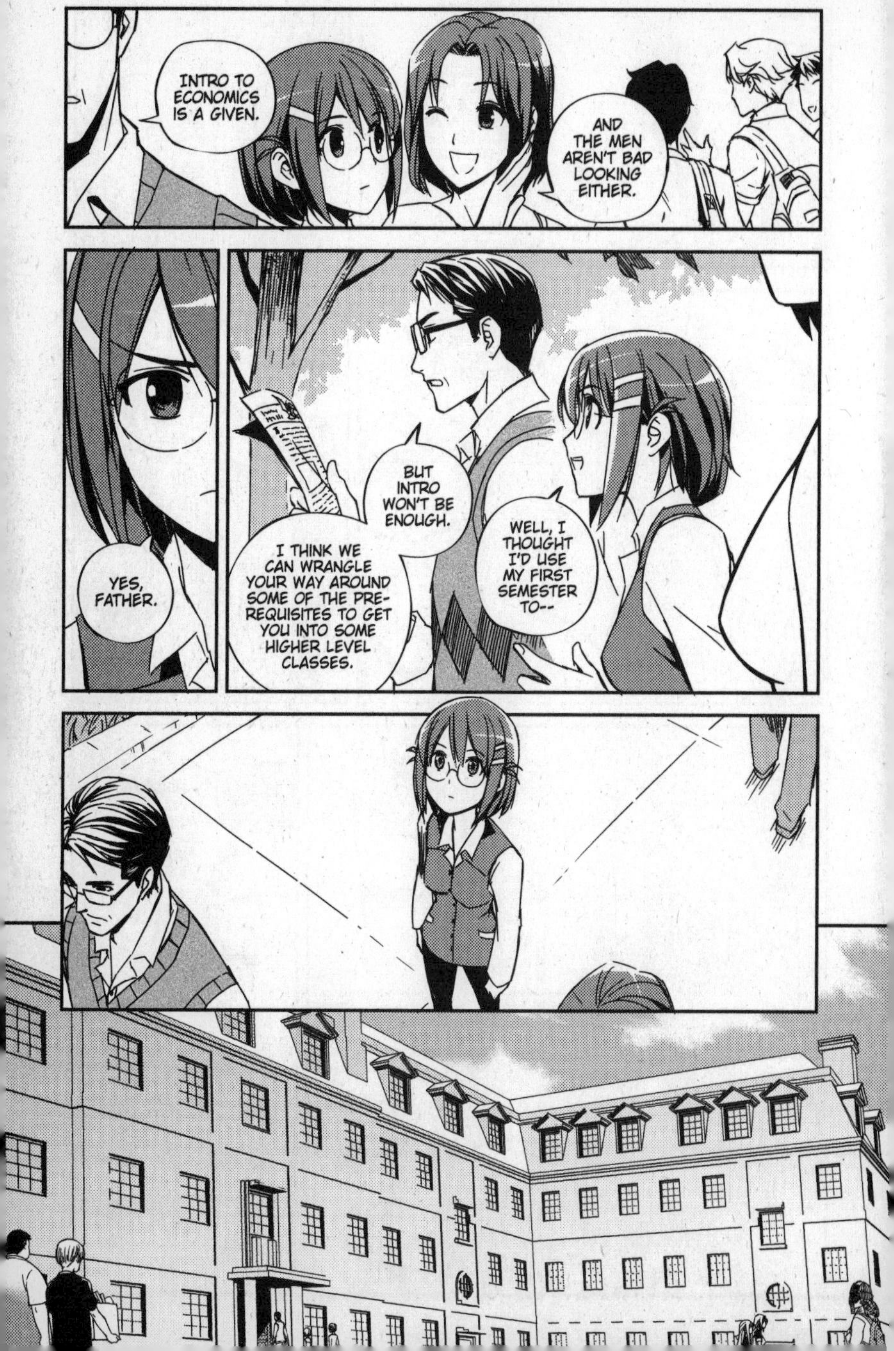
AND THE MEN AREN'T BAD LOOKING EITHER.
INTRO TO ECONOMICS IS A GIVEN.
WELL, I THOUGHT I'D USE MY FIRST SEMESTER TO--
BUT INTRO WON'T BE ENOUGH.
I THINK WE CAN WRANGLE YOUR WAY AROUND SOME OF THE PRE-REQUISITES TO GET YOU INTO SOME HIGHER LEVEL CLASSES.
YES, FATHER.

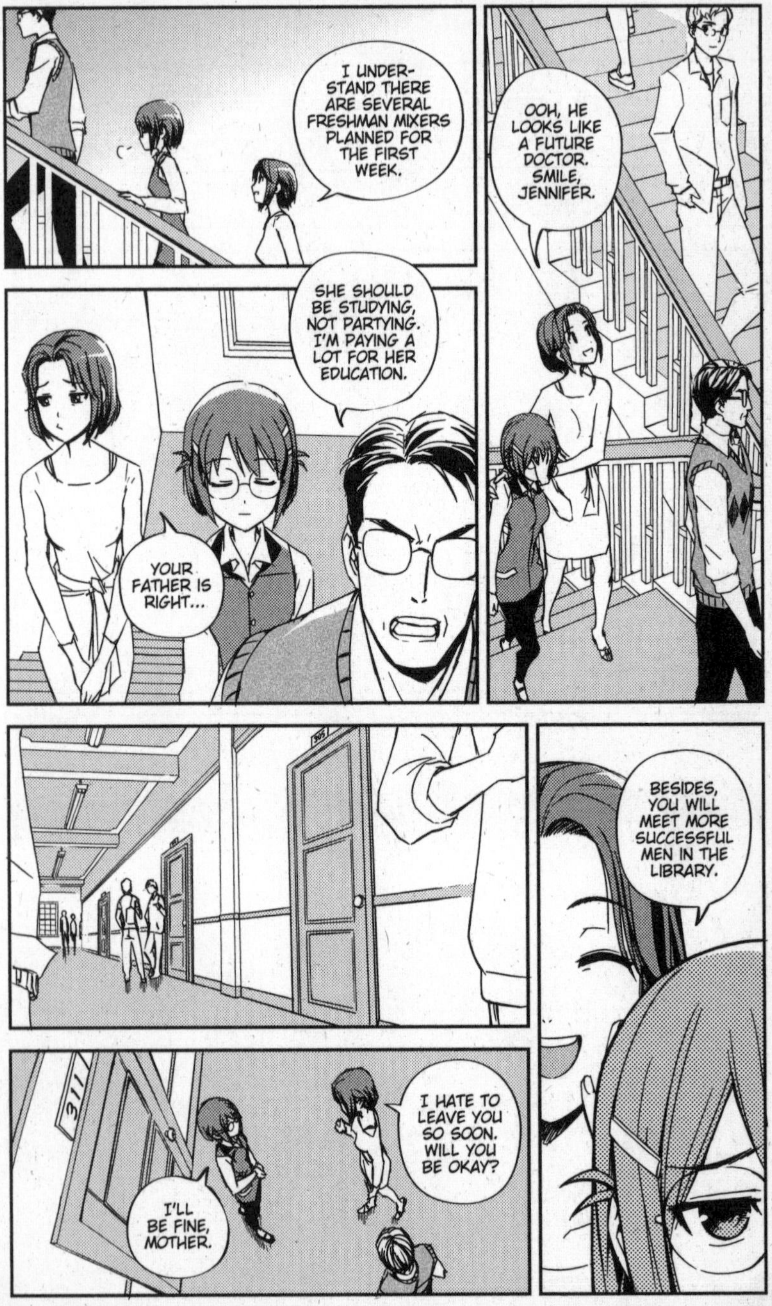
I UNDER-STAND THERE ARE SEVERAL FRESHMAN MIXERS PLANNED FOR THE FIRST WEEK.
SHE SHOULD BE STUDYING, NOT PARTYING. I'M PAYING A LOT FOR HER EDUCATION.
YOUR FATHER IS RIGHT...
OOH, HE LOOKS LIKE A FUTURE DOCTOR. SMILE, JENNIFER.
BESIDES, YOU WILL MEET MORE SUCCESSFUL MEN IN THE LIBRARY.
311
I HATE TO LEAVE YOU SO SOON. WILL YOU BE OKAY?
I'LL BE FINE, MOTHER.

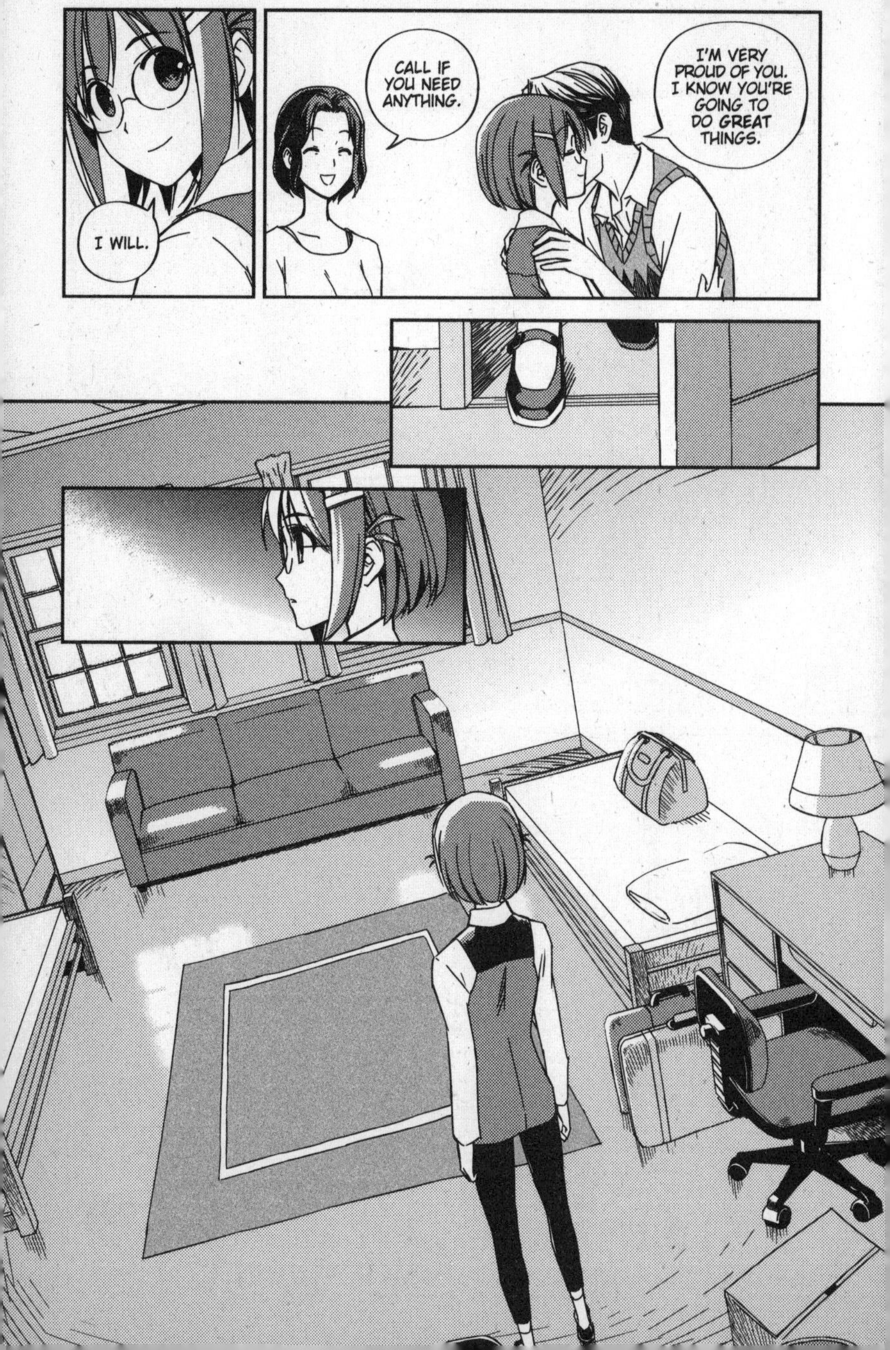
I'M VERY PROUD OF YOU. I KNOW YOU'RE GOING TO DO GREAT THINGS.
CALL IF YOU NEED ANYTHING.
I WILL.

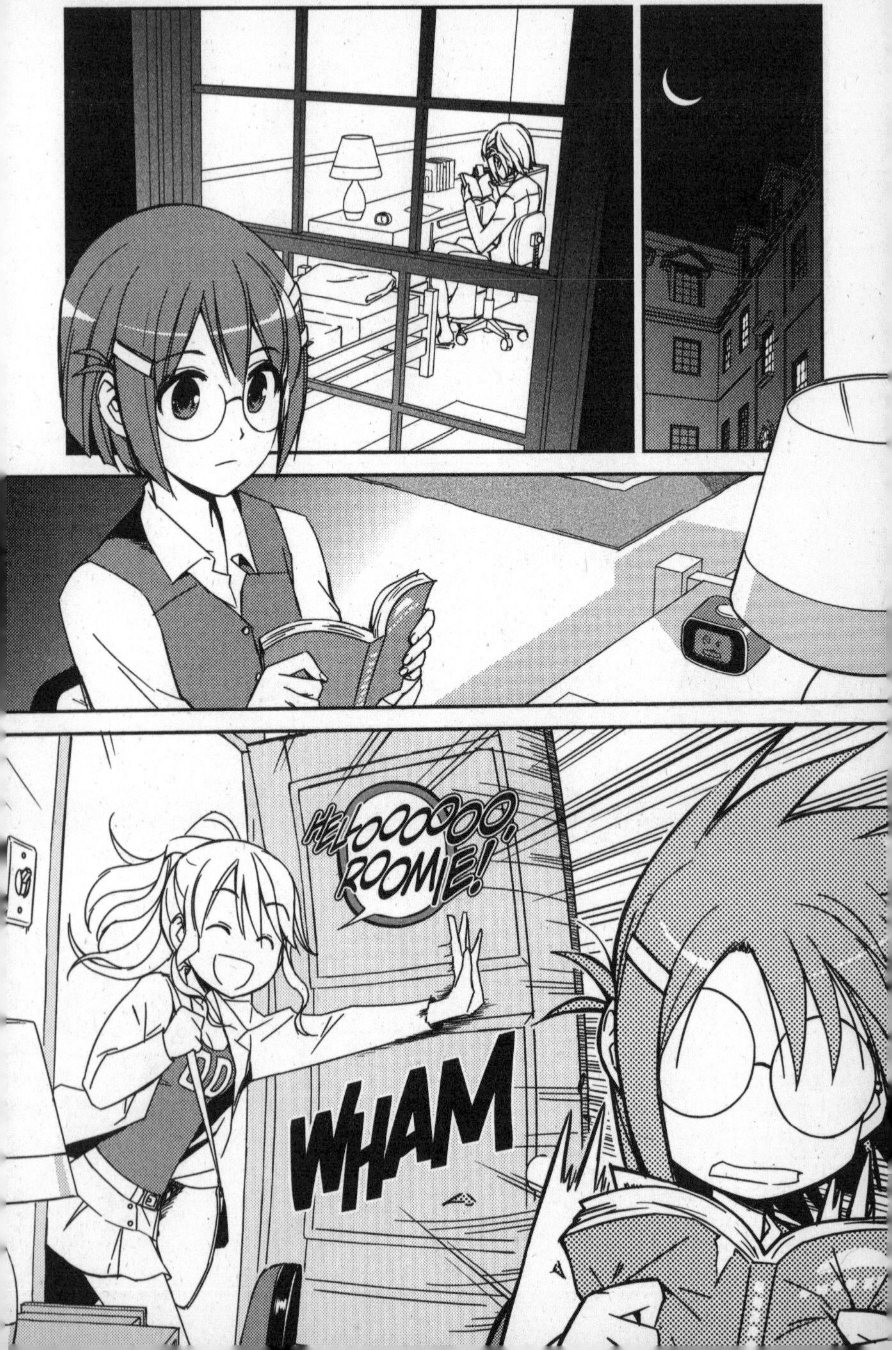
HELLOOOOOO, ROOMIE!
WHAM

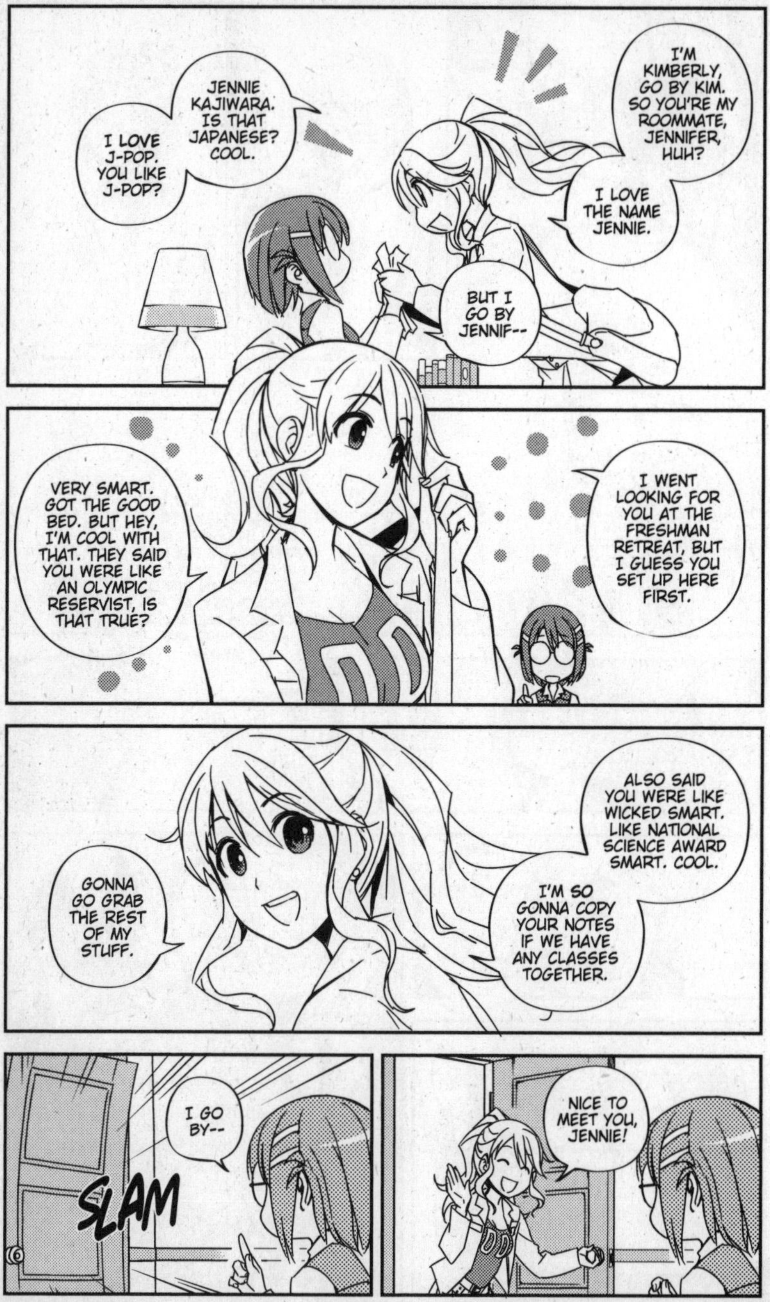

I'M KIMBERLY, GO BY KIM. SO YOU'RE MY ROOMMATE, JENNIFER, HUH?
I LOVE THE NAME JENNIE.
BUT I GO BY JENNIF--
JENNIE KAJIWARA. IS THAT JAPANESE? COOL.
I LOVE J-POP. YOU LIKE J-POP?
I WENT LOOKING FOR YOU AT THE FRESHMAN RETREAT, BUT I GUESS YOU SET UP HERE FIRST.
VERY SMART. GOT THE GOOD BED. BUT HEY, I'M COOL WITH THAT. THEY SAID YOU WERE LIKE AN OLYMPIC RESERVIST, IS THAT TRUE?
ALSO SAID YOU WERE LIKE WICKED SMART. LIKE NATIONAL SCIENCE AWARD SMART. COOL.
I'M SO GONNA COPY YOUR NOTES IF WE HAVE ANY CLASSES TOGETHER.
GONNA GO GRAB THE REST OF MY STUFF.
NICE TO MEET YOU, JENNIE!
I GO BY--
SLAM

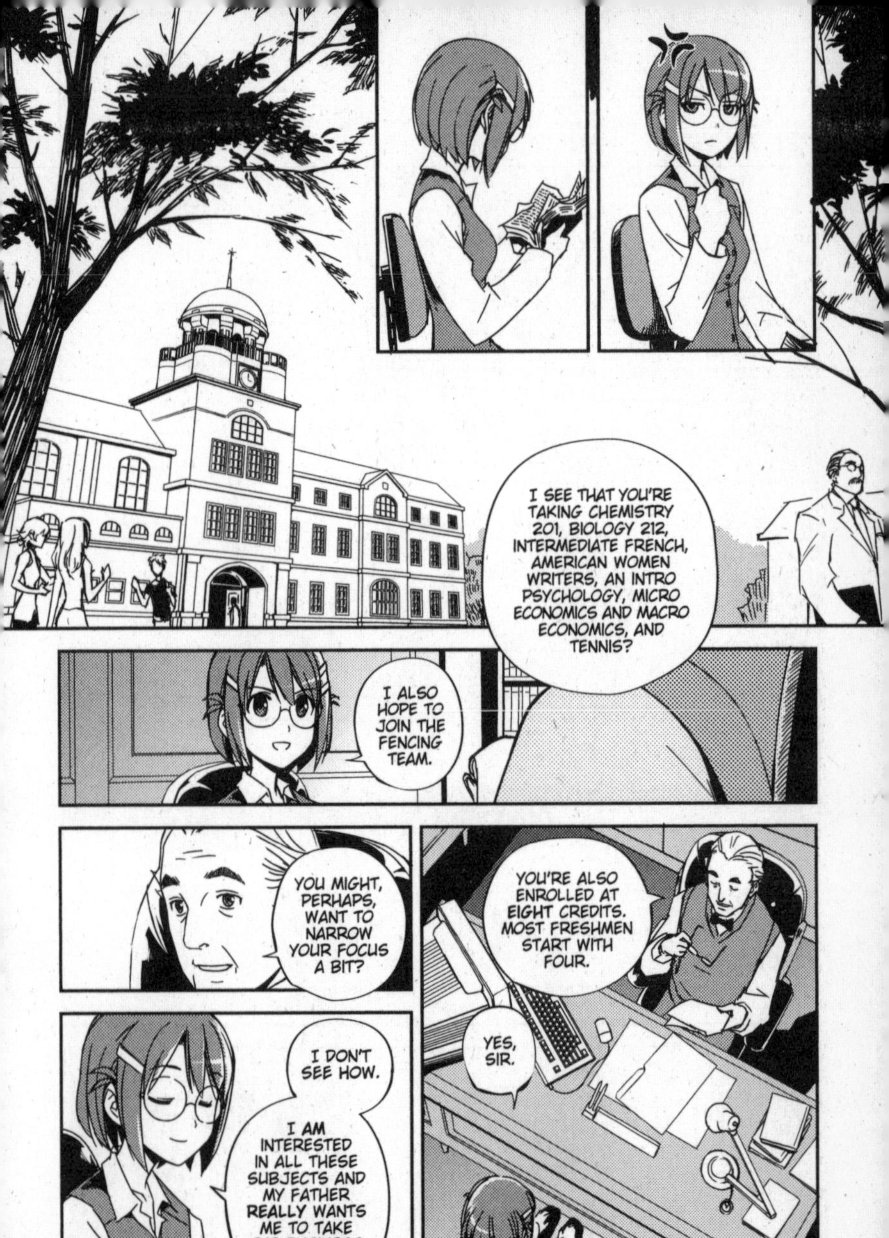
I SEE THAT YOU'RE TAKING CHEMISTRY 201, BIOLOGY 212, INTERMEDIATE FRENCH, AMERICAN WOMEN WRITERS, AN INTRO PSYCHOLOGY, MICRO ECONOMICS AND MACRO ECONOMICS, AND TENNIS?
I ALSO HOPE TO JOIN THE FENCING TEAM.
YOU'RE ALSO ENROLLED AT EIGHT CREDITS. MOST FRESHMEN START WITH FOUR.
YES, SIR.
YOU MIGHT, PERHAPS, WANT TO NARROW YOUR FOCUS A BIT?
I DON'T SEE HOW.
I AM INTERESTED IN ALL THESE SUBJECTS AND MY FATHER REALLY WANTS ME TO TAKE THE BUSINESS CLASSES.

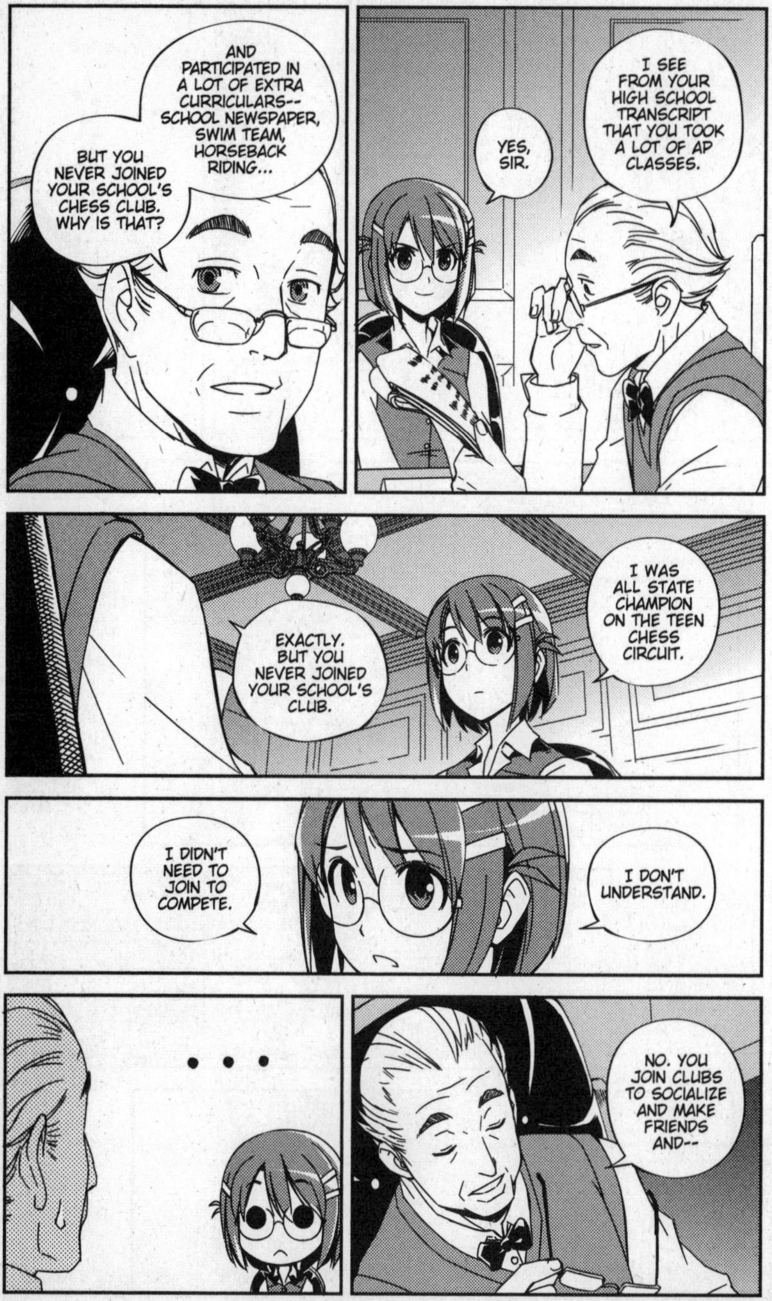
I SEE FROM YOUR HIGH SCHOOL TRANSCRIPT THAT YOU TOOK A LOT OF AP CLASSES.
YES, SIR.
AND PARTICIPATED IN A LOT OF EXTRA CURRICULARS-- SCHOOL NEWSPAPER, SWIM TEAM, HORSEBACK RIDING...
BUT YOU NEVER JOINED YOUR SCHOOL'S CHESS CLUB. WHY IS THAT?
I WAS ALL STATE CHAMPION ON THE TEEN CHESS CIRCUIT.
EXACTLY. BUT YOU NEVER JOINED YOUR SCHOOL'S CLUB.
I DON'T UNDERSTAND.
I DIDN'T NEED TO JOIN TO COMPETE.
NO. YOU JOIN CLUBS TO SOCIALIZE AND MAKE FRIENDS AND--
• • •

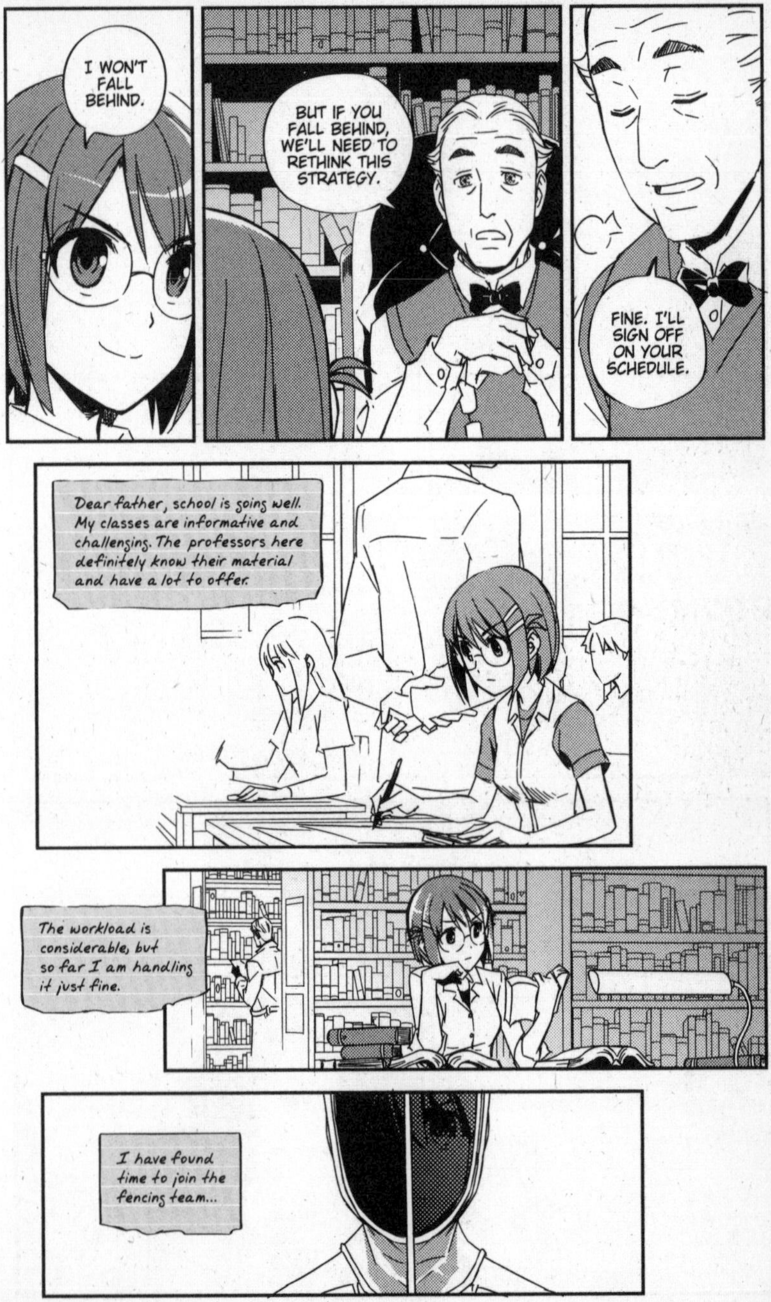
FINE. I'LL SIGN OFF ON YOUR SCHEDULE.
BUT IF YOU FALL BEHIND, WE'LL NEED TO RETHINK THIS STRATEGY.
I WON'T FALL BEHIND.
Dear father, school is going well. My classes are informative and challenging. The professors here definitely know their material and have a lot to offer.
The workload is considerable, but so far I am handling it just fine.
I have found time to join the fencing team...

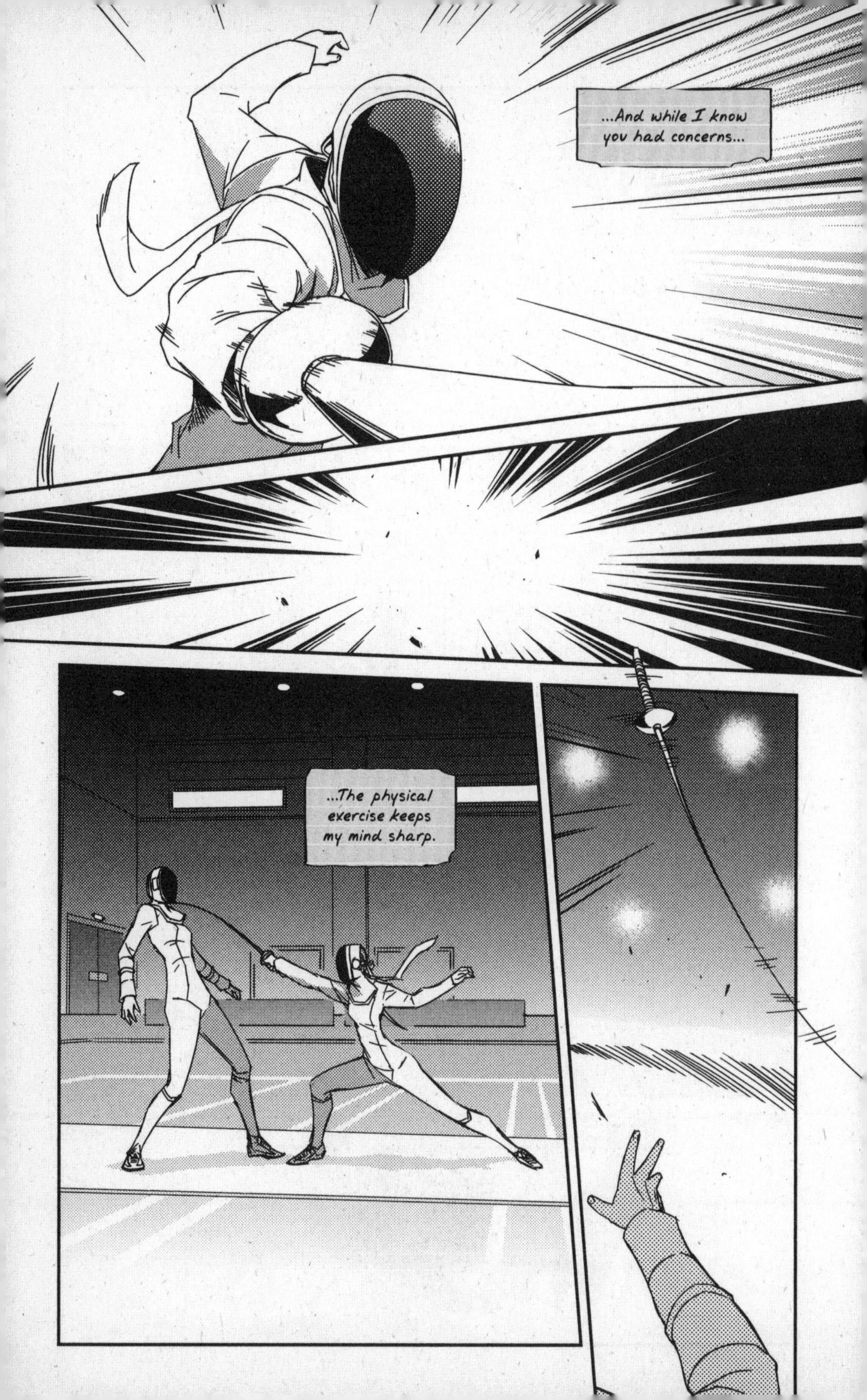
...And while I know you had concerns...
...The physical exercise keeps my mind sharp.

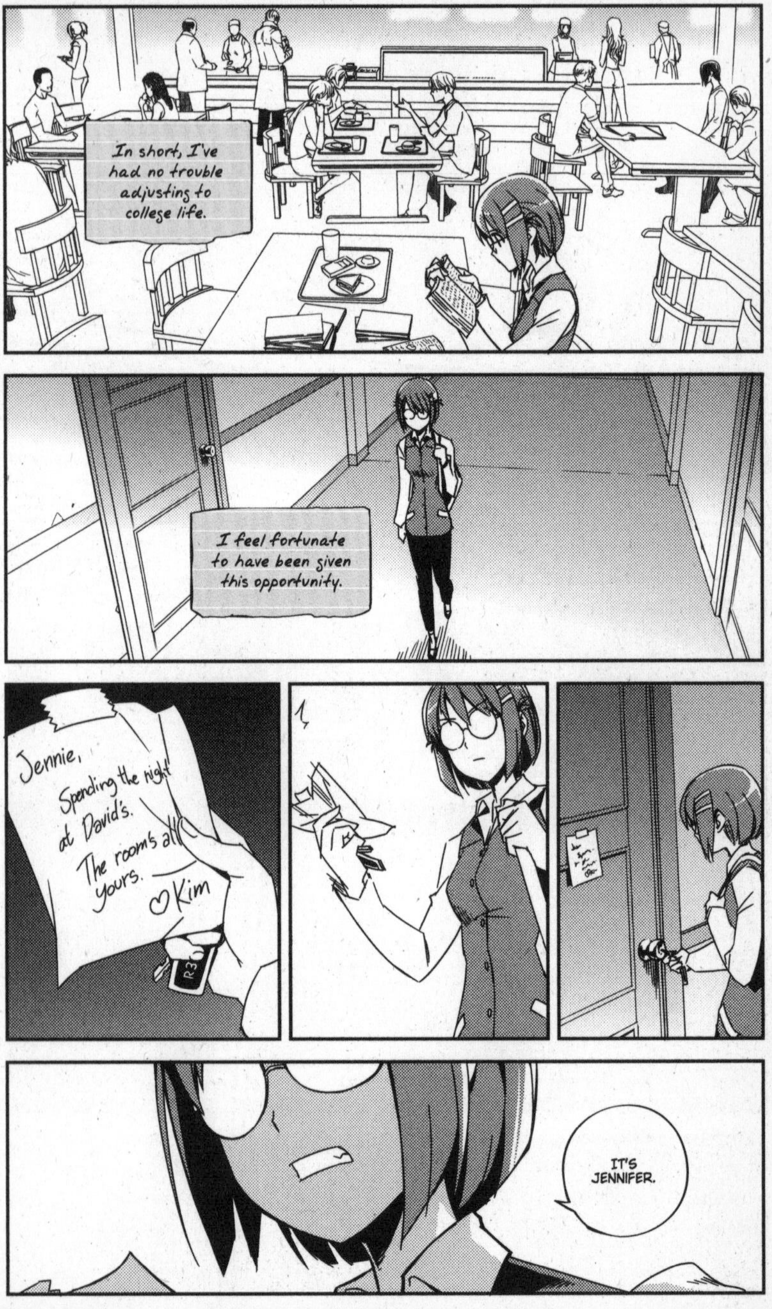
In short, I've had no trouble adjusting to college life.
I feel fortunate to have been given this opportunity.
Jennie, Spending the night at David's. The room's all yours. ♡Kim
IT'S JENNIFER.

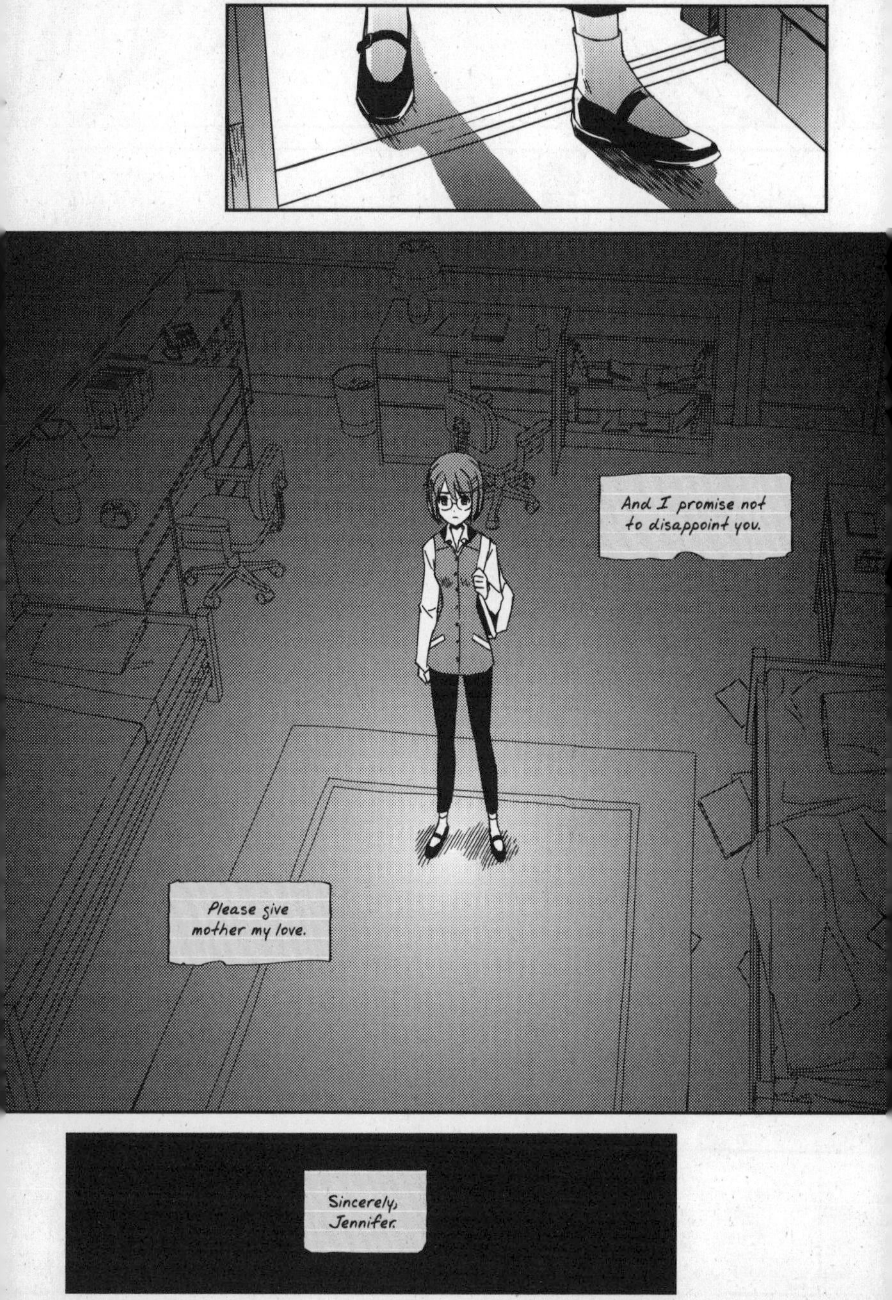
And I promise not to disappoint you.
Please give mother my love.
Sincerely, Jennifer.

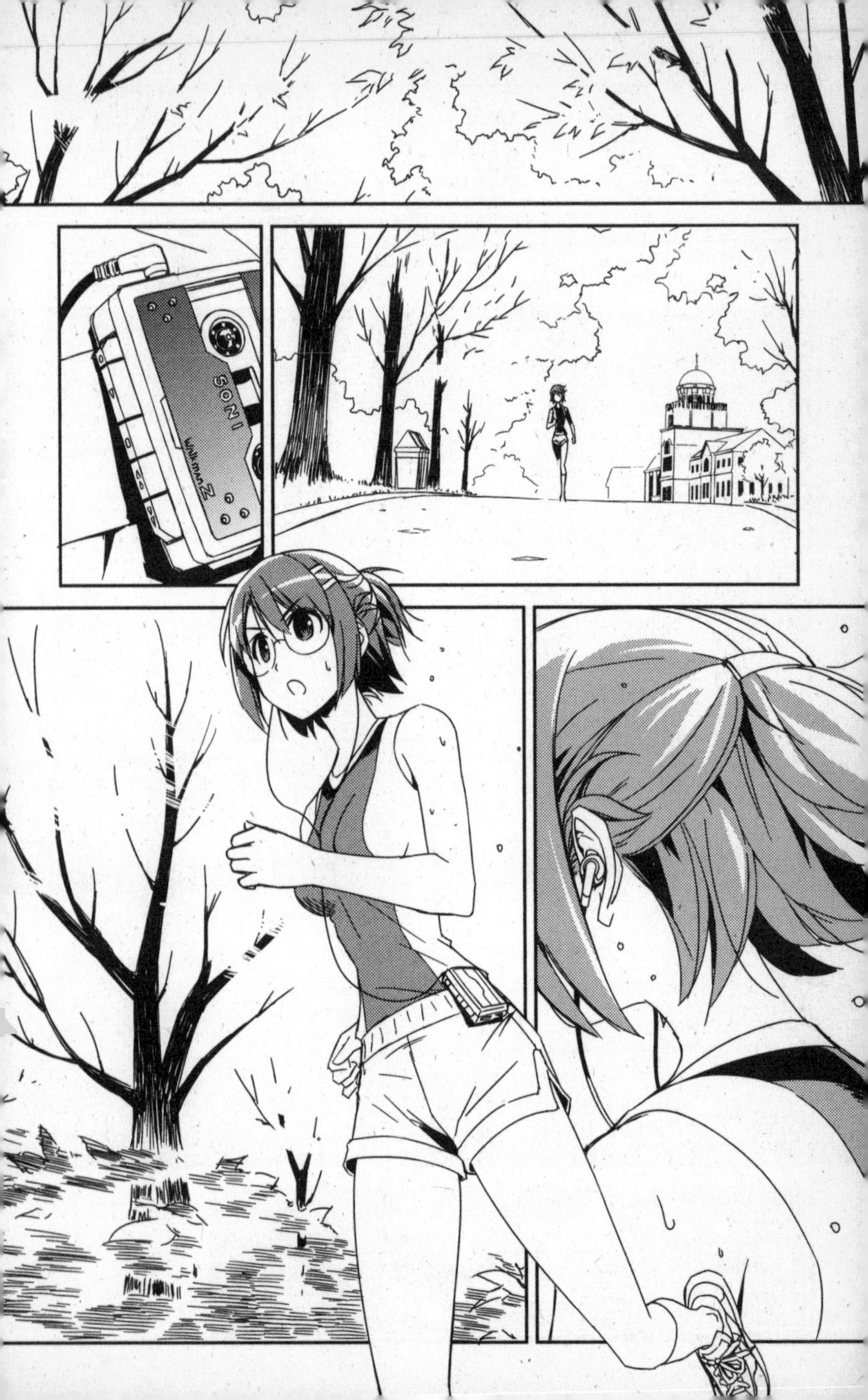
SONI
Walkman Z

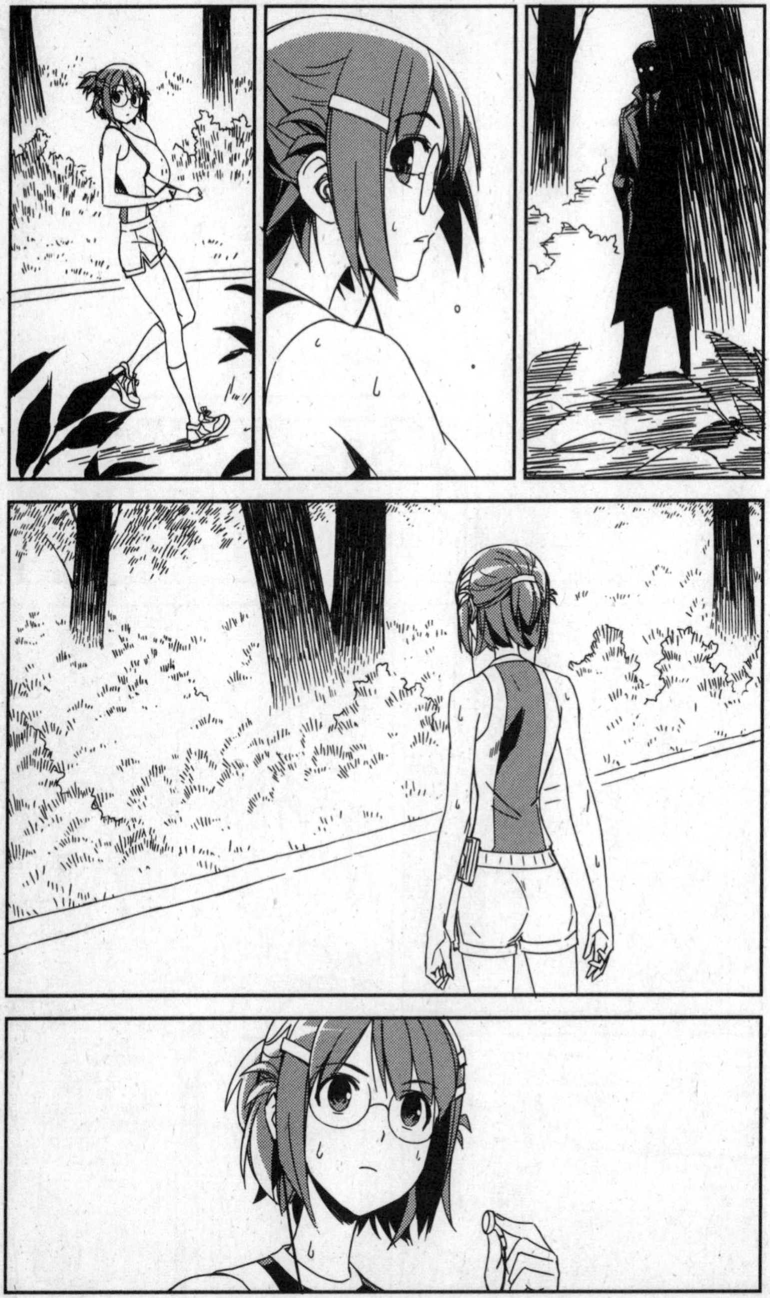

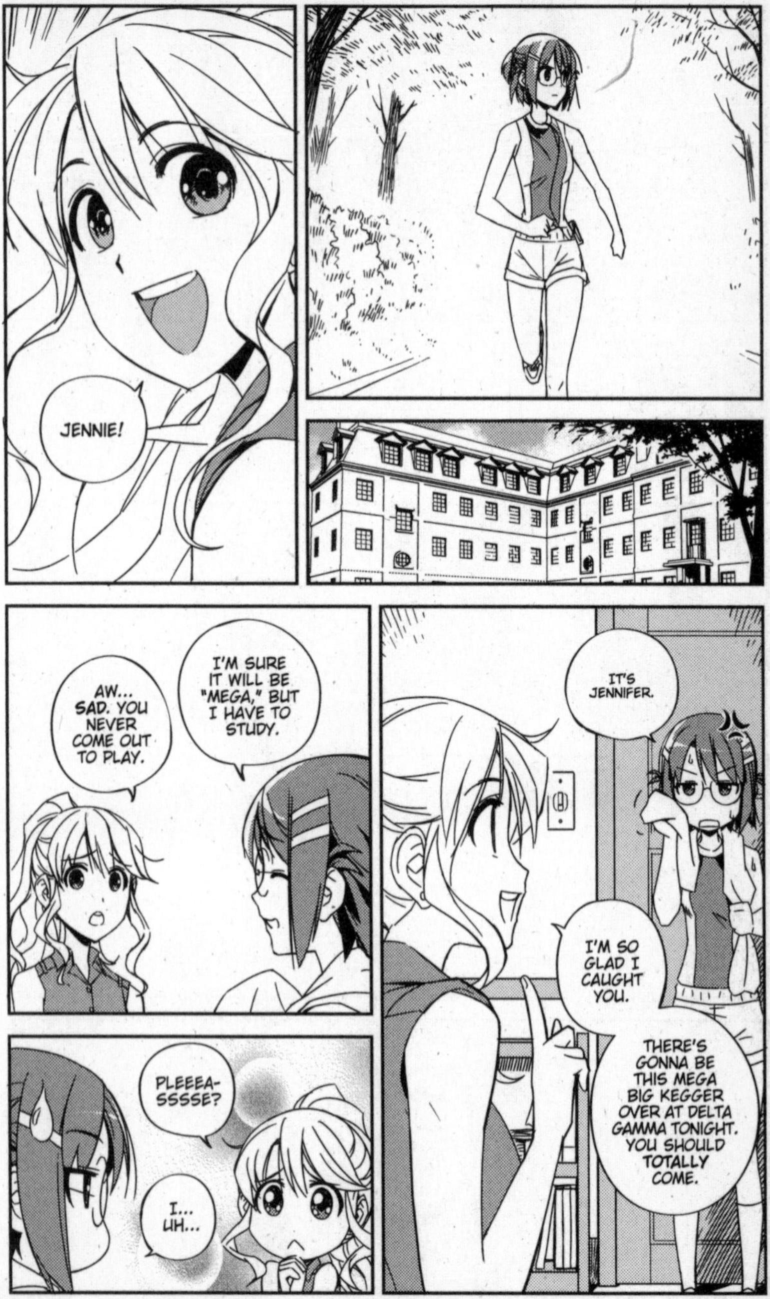
JENNIE!
IT'S JENNIFER.
I'M SO GLAD I CAUGHT YOU.
THERE'S GONNA BE THIS MEGA BIG KEGGER OVER AT DELTA GAMMA TONIGHT. YOU SHOULD TOTALLY COME.
I'M SURE IT WILL BE "MEGA," BUT I HAVE TO STUDY.
AW... SAD. YOU NEVER COME OUT TO PLAY.
PLEEEA-SSSSE?
I... UH...

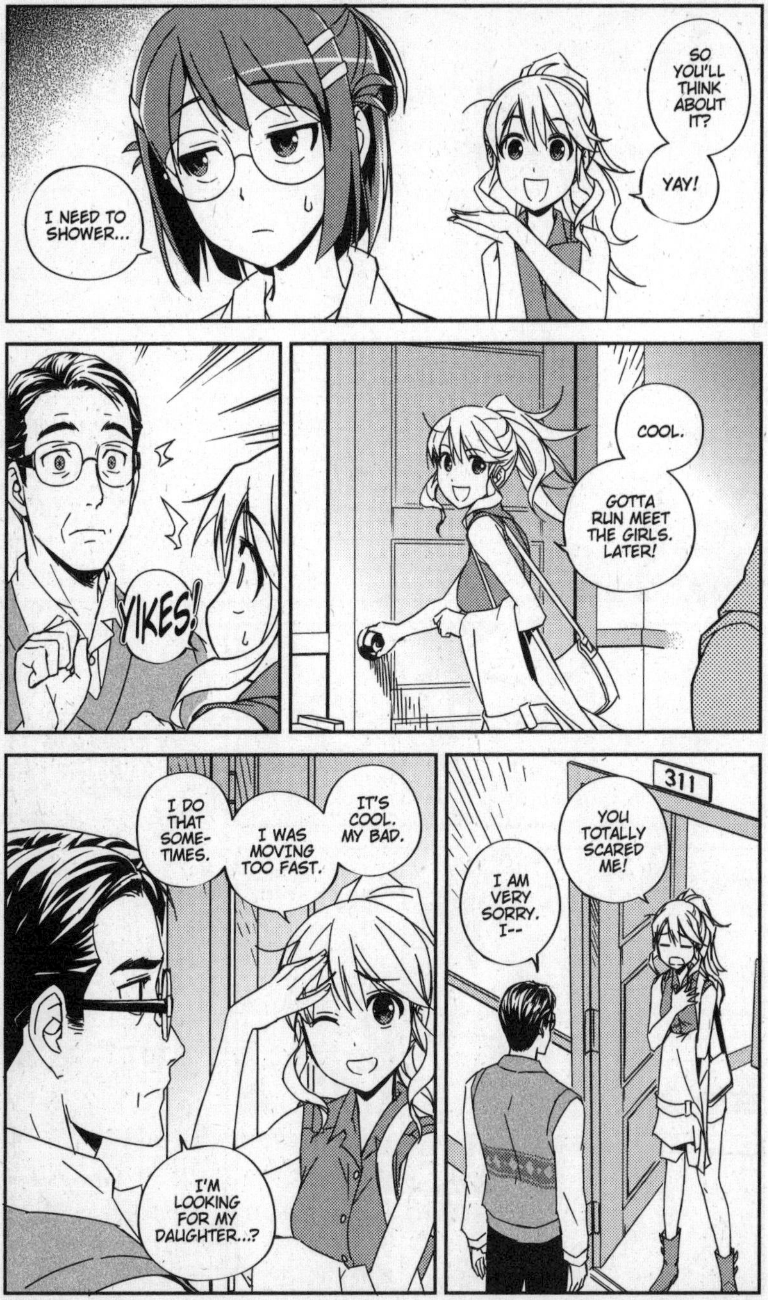
SO YOU'LL THINK ABOUT IT?
YAY!
I NEED TO SHOWER...
COOL.
GOTTA RUN MEET THE GIRLS. LATER!
YIKES!
YOU TOTALLY SCARED ME!
I AM VERY SORRY. I--
311
IT'S COOL. MY BAD.
I WAS MOVING TOO FAST.
I DO THAT SOME- TIMES.
I'M LOOKING FOR MY DAUGHTER...?

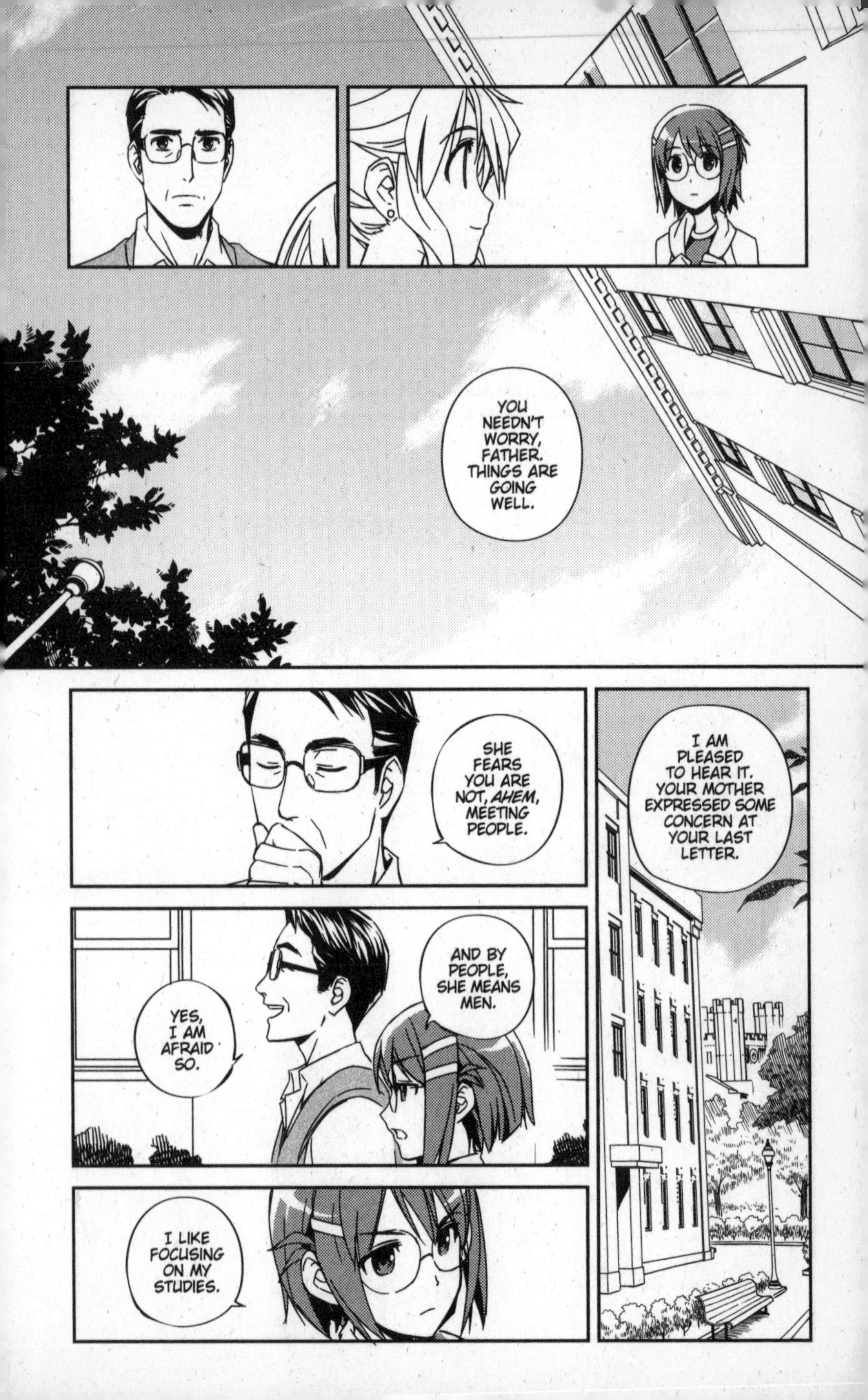
YOU NEEDN'T WORRY, FATHER. THINGS ARE GOING WELL.
I AM PLEASED TO HEAR IT. YOUR MOTHER EXPRESSED SOME CONCERN AT YOUR LAST LETTER.
SHE FEARS YOU ARE NOT, *AHEM*, MEETING PEOPLE.
AND BY PEOPLE, SHE MEANS MEN.
YES, I AM AFRAID SO.
I LIKE FOCUSING ON MY STUDIES.

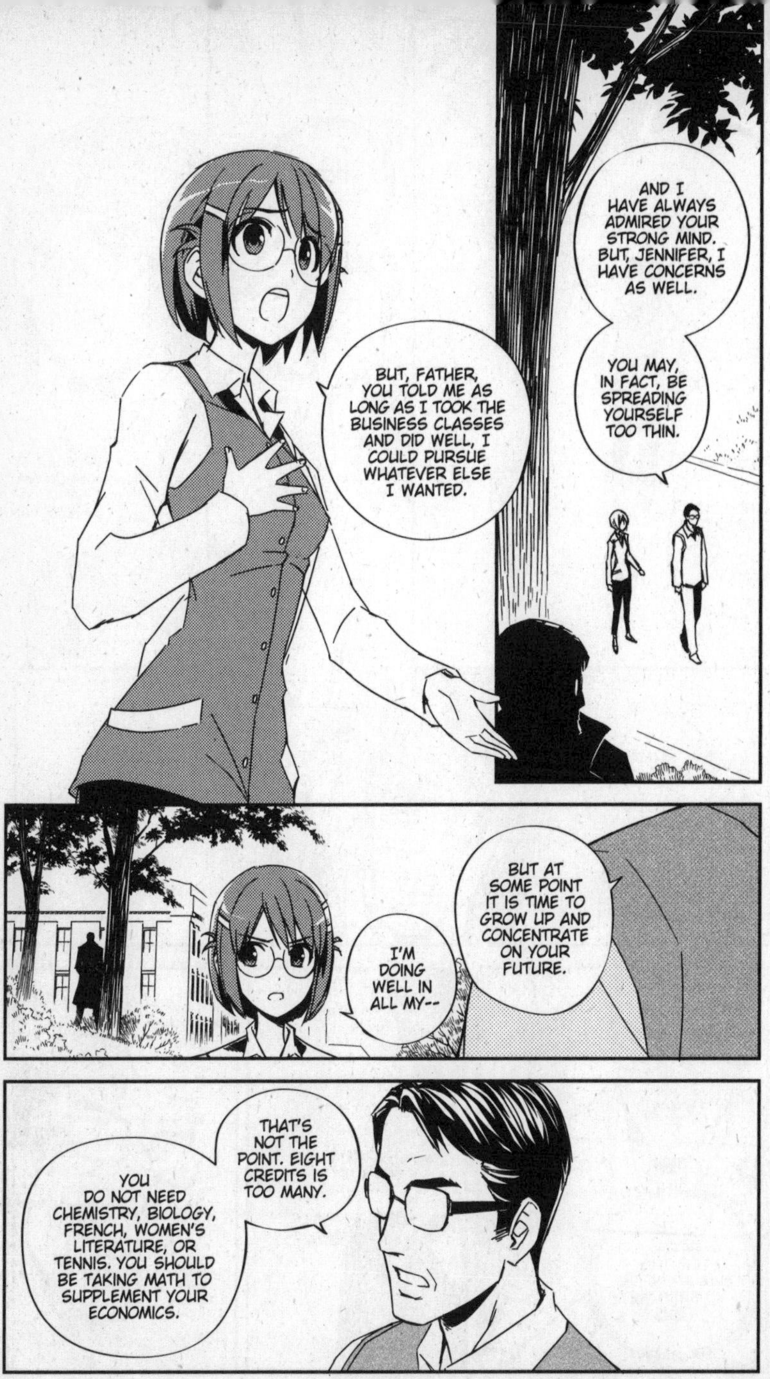
AND I HAVE ALWAYS ADMIRED YOUR STRONG MIND. BUT, JENNIFER, I HAVE CONCERNS AS WELL.
YOU MAY, IN FACT, BE SPREADING YOURSELF TOO THIN.
BUT, FATHER, YOU TOLD ME AS LONG AS I TOOK THE BUSINESS CLASSES AND DID WELL, I COULD PURSUE WHATEVER ELSE I WANTED.
BUT AT SOME POINT IT IS TIME TO GROW UP AND CONCENTRATE ON YOUR FUTURE.
I'M DOING WELL IN ALL MY--
THAT'S NOT THE POINT. EIGHT CREDITS IS TOO MANY.
YOU DO NOT NEED CHEMISTRY, BIOLOGY, FRENCH, WOMEN'S LITERATURE, OR TENNIS. YOU SHOULD BE TAKING MATH TO SUPPLEMENT YOUR ECONOMICS.

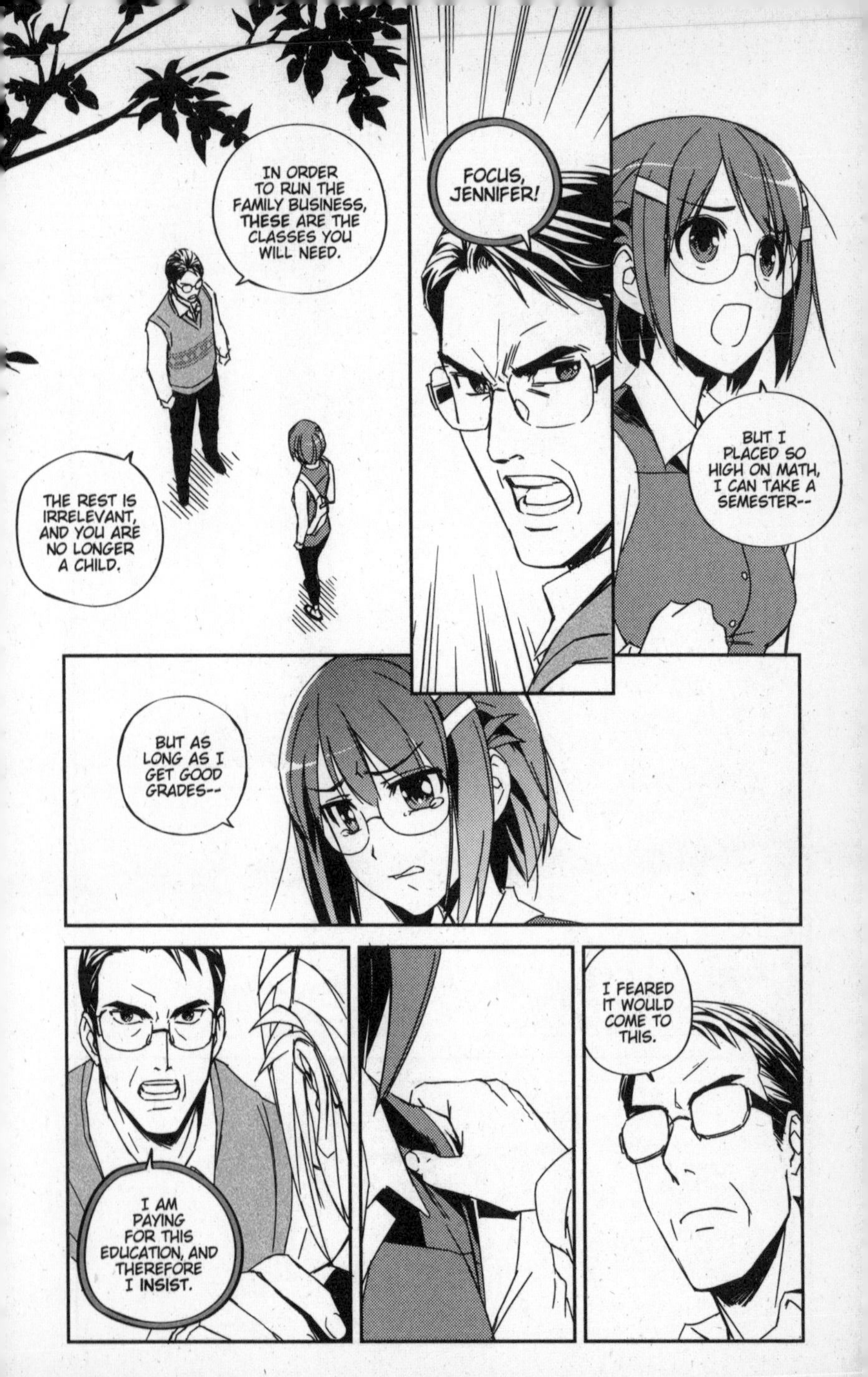
IN ORDER TO RUN THE FAMILY BUSINESS, THESE ARE THE CLASSES YOU WILL NEED.
THE REST IS IRRELEVANT, AND YOU ARE NO LONGER A CHILD.
FOCUS, JENNIFER!
BUT I PLACED SO HIGH ON MATH, I CAN TAKE A SEMESTER--
BUT AS LONG AS I GET GOOD GRADES--
I AM PAYING FOR THIS EDUCATION, AND THEREFORE I INSIST.
I FEARED IT WOULD COME TO THIS.

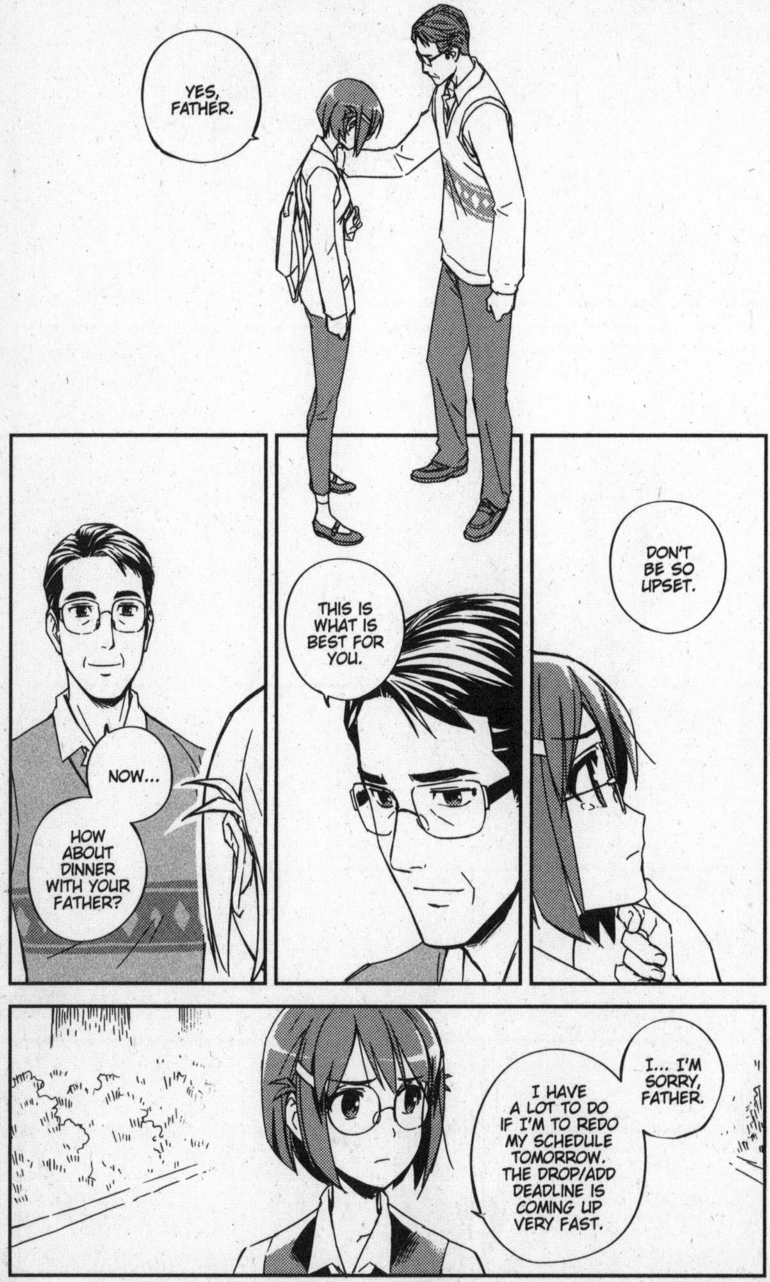
YES, FATHER.
DON'T BE SO UPSET.
THIS IS WHAT IS BEST FOR YOU.
NOW...
HOW ABOUT DINNER WITH YOUR FATHER?
I... I'M SORRY, FATHER.
I HAVE A LOT TO DO IF I'M TO REDO MY SCHEDULE TOMORROW. THE DROP/ADD DEADLINE IS COMING UP VERY FAST.

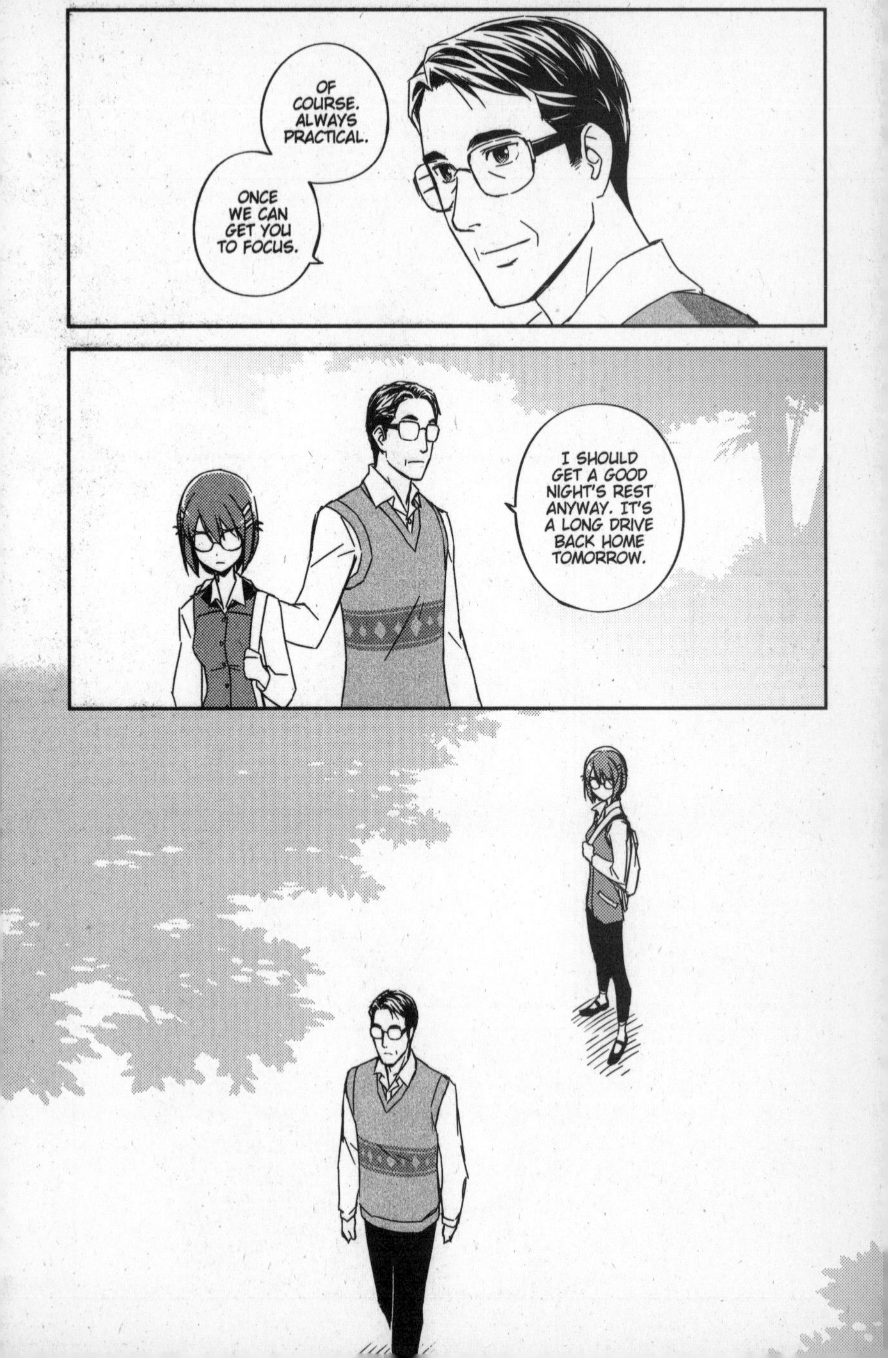
OF COURSE. ALWAYS PRACTICAL.
ONCE WE CAN GET YOU TO FOCUS.
I SHOULD GET A GOOD NIGHT'S REST ANYWAY. IT'S A LONG DRIVE BACK HOME TOMORROW.

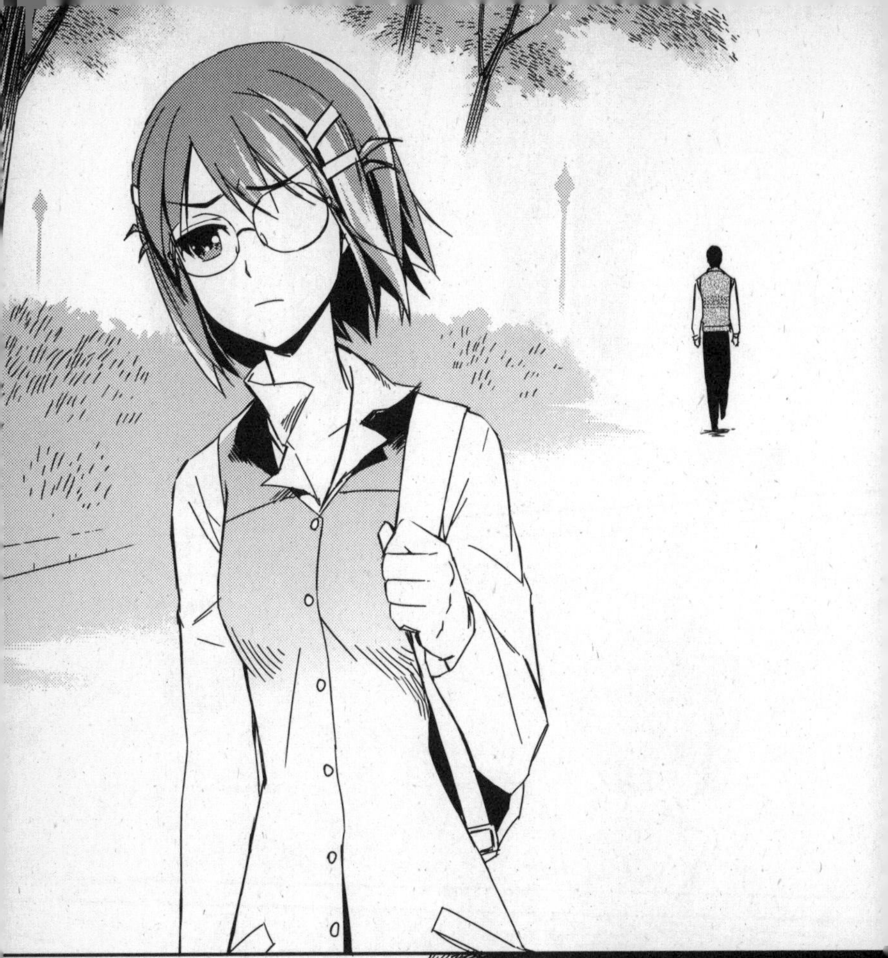
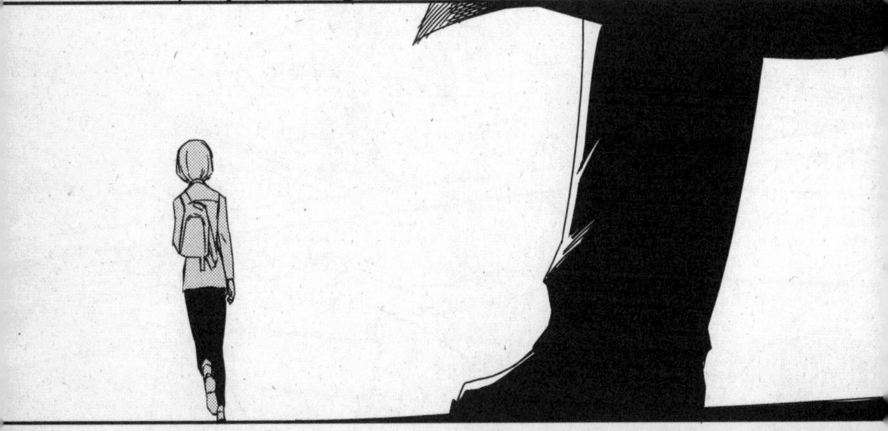

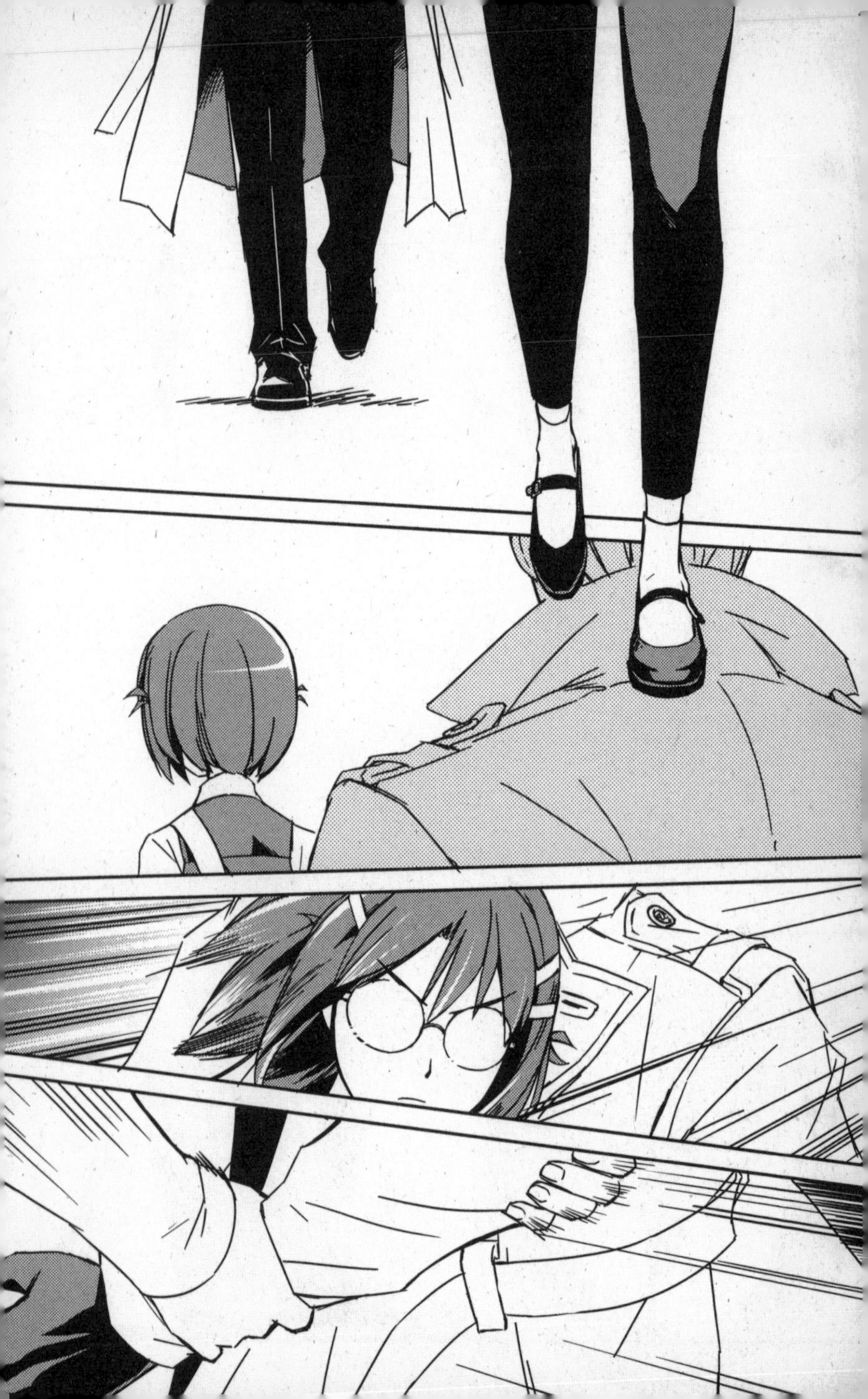

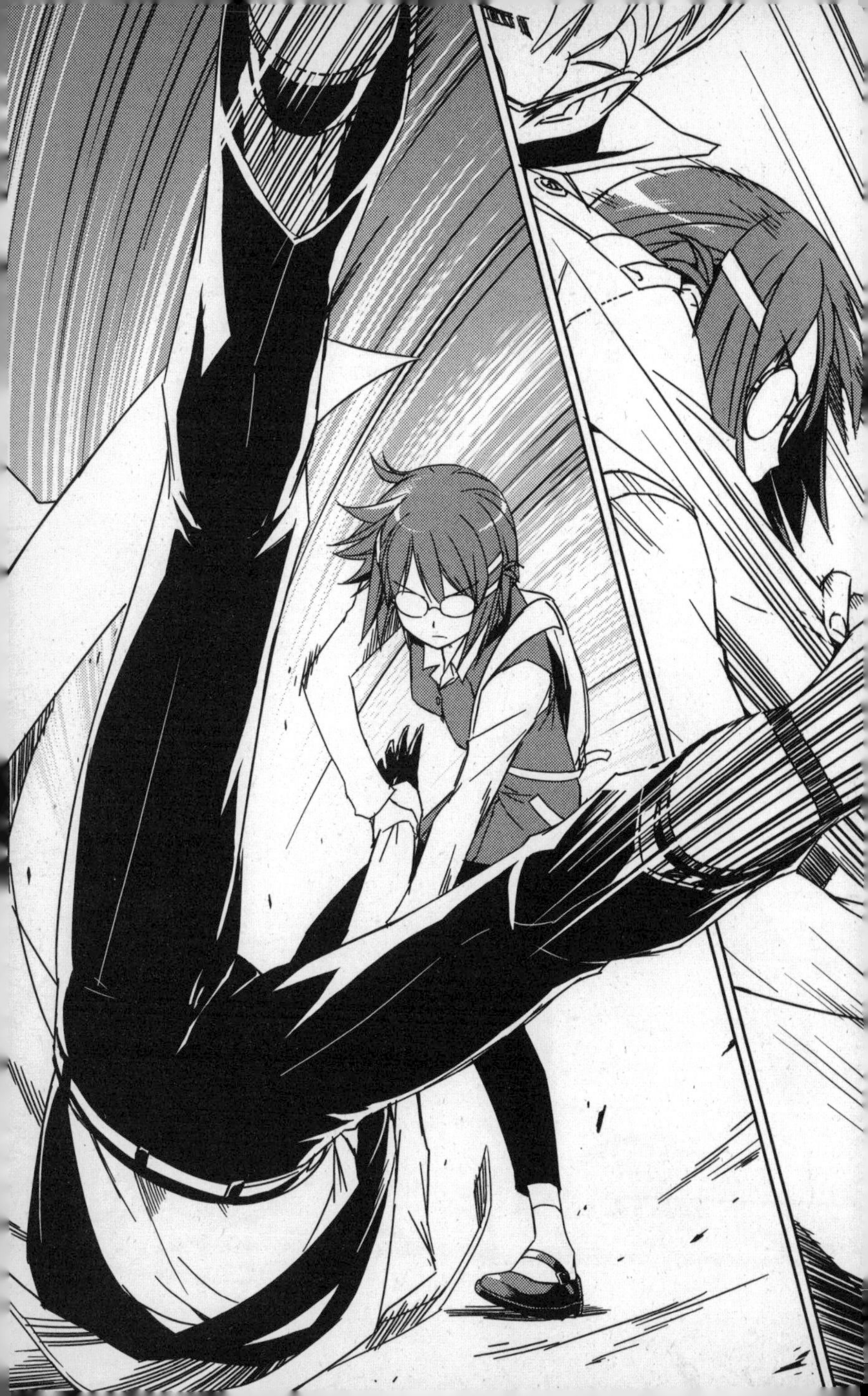

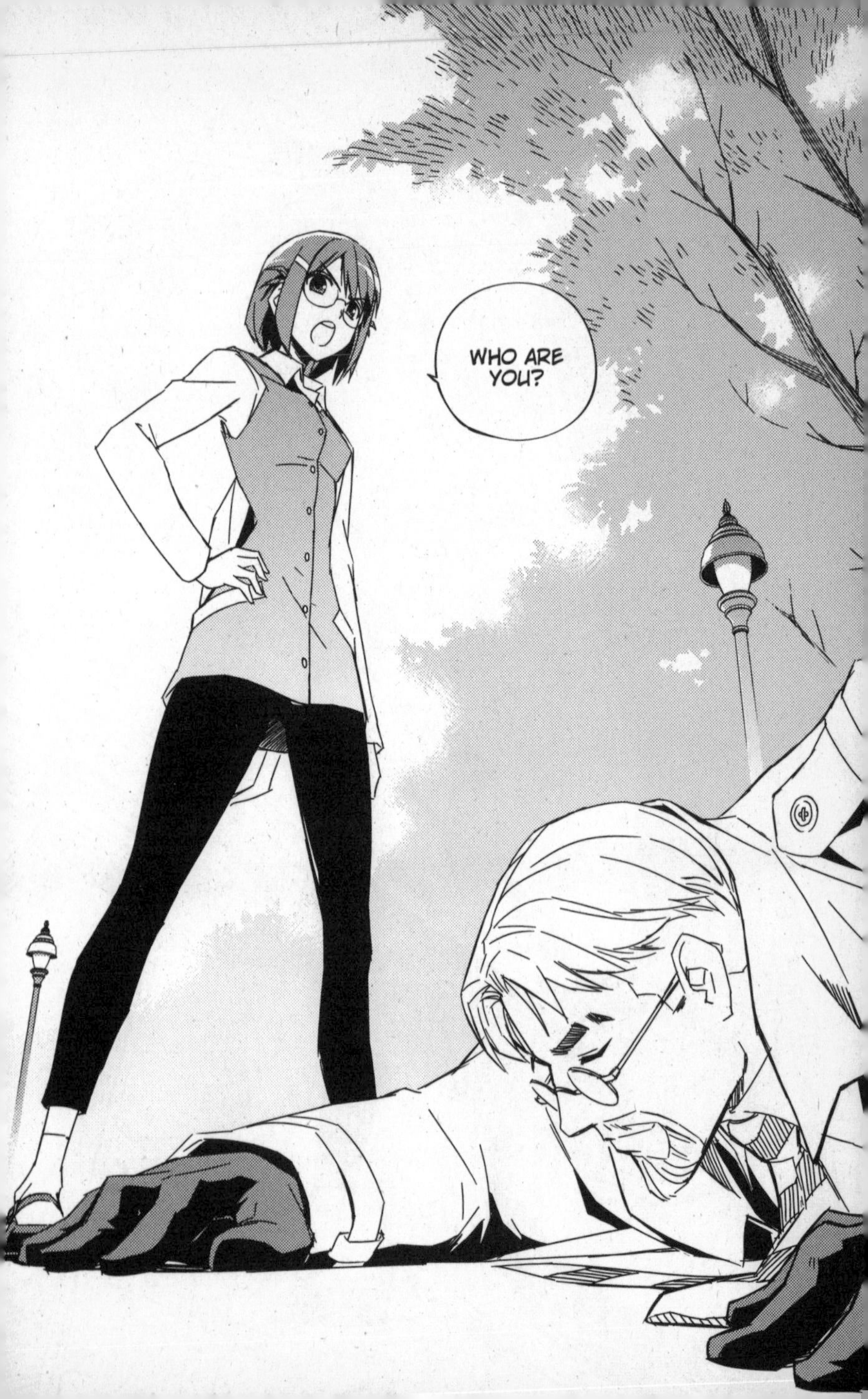
WHO ARE YOU?

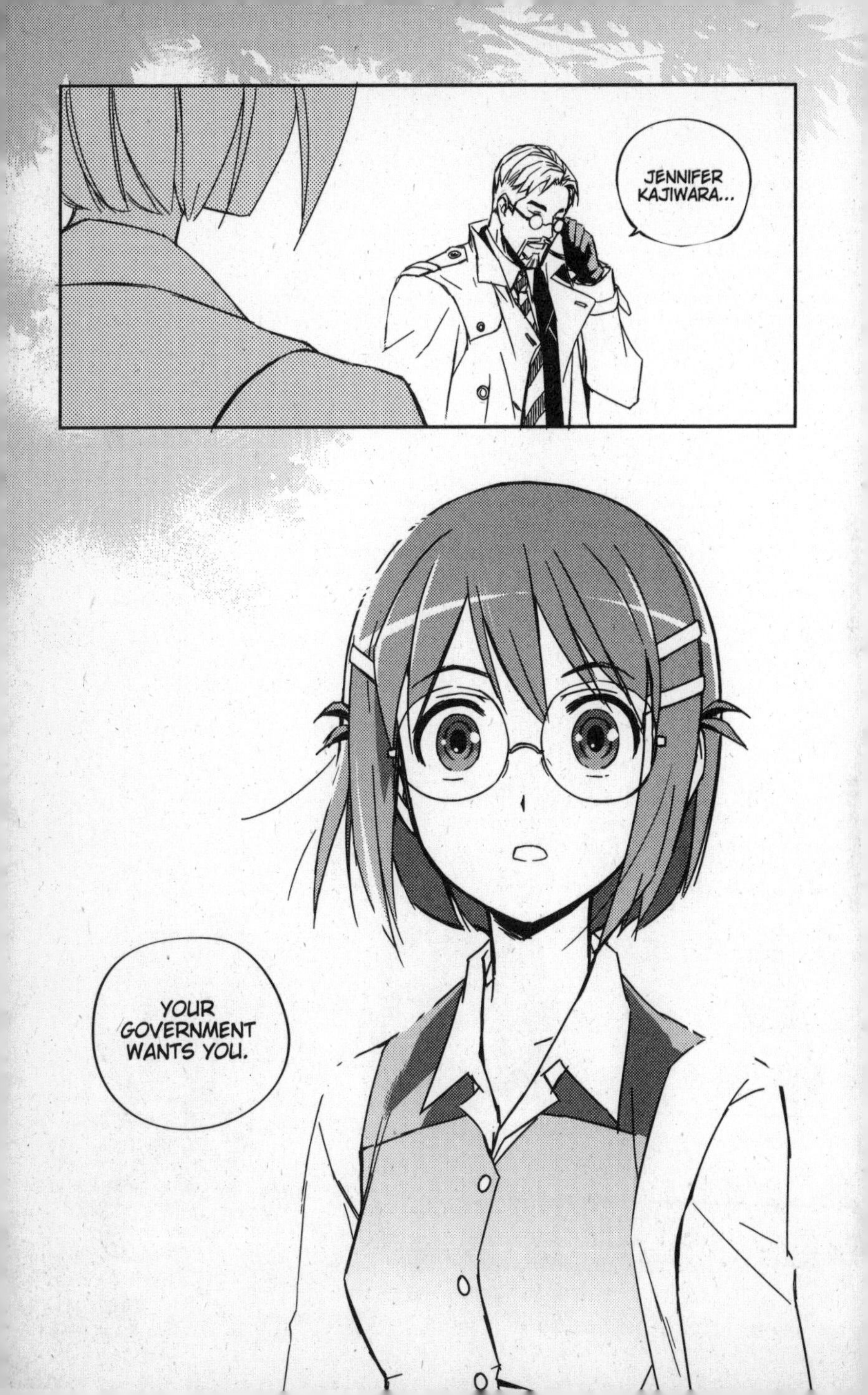
JENNIFER KAJIWARA...
YOUR GOVERNMENT WANTS YOU.

FILE 2:
NEW RECRUIT

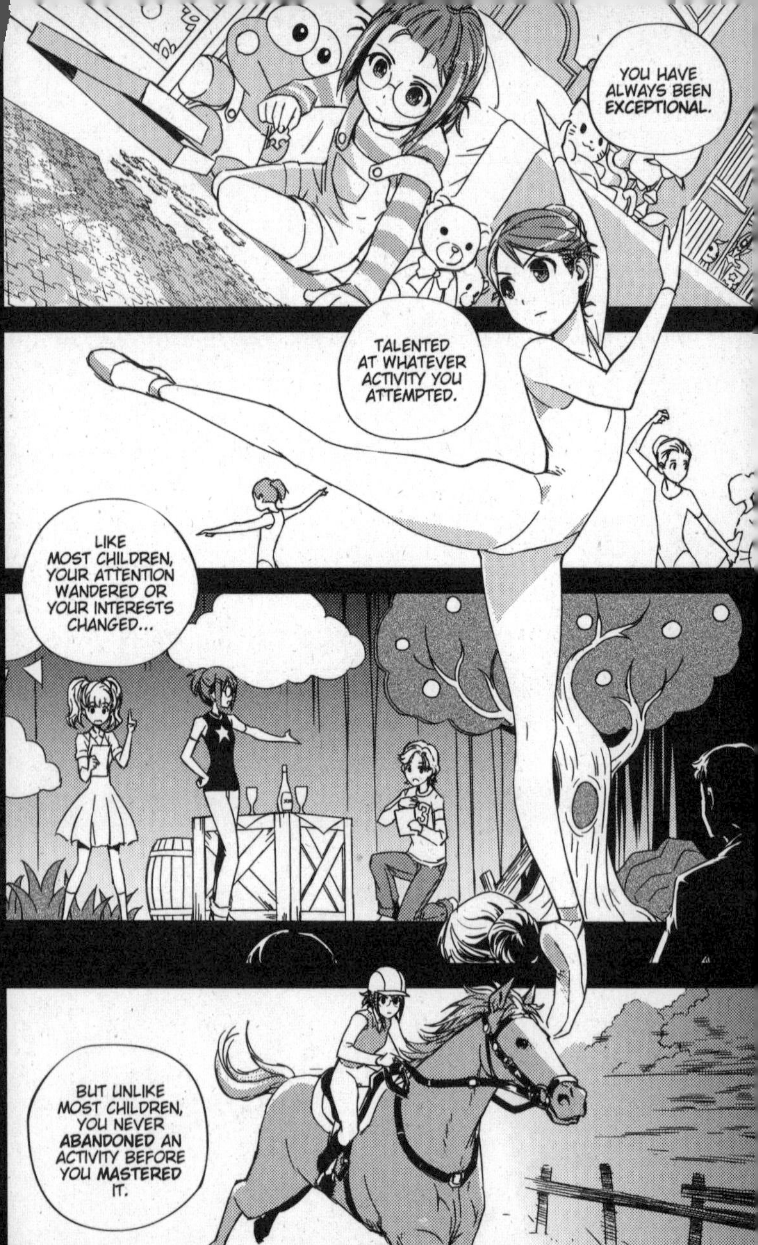
YOU HAVE ALWAYS BEEN EXCEPTIONAL.
TALENTED AT WHATEVER ACTIVITY YOU ATTEMPTED.
LIKE MOST CHILDREN, YOUR ATTENTION WANDERED OR YOUR INTERESTS CHANGED...
BUT UNLIKE MOST CHILDREN, YOU NEVER ABANDONED AN ACTIVITY BEFORE YOU MASTERED IT.

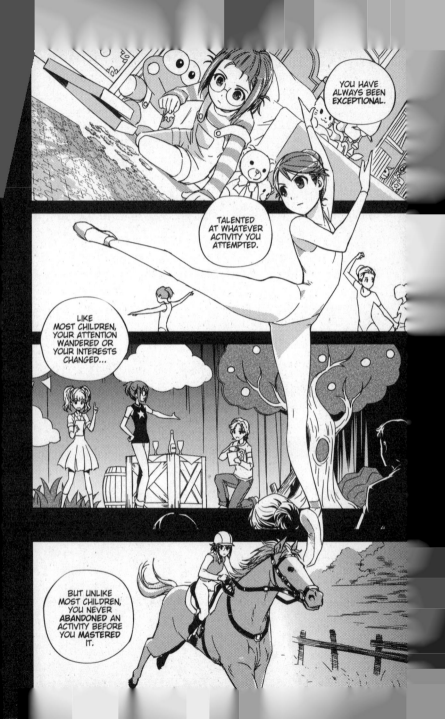

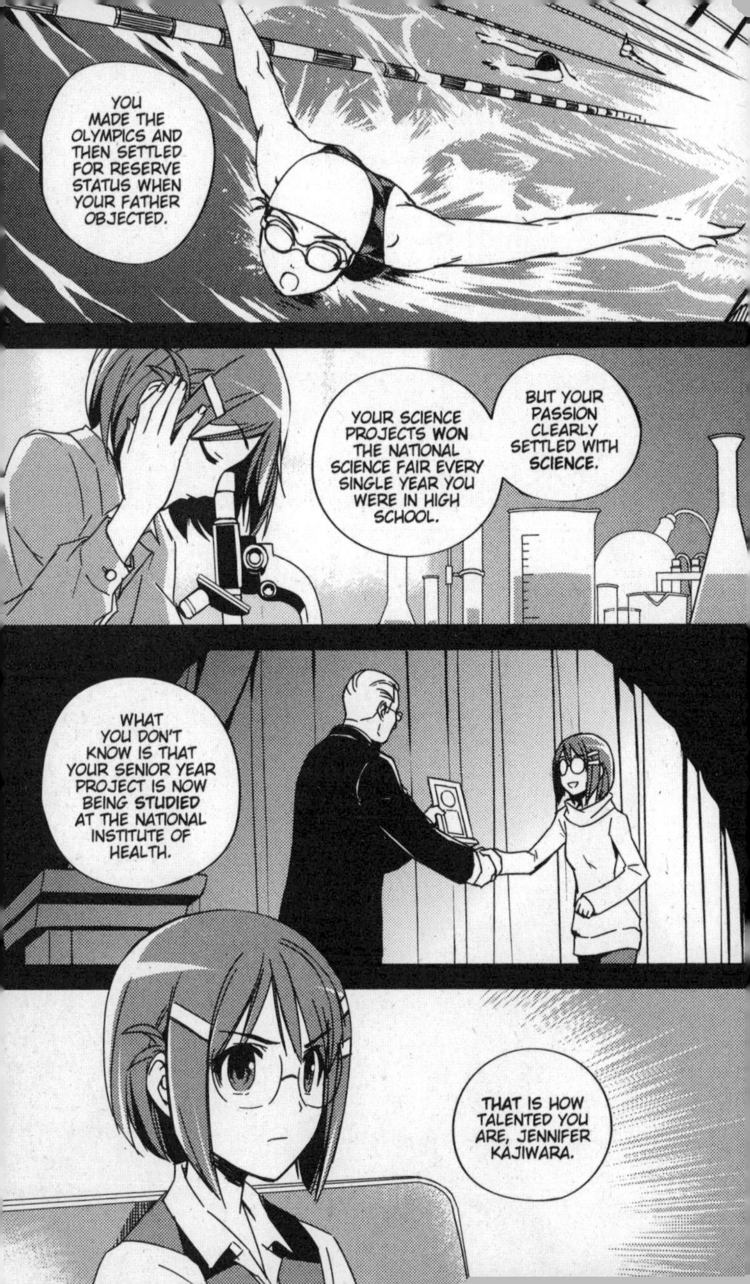
YOU MADE THE OLYMPICS AND THEN SETTLED FOR RESERVE STATUS WHEN YOUR FATHER OBJECTED.
BUT YOUR PASSION CLEARLY SETTLED WITH SCIENCE.
YOUR SCIENCE PROJECTS WON THE NATIONAL SCIENCE FAIR EVERY SINGLE YEAR YOU WERE IN HIGH SCHOOL.
WHAT YOU DON'T KNOW IS THAT YOUR SENIOR YEAR PROJECT IS NOW BEING STUDIED AT THE NATIONAL INSTITUTE OF HEALTH.
THAT IS HOW TALENTED YOU ARE, JENNIFER KAJIWARA.

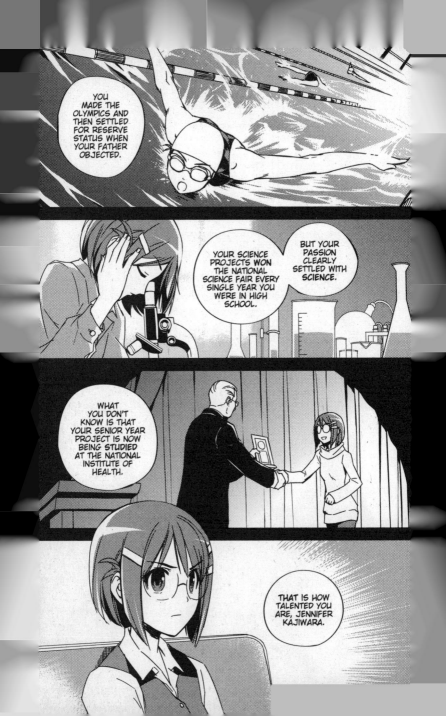

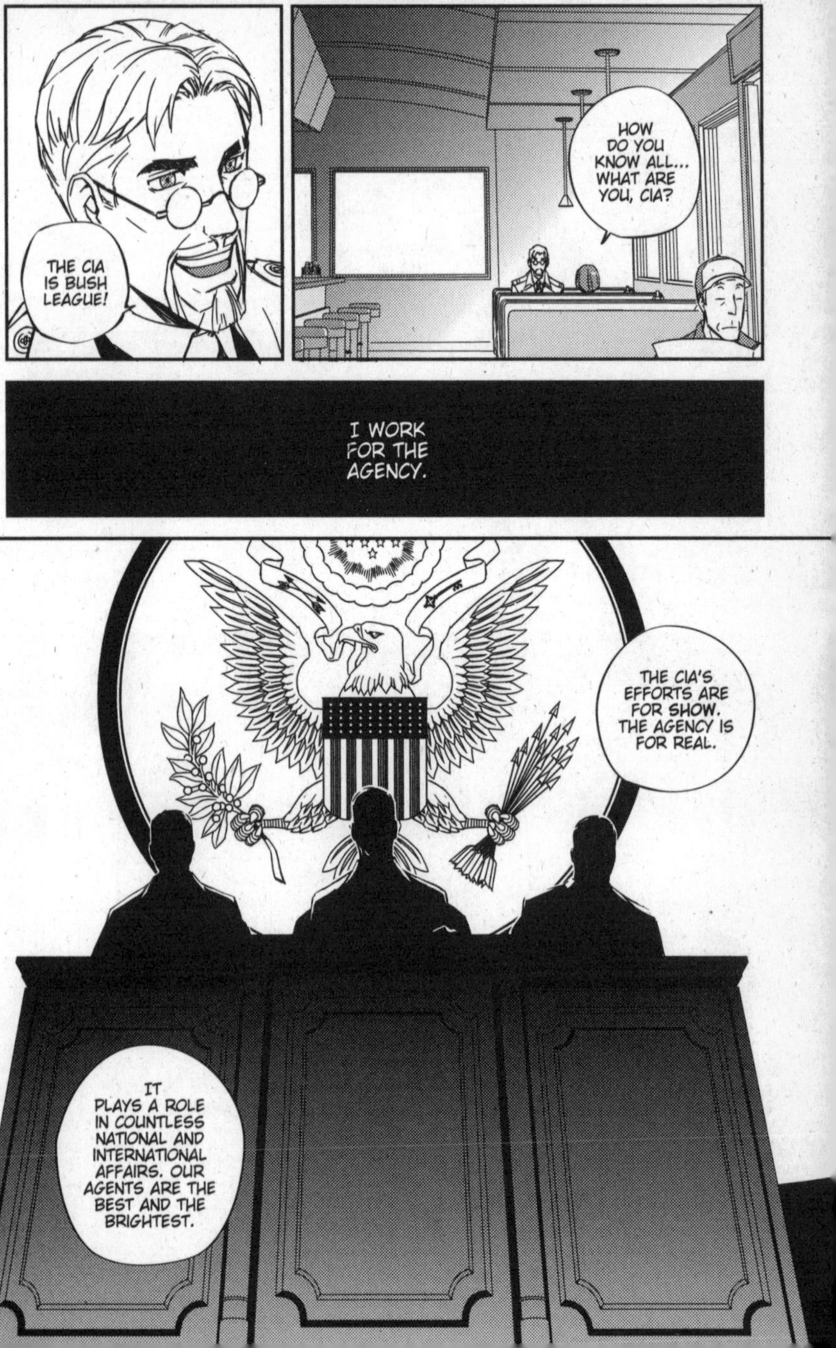
HOW DO YOU KNOW ALL... WHAT ARE YOU, CIA?
THE CIA IS BUSH LEAGUE!
I WORK FOR THE AGENCY.
THE CIA'S EFFORTS ARE FOR SHOW. THE AGENCY IS FOR REAL.
IT PLAYS A ROLE IN COUNTLESS NATIONAL AND INTERNATIONAL AFFAIRS. OUR AGENTS ARE THE BEST AND THE BRIGHTEST.

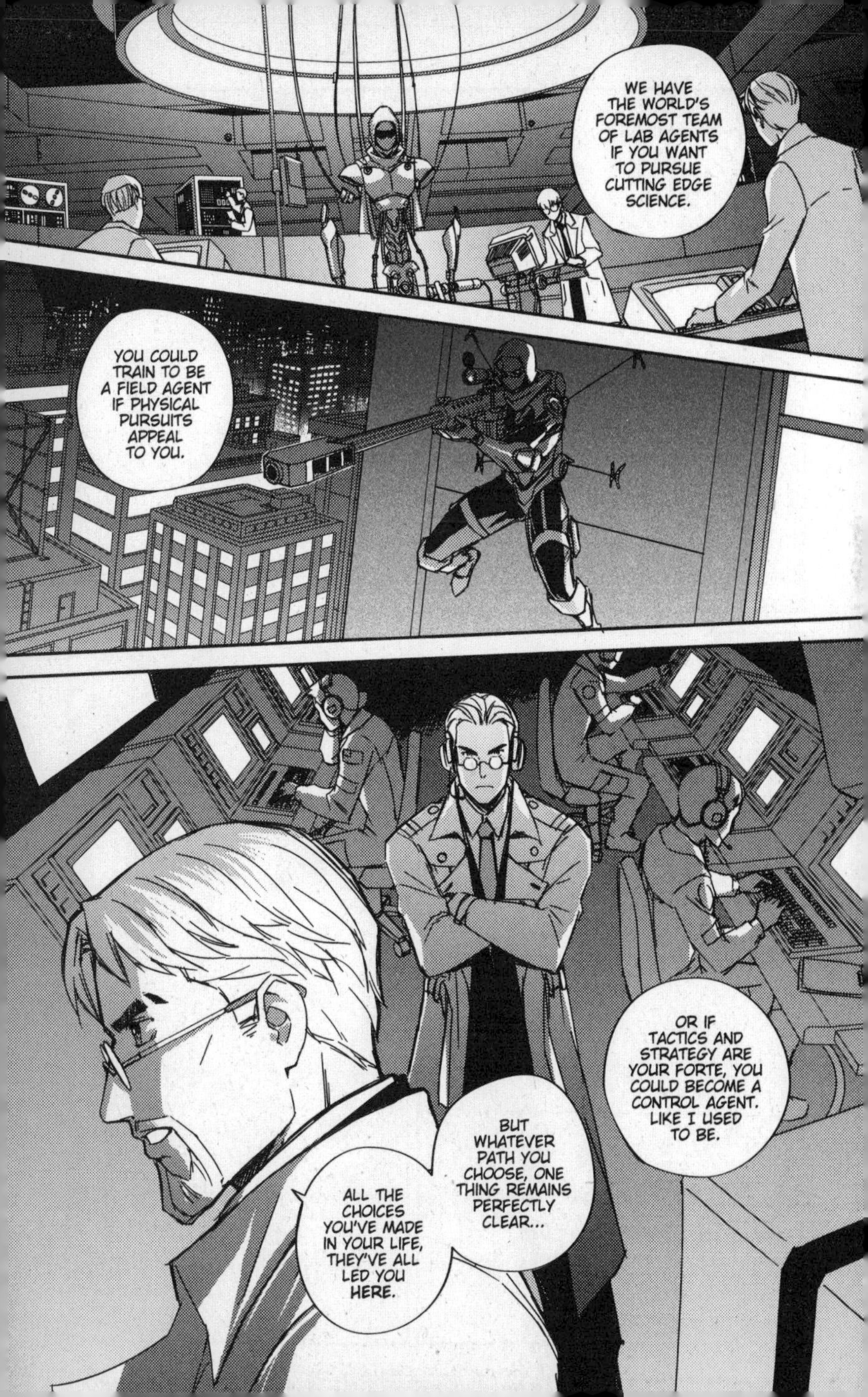
WE HAVE THE WORLD'S FOREMOST TEAM OF LAB AGENTS IF YOU WANT TO PURSUE CUTTING EDGE SCIENCE.
YOU COULD TRAIN TO BE A FIELD AGENT IF PHYSICAL PURSUITS APPEAL TO YOU.
OR IF TACTICS AND STRATEGY ARE YOUR FORTE, YOU COULD BECOME A CONTROL AGENT. LIKE I USED TO BE.
BUT WHATEVER PATH YOU CHOOSE, ONE THING REMAINS PERFECTLY CLEAR...
ALL THE CHOICES YOU'VE MADE IN YOUR LIFE, THEY'VE ALL LED YOU HERE.

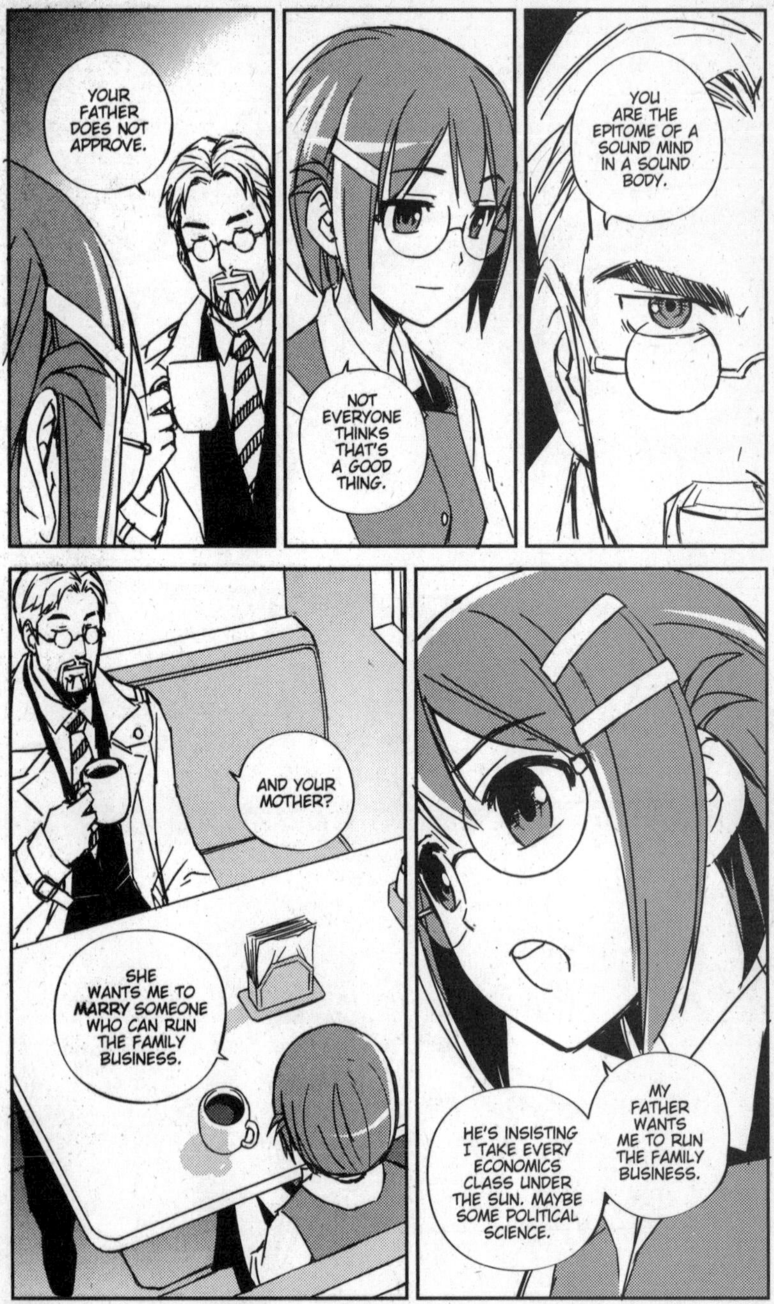
YOU ARE THE EPITOME OF A SOUND MIND IN A SOUND BODY.
NOT EVERYONE THINKS THAT'S A GOOD THING.
YOUR FATHER DOES NOT APPROVE.
MY FATHER WANTS ME TO RUN THE FAMILY BUSINESS.
HE'S INSISTING I TAKE EVERY ECONOMICS CLASS UNDER THE SUN. MAYBE SOME POLITICAL SCIENCE.
AND YOUR MOTHER?
SHE WANTS ME TO MARRY SOMEONE WHO CAN RUN THE FAMILY BUSINESS.

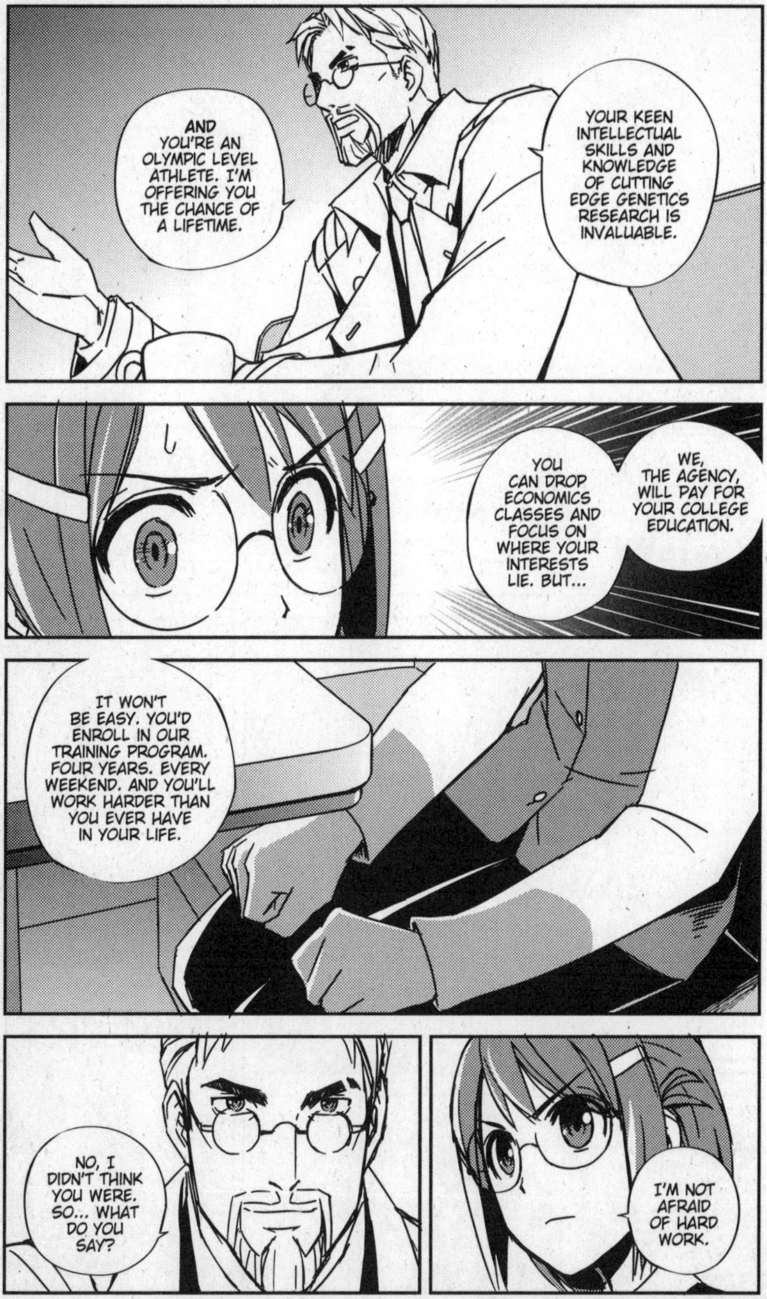
YOUR KEEN INTELLECTUAL SKILLS AND KNOWLEDGE OF CUTTING EDGE GENETICS RESEARCH IS INVALUABLE.
AND YOU'RE AN OLYMPIC LEVEL ATHLETE. I'M OFFERING YOU THE CHANCE OF A LIFETIME.
WE, THE AGENCY, WILL PAY FOR YOUR COLLEGE EDUCATION.
YOU CAN DROP ECONOMICS CLASSES AND FOCUS ON WHERE YOUR INTERESTS LIE. BUT...
IT WON'T BE EASY. YOU'D ENROLL IN OUR TRAINING PROGRAM. FOUR YEARS. EVERY WEEKEND. AND YOU'LL WORK HARDER THAN YOU EVER HAVE IN YOUR LIFE.
I'M NOT AFRAID OF HARD WORK.
NO, I DIDN'T THINK YOU WERE. SO... WHAT DO YOU SAY?

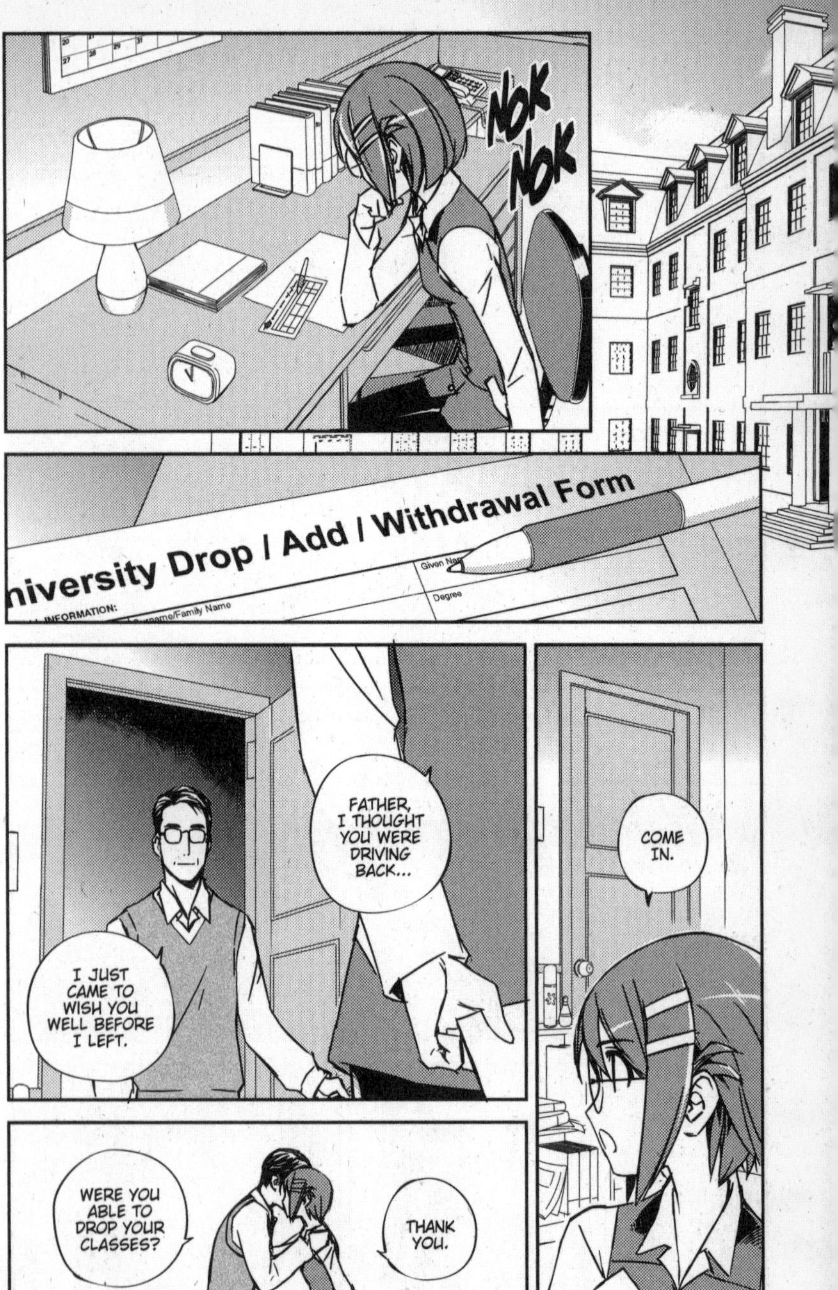
NOK NOK
niversity Drop / Add / Withdrawal Form
Given Na
Degree
INFORMATION:
Surname/Family Name
COME IN.
FATHER, I THOUGHT YOU WERE DRIVING BACK...
I JUST CAME TO WISH YOU WELL BEFORE I LEFT.
THANK YOU.
WERE YOU ABLE TO DROP YOUR CLASSES?

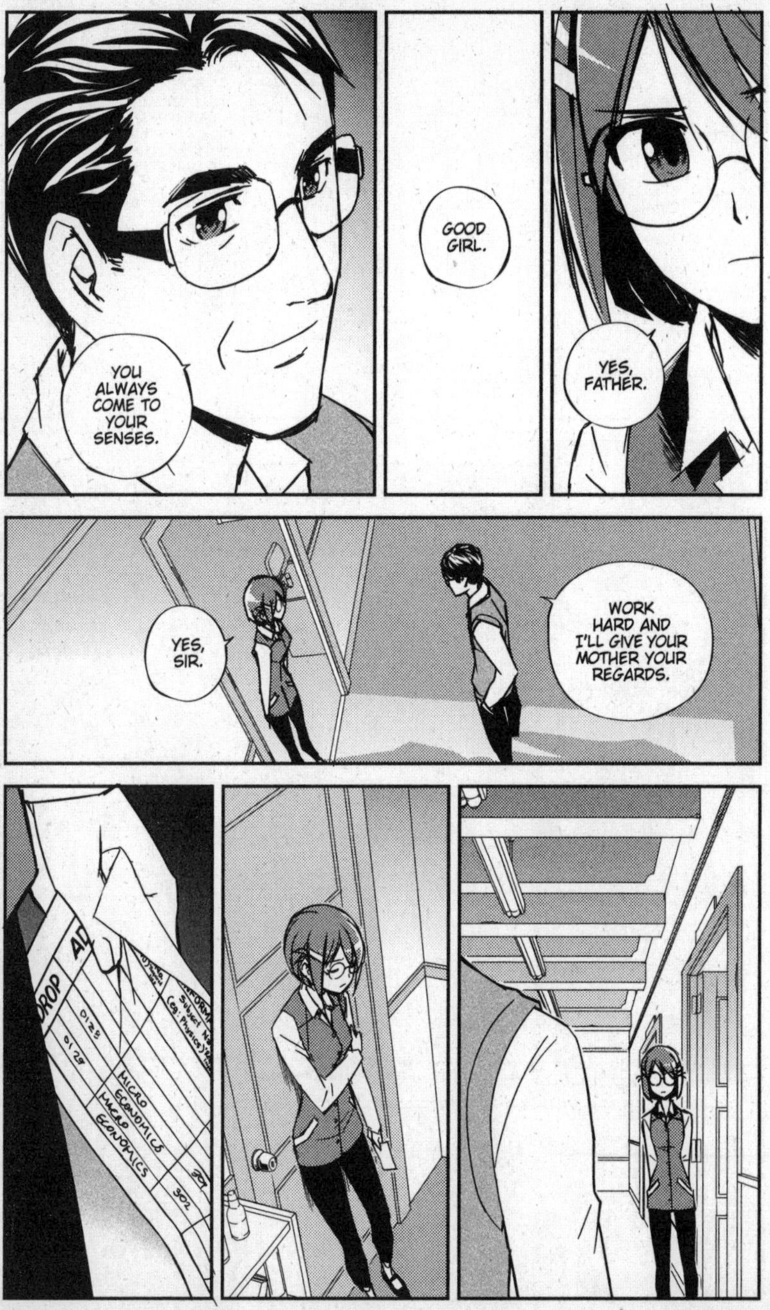

YES, FATHER.
GOOD GIRL.
YOU ALWAYS COME TO YOUR SENSES.
WORK HARD AND I'LL GIVE YOUR MOTHER YOUR REGARDS.
YES, SIR.
DROP
0128
MICRO ECONOMICS
307
0129
MACRO ECONOMICS
302

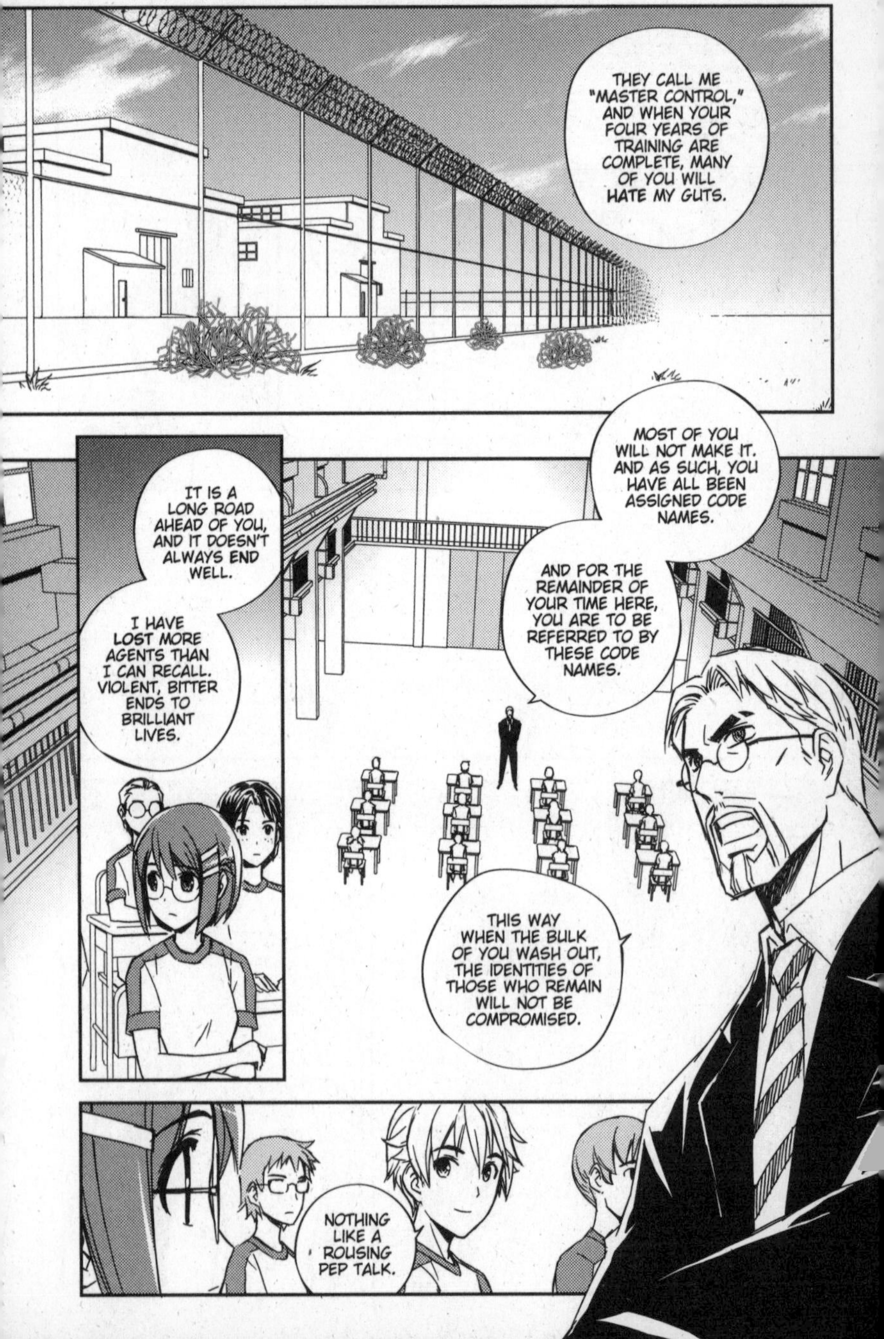
THEY CALL ME "MASTER CONTROL," AND WHEN YOUR FOUR YEARS OF TRAINING ARE COMPLETE, MANY OF YOU WILL HATE MY GUTS.
MOST OF YOU WILL NOT MAKE IT. AND AS SUCH, YOU HAVE ALL BEEN ASSIGNED CODE NAMES.
AND FOR THE REMAINDER OF YOUR TIME HERE, YOU ARE TO BE REFERRED TO BY THESE CODE NAMES.
THIS WAY WHEN THE BULK OF YOU WASH OUT, THE IDENTITIES OF THOSE WHO REMAIN WILL NOT BE COMPROMISED.
IT IS A LONG ROAD AHEAD OF YOU, AND IT DOESN'T ALWAYS END WELL.
I HAVE LOST MORE AGENTS THAN I CAN RECALL. VIOLENT, BITTER ENDS TO BRILLIANT LIVES.
NOTHING LIKE A ROUSING PEP TALK.

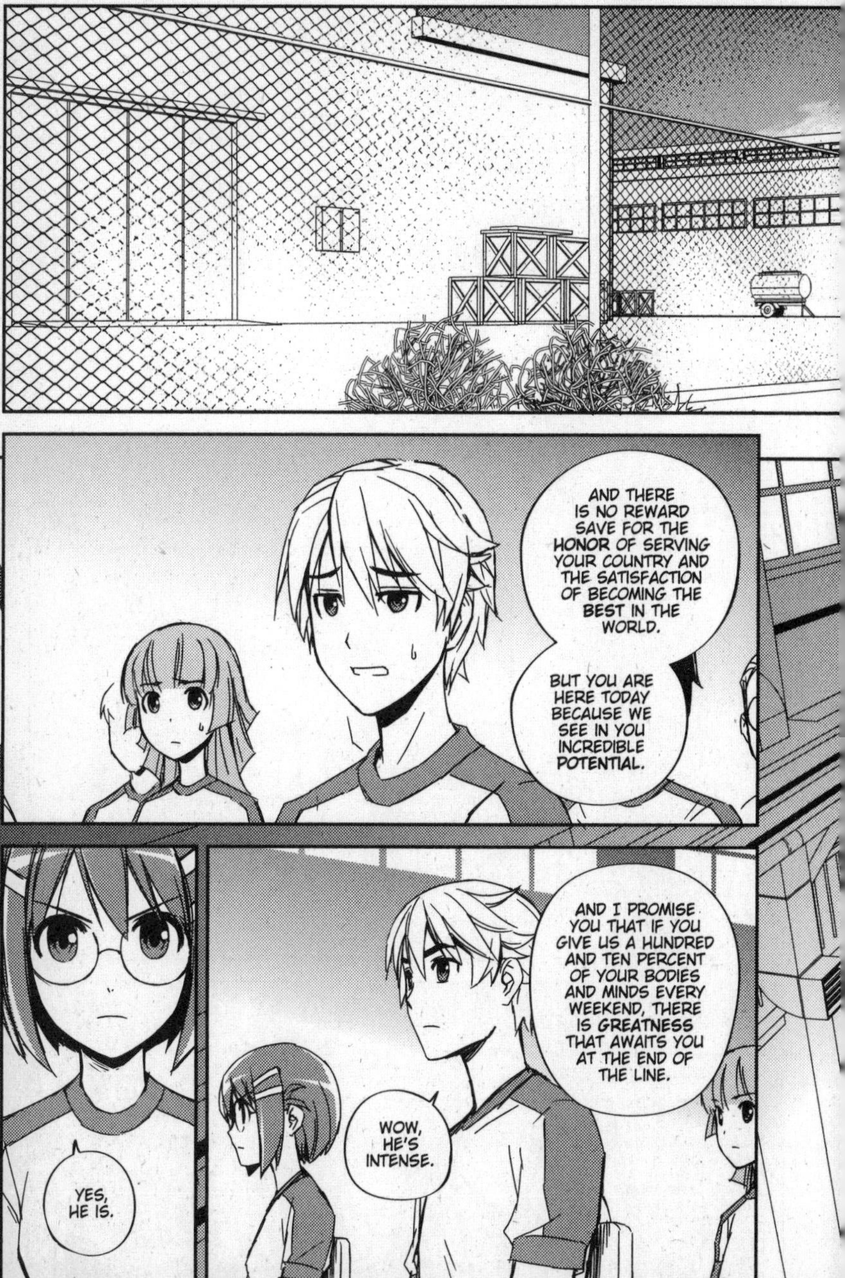
AND THERE IS NO REWARD SAVE FOR THE HONOR OF SERVING YOUR COUNTRY AND THE SATISFACTION OF BECOMING THE BEST IN THE WORLD.
BUT YOU ARE HERE TODAY BECAUSE WE SEE IN YOU INCREDIBLE POTENTIAL.
AND I PROMISE YOU THAT IF YOU GIVE US A HUNDRED AND TEN PERCENT OF YOUR BODIES AND MINDS EVERY WEEKEND, THERE IS GREATNESS THAT AWAITS YOU AT THE END OF THE LINE.
WOW, HE'S INTENSE.
YES, HE IS.

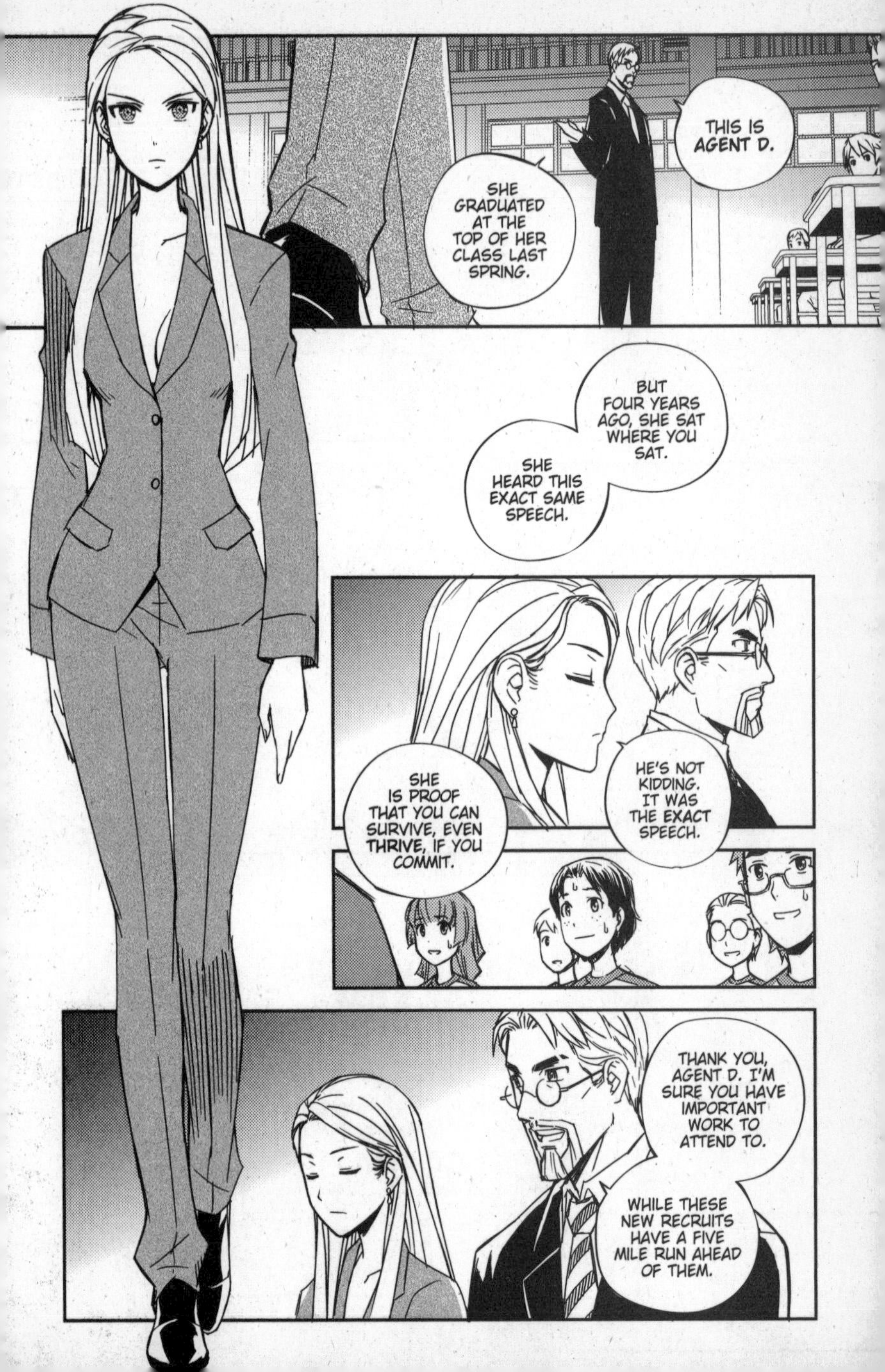
THIS IS AGENT D.
SHE GRADUATED AT THE TOP OF HER CLASS LAST SPRING.
BUT FOUR YEARS AGO, SHE SAT WHERE YOU SAT.
SHE HEARD THIS EXACT SAME SPEECH.
HE'S NOT KIDDING. IT WAS THE EXACT SPEECH.
SHE IS PROOF THAT YOU CAN SURVIVE, EVEN THRIVE, IF YOU COMMIT.
THANK YOU, AGENT D. I'M SURE YOU HAVE IMPORTANT WORK TO ATTEND TO.
WHILE THESE NEW RECRUITS HAVE A FIVE MILE RUN AHEAD OF THEM.

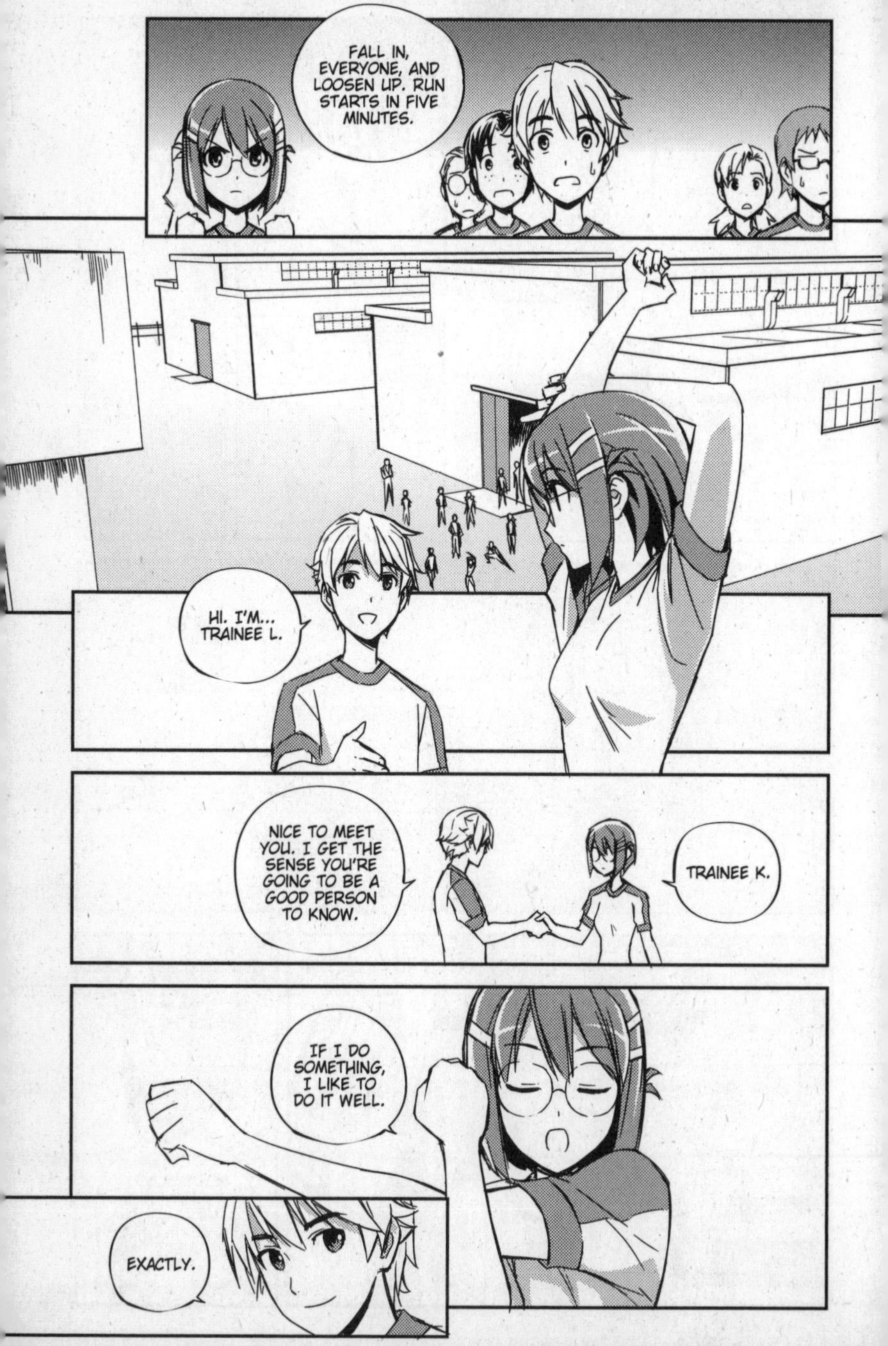
FALL IN, EVERYONE, AND LOOSEN UP. RUN STARTS IN FIVE MINUTES.
HI. I'M... TRAINEE L.
TRAINEE K.
NICE TO MEET YOU. I GET THE SENSE YOU'RE GOING TO BE A GOOD PERSON TO KNOW.
IF I DO SOMETHING, I LIKE TO DO IT WELL.
EXACTLY.

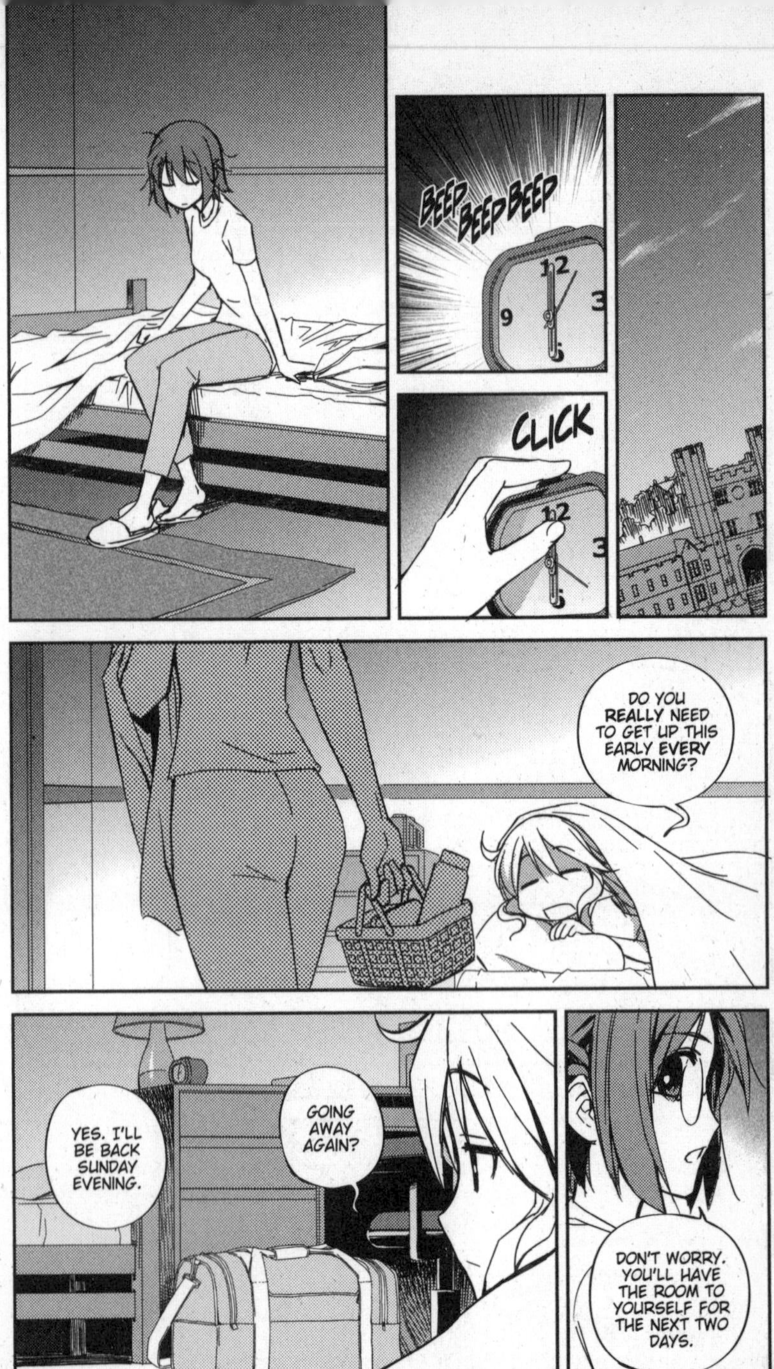
BEEP BEEP BEEP
CLICK
DO YOU REALLY NEED TO GET UP THIS EARLY EVERY MORNING?
DON'T WORRY. YOU'LL HAVE THE ROOM TO YOURSELF FOR THE NEXT TWO DAYS.
GOING AWAY AGAIN?
YES. I'LL BE BACK SUNDAY EVENING.

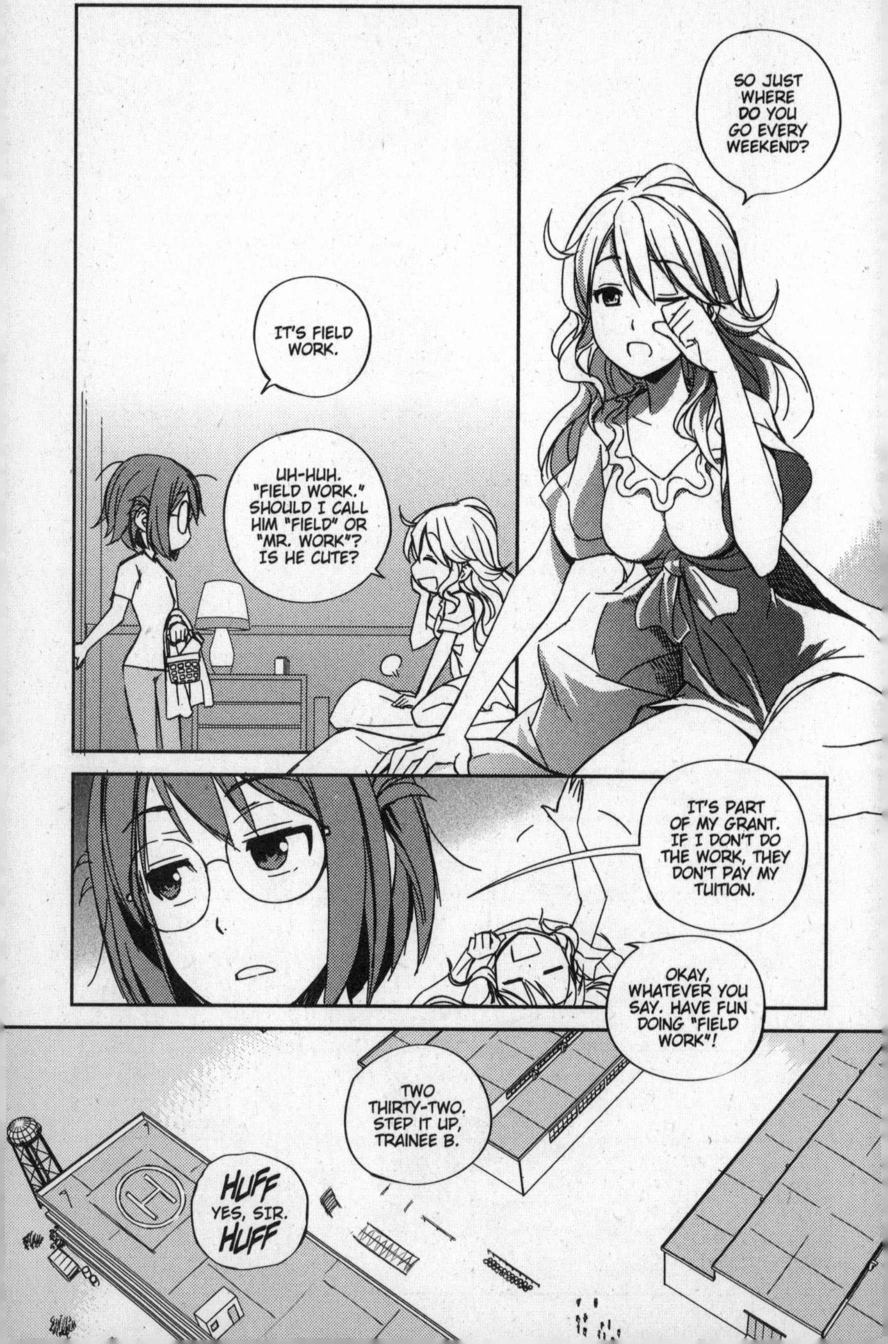
SO JUST WHERE DO YOU GO EVERY WEEKEND?
IT'S FIELD WORK.
UH-HUH. "FIELD WORK." SHOULD I CALL HIM "FIELD" OR "MR. WORK"? IS HE CUTE?
IT'S PART OF MY GRANT. IF I DON'T DO THE WORK, THEY DON'T PAY MY TUITION.
OKAY, WHATEVER YOU SAY. HAVE FUN DOING "FIELD WORK"!
TWO THIRTY-TWO. STEP IT UP, TRAINEE B.
HUFF YES, SIR. HUFF

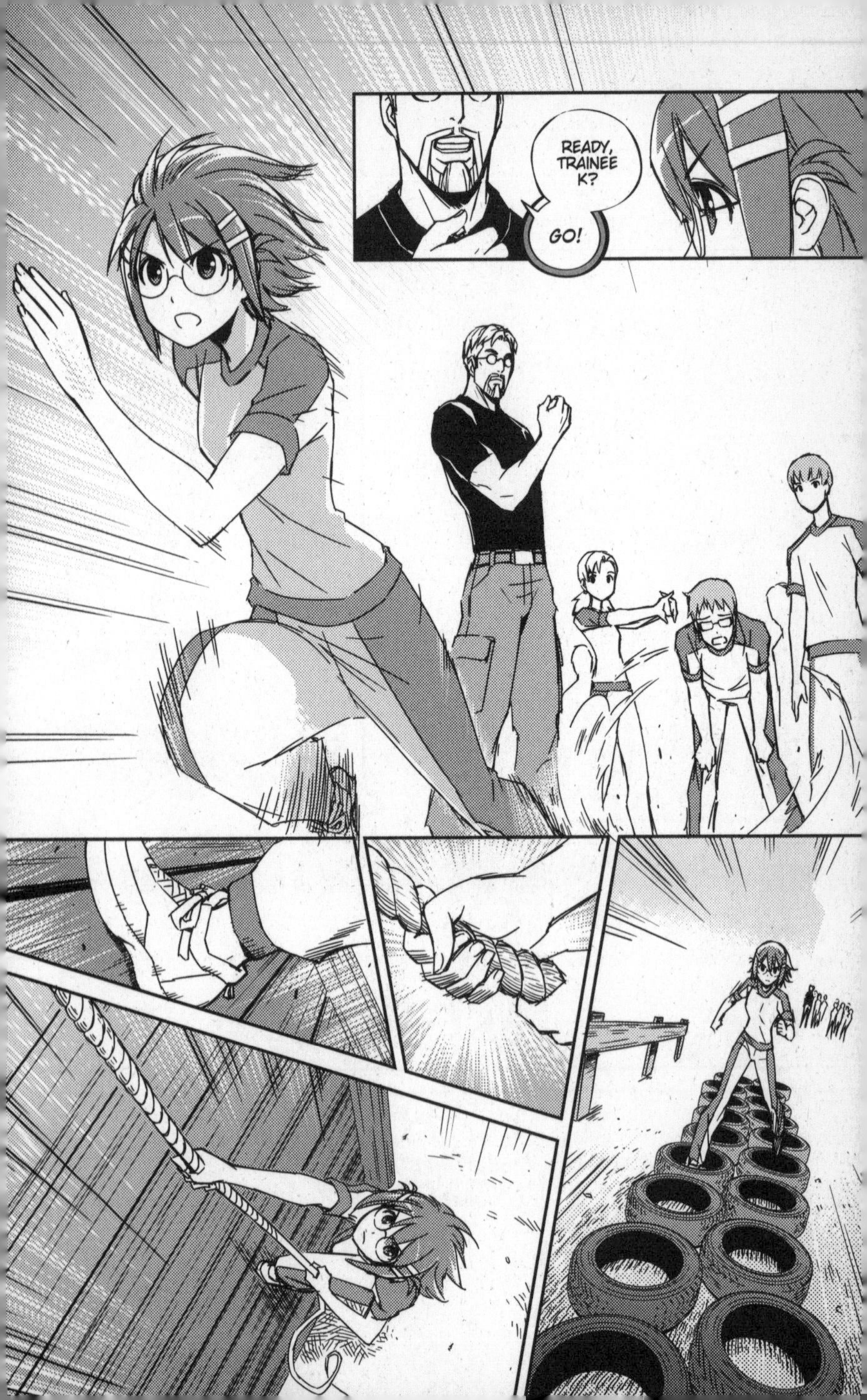
READY, TRAINEE K?
GO!

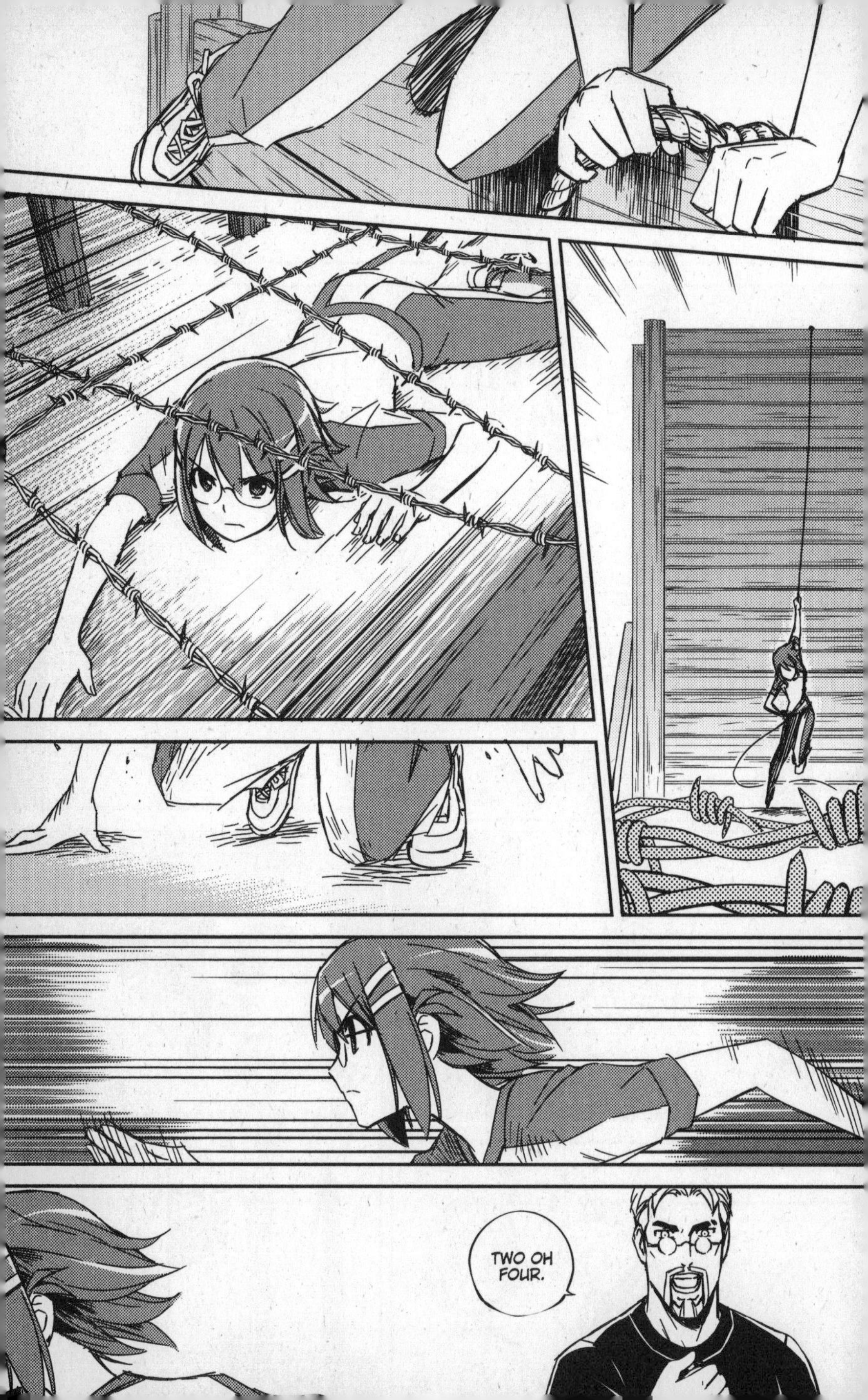
TWO OH FOUR.

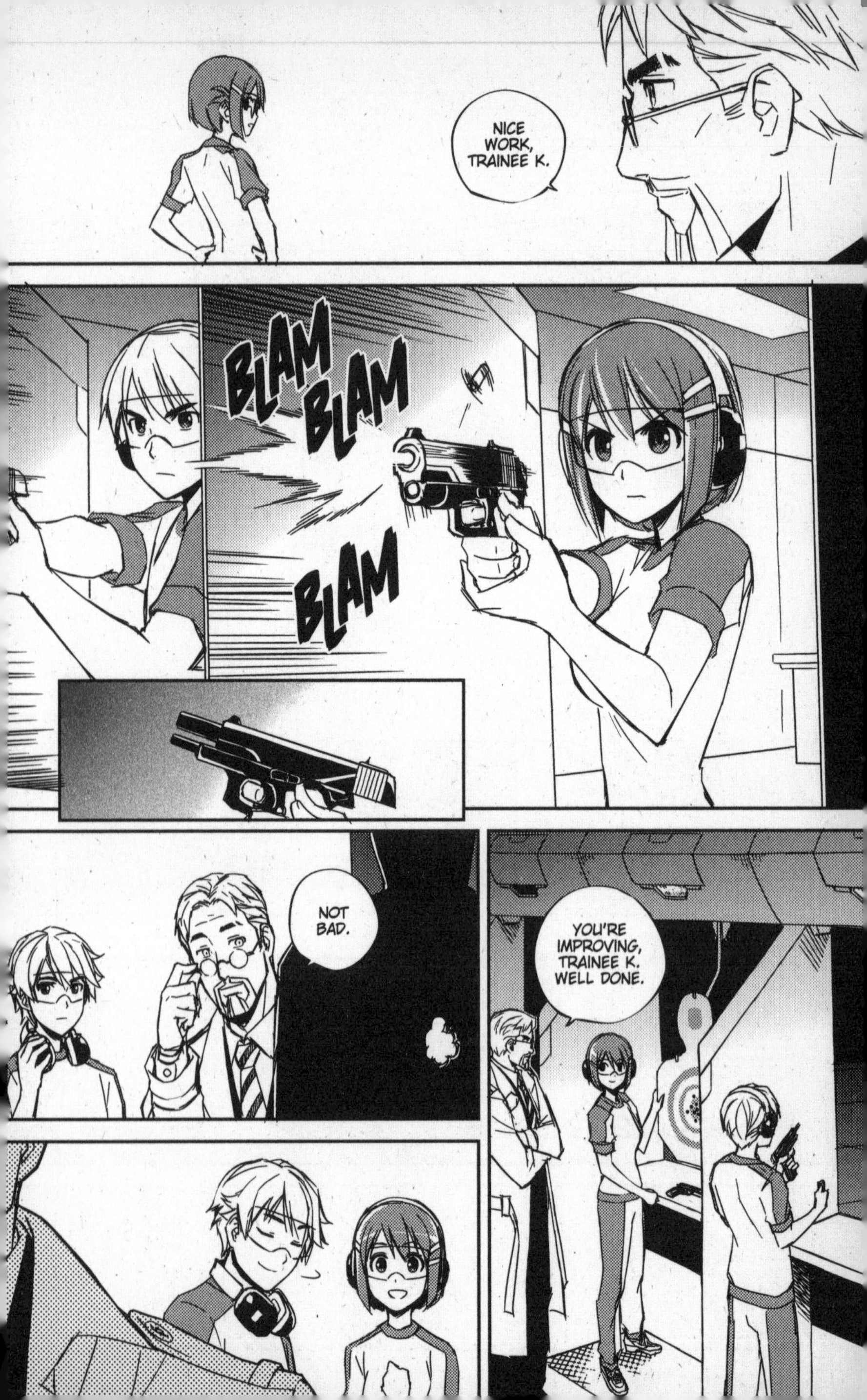
NICE WORK, TRAINEE K.
BLAM
BLAM
BLAM
YOU'RE IMPROVING, TRAINEE K. WELL DONE.
NOT BAD.

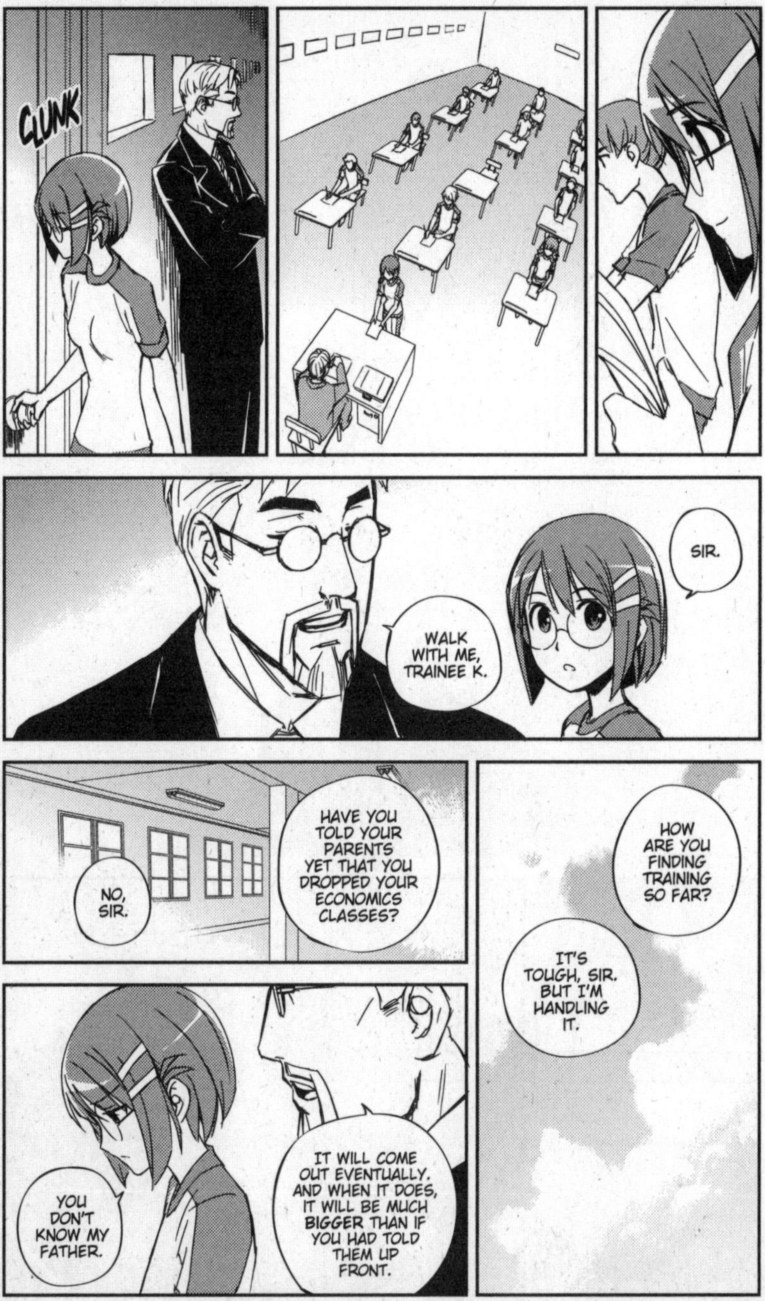
CLUNK
SIR.
WALK WITH ME, TRAINEE K.
HOW ARE YOU FINDING TRAINING SO FAR?
IT'S TOUGH, SIR. BUT I'M HANDLING IT.
HAVE YOU TOLD YOUR PARENTS YET THAT YOU DROPPED YOUR ECONOMICS CLASSES?
NO, SIR.
IT WILL COME OUT EVENTUALLY. AND WHEN IT DOES, IT WILL BE MUCH BIGGER THAN IF YOU HAD TOLD THEM UP FRONT.
YOU DON'T KNOW MY FATHER.

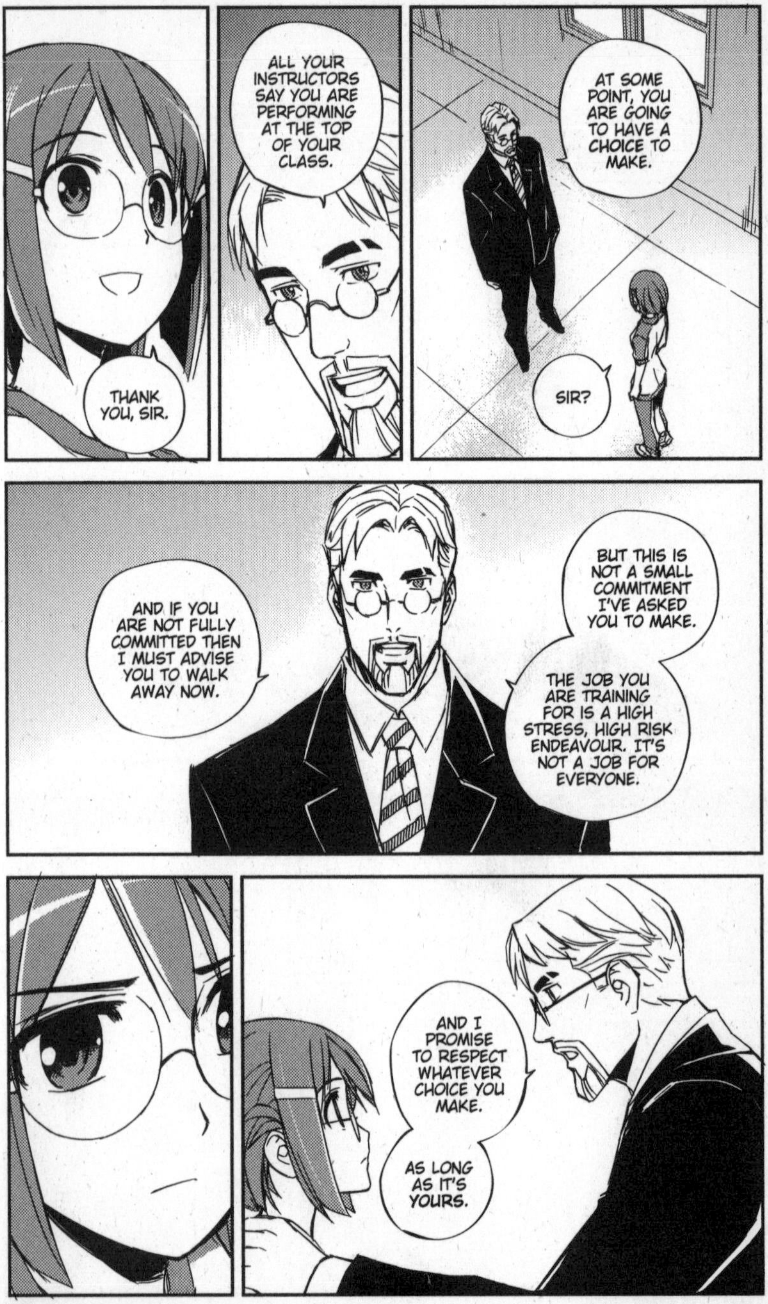
AT SOME POINT, YOU ARE GOING TO HAVE A CHOICE TO MAKE.
SIR?
ALL YOUR INSTRUCTORS SAY YOU ARE PERFORMING AT THE TOP OF YOUR CLASS.
THANK YOU, SIR.
BUT THIS IS NOT A SMALL COMMITMENT I'VE ASKED YOU TO MAKE.
THE JOB YOU ARE TRAINING FOR IS A HIGH STRESS, HIGH RISK ENDEAVOUR. IT'S NOT A JOB FOR EVERYONE.
AND IF YOU ARE NOT FULLY COMMITTED THEN I MUST ADVISE YOU TO WALK AWAY NOW.
AND I PROMISE TO RESPECT WHATEVER CHOICE YOU MAKE.
AS LONG AS IT'S YOURS.

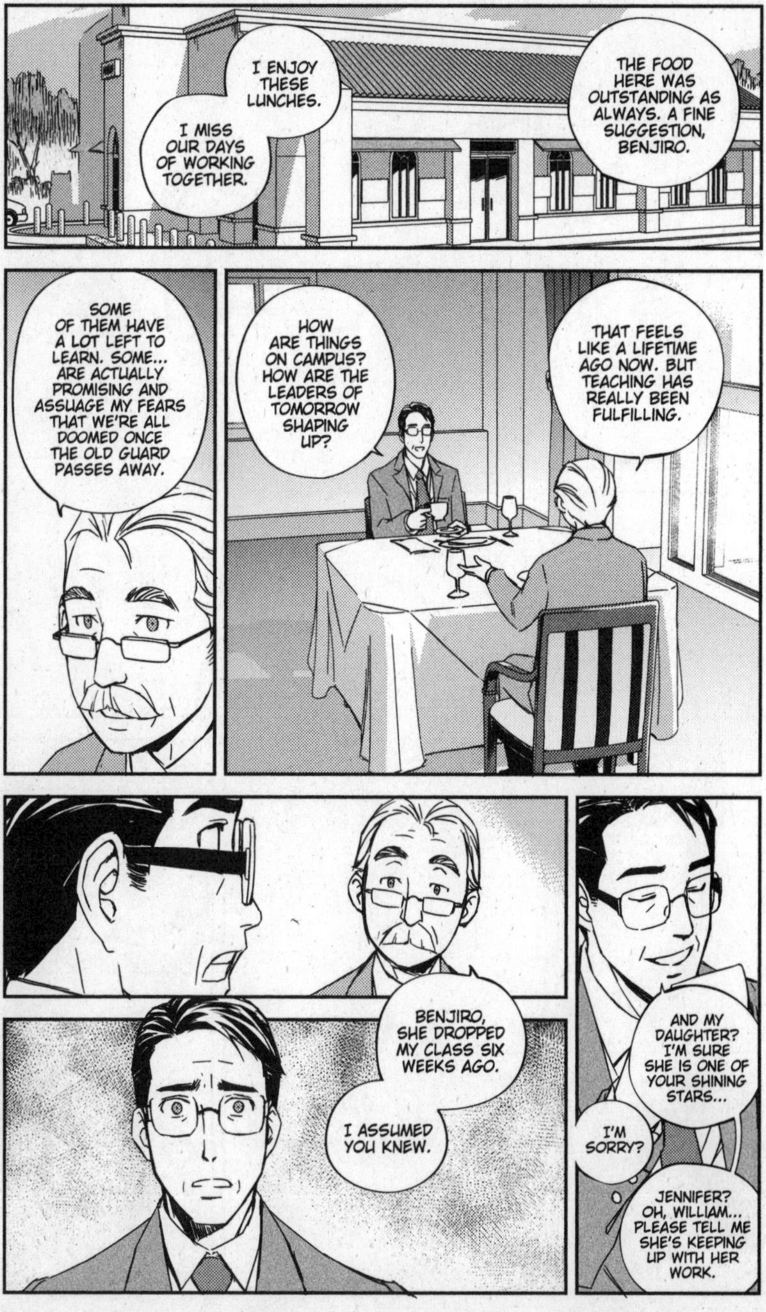
THE FOOD HERE WAS OUTSTANDING AS ALWAYS. A FINE SUGGESTION, BENJIRO.
I ENJOY THESE LUNCHES.
I MISS OUR DAYS OF WORKING TOGETHER.
THAT FEELS LIKE A LIFETIME AGO NOW. BUT TEACHING HAS REALLY BEEN FULFILLING.
HOW ARE THINGS ON CAMPUS? HOW ARE THE LEADERS OF TOMORROW SHAPING UP?
SOME OF THEM HAVE A LOT LEFT TO LEARN. SOME... ARE ACTUALLY PROMISING AND ASSUAGE MY FEARS THAT WE'RE ALL DOOMED ONCE THE OLD GUARD PASSES AWAY.
AND MY DAUGHTER? I'M SURE SHE IS ONE OF YOUR SHINING STARS...
I'M SORRY?
JENNIFER? OH, WILLIAM... PLEASE TELL ME SHE'S KEEPING UP WITH HER WORK.
BENJIRO, SHE DROPPED MY CLASS SIX WEEKS AGO.
I ASSUMED YOU KNEW.

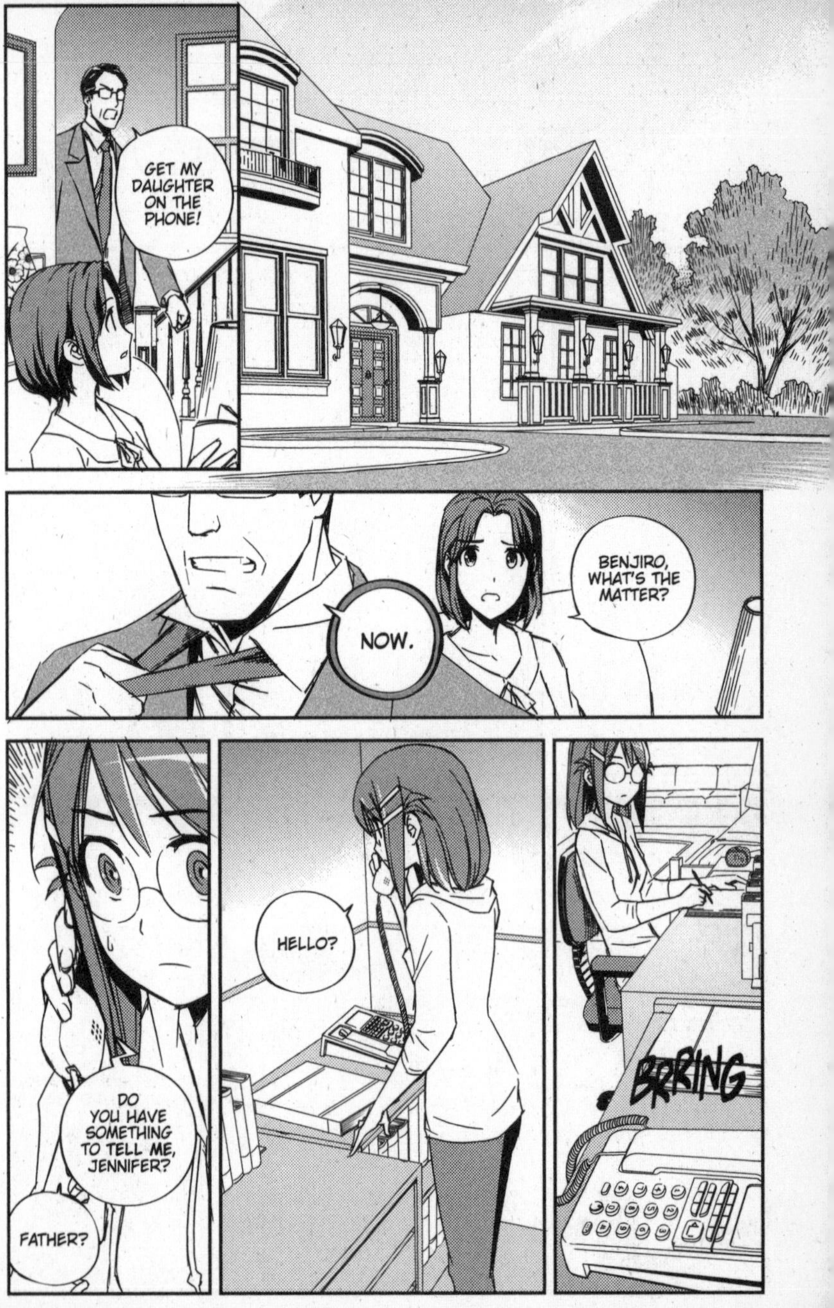
GET MY DAUGHTER ON THE PHONE!
BENJIRO, WHAT'S THE MATTER?
NOW.
BRRING
HELLO?
FATHER?
DO YOU HAVE SOMETHING TO TELL ME, JENNIFER?

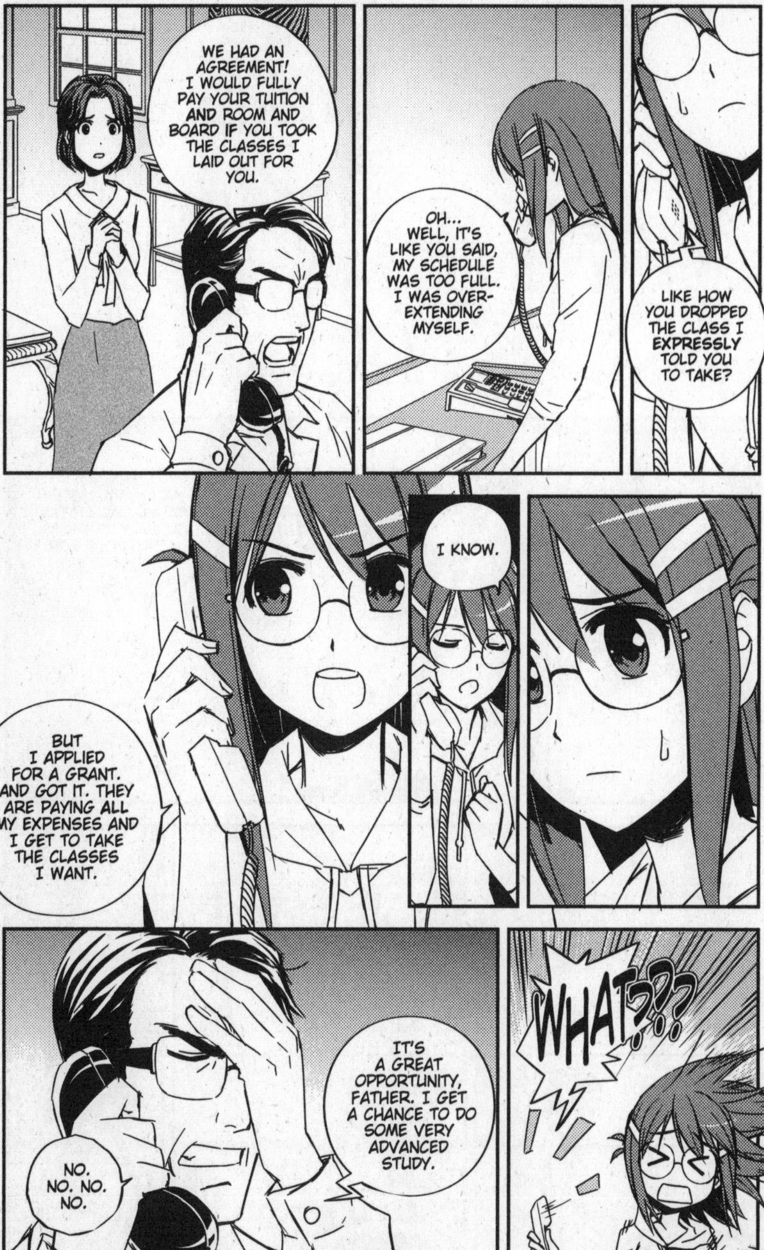
LIKE HOW YOU DROPPED THE CLASS I EXPRESSLY TOLD YOU TO TAKE?
OH... WELL, IT'S LIKE YOU SAID, MY SCHEDULE WAS TOO FULL. I WAS OVER-EXTENDING MYSELF.
WE HAD AN AGREEMENT! I WOULD FULLY PAY YOUR TUITION AND ROOM AND BOARD IF YOU TOOK THE CLASSES I LAID OUT FOR YOU.
I KNOW.
BUT I APPLIED FOR A GRANT. AND GOT IT. THEY ARE PAYING ALL MY EXPENSES AND I GET TO TAKE THE CLASSES I WANT.
WHAT???
IT'S A GREAT OPPORTUNITY, FATHER. I GET A CHANCE TO DO SOME VERY ADVANCED STUDY.
NO. NO. NO. NO.

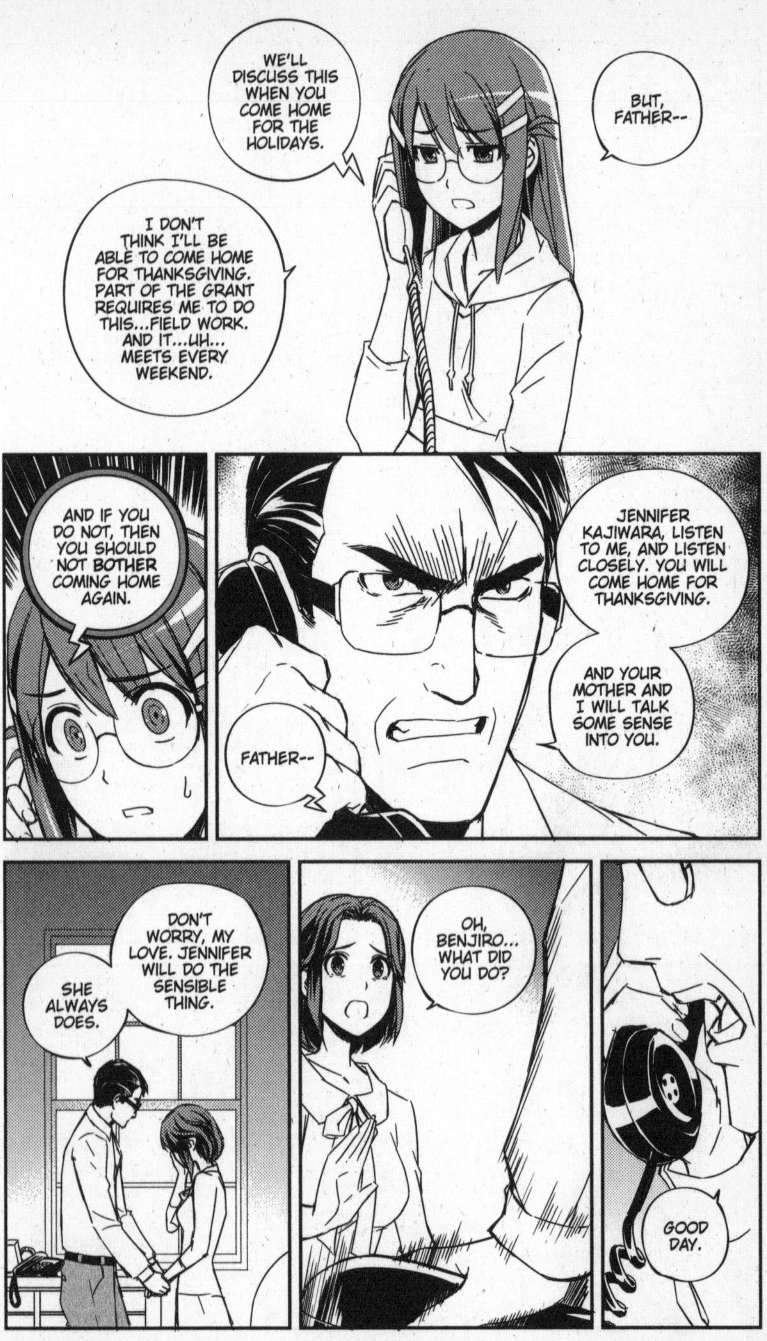
BUT, FATHER--
WE'LL DISCUSS THIS WHEN YOU COME HOME FOR THE HOLIDAYS.
I DON'T THINK I'LL BE ABLE TO COME HOME FOR THANKSGIVING. PART OF THE GRANT REQUIRES ME TO DO THIS...FIELD WORK. AND IT...UH... MEETS EVERY WEEKEND.
JENNIFER KAJIWARA, LISTEN TO ME, AND LISTEN CLOSELY. YOU WILL COME HOME FOR THANKSGIVING.
FATHER--
AND YOUR MOTHER AND I WILL TALK SOME SENSE INTO YOU.
AND IF YOU DO NOT, THEN YOU SHOULD NOT BOTHER COMING HOME AGAIN.
GOOD DAY.
OH, BENJIRO... WHAT DID YOU DO?
DON'T WORRY, MY LOVE. JENNIFER WILL DO THE SENSIBLE THING.
SHE ALWAYS DOES.

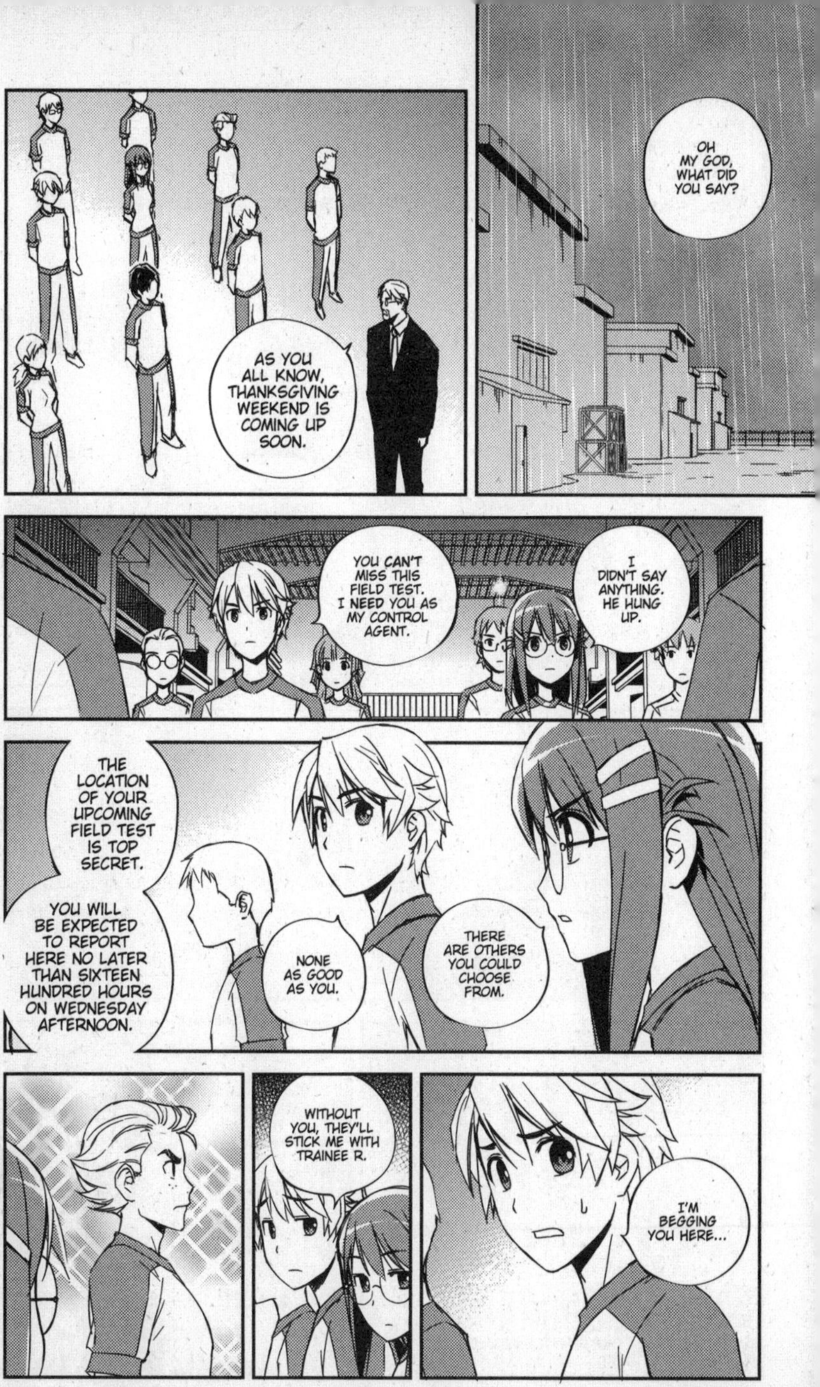
OH MY GOD, WHAT DID YOU SAY?
AS YOU ALL KNOW, THANKSGIVING WEEKEND IS COMING UP SOON.
I DIDN'T SAY ANYTHING. HE HUNG UP.
YOU CAN'T MISS THIS FIELD TEST. I NEED YOU AS MY CONTROL AGENT.
THERE ARE OTHERS YOU COULD CHOOSE FROM.
NONE AS GOOD AS YOU.
THE LOCATION OF YOUR UPCOMING FIELD TEST IS TOP SECRET.
YOU WILL BE EXPECTED TO REPORT HERE NO LATER THAN SIXTEEN HUNDRED HOURS ON WEDNESDAY AFTERNOON.
I'M BEGGING YOU HERE...
WITHOUT YOU, THEY'LL STICK ME WITH TRAINEE R.

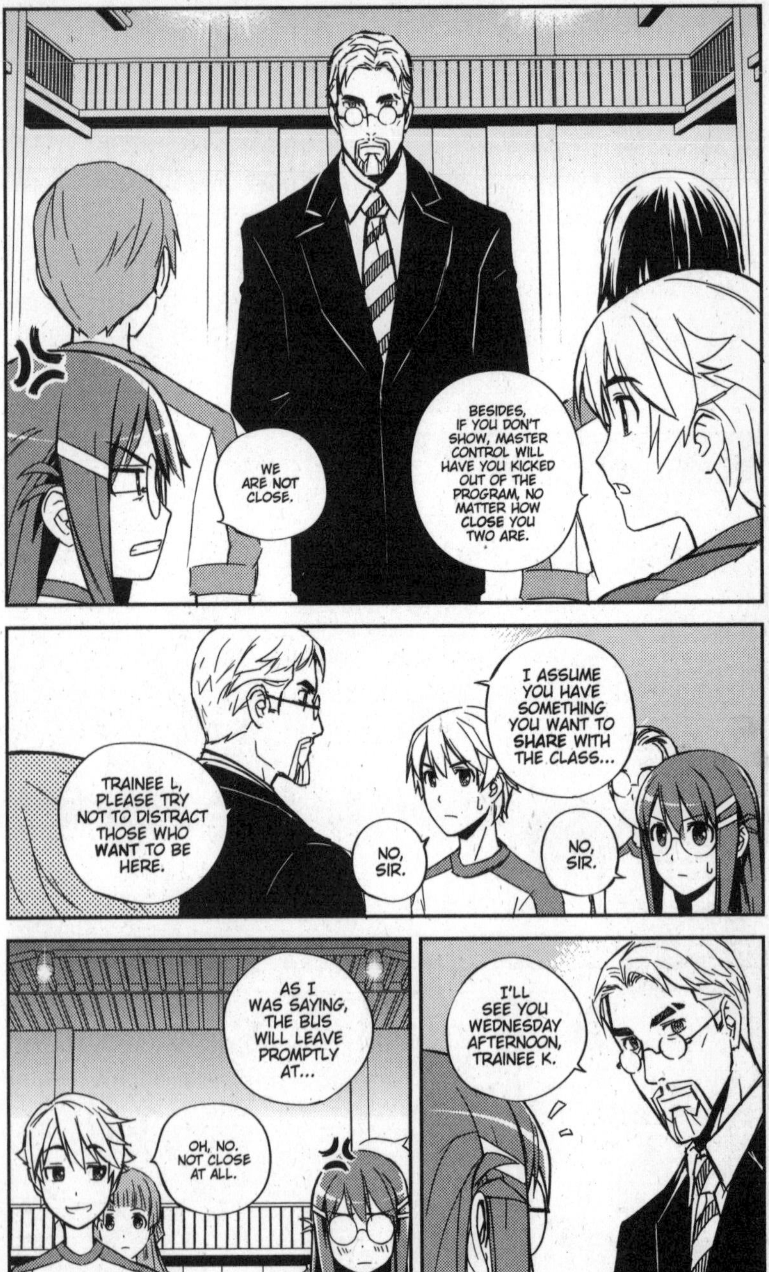
BESIDES, IF YOU DON'T SHOW, MASTER CONTROL WILL HAVE YOU KICKED OUT OF THE PROGRAM, NO MATTER HOW CLOSE YOU TWO ARE.
WE ARE NOT CLOSE.
I ASSUME YOU HAVE SOMETHING YOU WANT TO SHARE WITH THE CLASS...
NO, SIR.
NO, SIR.
TRAINEE L, PLEASE TRY NOT TO DISTRACT THOSE WHO WANT TO BE HERE.
I'LL SEE YOU WEDNESDAY AFTERNOON, TRAINEE K.
AS I WAS SAYING, THE BUS WILL LEAVE PROMPTLY AT...
OH, NO. NOT CLOSE AT ALL.

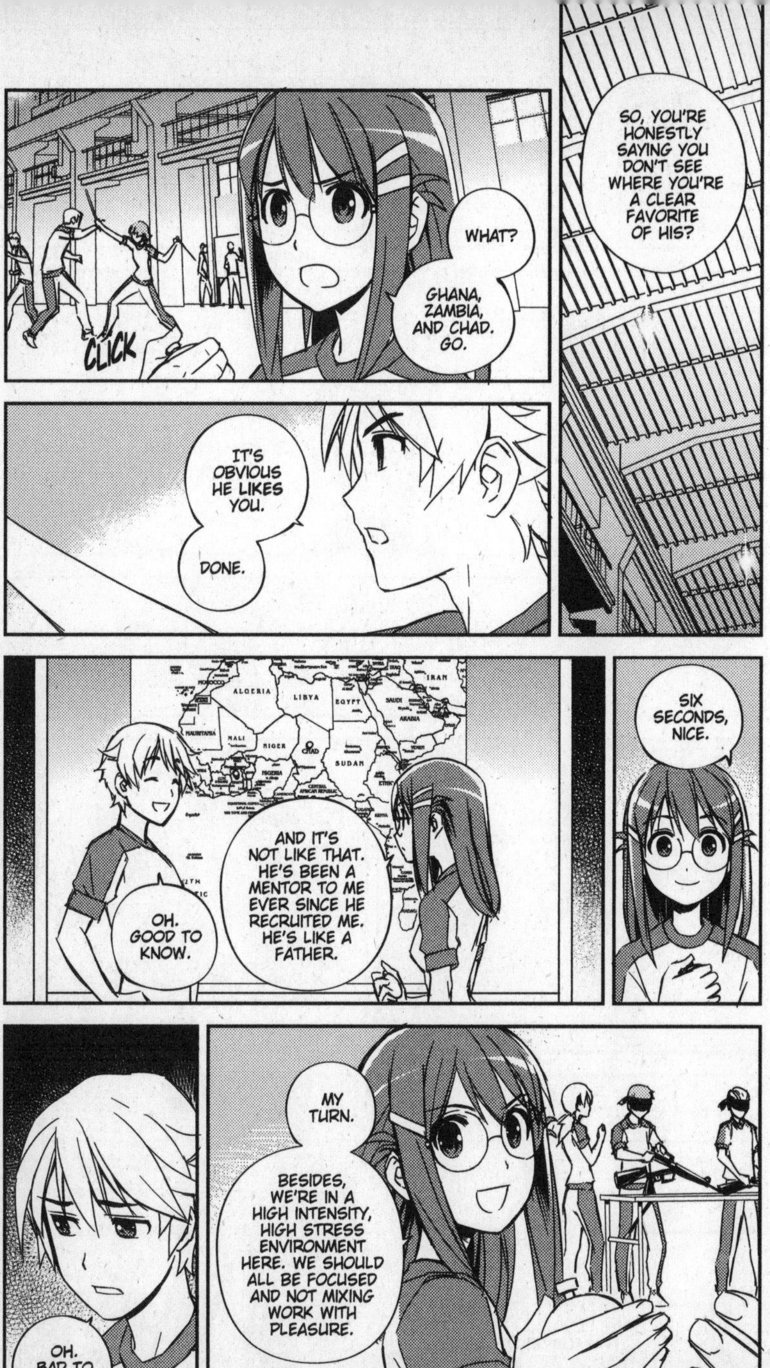
SO, YOU'RE HONESTLY SAYING YOU DON'T SEE WHERE YOU'RE A CLEAR FAVORITE OF HIS?
WHAT?
GHANA, ZAMBIA, AND CHAD. GO.
CLICK
IT'S OBVIOUS HE LIKES YOU.
DONE.
SIX SECONDS, NICE.
AND IT'S NOT LIKE THAT. HE'S BEEN A MENTOR TO ME EVER SINCE HE RECRUITED ME. HE'S LIKE A FATHER.
OH. GOOD TO KNOW.
MY TURN.
BESIDES, WE'RE IN A HIGH INTENSITY, HIGH STRESS ENVIRONMENT HERE. WE SHOULD ALL BE FOCUSED AND NOT MIXING WORK WITH PLEASURE.
OH. BAD TO KNOW.

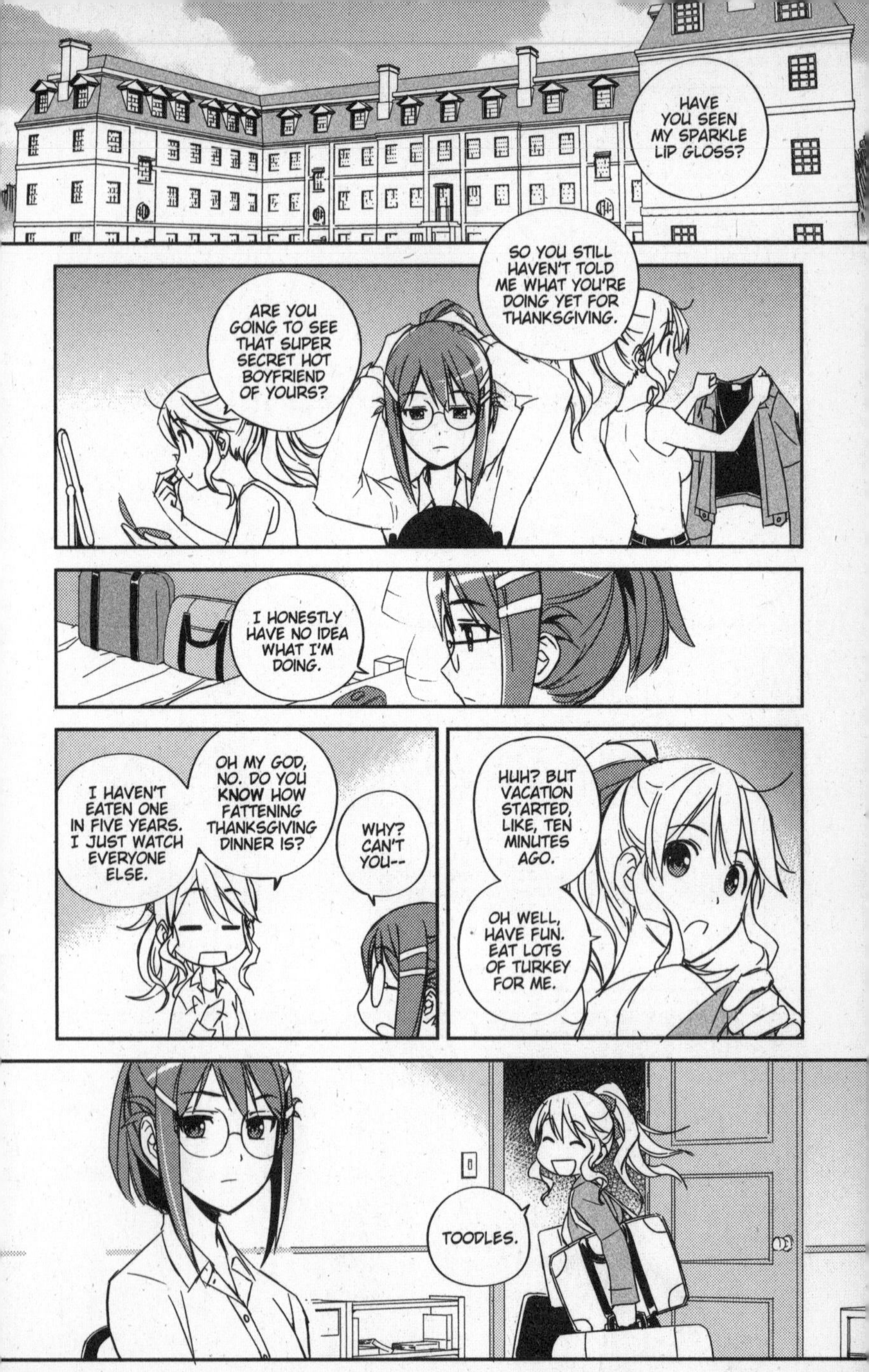
HAVE YOU SEEN MY SPARKLE LIP GLOSS?
SO YOU STILL HAVEN'T TOLD ME WHAT YOU'RE DOING YET FOR THANKSGIVING.
ARE YOU GOING TO SEE THAT SUPER SECRET HOT BOYFRIEND OF YOURS?
I HONESTLY HAVE NO IDEA WHAT I'M DOING.
HUH? BUT VACATION STARTED, LIKE, TEN MINUTES AGO.
OH WELL, HAVE FUN. EAT LOTS OF TURKEY FOR ME.
WHY? CAN'T YOU--
OH MY GOD, NO. DO YOU KNOW HOW FATTENING THANKSGIVING DINNER IS?
I HAVEN'T EATEN ONE IN FIVE YEARS. I JUST WATCH EVERYONE ELSE.
TOODLES.

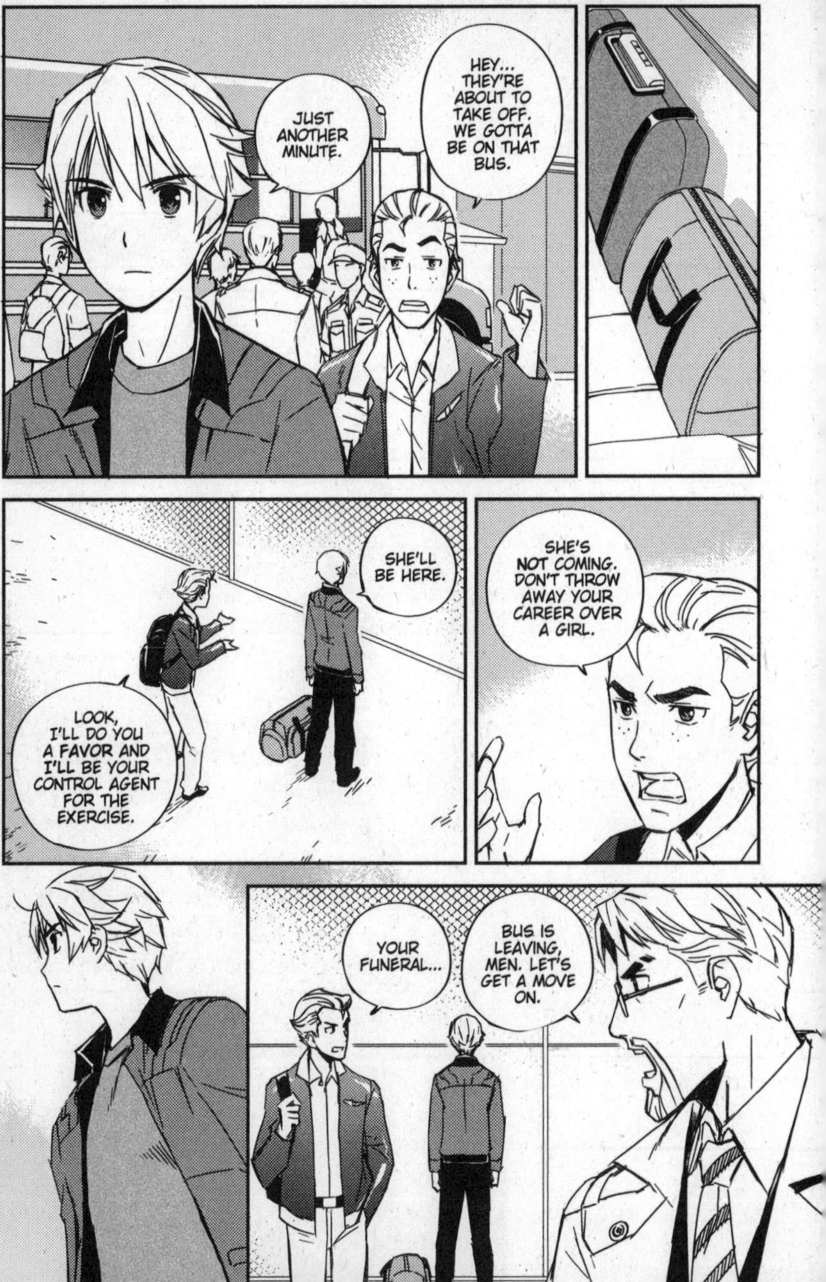
HEY... THEY'RE ABOUT TO TAKE OFF. WE GOTTA BE ON THAT BUS.
JUST ANOTHER MINUTE.
SHE'S NOT COMING. DON'T THROW AWAY YOUR CAREER OVER A GIRL.
SHE'LL BE HERE.
LOOK, I'LL DO YOU A FAVOR AND I'LL BE YOUR CONTROL AGENT FOR THE EXERCISE.
BUS IS LEAVING, MEN. LET'S GET A MOVE ON.
YOUR FUNERAL...

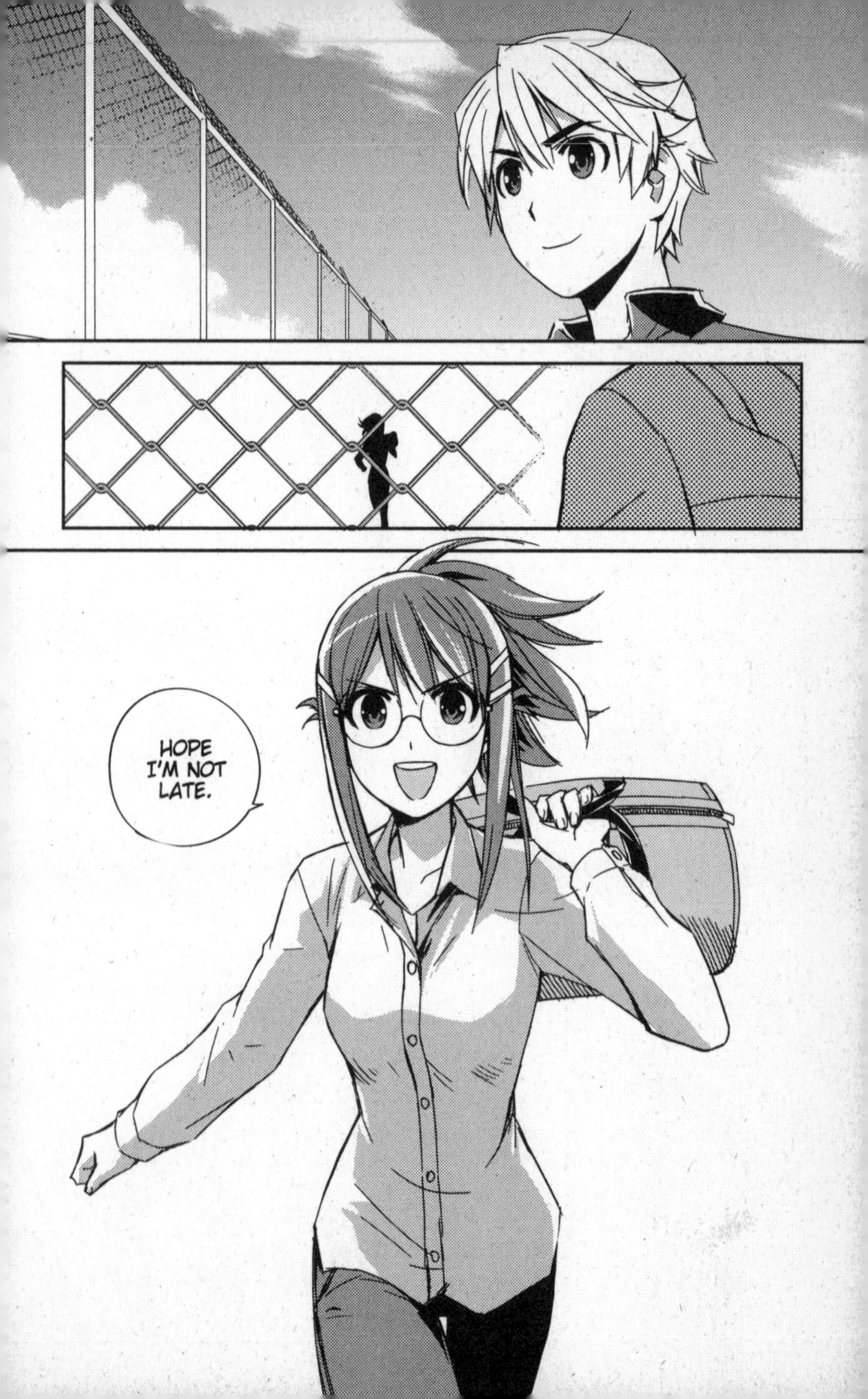
HOPE I'M NOT LATE.

FILE 3:
THE DEVICE

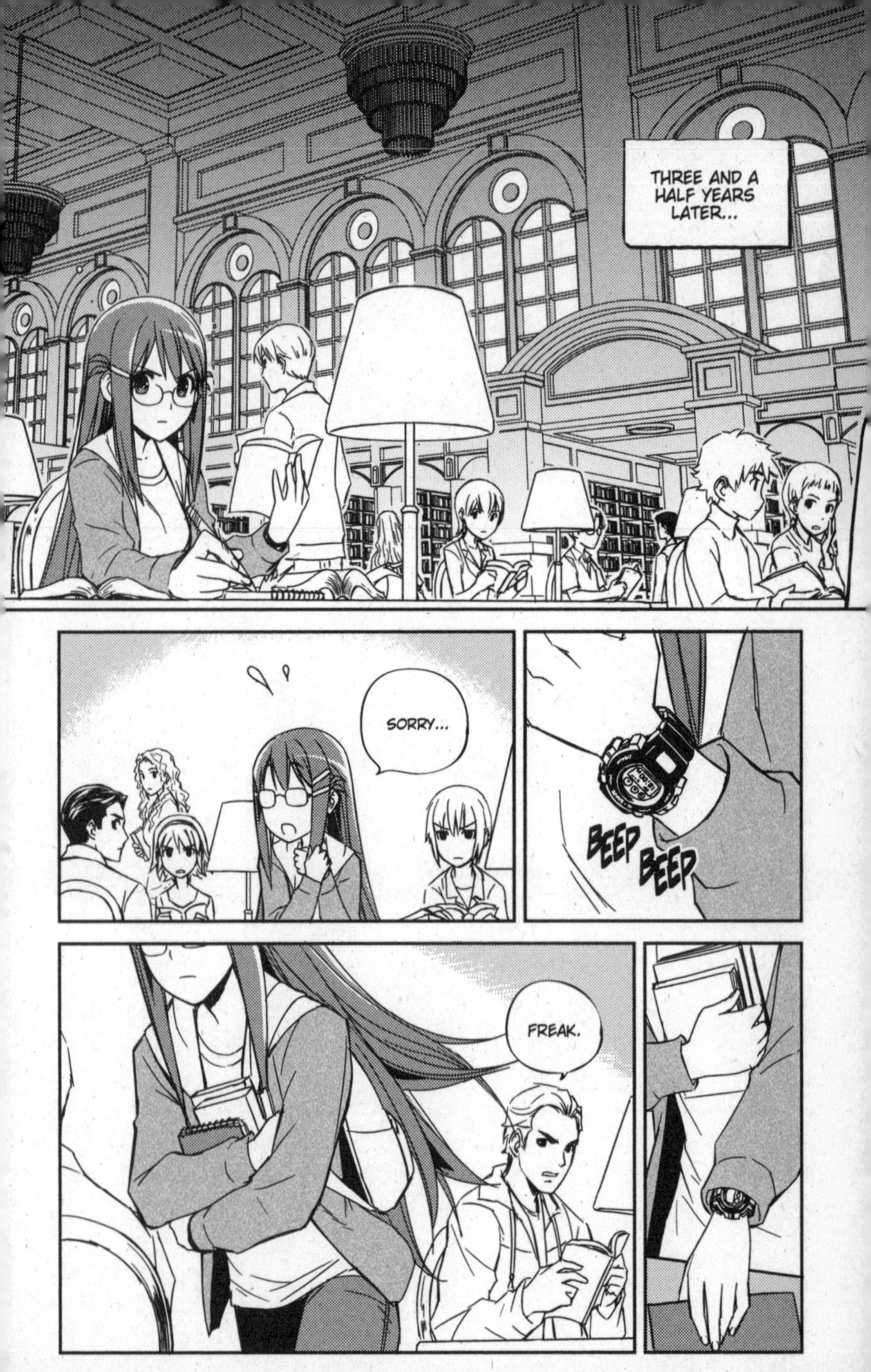
THREE AND A HALF YEARS LATER...
BEEP BEEP
SORRY...
FREAK.

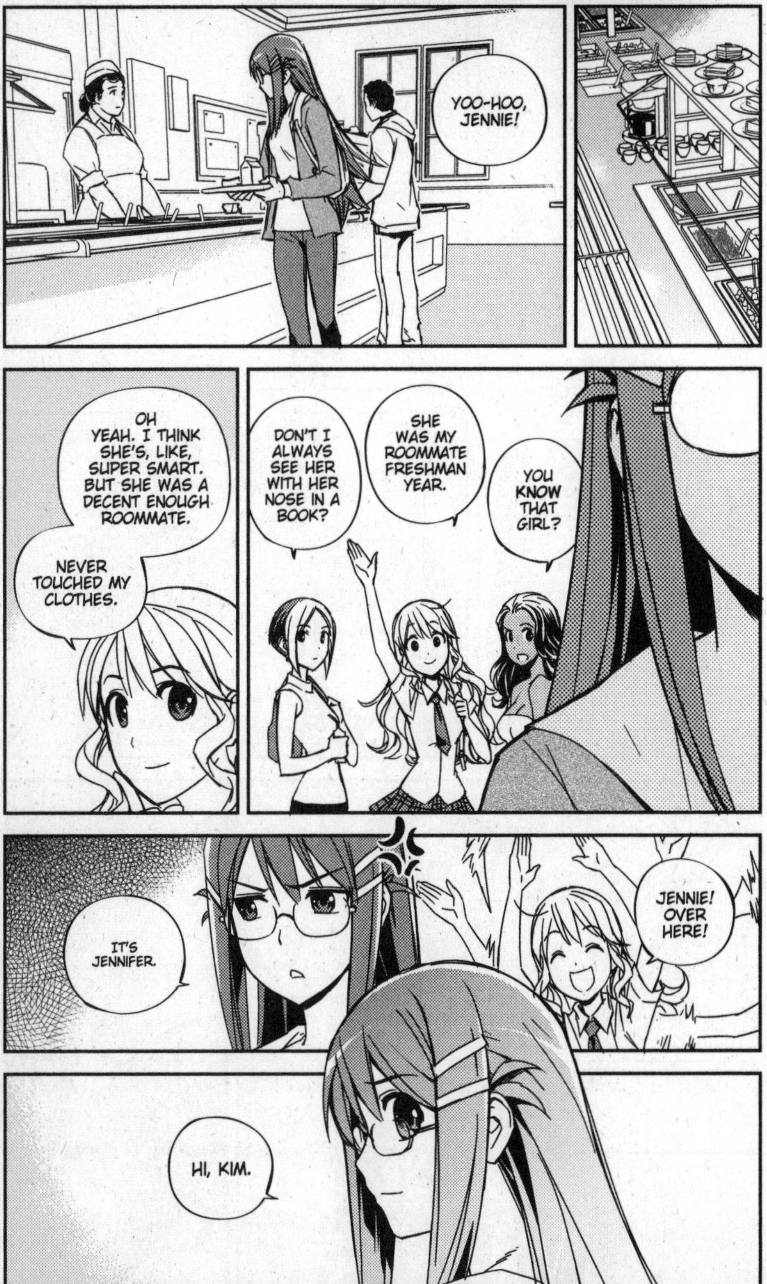
YOO-HOO, JENNIE!
YOU KNOW THAT GIRL?
SHE WAS MY ROOMMATE FRESHMAN YEAR.
DON'T I ALWAYS SEE HER WITH HER NOSE IN A BOOK?
OH YEAH. I THINK SHE'S, LIKE, SUPER SMART. BUT SHE WAS A DECENT ENOUGH ROOMMATE.
NEVER TOUCHED MY CLOTHES.
JENNIE! OVER HERE!
IT'S JENNIFER.
HI, KIM.

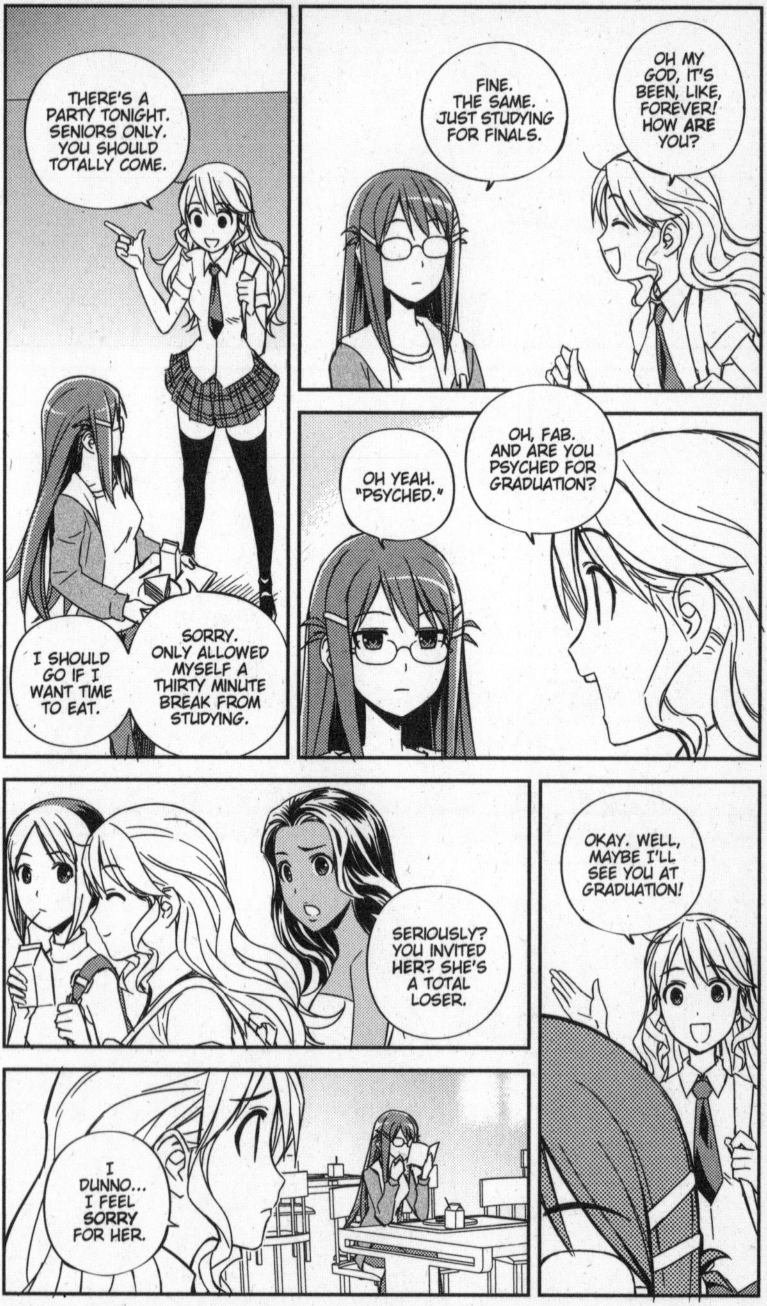
OH MY GOD, IT'S BEEN, LIKE, FOREVER! HOW ARE YOU?
FINE. THE SAME. JUST STUDYING FOR FINALS.
OH, FAB. AND ARE YOU PSYCHED FOR GRADUATION?
OH YEAH. "PSYCHED."
THERE'S A PARTY TONIGHT. SENIORS ONLY. YOU SHOULD TOTALLY COME.
SORRY. ONLY ALLOWED MYSELF A THIRTY MINUTE BREAK FROM STUDYING.
I SHOULD GO IF I WANT TIME TO EAT.
OKAY. WELL, MAYBE I'LL SEE YOU AT GRADUATION!
SERIOUSLY? YOU INVITED HER? SHE'S A TOTAL LOSER.
I DUNNO... I FEEL SORRY FOR HER.

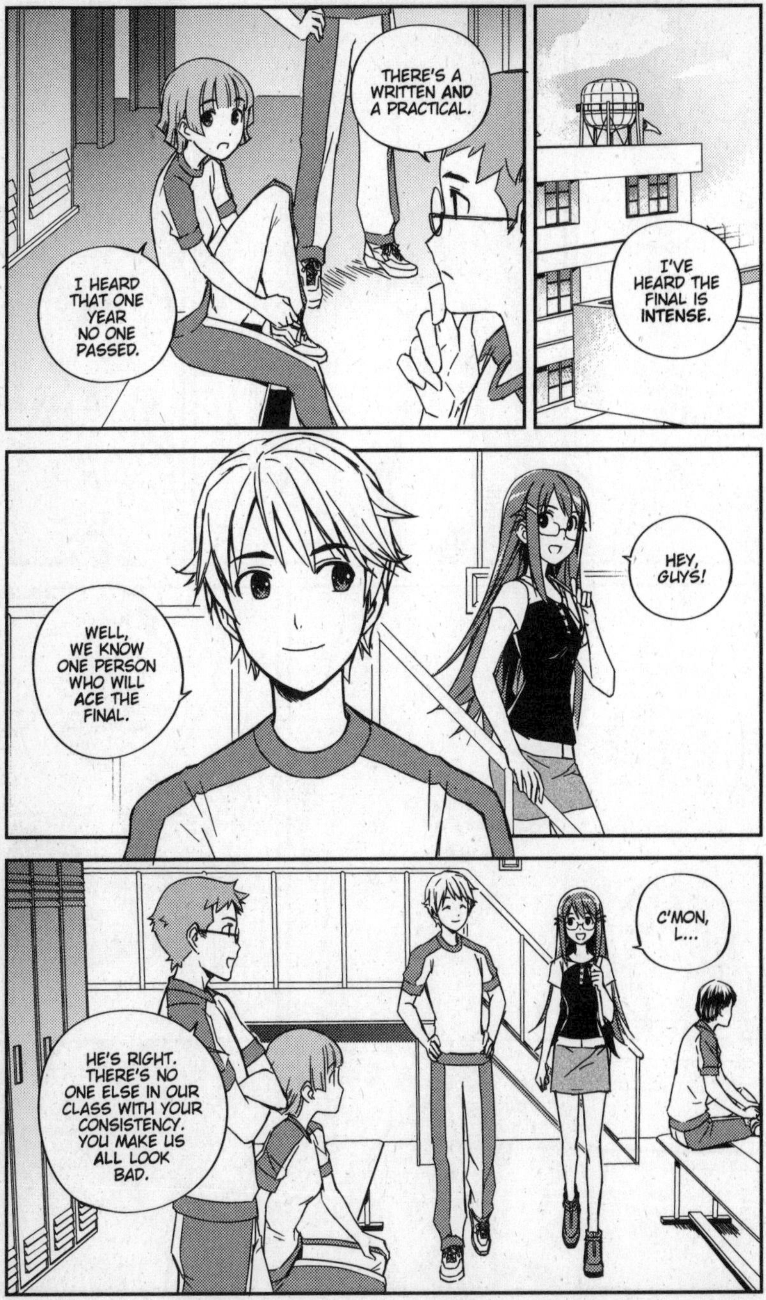
I'VE HEARD THE FINAL IS INTENSE.
THERE'S A WRITTEN AND A PRACTICAL.
I HEARD THAT ONE YEAR NO ONE PASSED.
HEY, GUYS!
WELL, WE KNOW ONE PERSON WHO WILL ACE THE FINAL.
C'MON, L...
HE'S RIGHT. THERE'S NO ONE ELSE IN OUR CLASS WITH YOUR CONSISTENCY. YOU MAKE US ALL LOOK BAD.

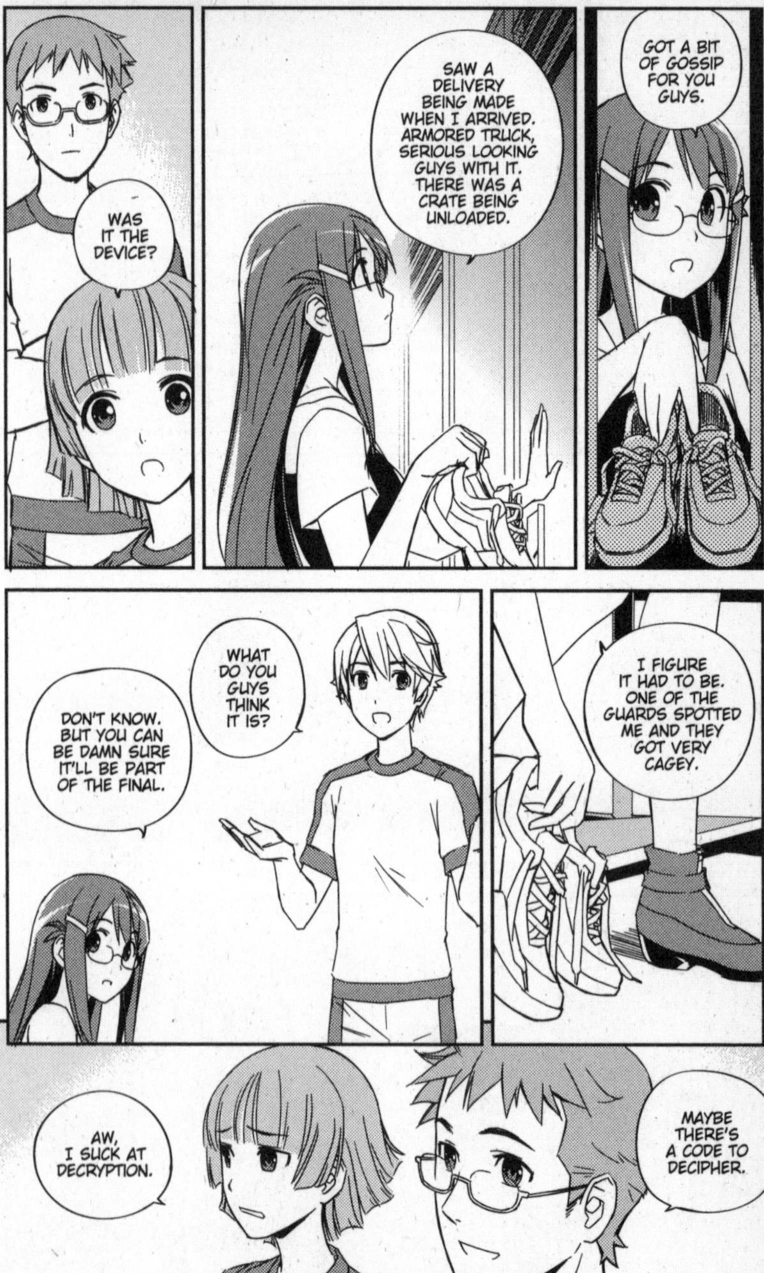
GOT A BIT OF GOSSIP FOR YOU GUYS.
SAW A DELIVERY BEING MADE WHEN I ARRIVED. ARMORED TRUCK, SERIOUS LOOKING GUYS WITH IT. THERE WAS A CRATE BEING UNLOADED.
WAS IT THE DEVICE?
I FIGURE IT HAD TO BE. ONE OF THE GUARDS SPOTTED ME AND THEY GOT VERY CAGEY.
WHAT DO YOU GUYS THINK IT IS?
DON'T KNOW. BUT YOU CAN BE DAMN SURE IT'LL BE PART OF THE FINAL.
MAYBE THERE'S A CODE TO DECIPHER.
AW, I SUCK AT DECRYPTION.

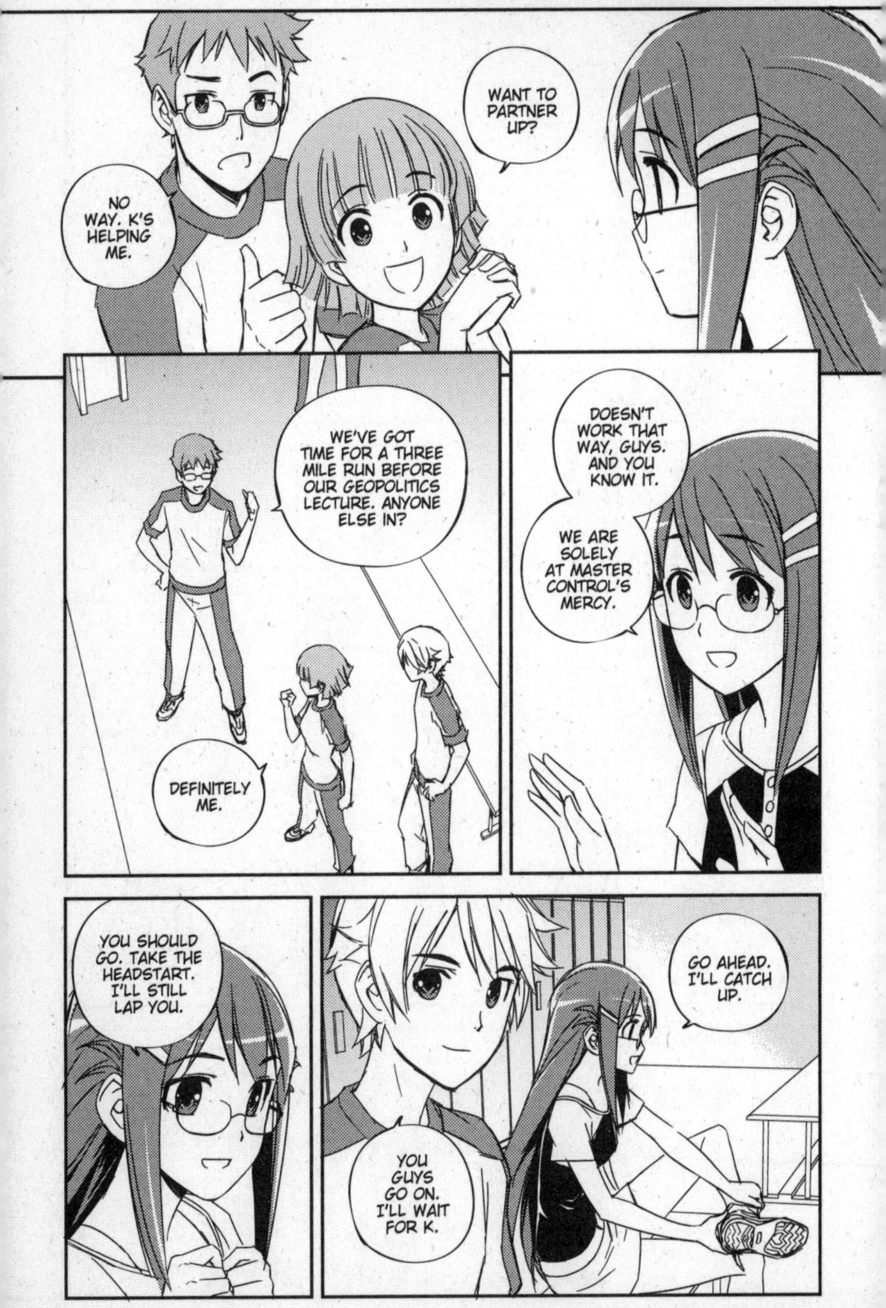
WANT TO PARTNER UP?
NO WAY. K'S HELPING ME.
DOESN'T WORK THAT WAY, GUYS. AND YOU KNOW IT.
WE ARE SOLELY AT MASTER CONTROL'S MERCY.
WE'VE GOT TIME FOR A THREE MILE RUN BEFORE OUR GEOPOLITICS LECTURE. ANYONE ELSE IN?
DEFINITELY ME.
GO AHEAD. I'LL CATCH UP.
YOU GUYS GO ON. I'LL WAIT FOR K.
YOU SHOULD GO. TAKE THE HEADSTART. I'LL STILL LAP YOU.

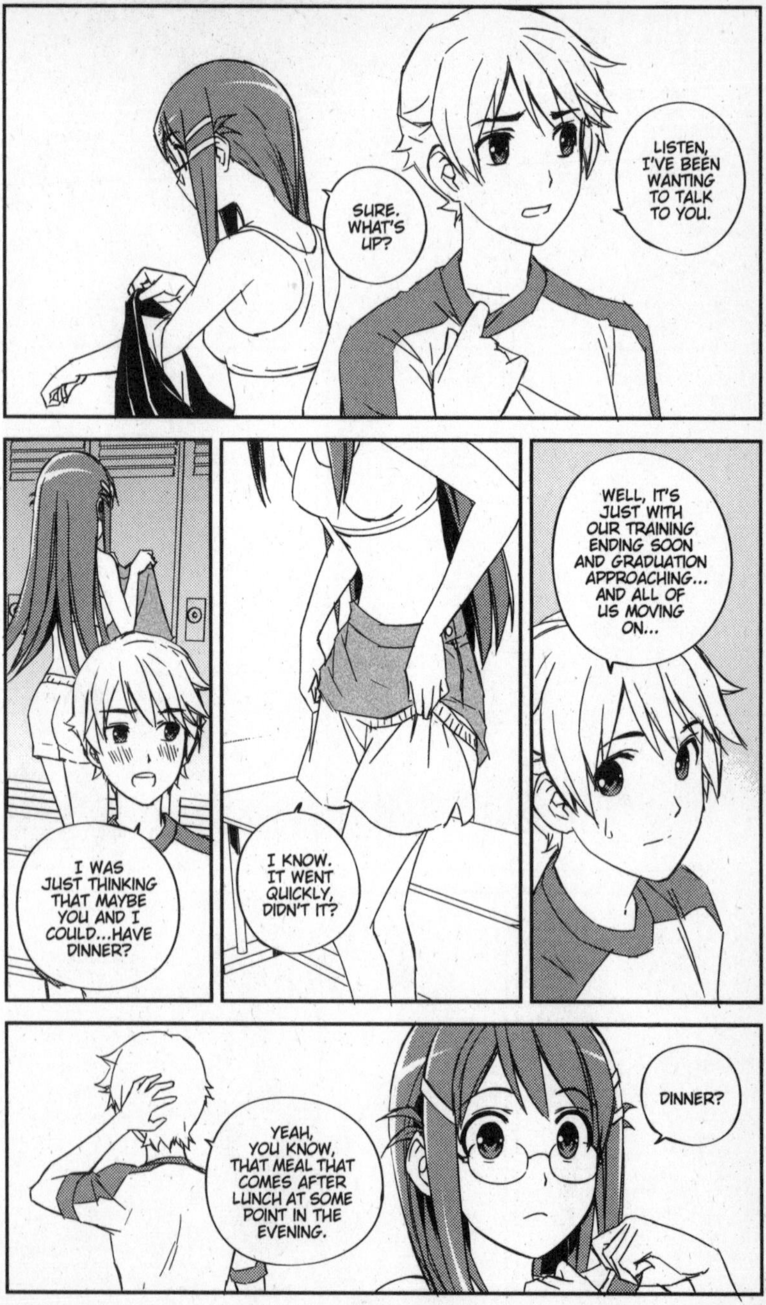
LISTEN, I'VE BEEN WANTING TO TALK TO YOU.
SURE. WHAT'S UP?
WELL, IT'S JUST WITH OUR TRAINING ENDING SOON AND GRADUATION APPROACHING... AND ALL OF US MOVING ON...
I KNOW. IT WENT QUICKLY, DIDN'T IT?
I WAS JUST THINKING THAT MAYBE YOU AND I COULD...HAVE DINNER?
DINNER?
YEAH, YOU KNOW, THAT MEAL THAT COMES AFTER LUNCH AT SOME POINT IN THE EVENING.

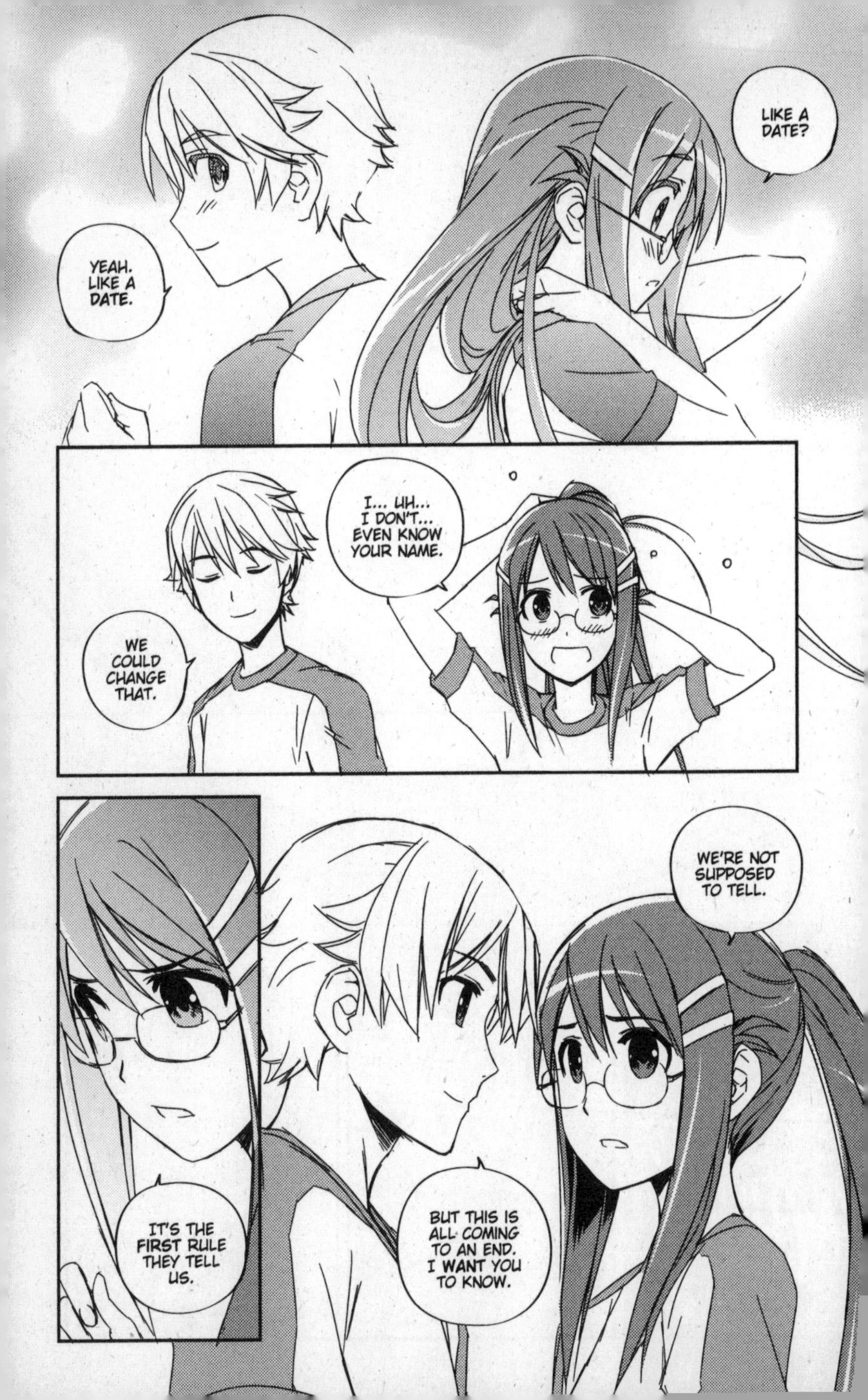
LIKE A DATE?
YEAH. LIKE A DATE.
I... UH... I DON'T... EVEN KNOW YOUR NAME.
WE COULD CHANGE THAT.
WE'RE NOT SUPPOSED TO TELL.
IT'S THE FIRST RULE THEY TELL US.
BUT THIS IS ALL COMING TO AN END. I WANT YOU TO KNOW.

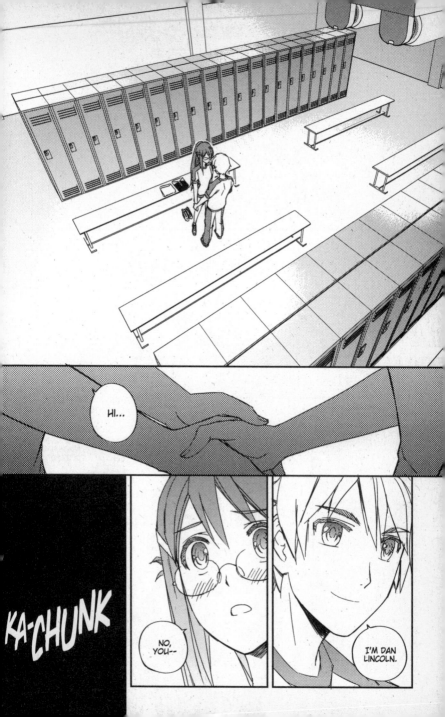

HI...

KA-CHUNK

NO, YOU--

I'M DAN LINCOLN.

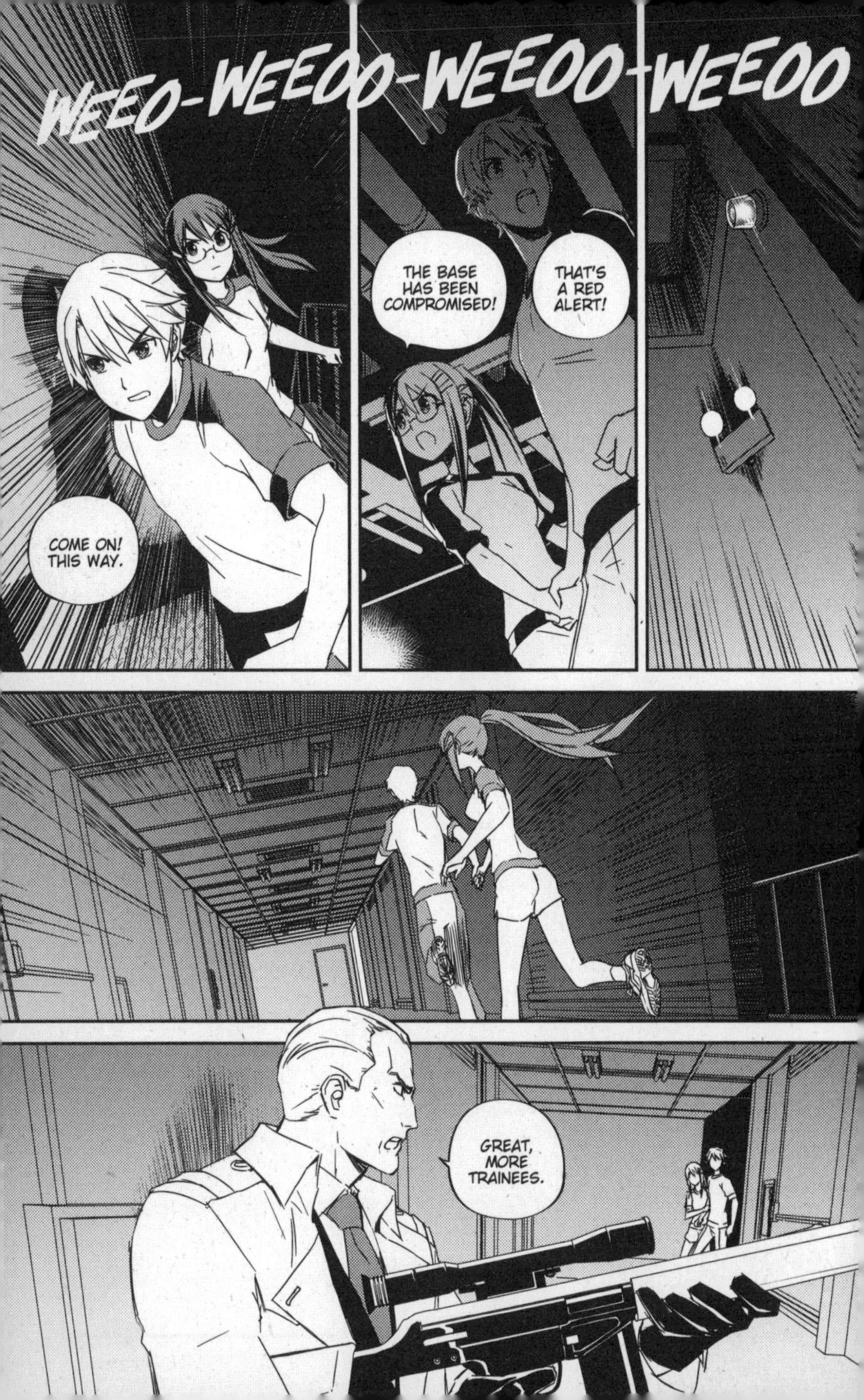
WEEO-WEEOO-WEEOO-WEEOO
THAT'S A RED ALERT!
THE BASE HAS BEEN COMPROMISED!
COME ON! THIS WAY.
GREAT, MORE TRAINEES.

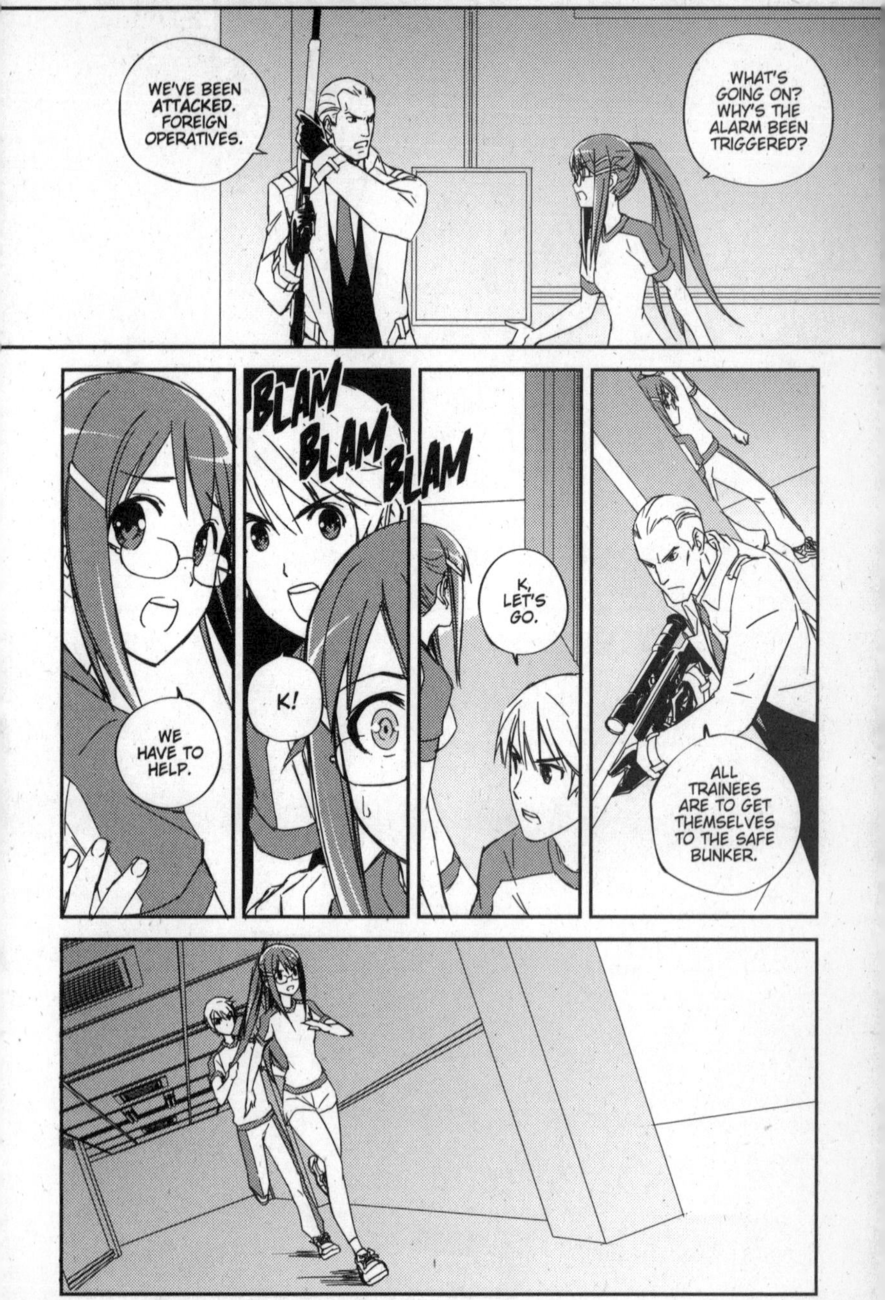
WHAT'S GOING ON? WHY'S THE ALARM BEEN TRIGGERED?
WE'VE BEEN ATTACKED. FOREIGN OPERATIVES.
ALL TRAINEES ARE TO GET THEMSELVES TO THE SAFE BUNKER.
K, LET'S GO.
BLAM BLAM BLAM
K!
WE HAVE TO HELP.

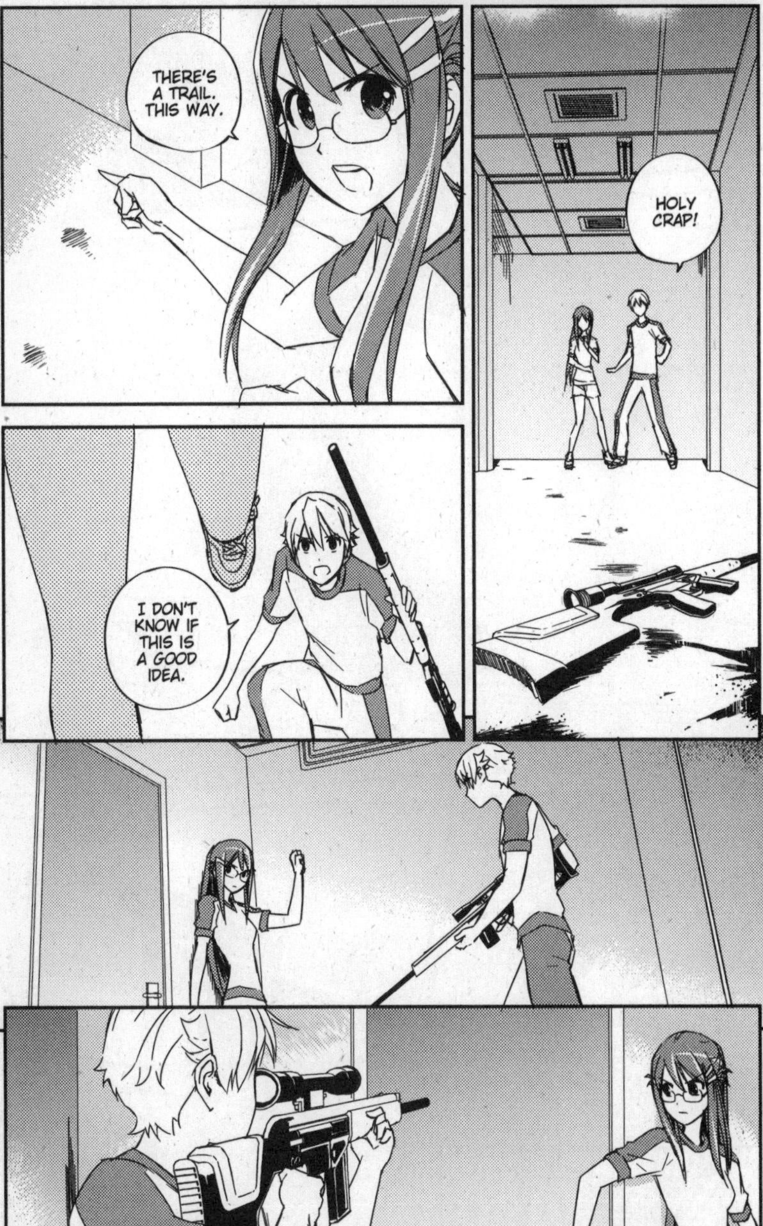
THERE'S A TRAIL. THIS WAY.
I DON'T KNOW IF THIS IS A GOOD IDEA.
HOLY CRAP!

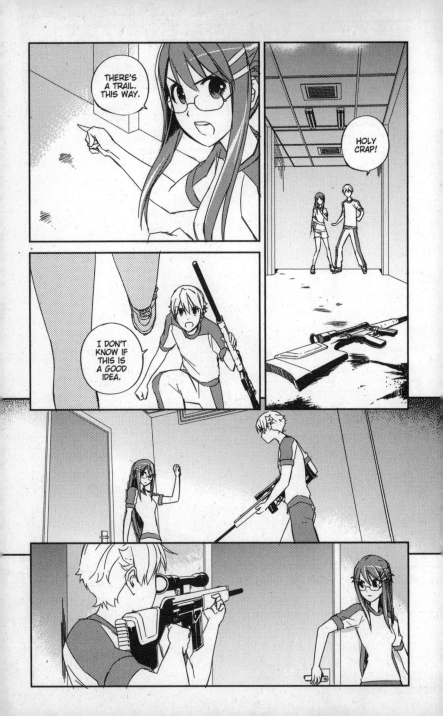

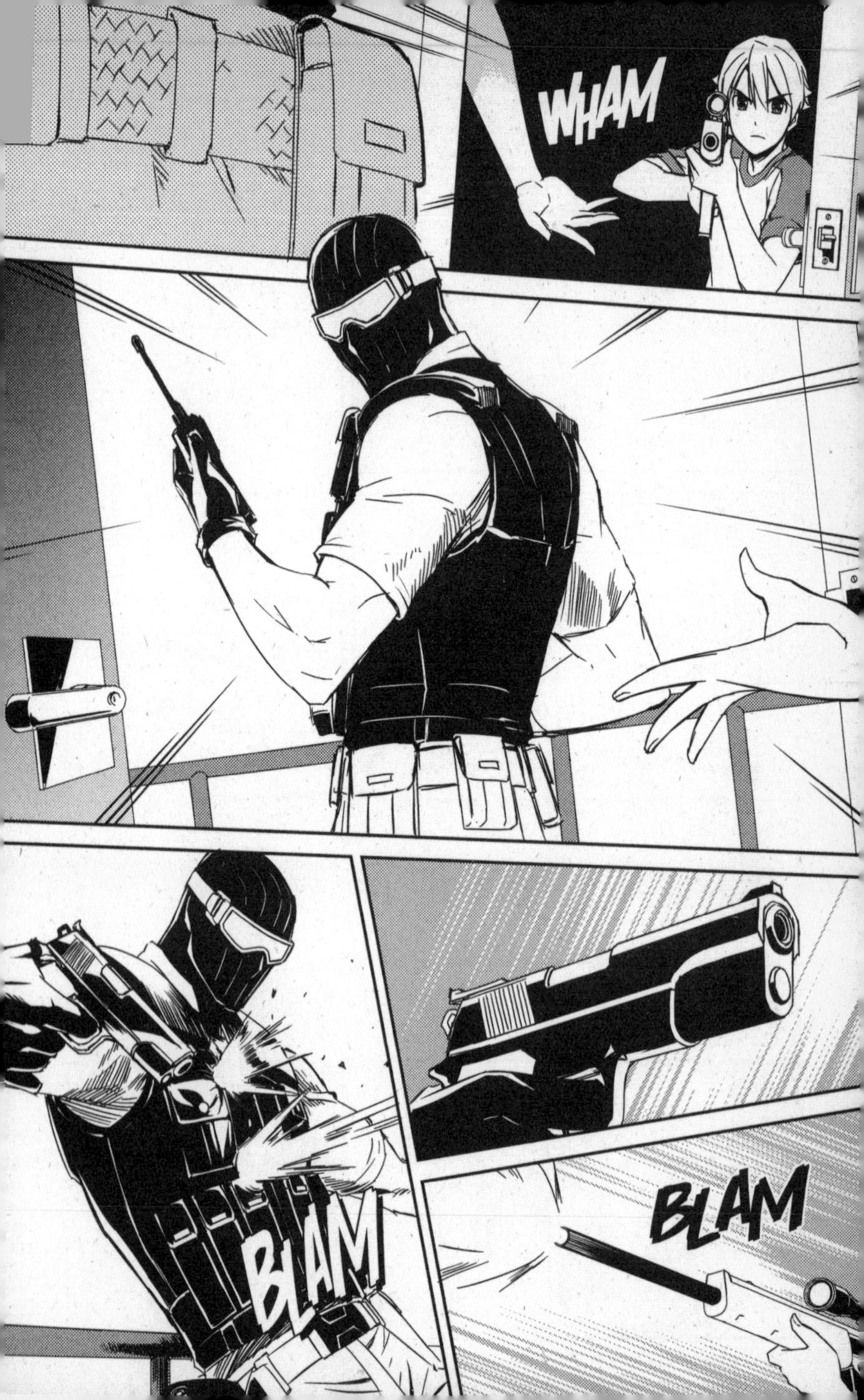
WHAM
BLAM
BLAM

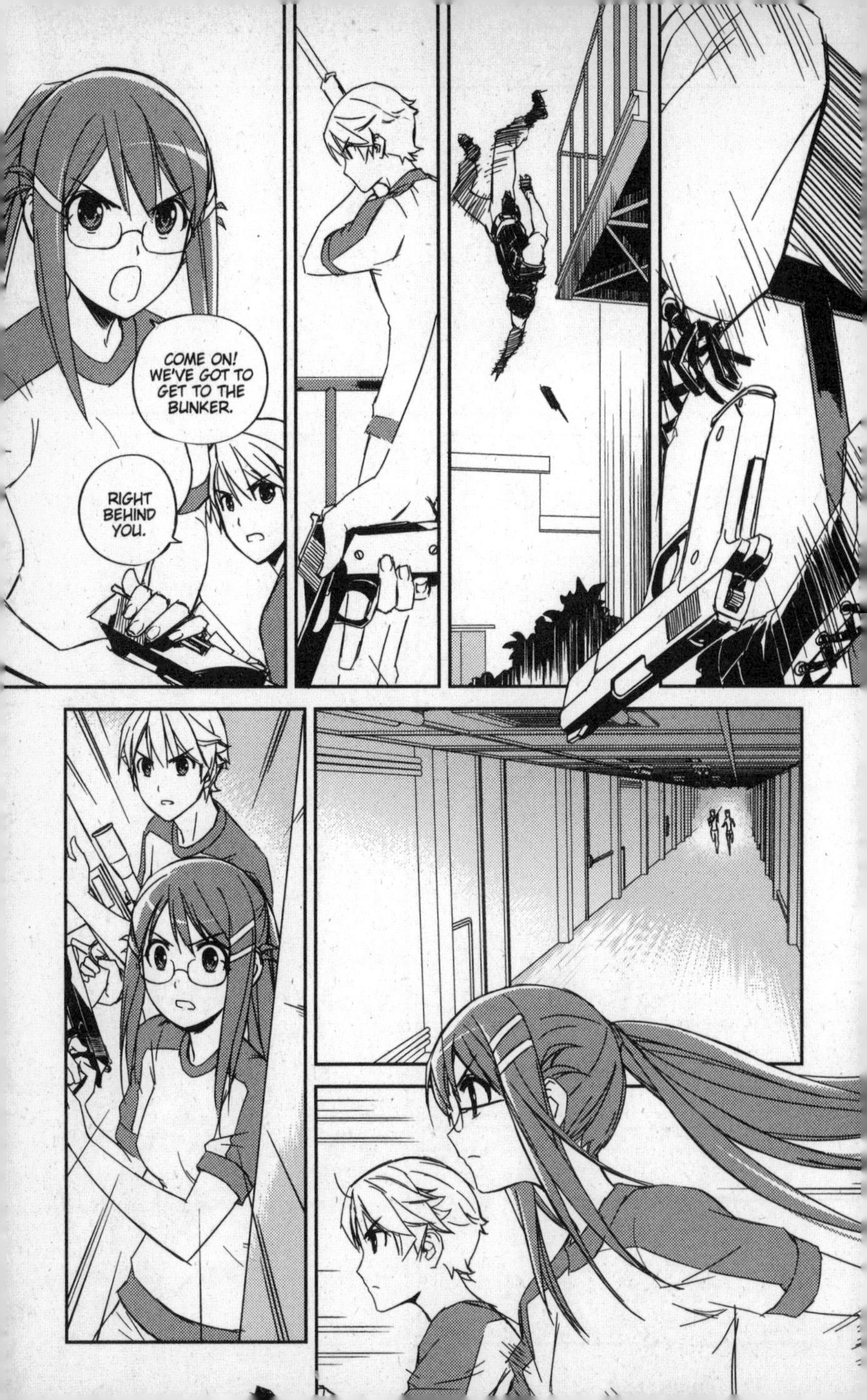
COME ON! WE'VE GOT TO GET TO THE BUNKER.
RIGHT BEHIND YOU.

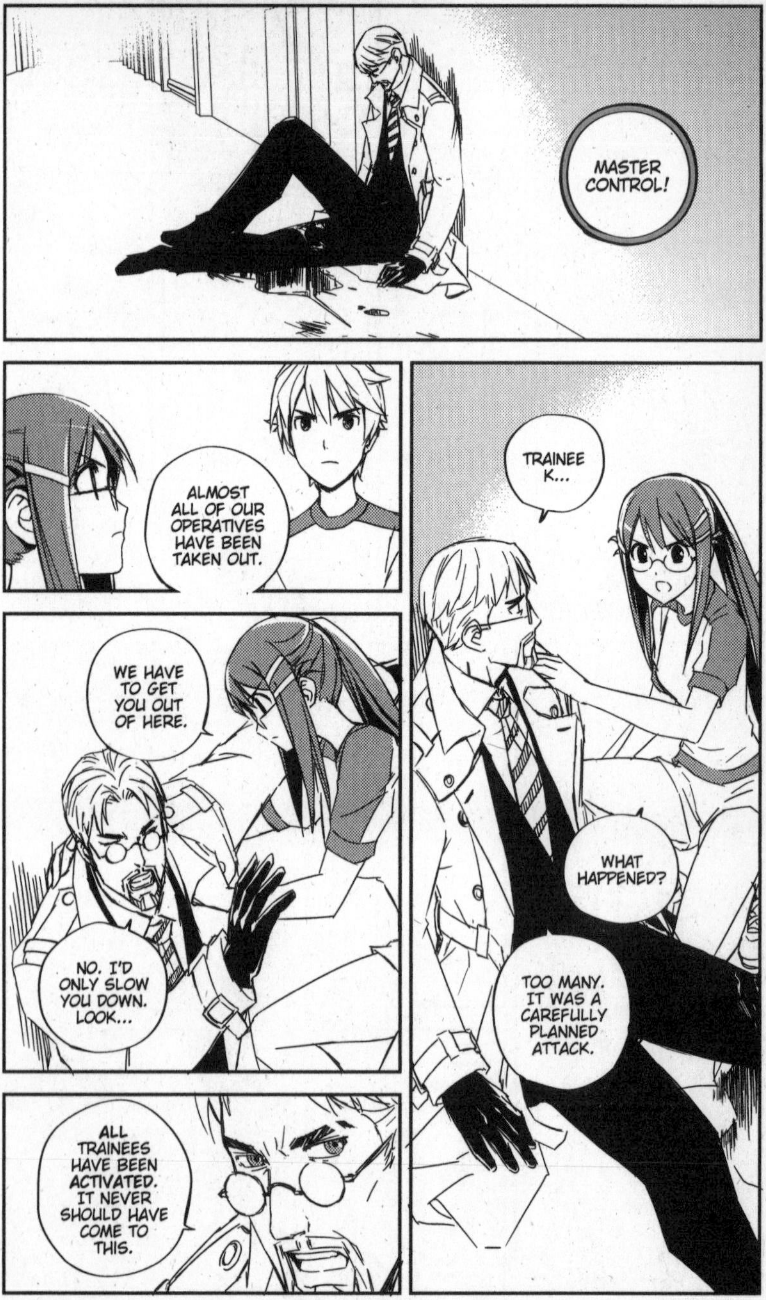
MASTER CONTROL!
TRAINEE K...
WHAT HAPPENED?
TOO MANY. IT WAS A CAREFULLY PLANNED ATTACK.
ALMOST ALL OF OUR OPERATIVES HAVE BEEN TAKEN OUT.
WE HAVE TO GET YOU OUT OF HERE.
NO. I'D ONLY SLOW YOU DOWN. LOOK...
ALL TRAINEES HAVE BEEN ACTIVATED. IT NEVER SHOULD HAVE COME TO THIS.

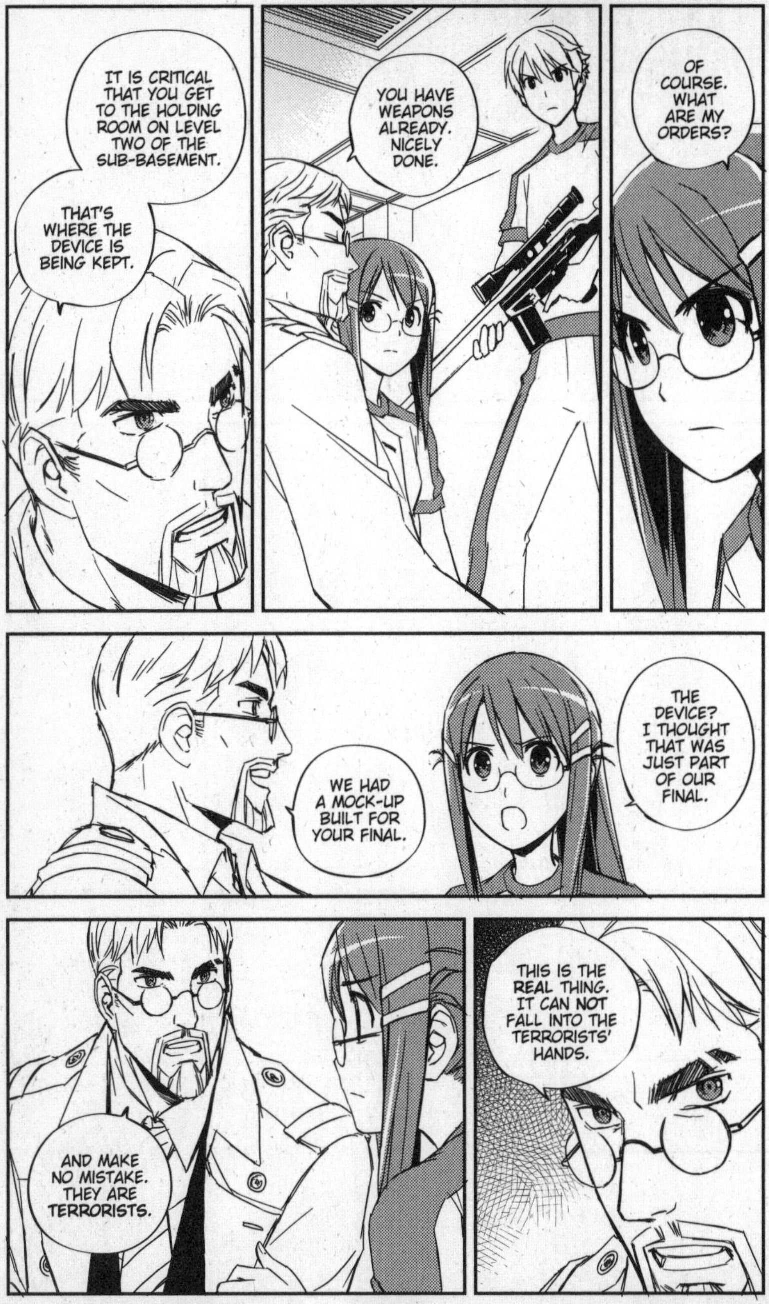
OF COURSE. WHAT ARE MY ORDERS?
YOU HAVE WEAPONS ALREADY. NICELY DONE.
IT IS CRITICAL THAT YOU GET TO THE HOLDING ROOM ON LEVEL TWO OF THE SUB-BASEMENT.
THAT'S WHERE THE DEVICE IS BEING KEPT.
THE DEVICE? I THOUGHT THAT WAS JUST PART OF OUR FINAL.
WE HAD A MOCK-UP BUILT FOR YOUR FINAL.
THIS IS THE REAL THING. IT CAN NOT FALL INTO THE TERRORISTS' HANDS.
AND MAKE NO MISTAKE. THEY ARE TERRORISTS.

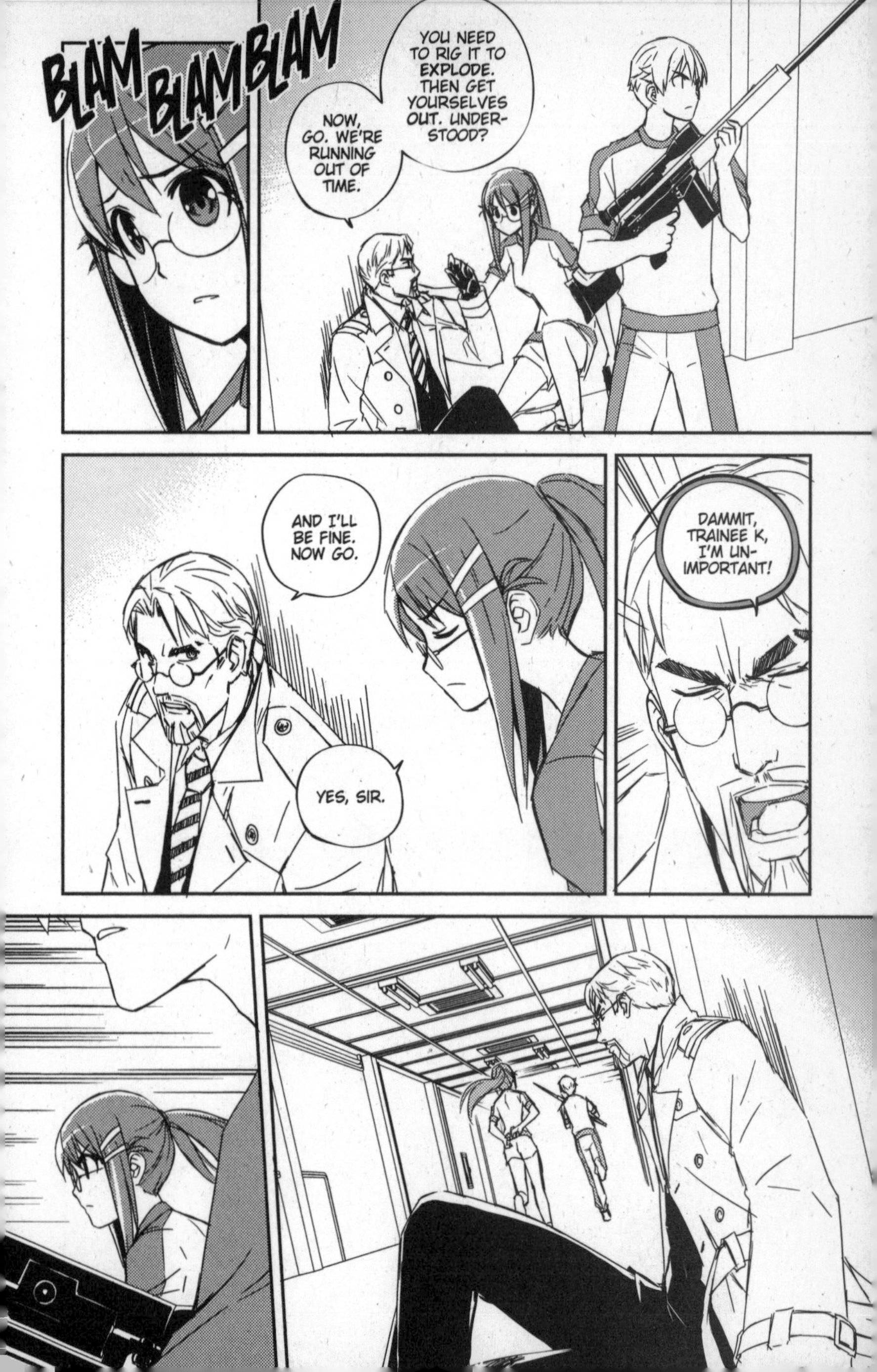
YOU NEED TO RIG IT TO EXPLODE. THEN GET YOURSELVES OUT. UNDER-STOOD?
NOW, GO. WE'RE RUNNING OUT OF TIME.
BLAM BLAM BLAM
DAMMIT, TRAINEE K, I'M UN-IMPORTANT!
AND I'LL BE FINE. NOW GO.
YES, SIR.

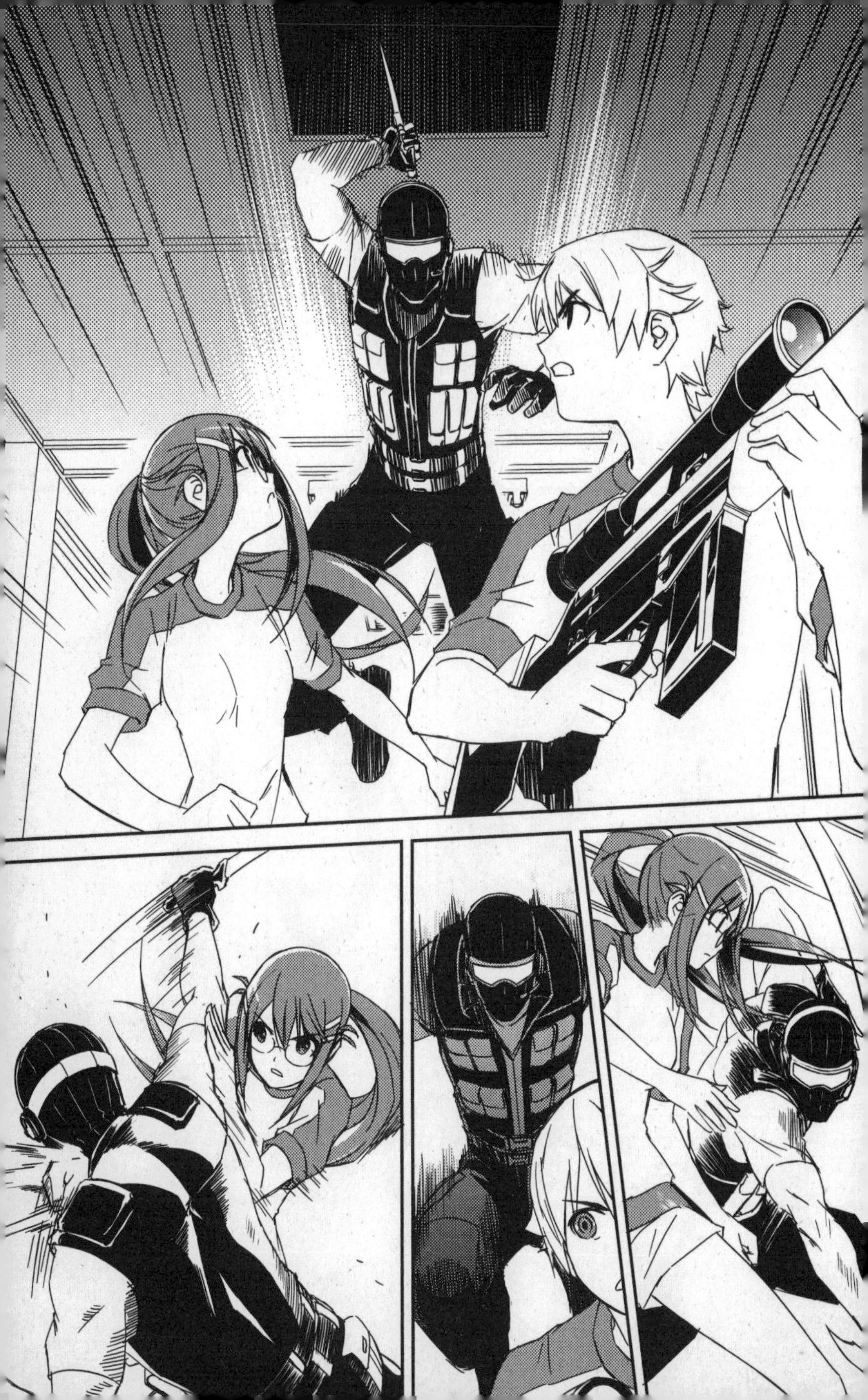

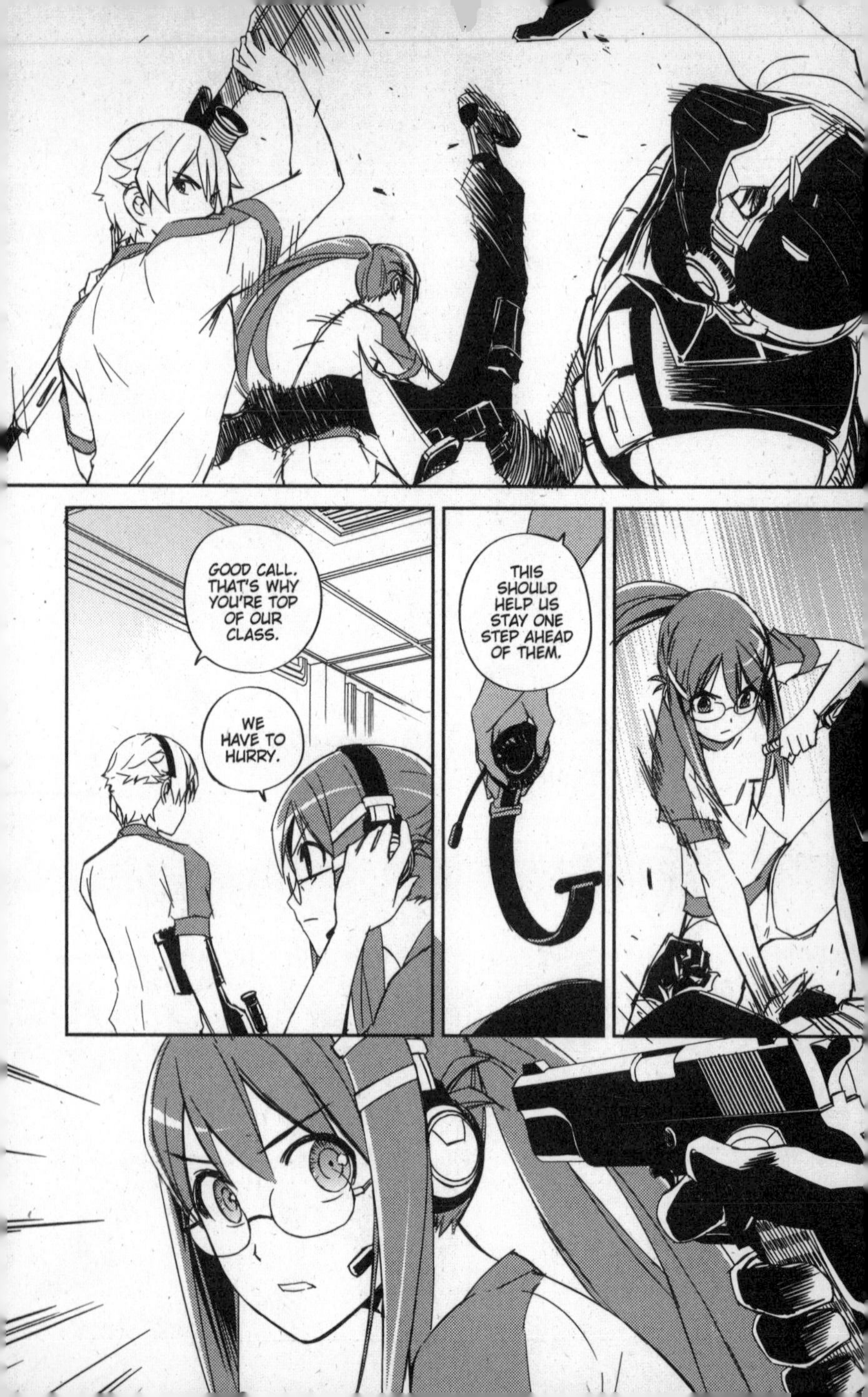
THIS SHOULD HELP US STAY ONE STEP AHEAD OF THEM.
GOOD CALL. THAT'S WHY YOU'RE TOP OF OUR CLASS.
WE HAVE TO HURRY.

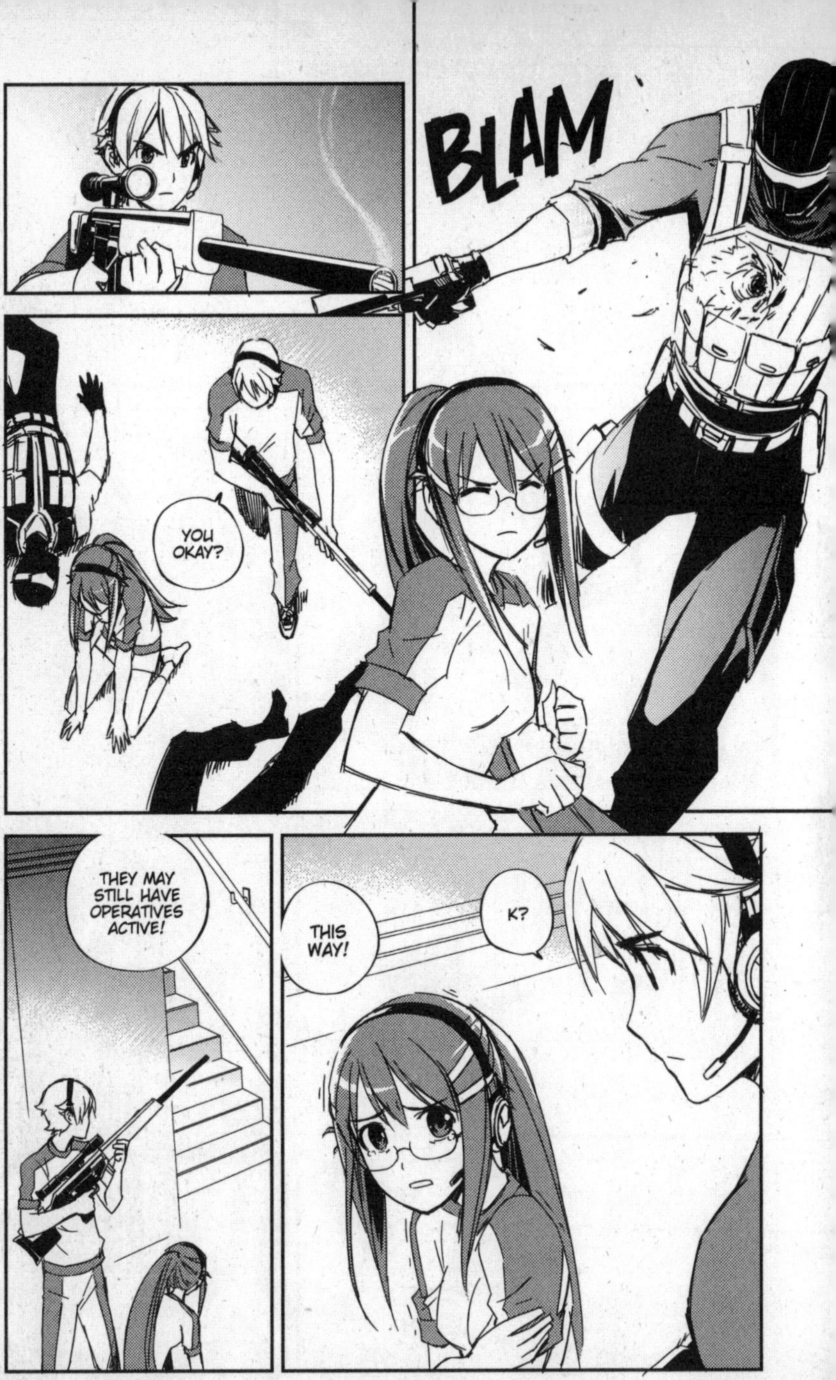
BLAM
YOU OKAY?
K?
THIS WAY!
THEY MAY STILL HAVE OPERATIVES ACTIVE!

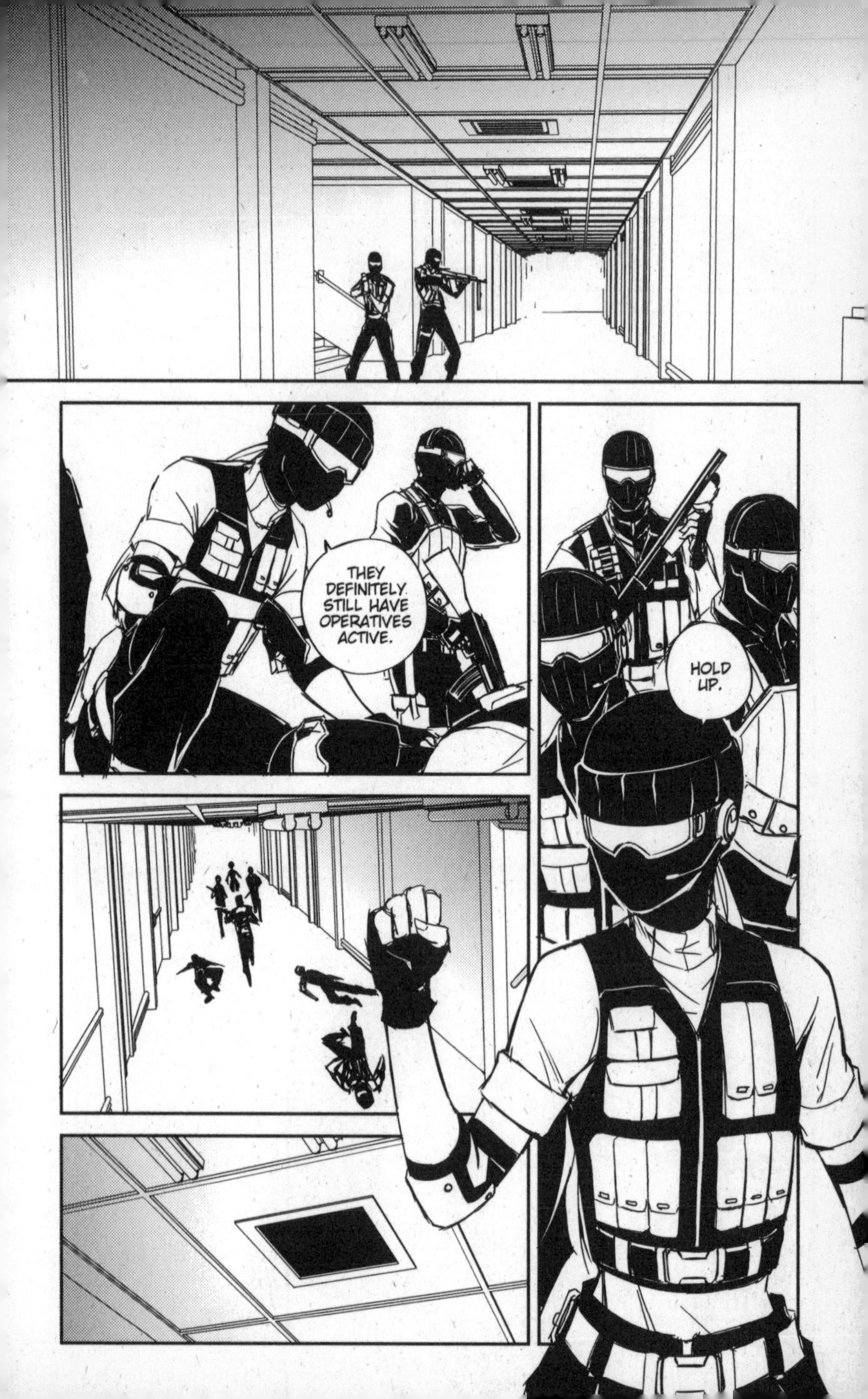
HOLD UP.
THEY DEFINITELY STILL HAVE OPERATIVES ACTIVE.

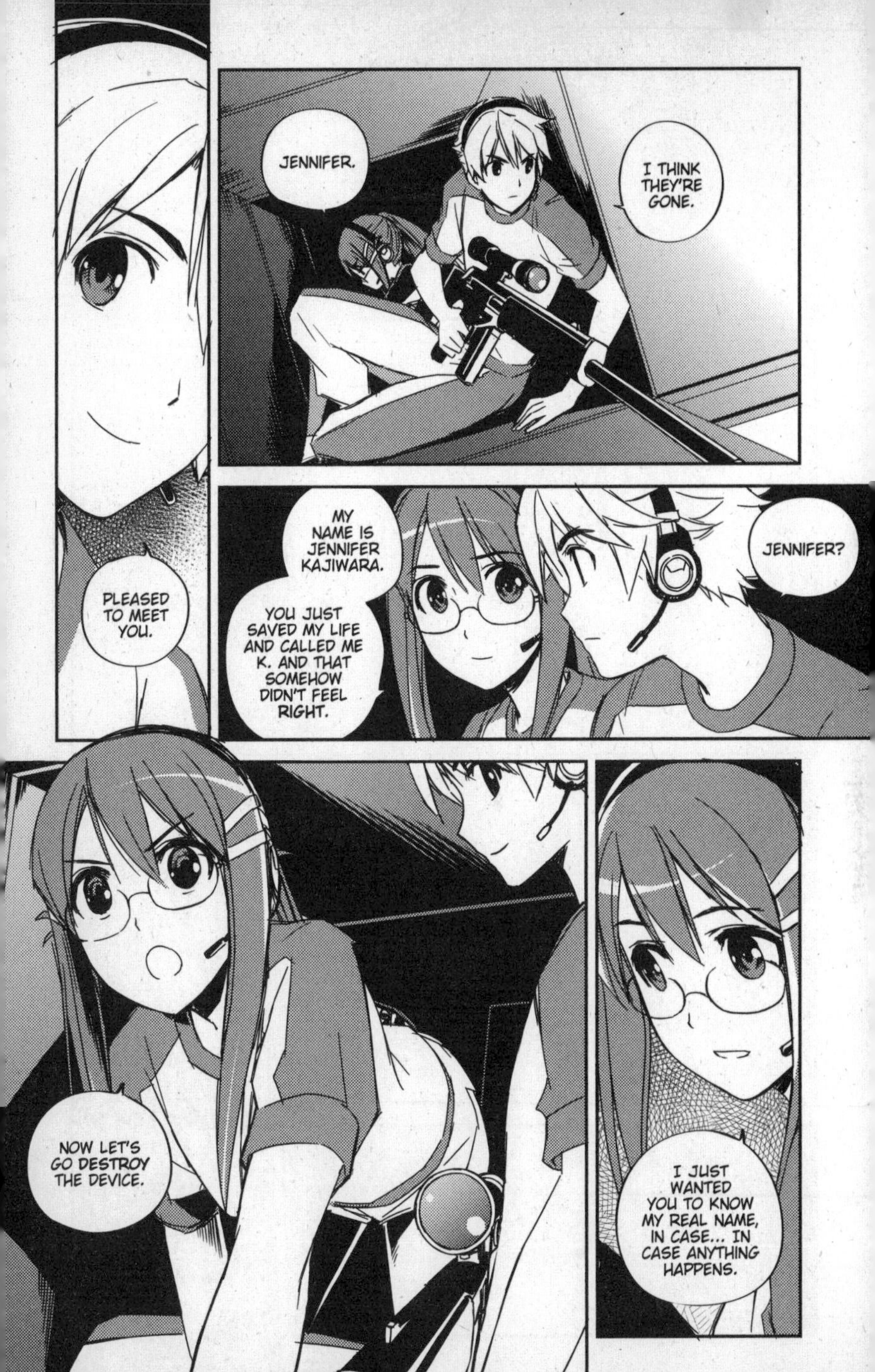
I THINK THEY'RE GONE.
JENNIFER.
JENNIFER?
MY NAME IS JENNIFER KAJIWARA.
YOU JUST SAVED MY LIFE AND CALLED ME K. AND THAT SOMEHOW DIDN'T FEEL RIGHT.
PLEASED TO MEET YOU.
I JUST WANTED YOU TO KNOW MY REAL NAME, IN CASE... IN CASE ANYTHING HAPPENS.
NOW LET'S GO DESTROY THE DEVICE.

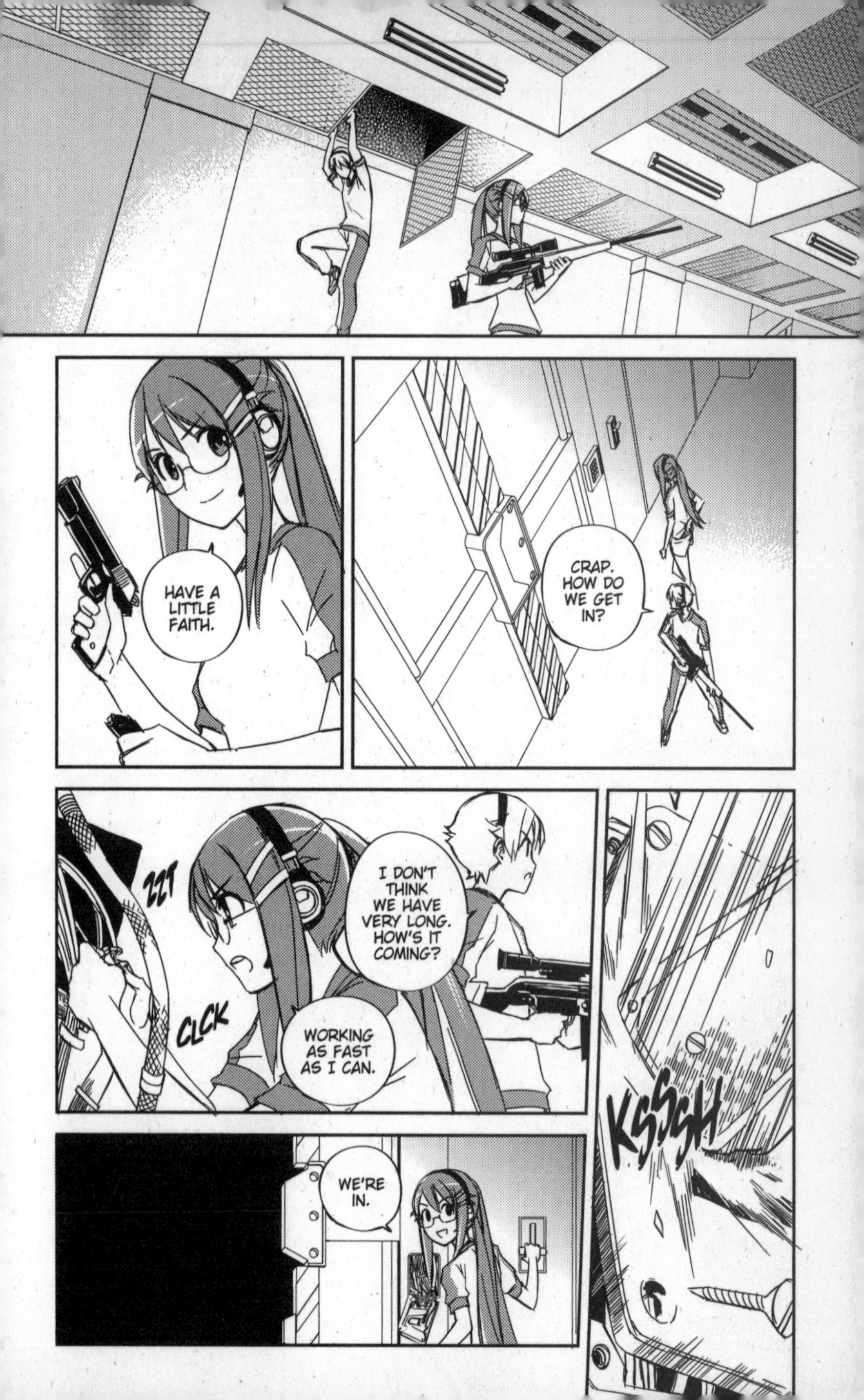
CRAP. HOW DO WE GET IN?
HAVE A LITTLE FAITH.
KSSSH
I DON'T THINK WE HAVE VERY LONG. HOW'S IT COMING?
ZZT
CLCK
WORKING AS FAST AS I CAN.
WE'RE IN.

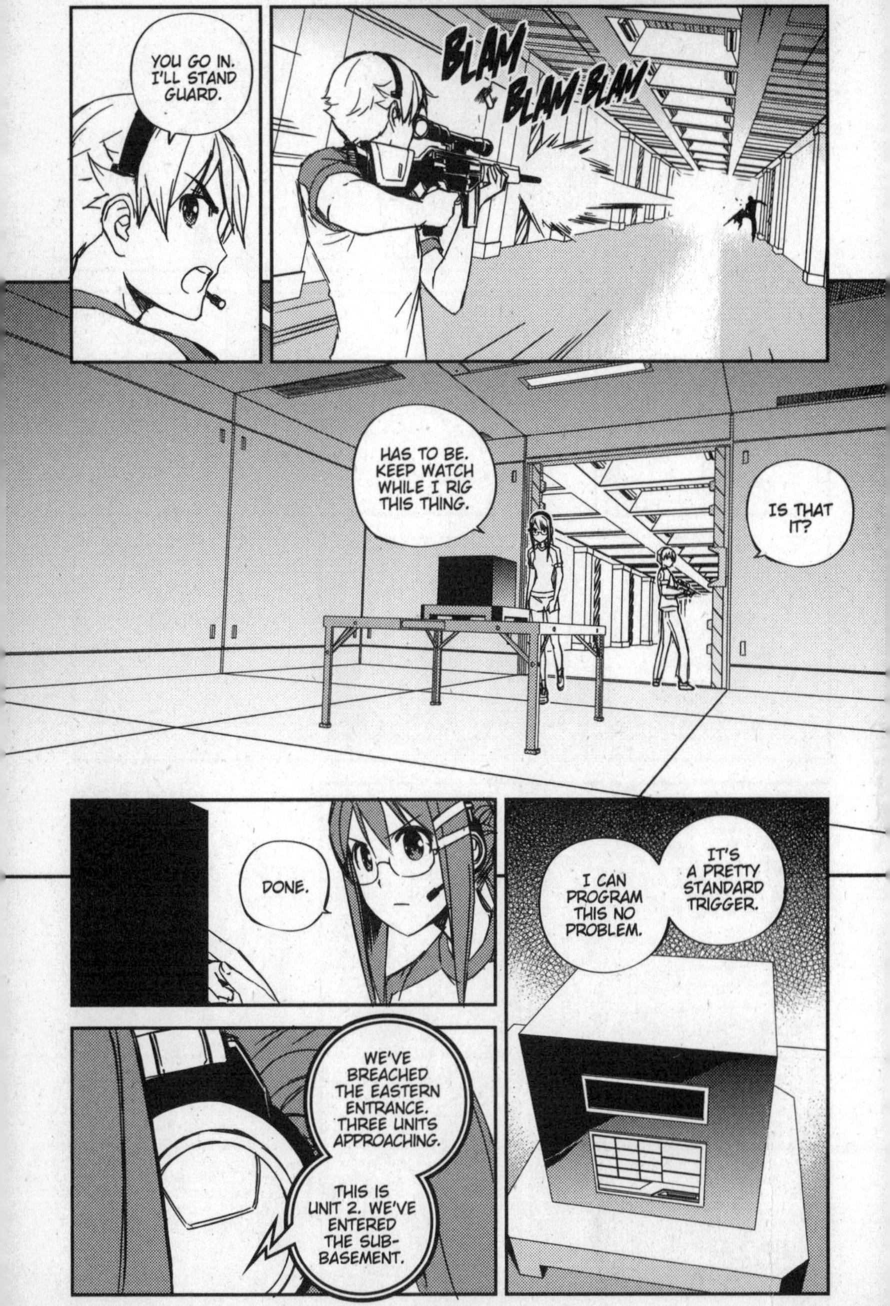
BLAM
BLAM BLAM
YOU GO IN. I'LL STAND GUARD.
IS THAT IT?
HAS TO BE. KEEP WATCH WHILE I RIG THIS THING.
IT'S A PRETTY STANDARD TRIGGER.
I CAN PROGRAM THIS NO PROBLEM.
DONE.
WE'VE BREACHED THE EASTERN ENTRANCE. THREE UNITS APPROACHING.
THIS IS UNIT 2. WE'VE ENTERED THE SUB-BASEMENT.

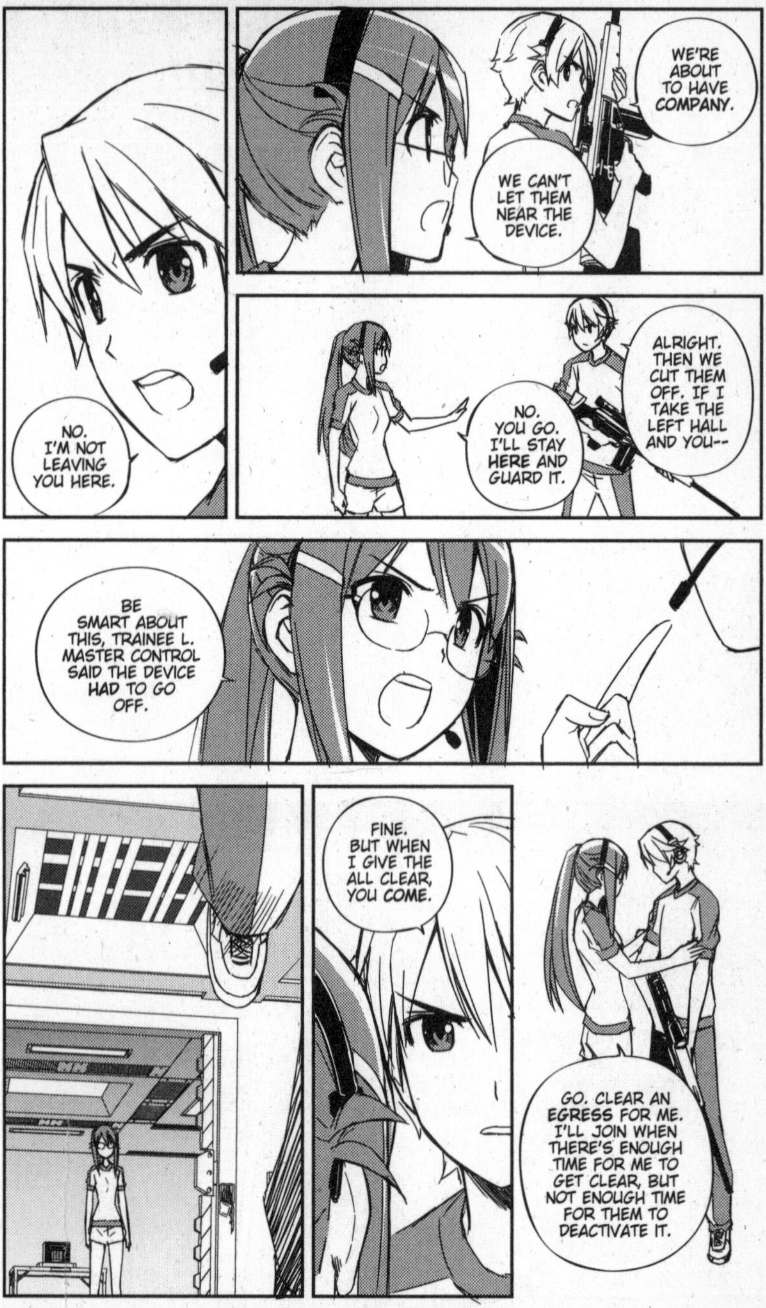
WE'RE ABOUT TO HAVE COMPANY.
WE CAN'T LET THEM NEAR THE DEVICE.
ALRIGHT. THEN WE CUT THEM OFF. IF I TAKE THE LEFT HALL AND YOU--
NO. YOU GO. I'LL STAY HERE AND GUARD IT.
NO. I'M NOT LEAVING YOU HERE.
BE SMART ABOUT THIS, TRAINEE L. MASTER CONTROL SAID THE DEVICE HAD TO GO OFF.
GO. CLEAR AN EGRESS FOR ME. I'LL JOIN WHEN THERE'S ENOUGH TIME FOR ME TO GET CLEAR, BUT NOT ENOUGH TIME FOR THEM TO DEACTIVATE IT.
FINE. BUT WHEN I GIVE THE ALL CLEAR, YOU COME.

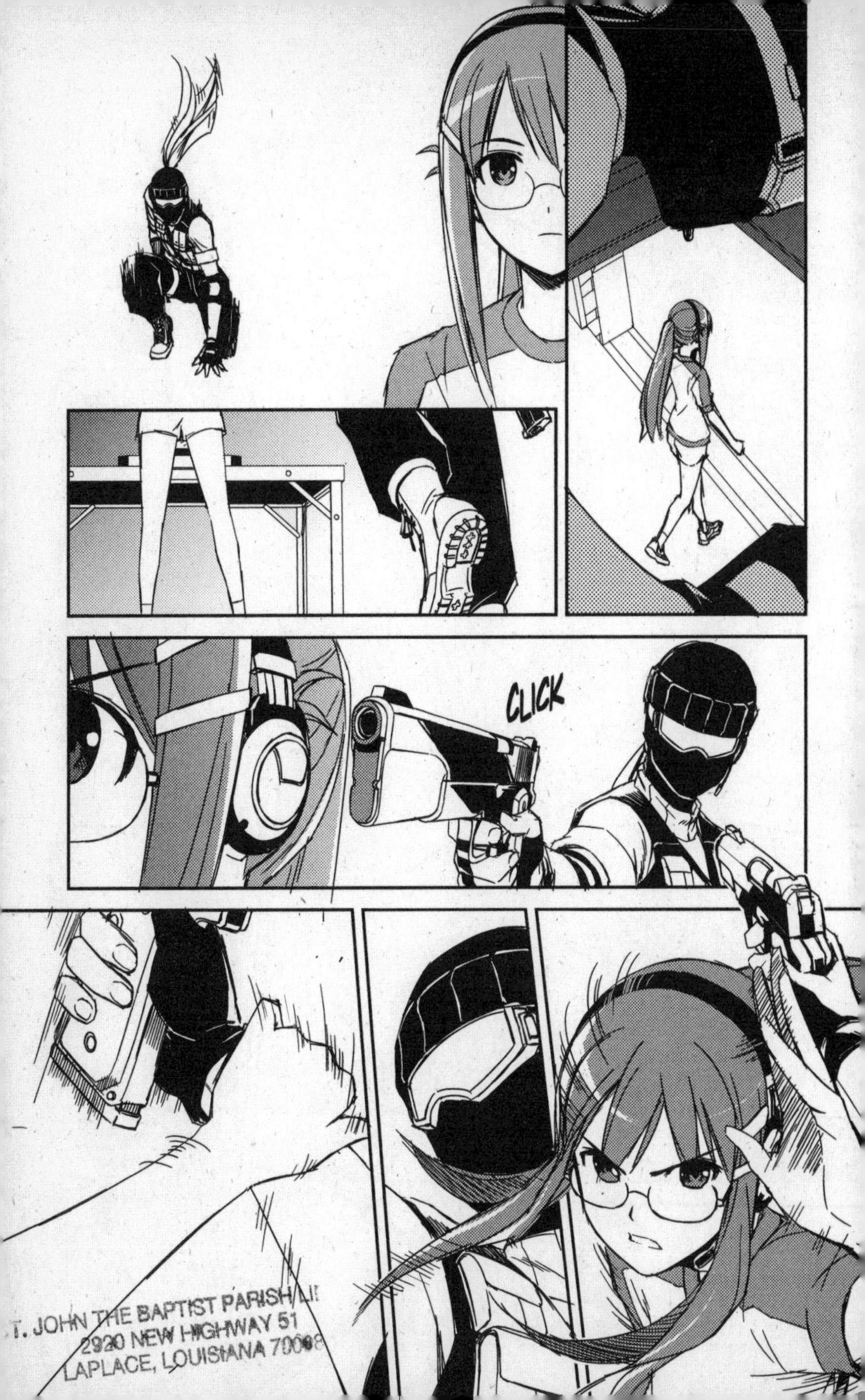
CLICK

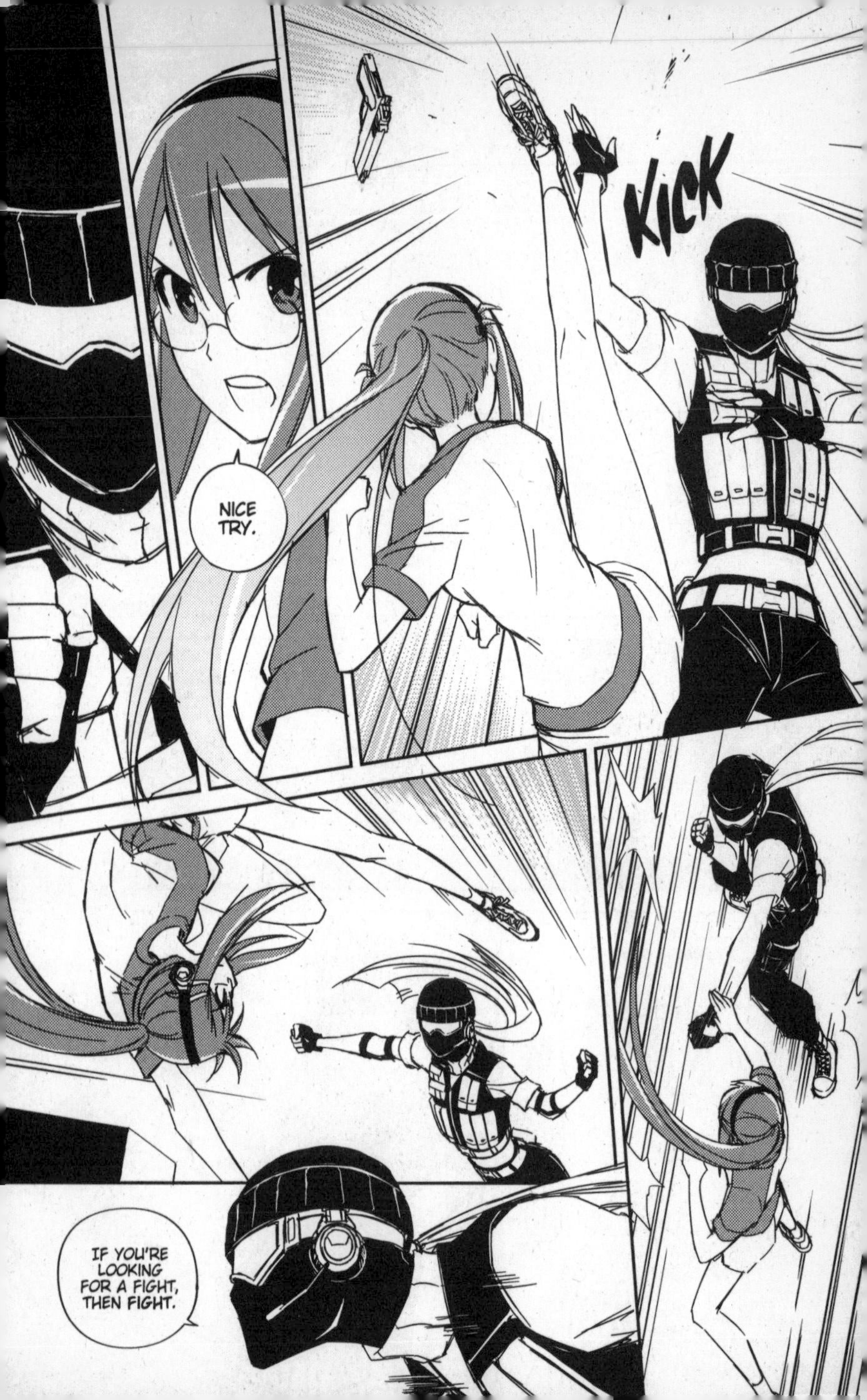
KICK
NICE TRY.
IF YOU'RE LOOKING FOR A FIGHT, THEN FIGHT.

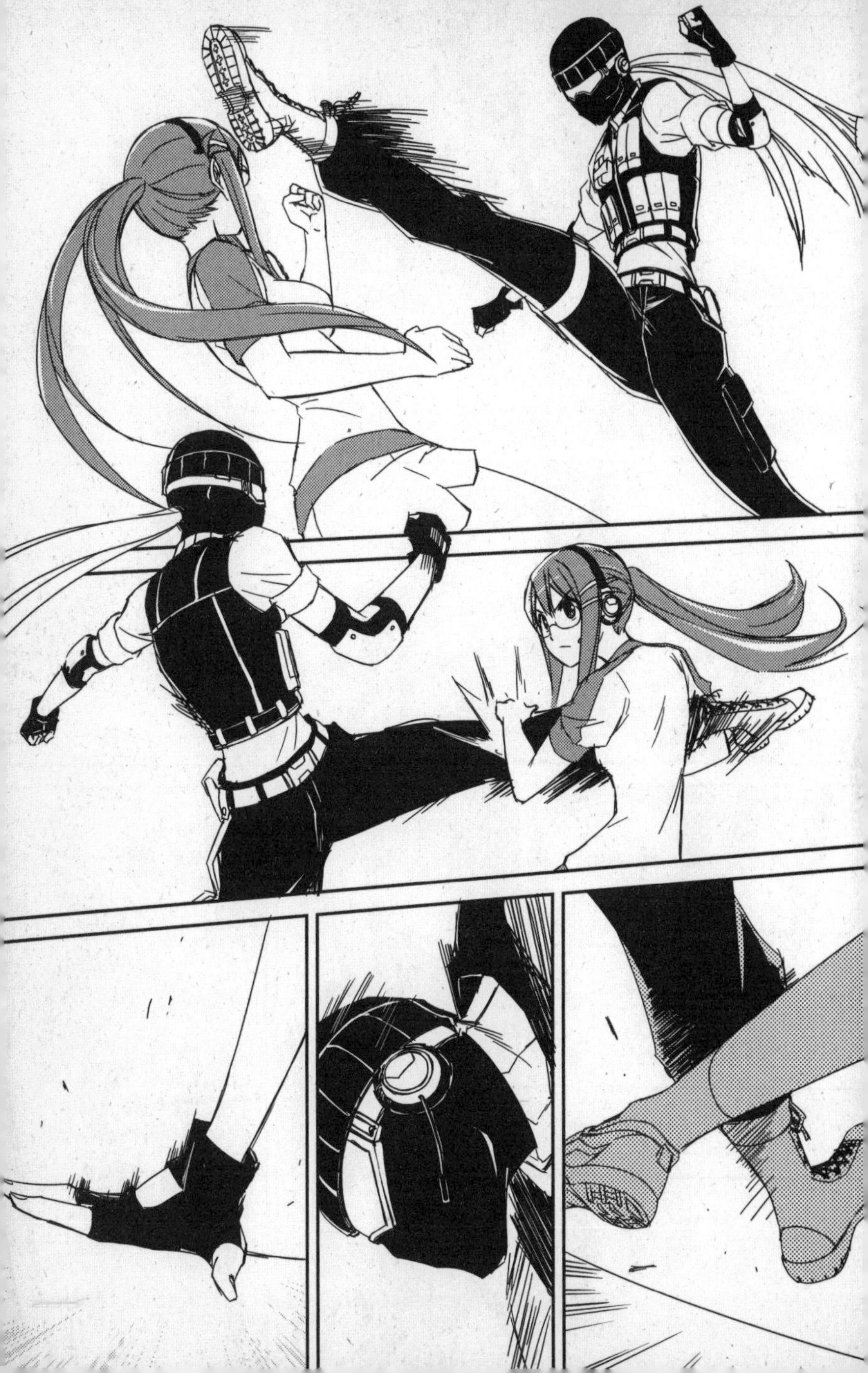

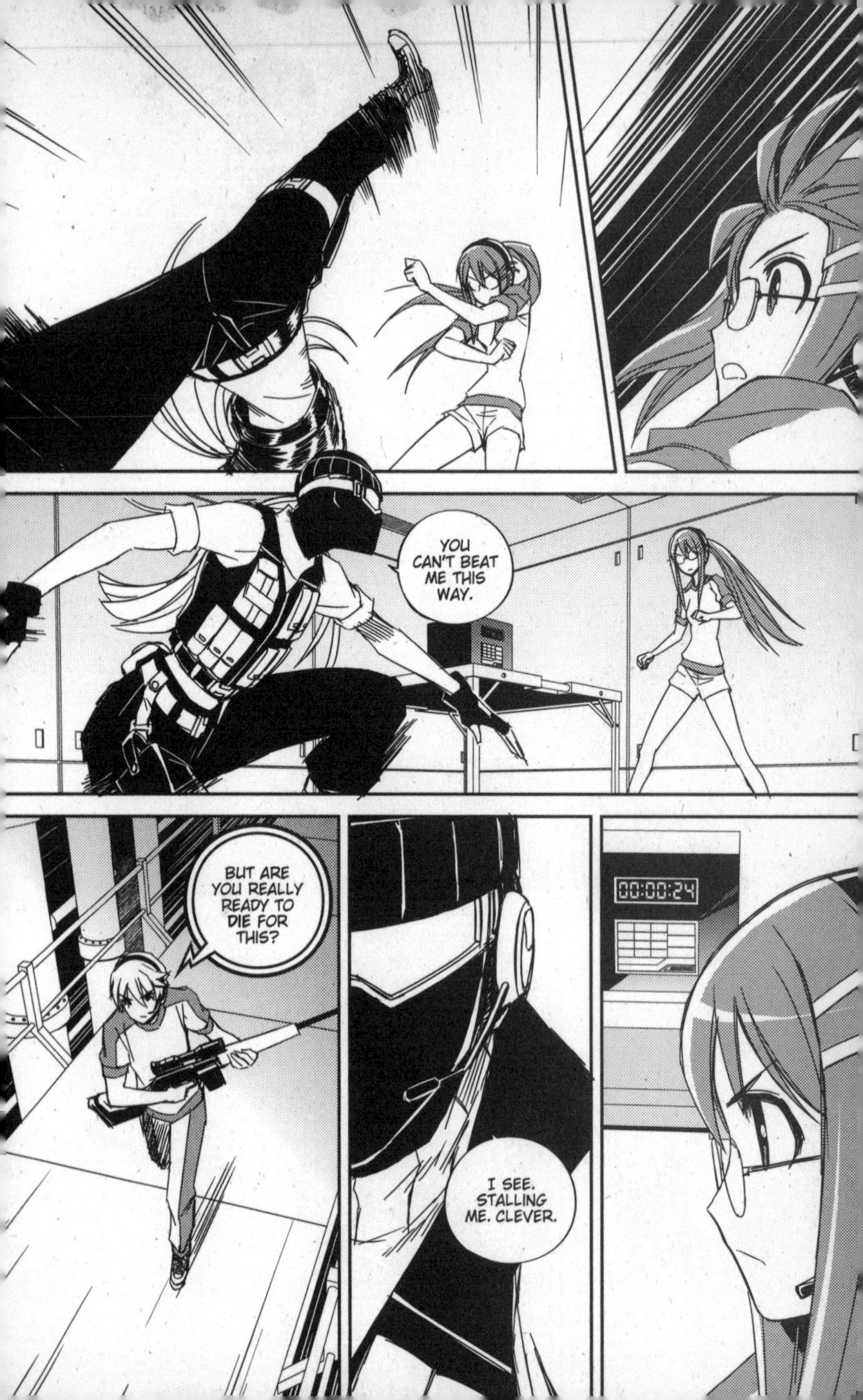
YOU CAN'T BEAT ME THIS WAY.
BUT ARE YOU REALLY READY TO DIE FOR THIS?
I SEE. STALLING ME. CLEVER.
00:00:24

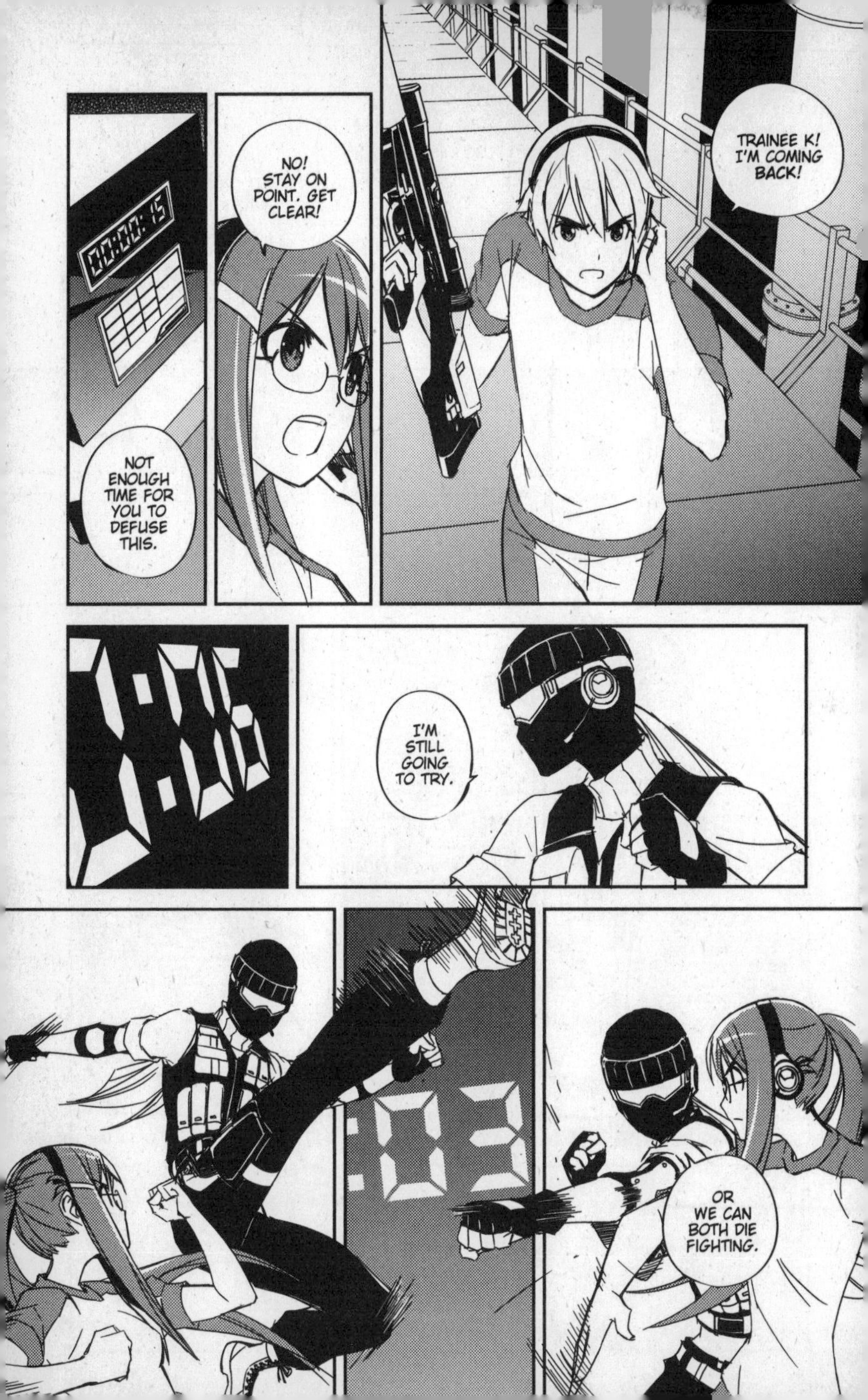
TRAINEE K! I'M COMING BACK!
NO! STAY ON POINT. GET CLEAR!
00:00:15
NOT ENOUGH TIME FOR YOU TO DEFUSE THIS.
I'M STILL GOING TO TRY.
OR WE CAN BOTH DIE FIGHTING.

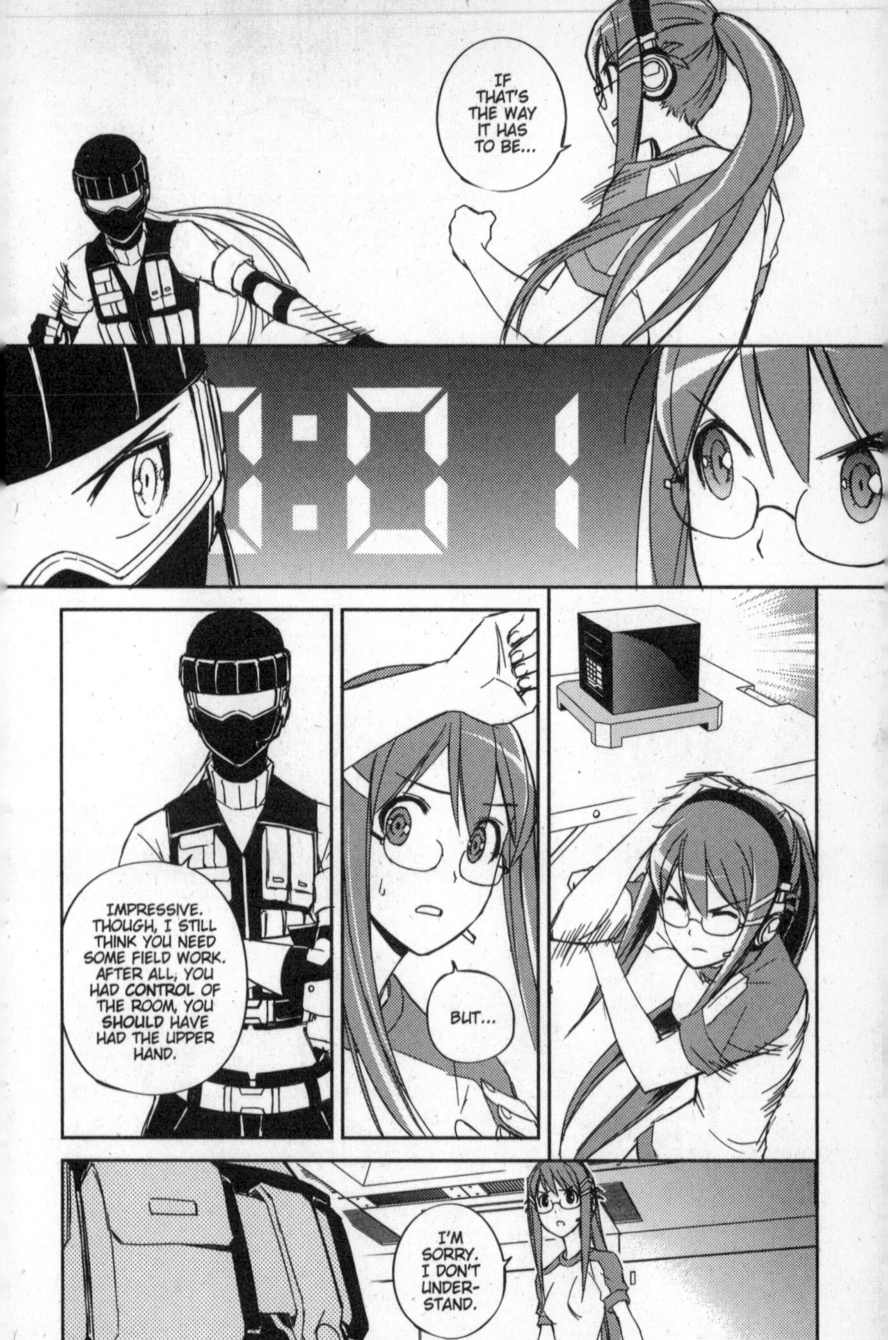
IF THAT'S THE WAY IT HAS TO BE...
BUT...
IMPRESSIVE. THOUGH, I STILL THINK YOU NEED SOME FIELD WORK. AFTER ALL, YOU HAD CONTROL OF THE ROOM, YOU SHOULD HAVE HAD THE UPPER HAND.
I'M SORRY. I DON'T UNDER-STAND.

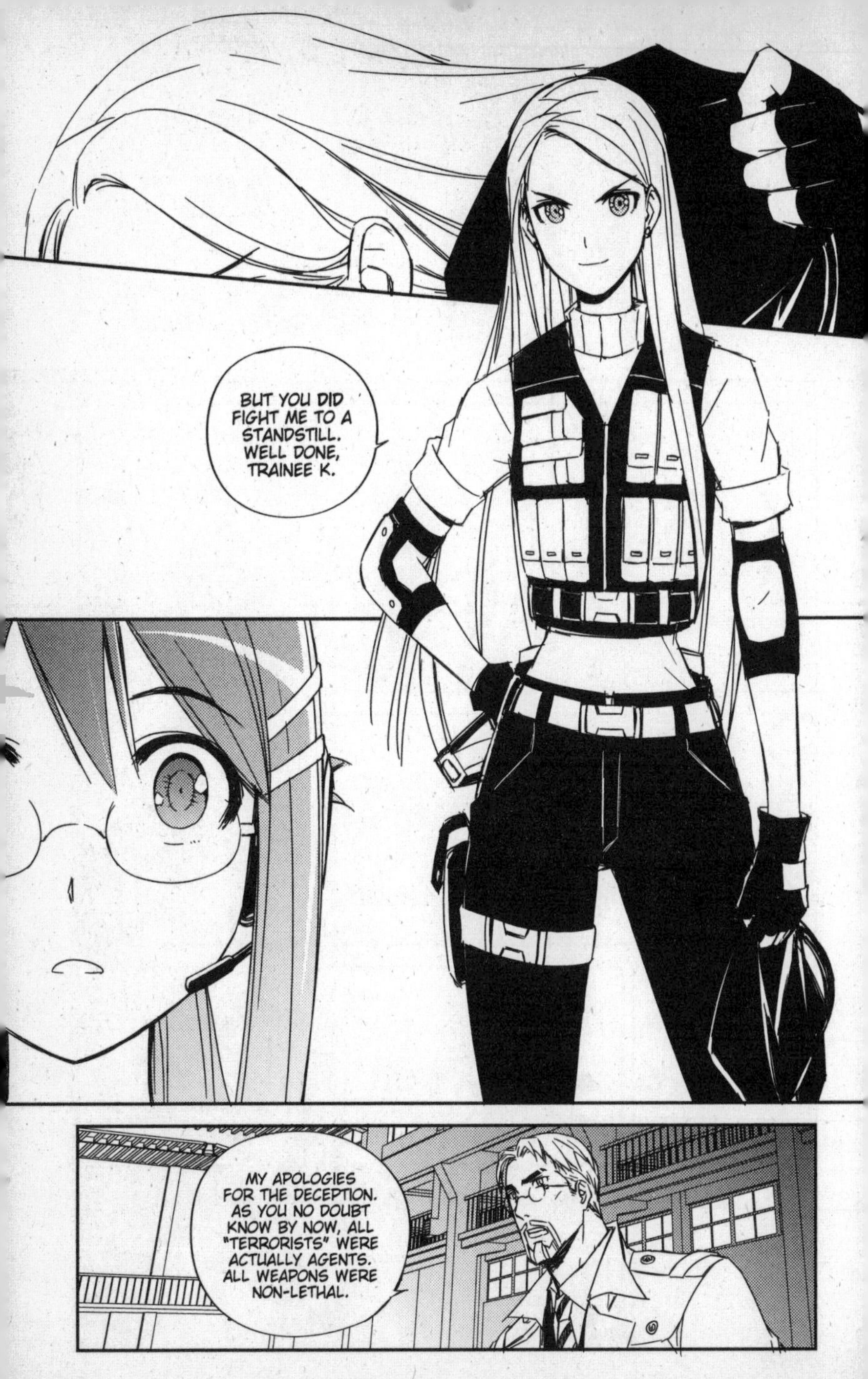
BUT YOU DID FIGHT ME TO A STANDSTILL. WELL DONE, TRAINEE K.
MY APOLOGIES FOR THE DECEPTION. AS YOU NO DOUBT KNOW BY NOW, ALL "TERRORISTS" WERE ACTUALLY AGENTS. ALL WEAPONS WERE NON-LETHAL.

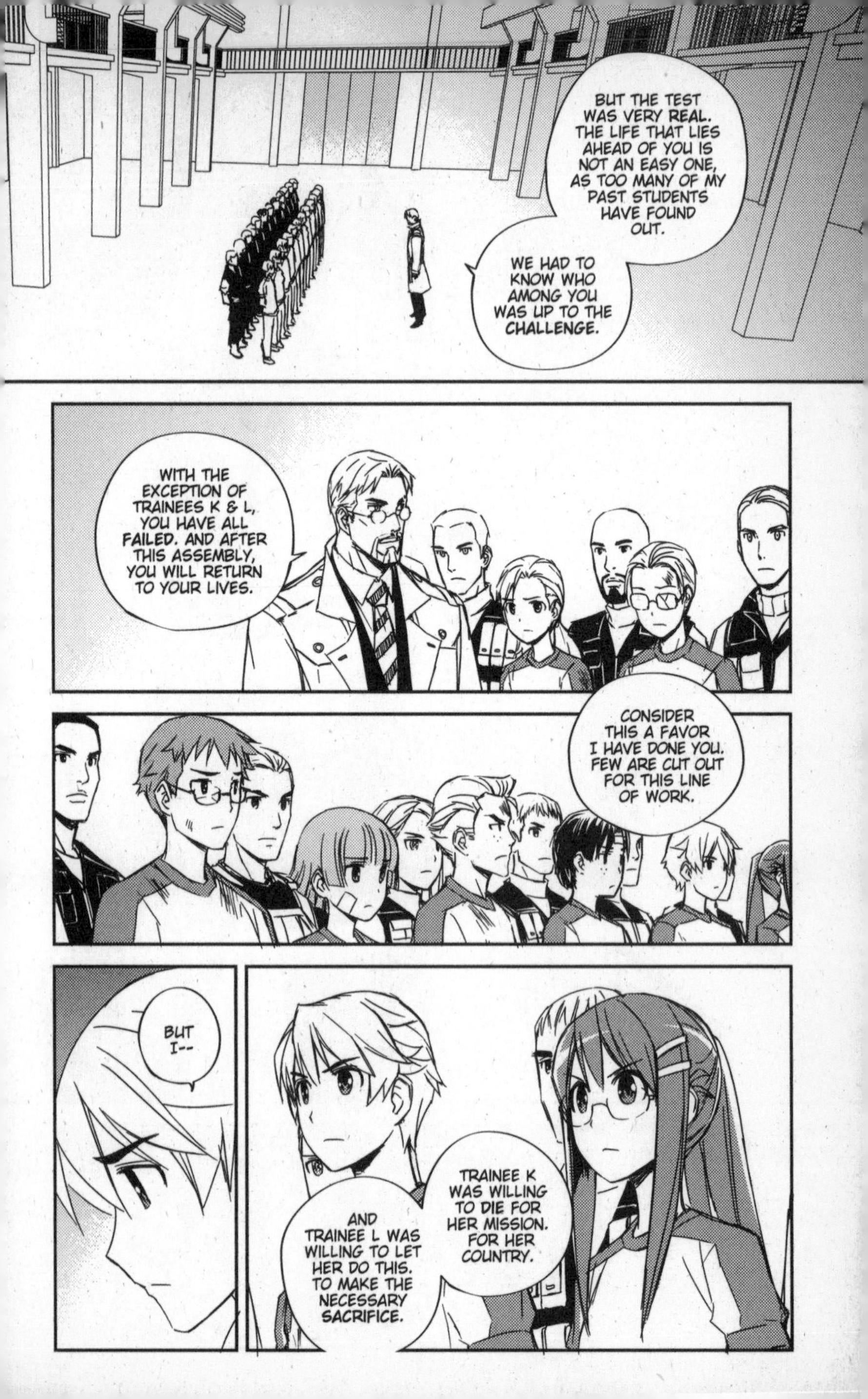
BUT THE TEST WAS VERY REAL. THE LIFE THAT LIES AHEAD OF YOU IS NOT AN EASY ONE, AS TOO MANY OF MY PAST STUDENTS HAVE FOUND OUT.
WE HAD TO KNOW WHO AMONG YOU WAS UP TO THE CHALLENGE.
WITH THE EXCEPTION OF TRAINEES K & L, YOU HAVE ALL FAILED. AND AFTER THIS ASSEMBLY, YOU WILL RETURN TO YOUR LIVES.
CONSIDER THIS A FAVOR I HAVE DONE YOU. FEW ARE CUT OUT FOR THIS LINE OF WORK.
TRAINEE K WAS WILLING TO DIE FOR HER MISSION. FOR HER COUNTRY.
AND TRAINEE L WAS WILLING TO LET HER DO THIS. TO MAKE THE NECESSARY SACRIFICE.
BUT I--

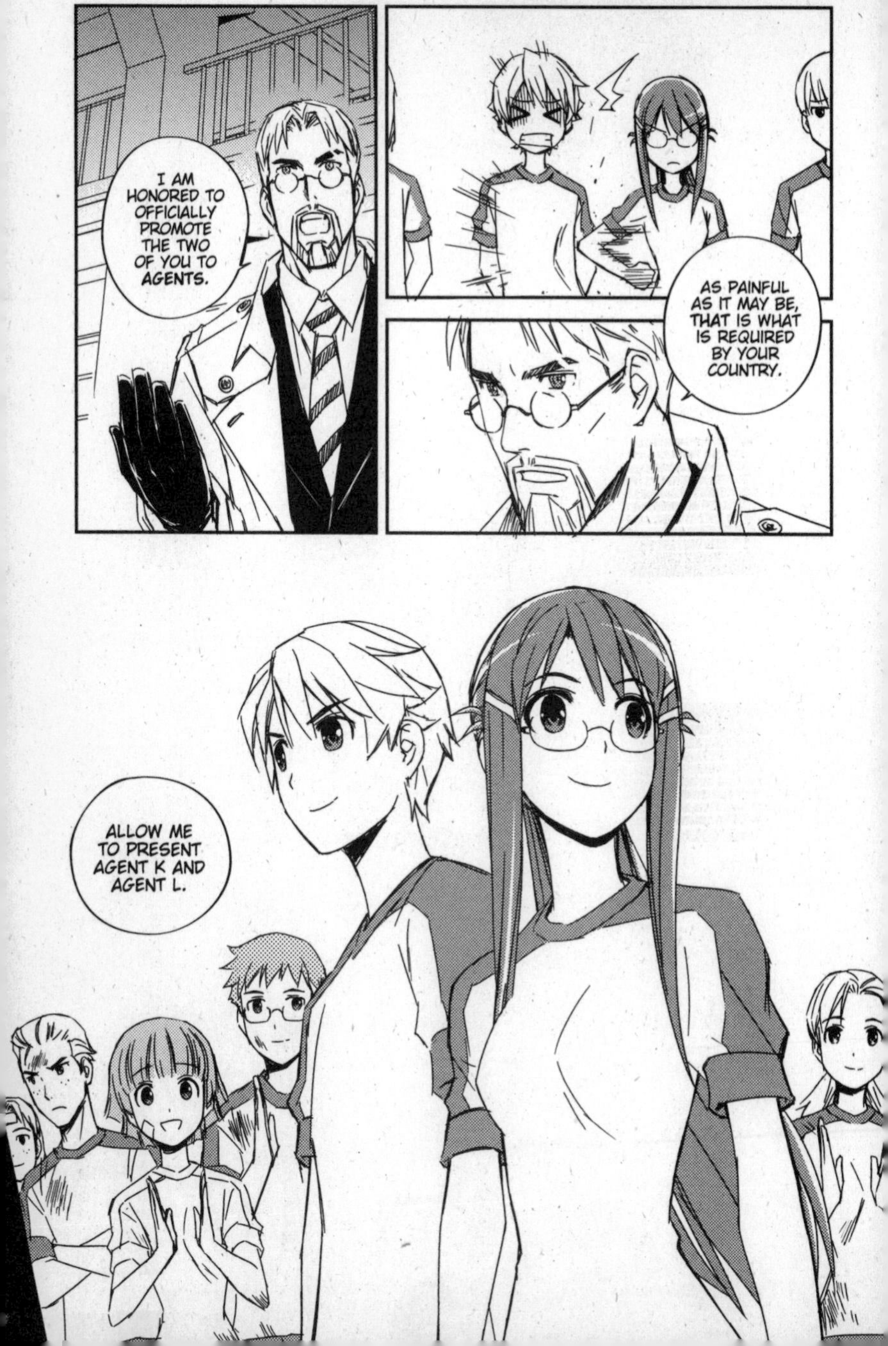
I AM HONORED TO OFFICIALLY PROMOTE THE TWO OF YOU TO AGENTS.
AS PAINFUL AS IT MAY BE, THAT IS WHAT IS REQUIRED BY YOUR COUNTRY.
ALLOW ME TO PRESENT AGENT K AND AGENT L.

FILE 4:
GRADUATION DAY

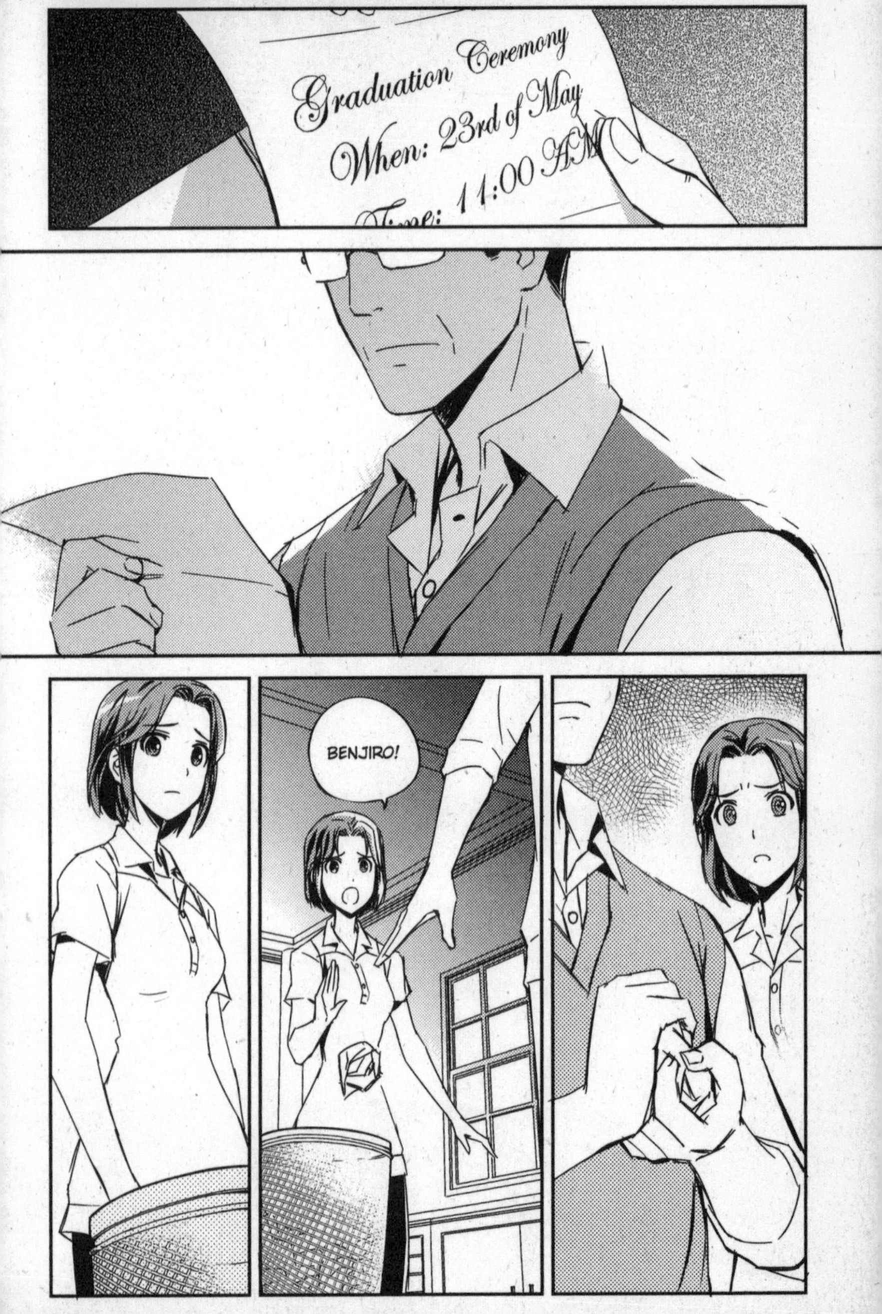
Graduation Ceremony
When: 23rd of May
Time: 11:00 AM
BENJIRO!

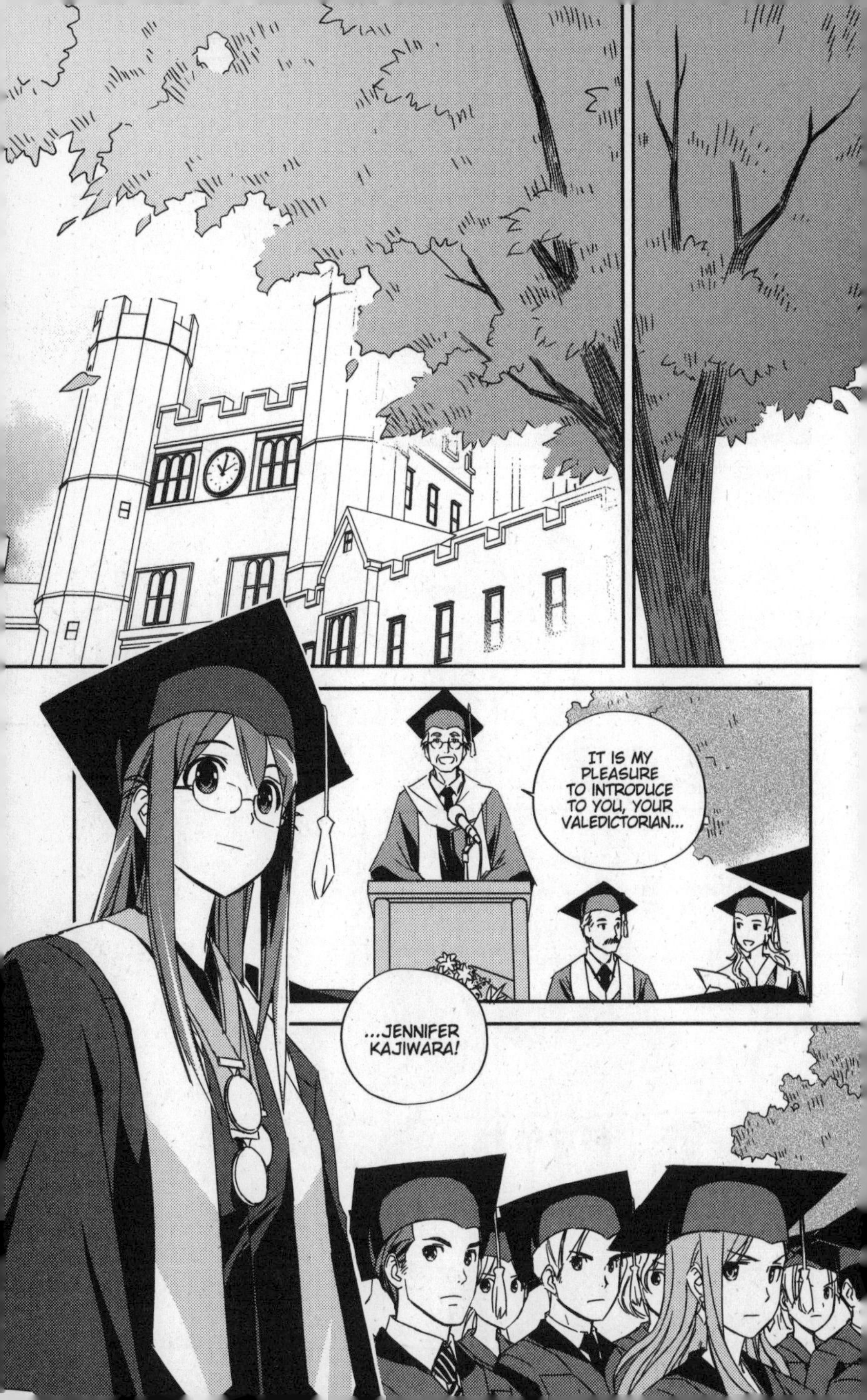
IT IS MY PLEASURE TO INTRODUCE TO YOU, YOUR VALEDICTORIAN...
...JENNIFER KAJIWARA!

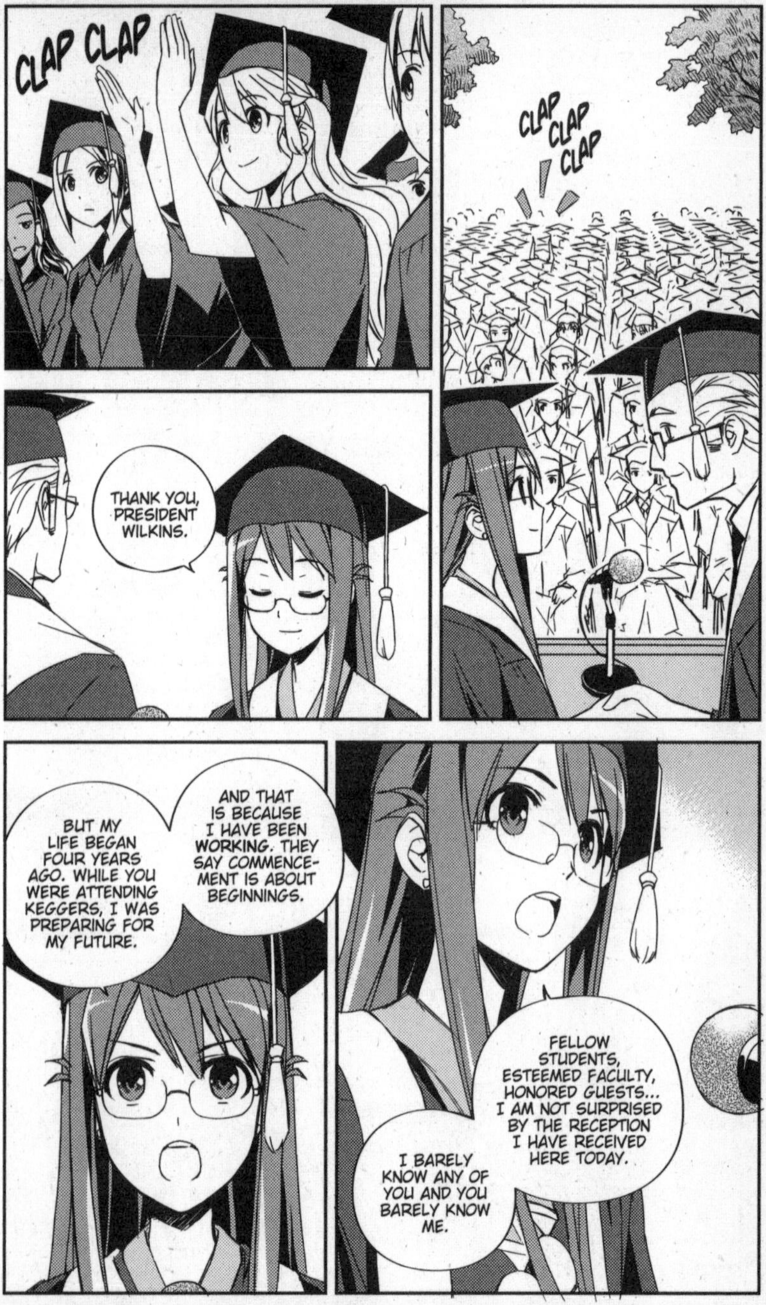
CLAP CLAP CLAP
CLAP CLAP
THANK YOU, PRESIDENT WILKINS.
FELLOW STUDENTS, ESTEEMED FACULTY, HONORED GUESTS... I AM NOT SURPRISED BY THE RECEPTION I HAVE RECEIVED HERE TODAY.
I BARELY KNOW ANY OF YOU AND YOU BARELY KNOW ME.
AND THAT IS BECAUSE I HAVE BEEN WORKING. THEY SAY COMMENCEMENT IS ABOUT BEGINNINGS.
BUT MY LIFE BEGAN FOUR YEARS AGO. WHILE YOU WERE ATTENDING KEGGERS, I WAS PREPARING FOR MY FUTURE.

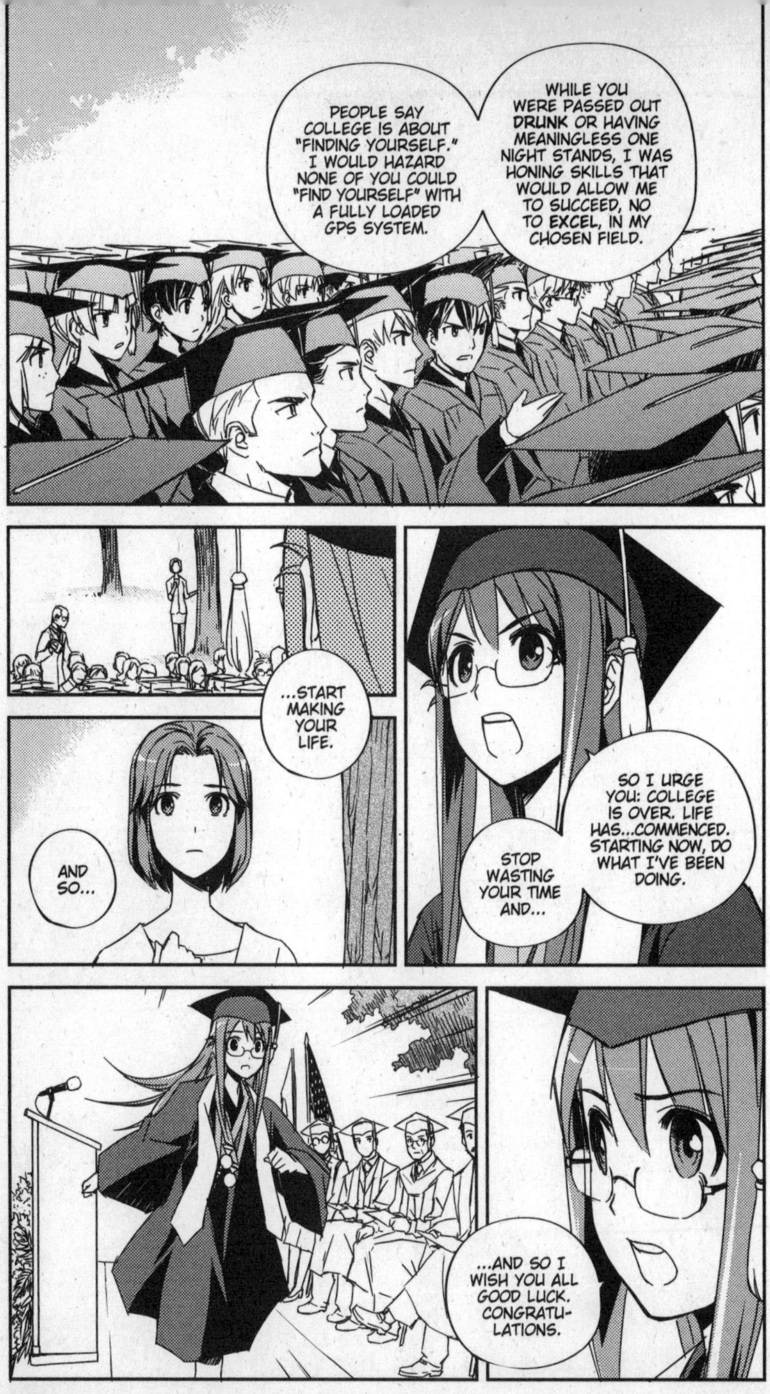
WHILE YOU WERE PASSED OUT **DRUNK** OR HAVING MEANINGLESS ONE NIGHT STANDS, I WAS HONING SKILLS THAT WOULD ALLOW ME TO SUCCEED, NO TO **EXCEL**, IN MY CHOSEN FIELD.
PEOPLE SAY COLLEGE IS ABOUT "FINDING YOURSELF." I WOULD HAZARD NONE OF YOU COULD "FIND YOURSELF" WITH A FULLY LOADED GPS SYSTEM.
SO I URGE YOU: COLLEGE IS OVER. LIFE HAS...COMMENCED. STARTING NOW, DO WHAT I'VE BEEN DOING.
STOP WASTING YOUR TIME AND...
...START MAKING YOUR LIFE.
AND SO...
...AND SO I WISH YOU ALL GOOD LUCK. CONGRATULATIONS.

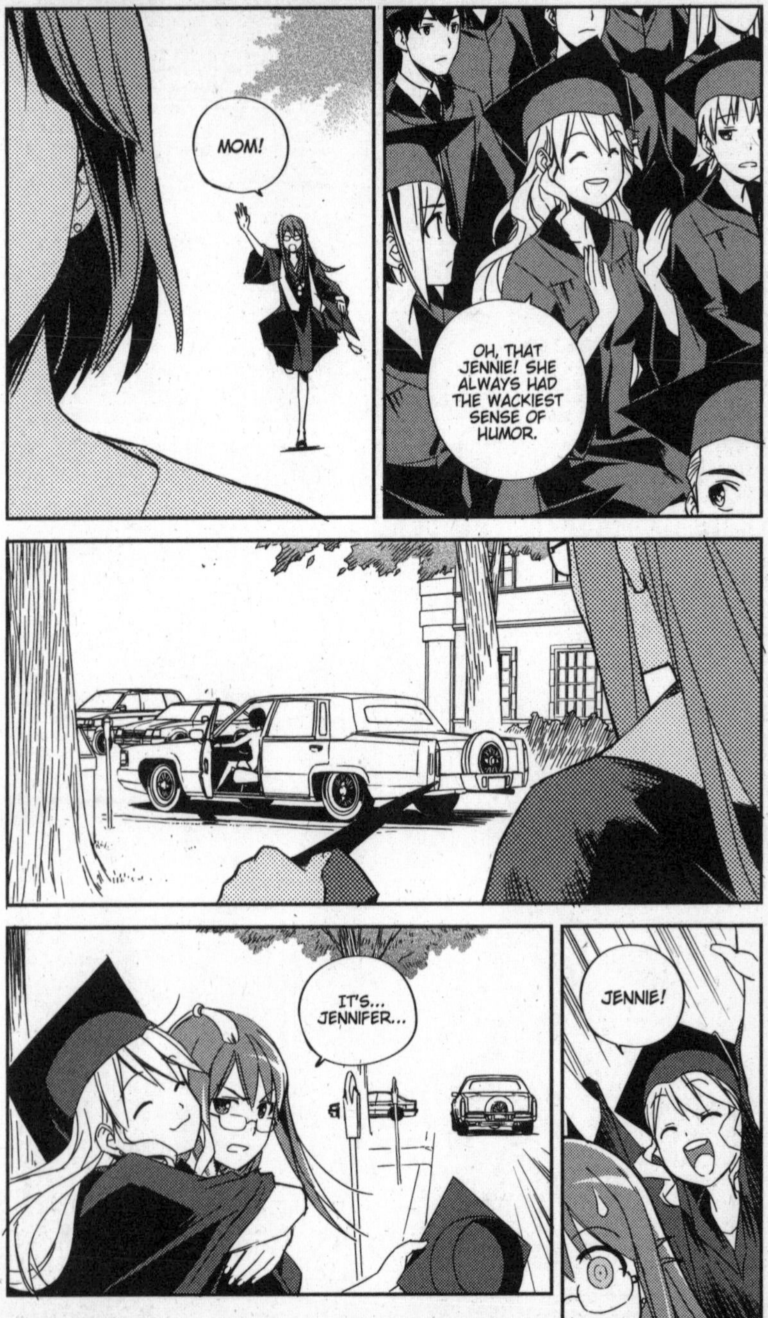
OH, THAT JENNIE! SHE ALWAYS HAD THE WACKIEST SENSE OF HUMOR.
MOM!
JENNIE!
IT'S... JENNIFER...

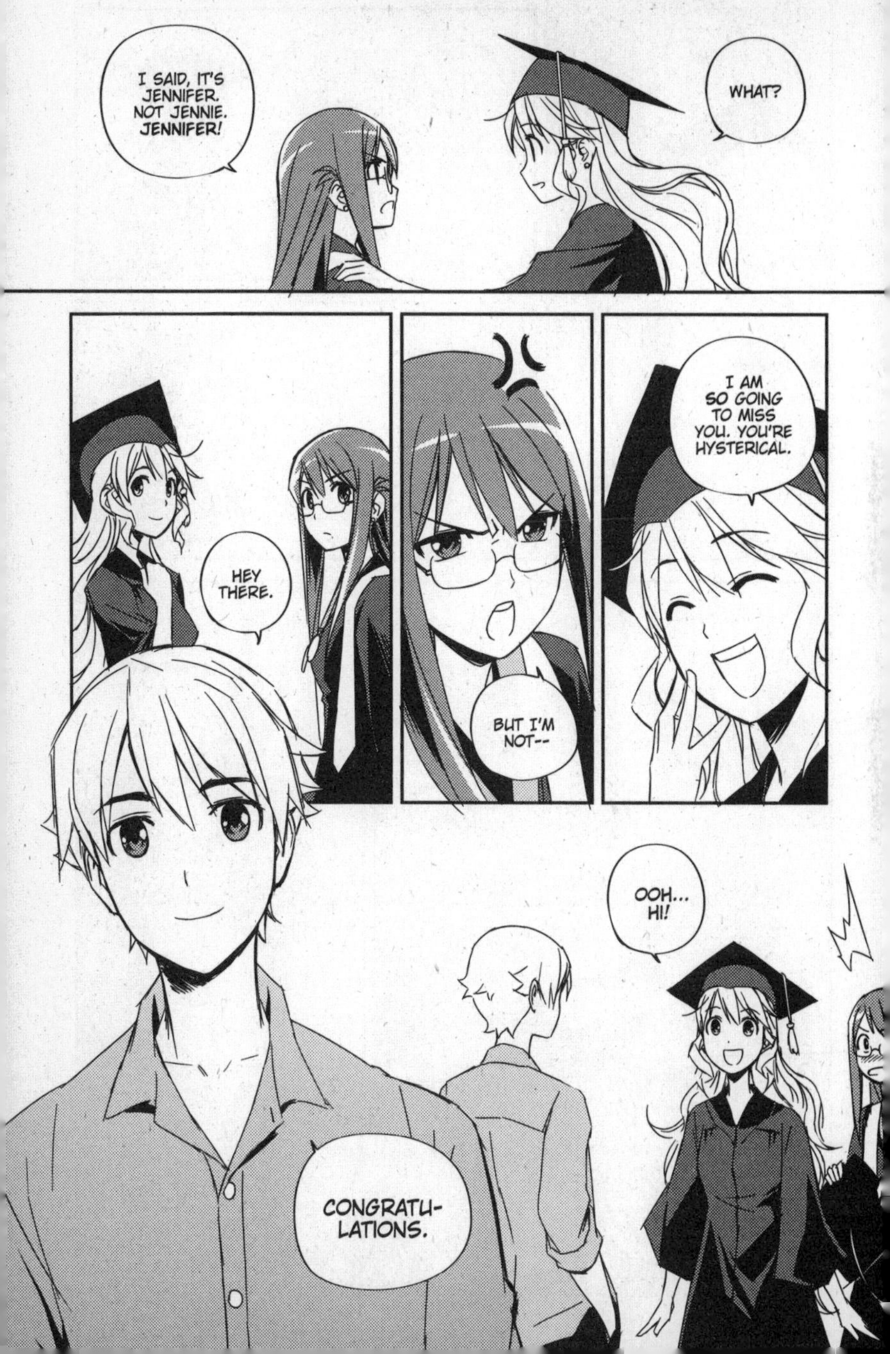
WHAT?
I SAID, IT'S JENNIFER. NOT JENNIE. JENNIFER!
I AM SO GOING TO MISS YOU. YOU'RE HYSTERICAL.
BUT I'M NOT--
HEY THERE.
OOH... HI!
CONGRATU-LATIONS.

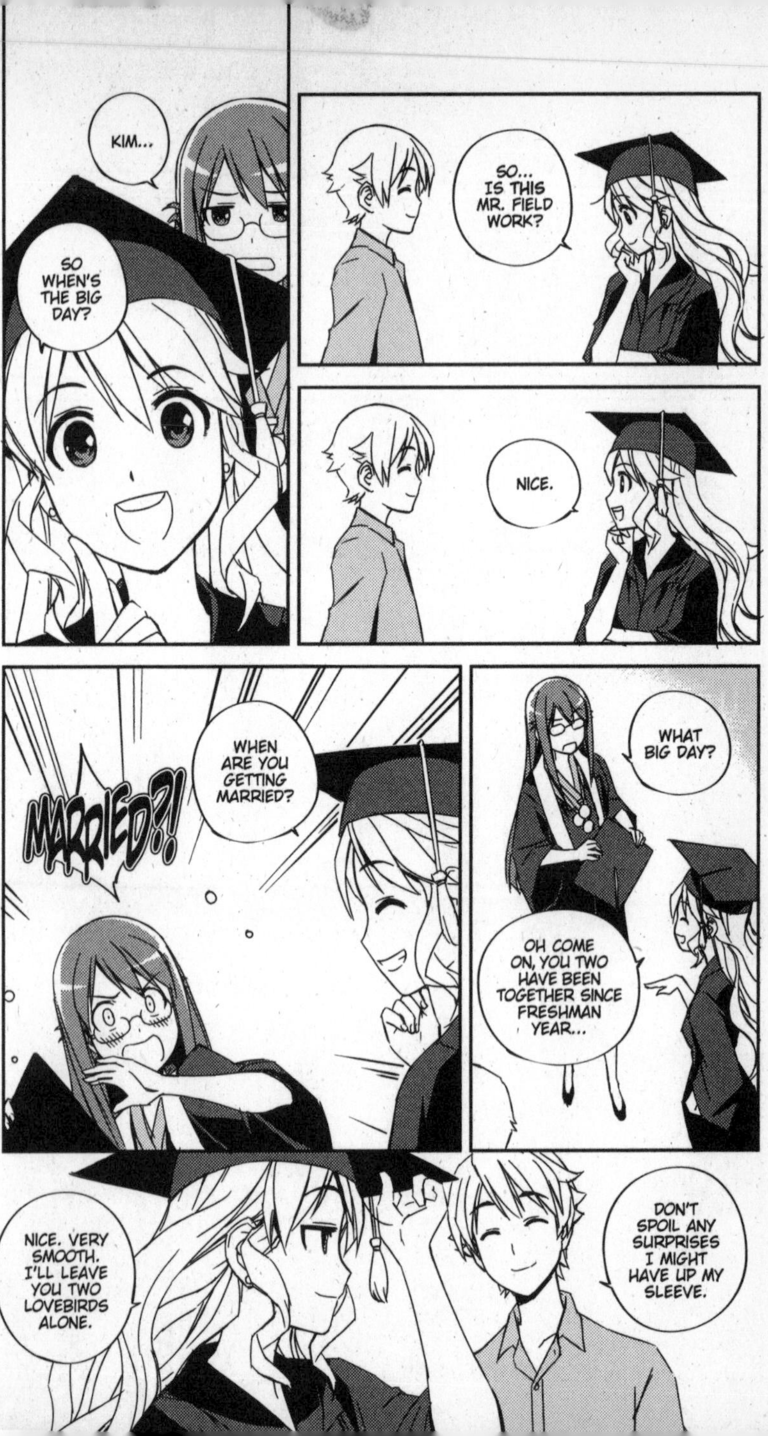
SO... IS THIS MR. FIELD WORK?
NICE.
KIM...
SO WHEN'S THE BIG DAY?
WHAT BIG DAY?
OH COME ON, YOU TWO HAVE BEEN TOGETHER SINCE FRESHMAN YEAR...
WHEN ARE YOU GETTING MARRIED?
MARRIED?!
DON'T SPOIL ANY SURPRISES I MIGHT HAVE UP MY SLEEVE.
NICE. VERY SMOOTH. I'LL LEAVE YOU TWO LOVEBIRDS ALONE.

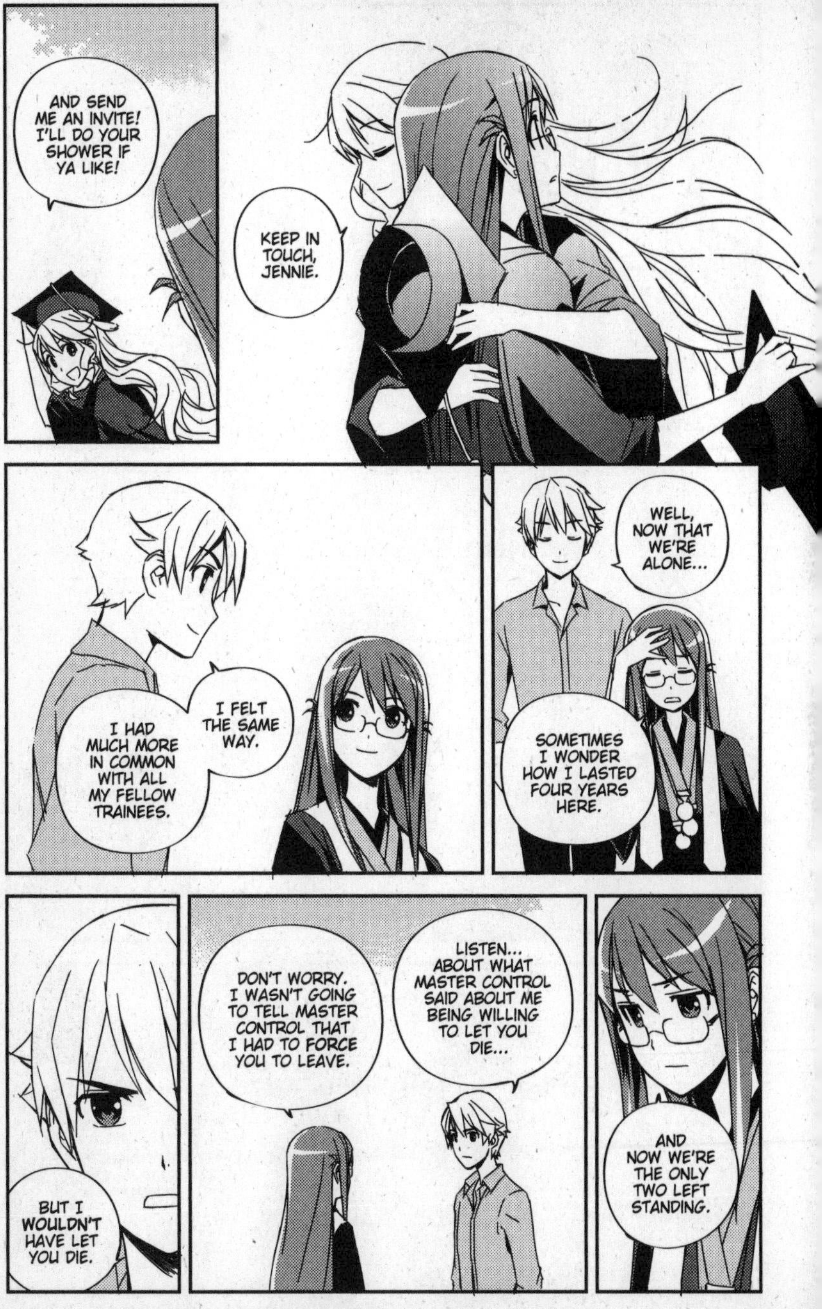
KEEP IN TOUCH, JENNIE.
AND SEND ME AN INVITE! I'LL DO YOUR SHOWER IF YA LIKE!
WELL, NOW THAT WE'RE ALONE...
SOMETIMES I WONDER HOW I LASTED FOUR YEARS HERE.
I HAD MUCH MORE IN COMMON WITH ALL MY FELLOW TRAINEES.
I FELT THE SAME WAY.
AND NOW WE'RE THE ONLY TWO LEFT STANDING.
LISTEN... ABOUT WHAT MASTER CONTROL SAID ABOUT ME BEING WILLING TO LET YOU DIE...
DON'T WORRY. I WASN'T GOING TO TELL MASTER CONTROL THAT I HAD TO FORCE YOU TO LEAVE.
BUT I WOULDN'T HAVE LET YOU DIE.

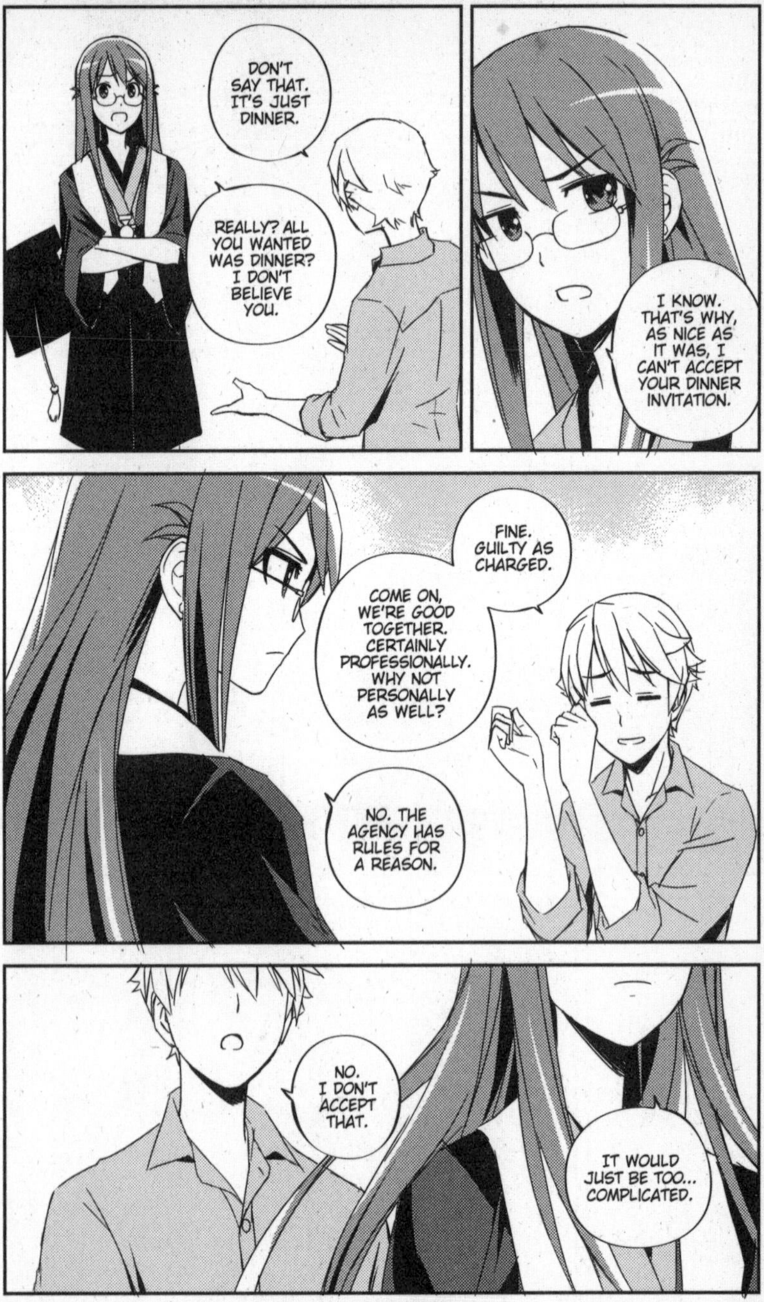
DON'T SAY THAT. IT'S JUST DINNER.
REALLY? ALL YOU WANTED WAS DINNER? I DON'T BELIEVE YOU.
I KNOW. THAT'S WHY, AS NICE AS IT WAS, I CAN'T ACCEPT YOUR DINNER INVITATION.
FINE. GUILTY AS CHARGED.
COME ON, WE'RE GOOD TOGETHER. CERTAINLY PROFESSIONALLY. WHY NOT PERSONALLY AS WELL?
NO. THE AGENCY HAS RULES FOR A REASON.
NO. I DON'T ACCEPT THAT.
IT WOULD JUST BE TOO... COMPLICATED.

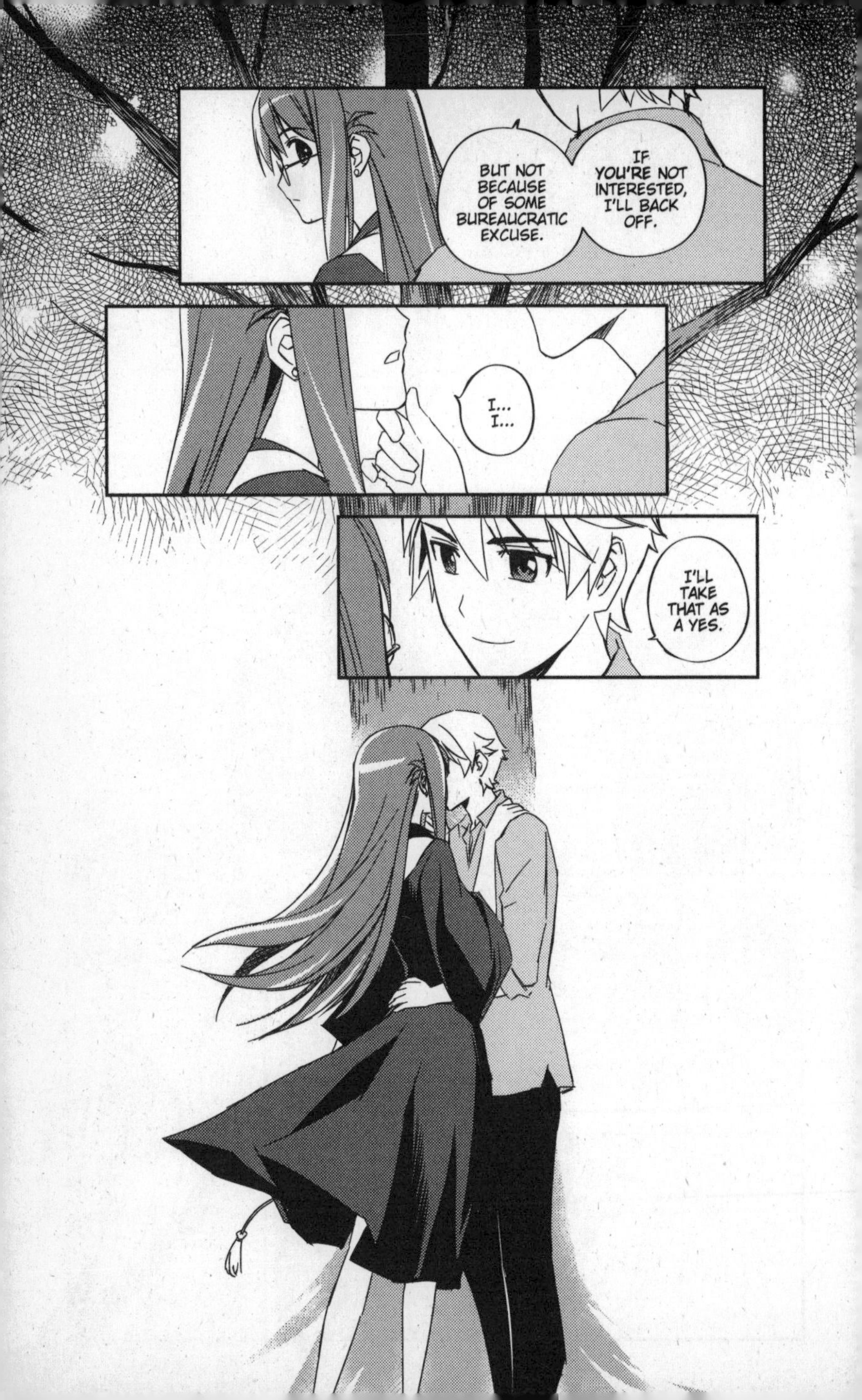
IF YOU'RE NOT INTERESTED, I'LL BACK OFF.
BUT NOT BECAUSE OF SOME BUREAUCRATIC EXCUSE.
I... I...
I'LL TAKE THAT AS A YES.

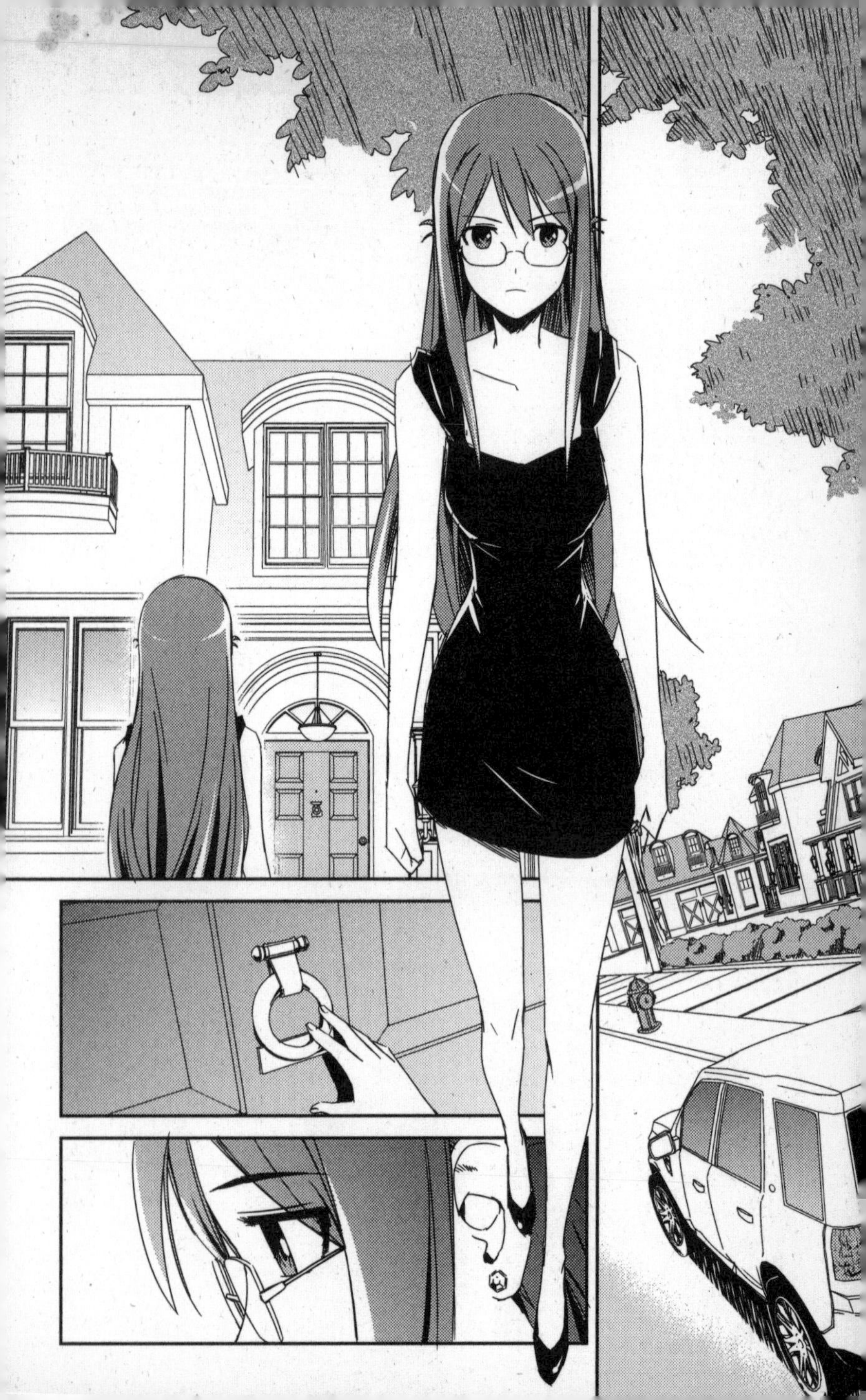

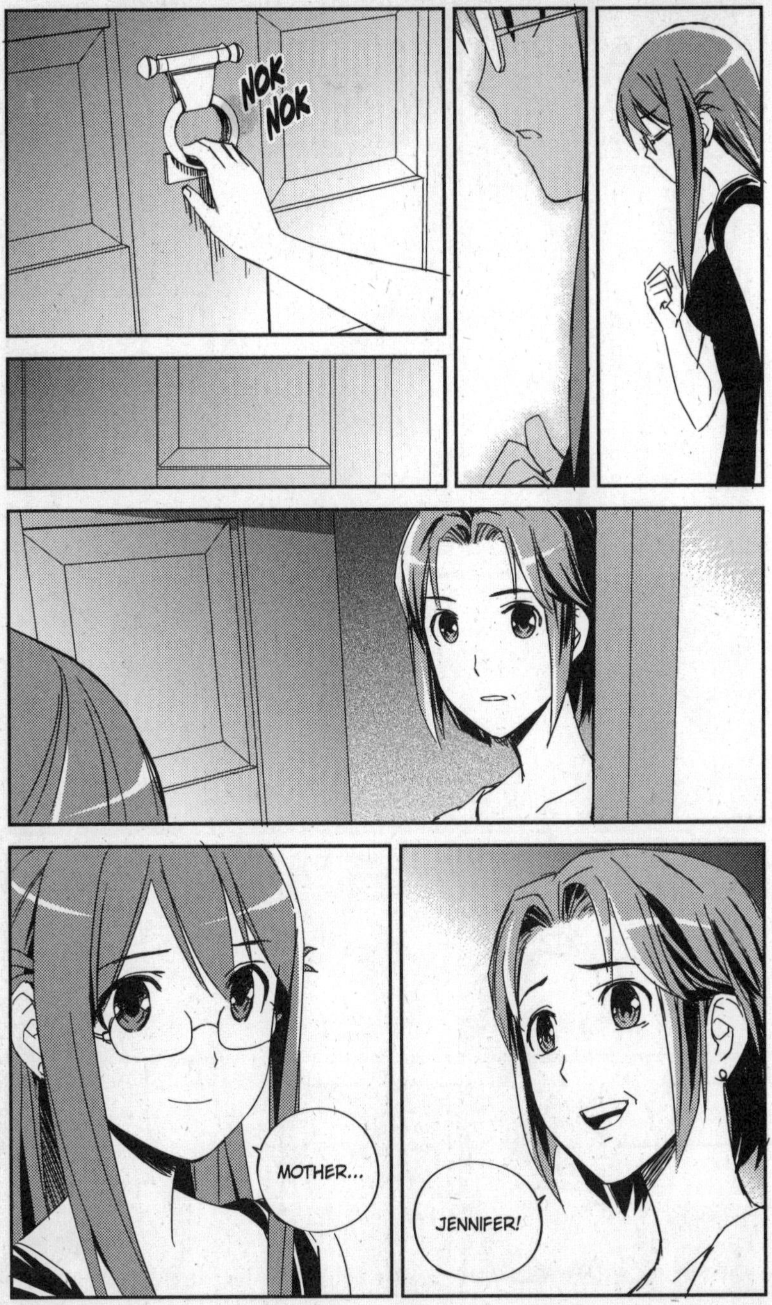
NOK NOK
JENNIFER!
MOTHER...

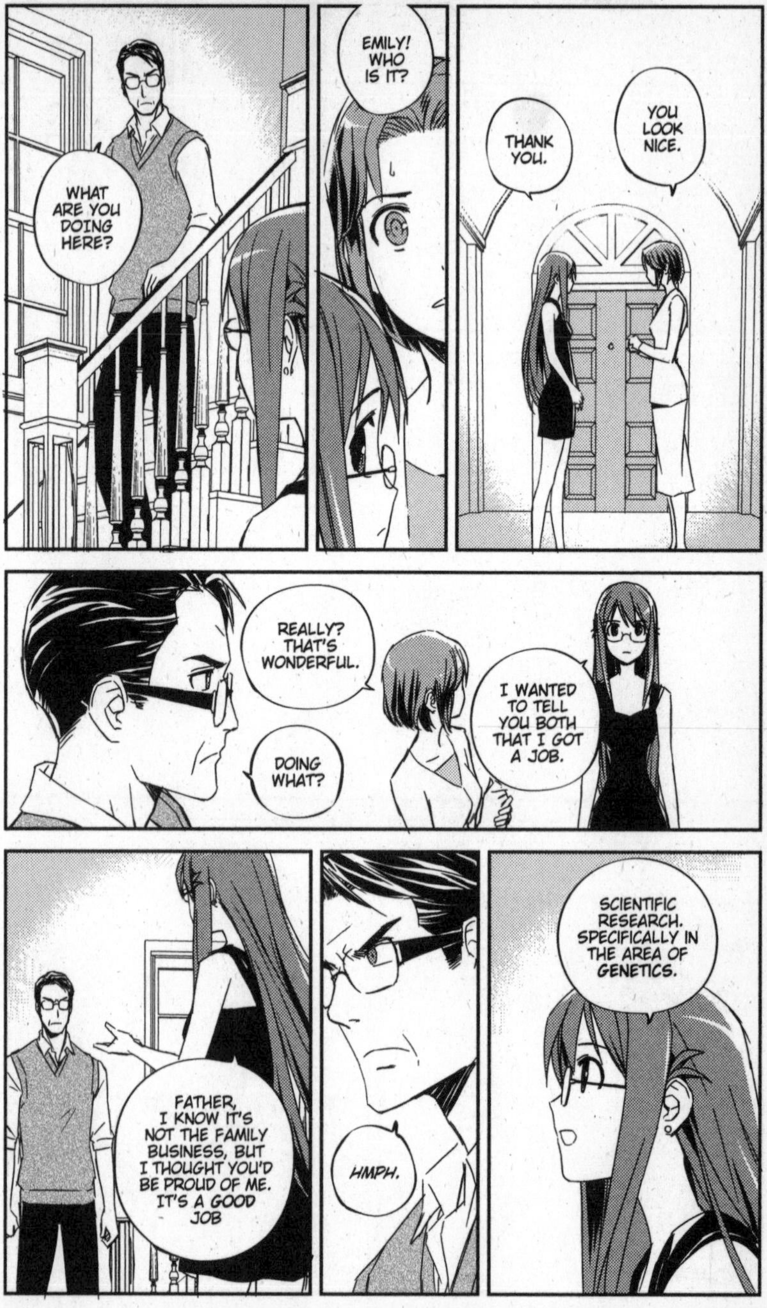
YOU LOOK NICE.
THANK YOU.
EMILY! WHO IS IT?
WHAT ARE YOU DOING HERE?
I WANTED TO TELL YOU BOTH THAT I GOT A JOB.
REALLY? THAT'S WONDERFUL.
DOING WHAT?
SCIENTIFIC RESEARCH. SPECIFICALLY IN THE AREA OF GENETICS.
HMPH.
FATHER, I KNOW IT'S NOT THE FAMILY BUSINESS, BUT I THOUGHT YOU'D BE PROUD OF ME. IT'S A GOOD JOB

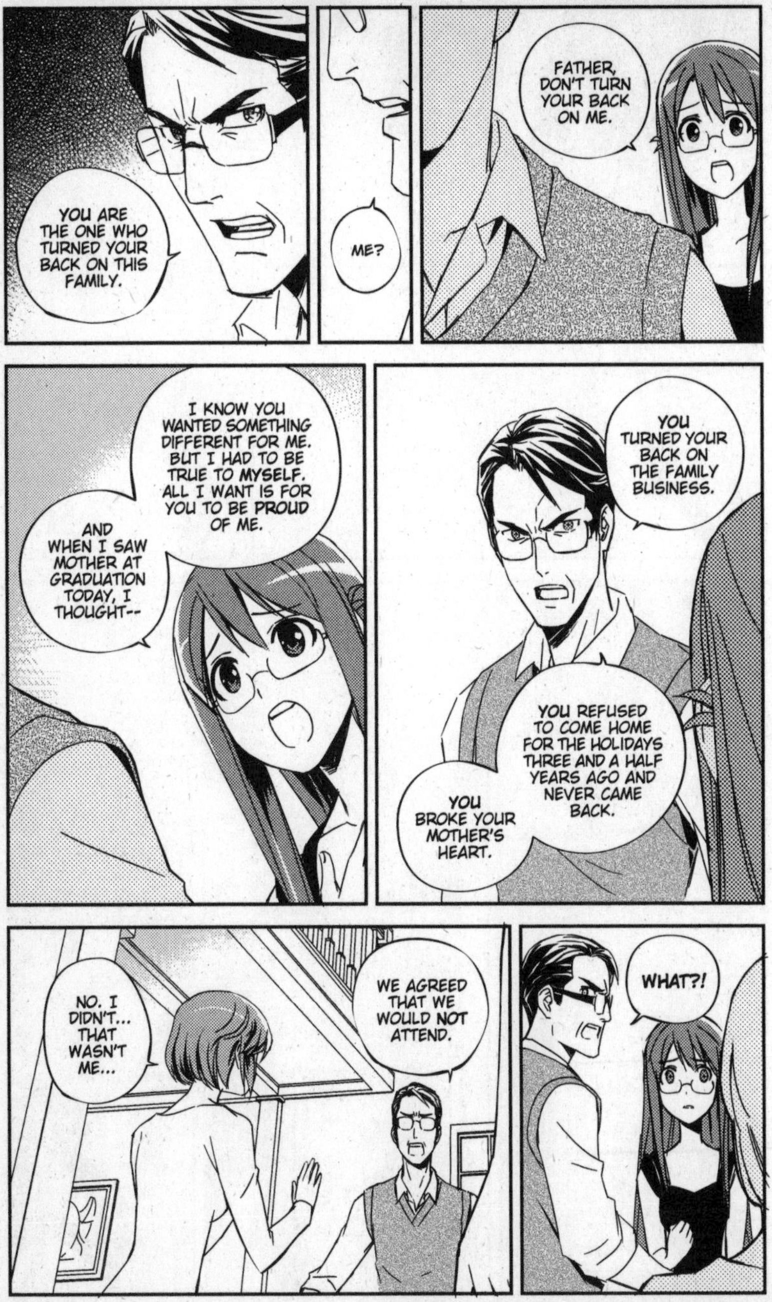
FATHER, DON'T TURN YOUR BACK ON ME.
ME?
YOU ARE THE ONE WHO TURNED YOUR BACK ON THIS FAMILY.
YOU TURNED YOUR BACK ON THE FAMILY BUSINESS.
YOU REFUSED TO COME HOME FOR THE HOLIDAYS THREE AND A HALF YEARS AGO AND NEVER CAME BACK.
YOU BROKE YOUR MOTHER'S HEART.
I KNOW YOU WANTED SOMETHING DIFFERENT FOR ME. BUT I HAD TO BE TRUE TO MYSELF. ALL I WANT IS FOR YOU TO BE PROUD OF ME.
AND WHEN I SAW MOTHER AT GRADUATION TODAY, I THOUGHT--
WHAT?!
WE AGREED THAT WE WOULD NOT ATTEND.
NO. I DIDN'T... THAT WASN'T ME...

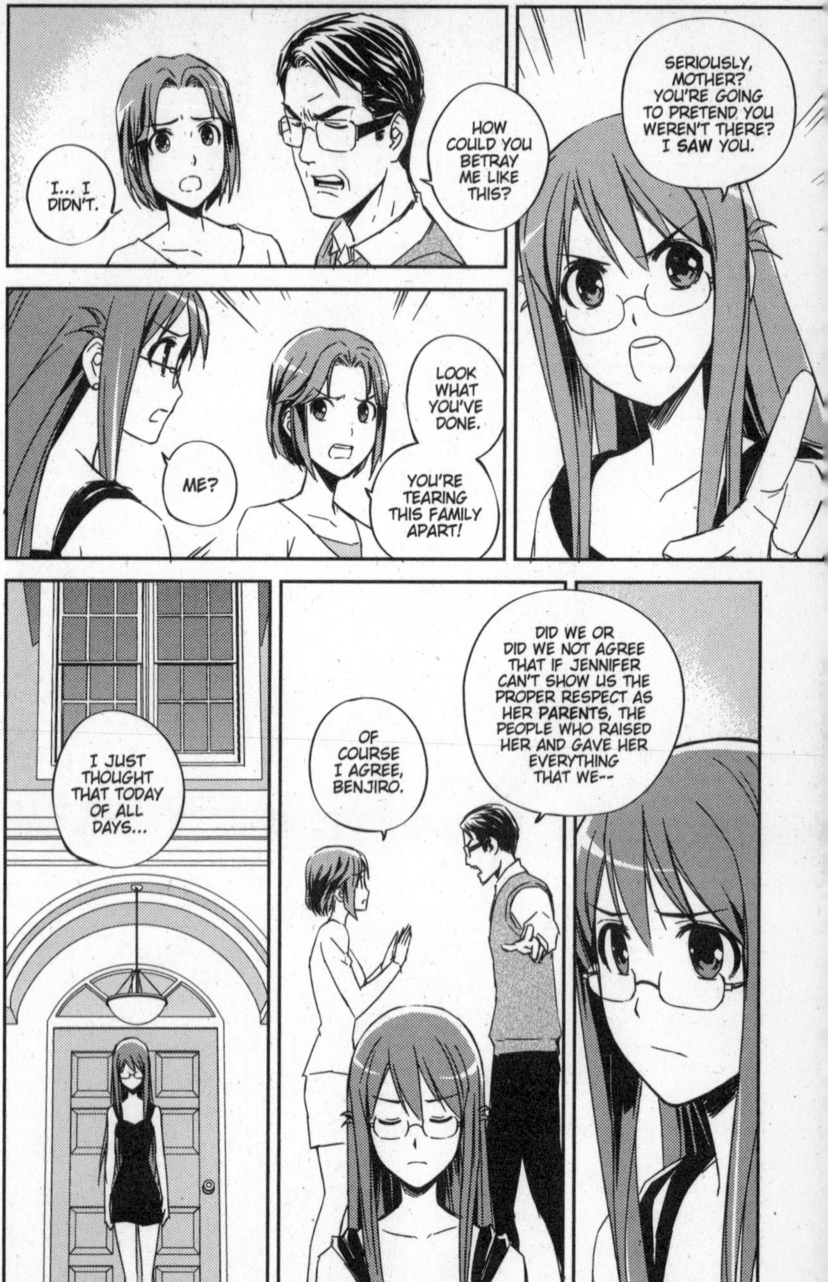
SERIOUSLY, MOTHER? YOU'RE GOING TO PRETEND YOU WEREN'T THERE? I SAW YOU.
HOW COULD YOU BETRAY ME LIKE THIS?
I... I DIDN'T.
LOOK WHAT YOU'VE DONE.
ME?
YOU'RE TEARING THIS FAMILY APART!
DID WE OR DID WE NOT AGREE THAT IF JENNIFER CAN'T SHOW US THE PROPER RESPECT AS HER PARENTS, THE PEOPLE WHO RAISED HER AND GAVE HER EVERYTHING THAT WE--
OF COURSE I AGREE, BENJIRO.
I JUST THOUGHT THAT TODAY OF ALL DAYS...

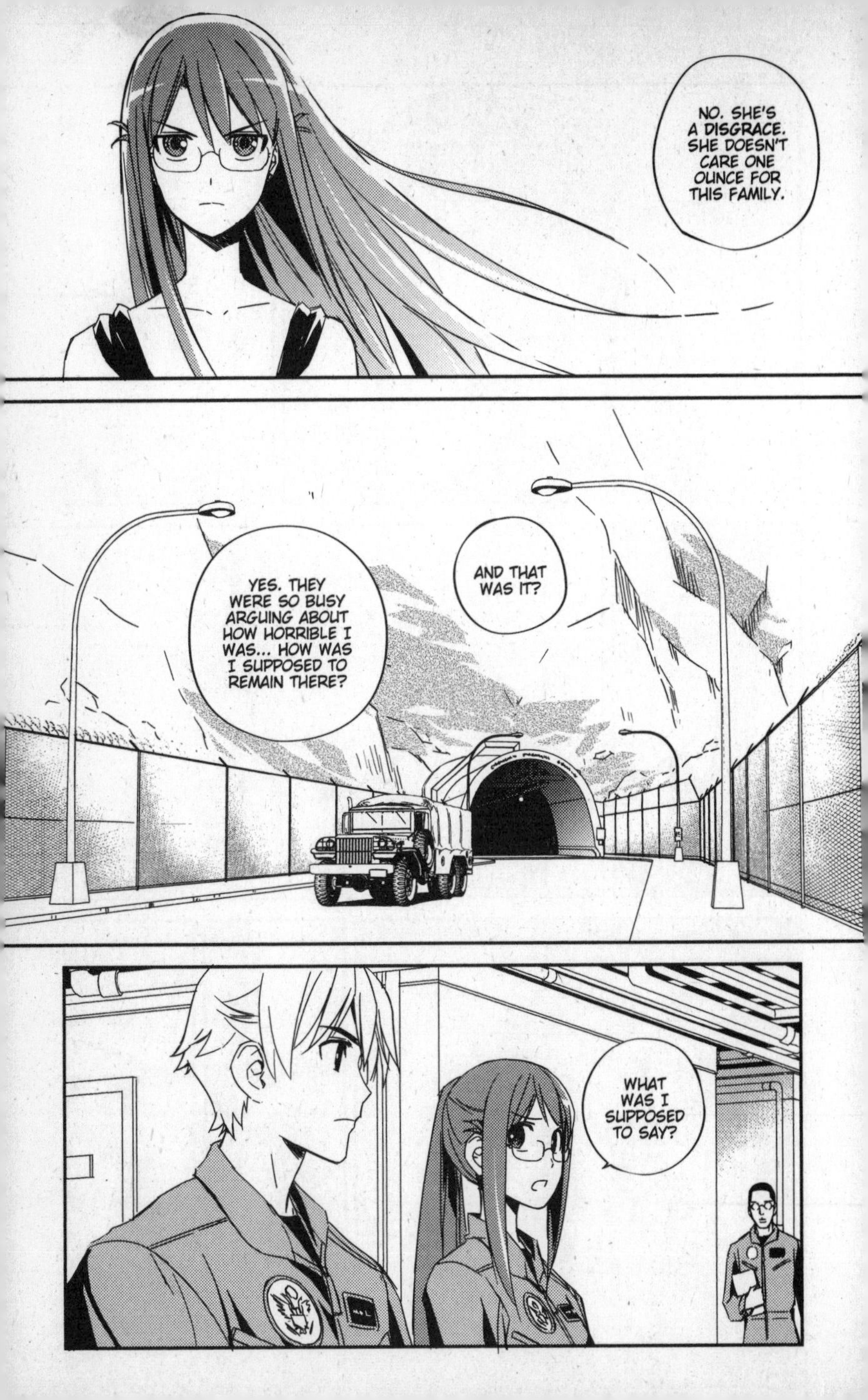
NO. SHE'S A DISGRACE. SHE DOESN'T CARE ONE OUNCE FOR THIS FAMILY.
AND THAT WAS IT?
YES. THEY WERE SO BUSY ARGUING ABOUT HOW HORRIBLE I WAS... HOW WAS I SUPPOSED TO REMAIN THERE?
WHAT WAS I SUPPOSED TO SAY?

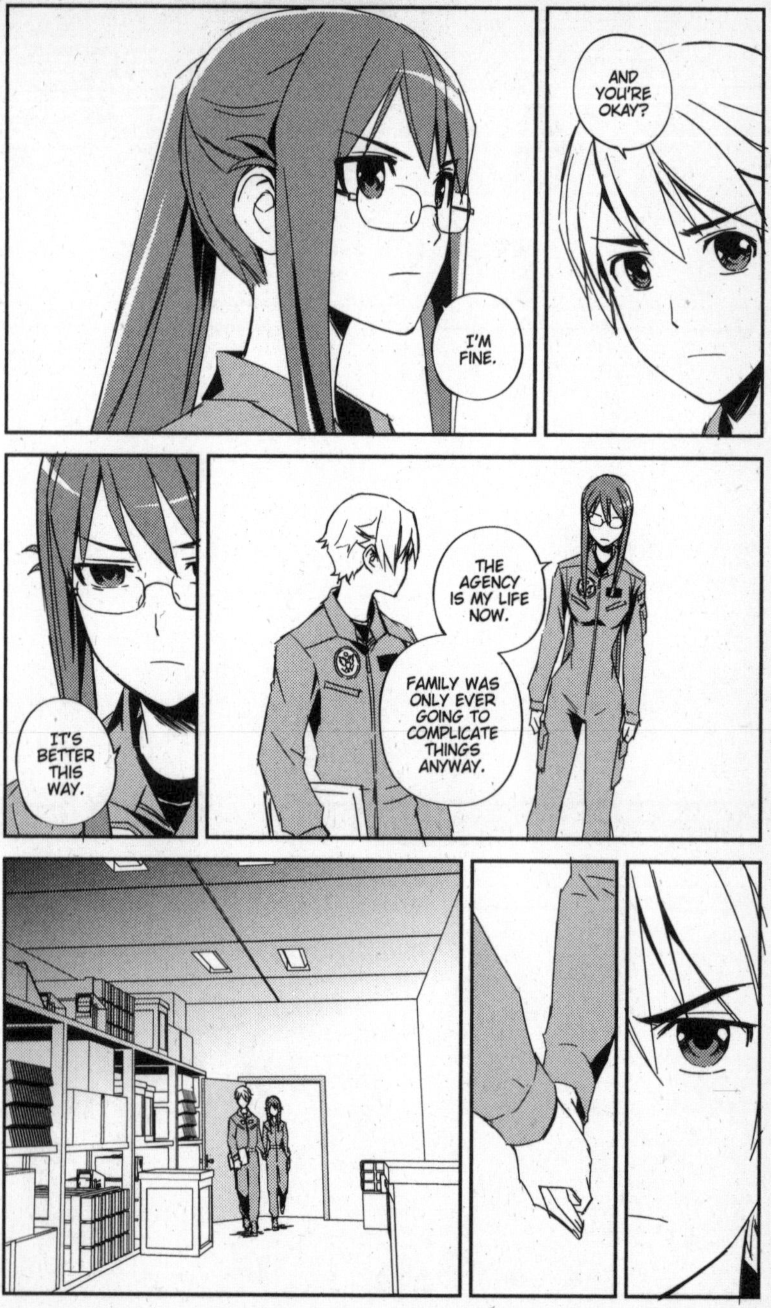
AND YOU'RE OKAY?
I'M FINE.
THE AGENCY IS MY LIFE NOW.
FAMILY WAS ONLY EVER GOING TO COMPLICATE THINGS ANYWAY.
IT'S BETTER THIS WAY.

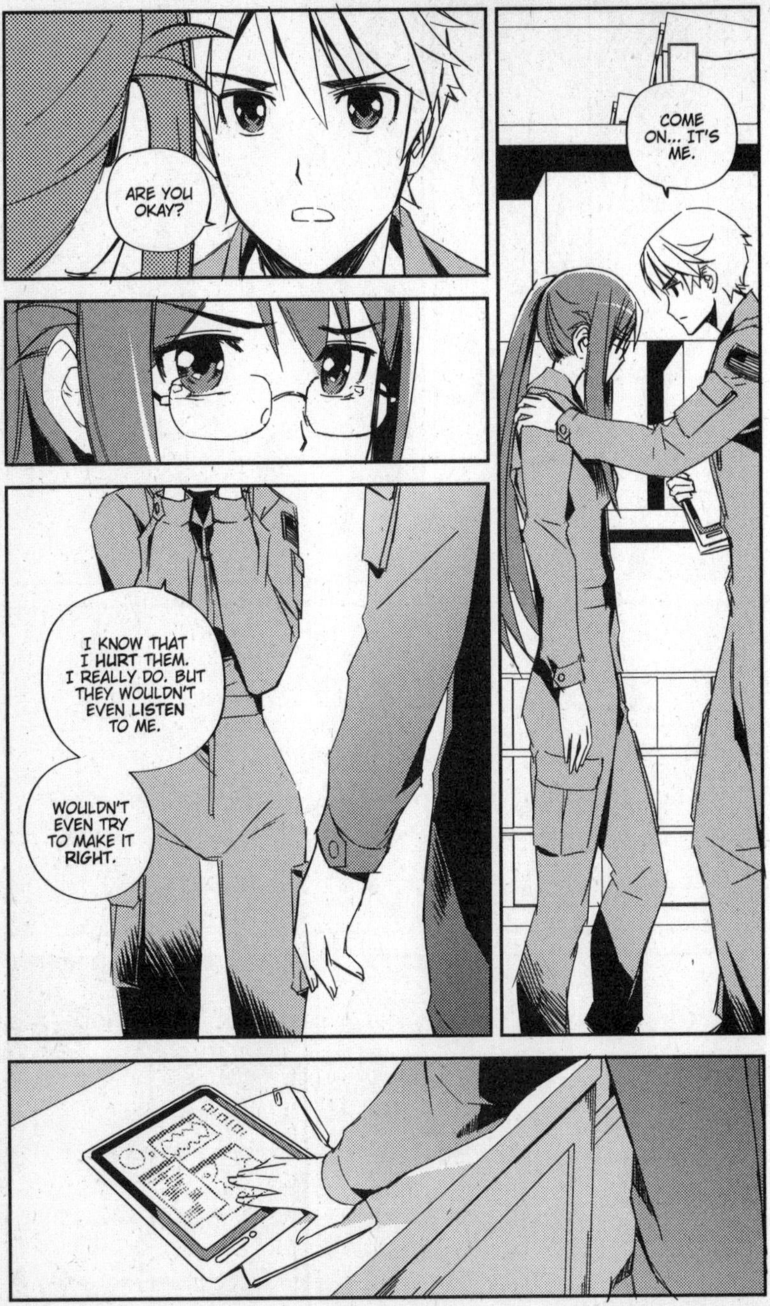
COME ON... IT'S ME.
ARE YOU OKAY?
I KNOW THAT I HURT THEM. I REALLY DO. BUT THEY WOULDN'T EVEN LISTEN TO ME.
WOULDN'T EVEN TRY TO MAKE IT RIGHT.

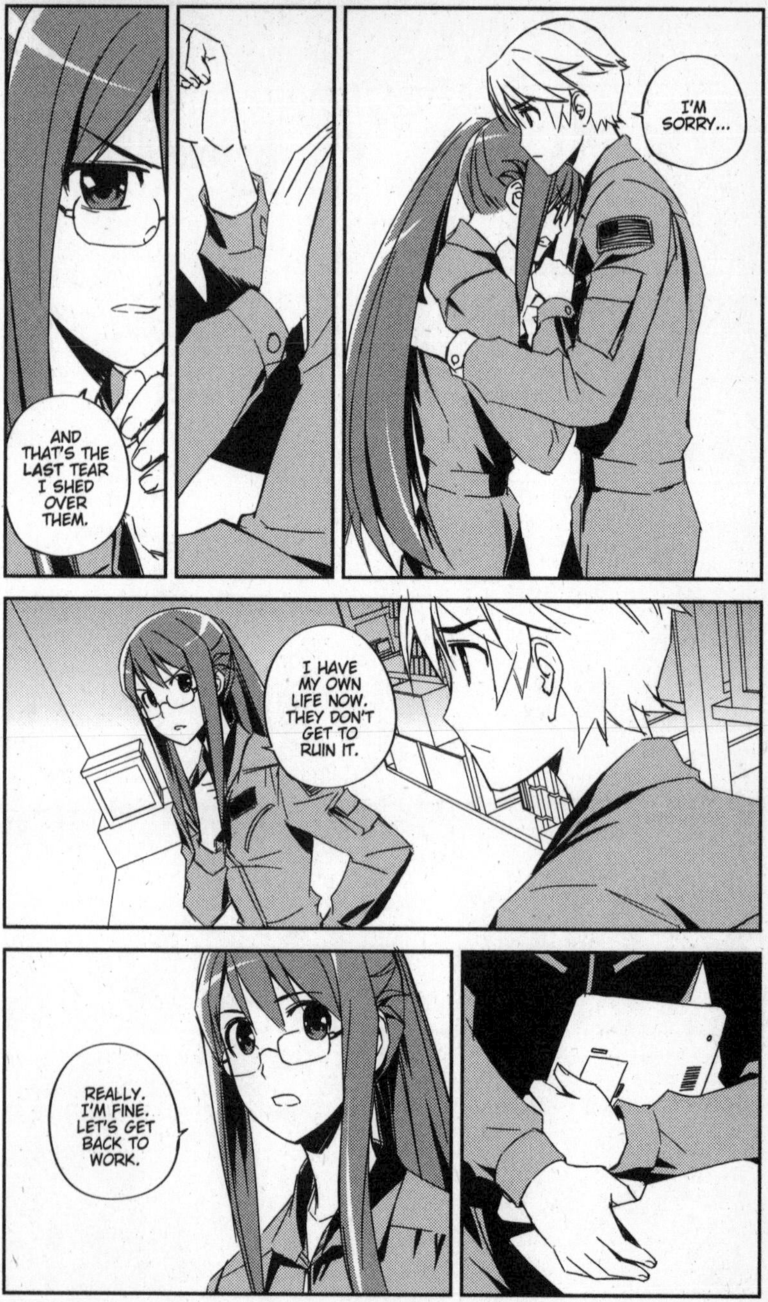
I'M SORRY...
AND THAT'S THE LAST TEAR I SHED OVER THEM.
I HAVE MY OWN LIFE NOW. THEY DON'T GET TO RUIN IT.
REALLY. I'M FINE. LET'S GET BACK TO WORK.

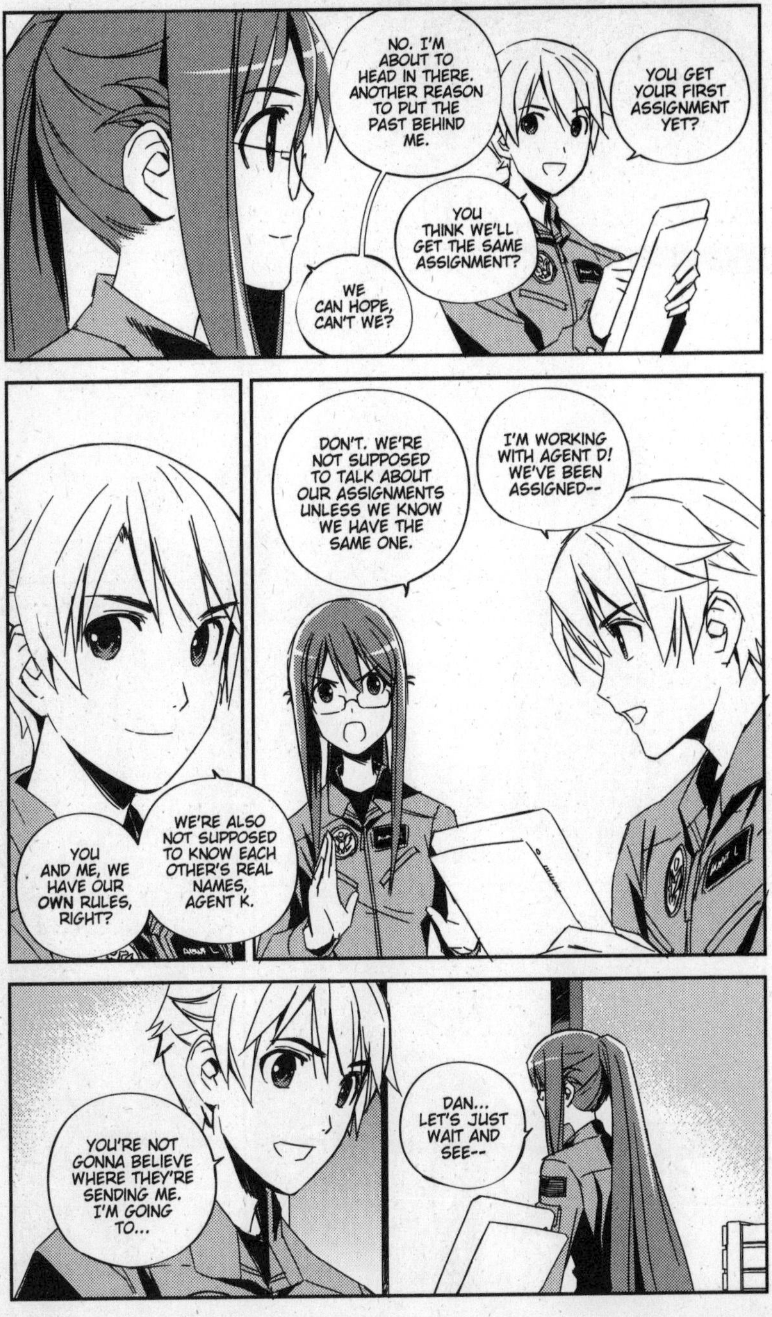
YOU GET YOUR FIRST ASSIGNMENT YET?
NO. I'M ABOUT TO HEAD IN THERE. ANOTHER REASON TO PUT THE PAST BEHIND ME.
YOU THINK WE'LL GET THE SAME ASSIGNMENT?
WE CAN HOPE, CAN'T WE?
I'M WORKING WITH AGENT D! WE'VE BEEN ASSIGNED--
DON'T. WE'RE NOT SUPPOSED TO TALK ABOUT OUR ASSIGNMENTS UNLESS WE KNOW WE HAVE THE SAME ONE.
WE'RE ALSO NOT SUPPOSED TO KNOW EACH OTHER'S REAL NAMES, AGENT K.
YOU AND ME, WE HAVE OUR OWN RULES, RIGHT?
DAN... LET'S JUST WAIT AND SEE--
YOU'RE NOT GONNA BELIEVE WHERE THEY'RE SENDING ME. I'M GOING TO...

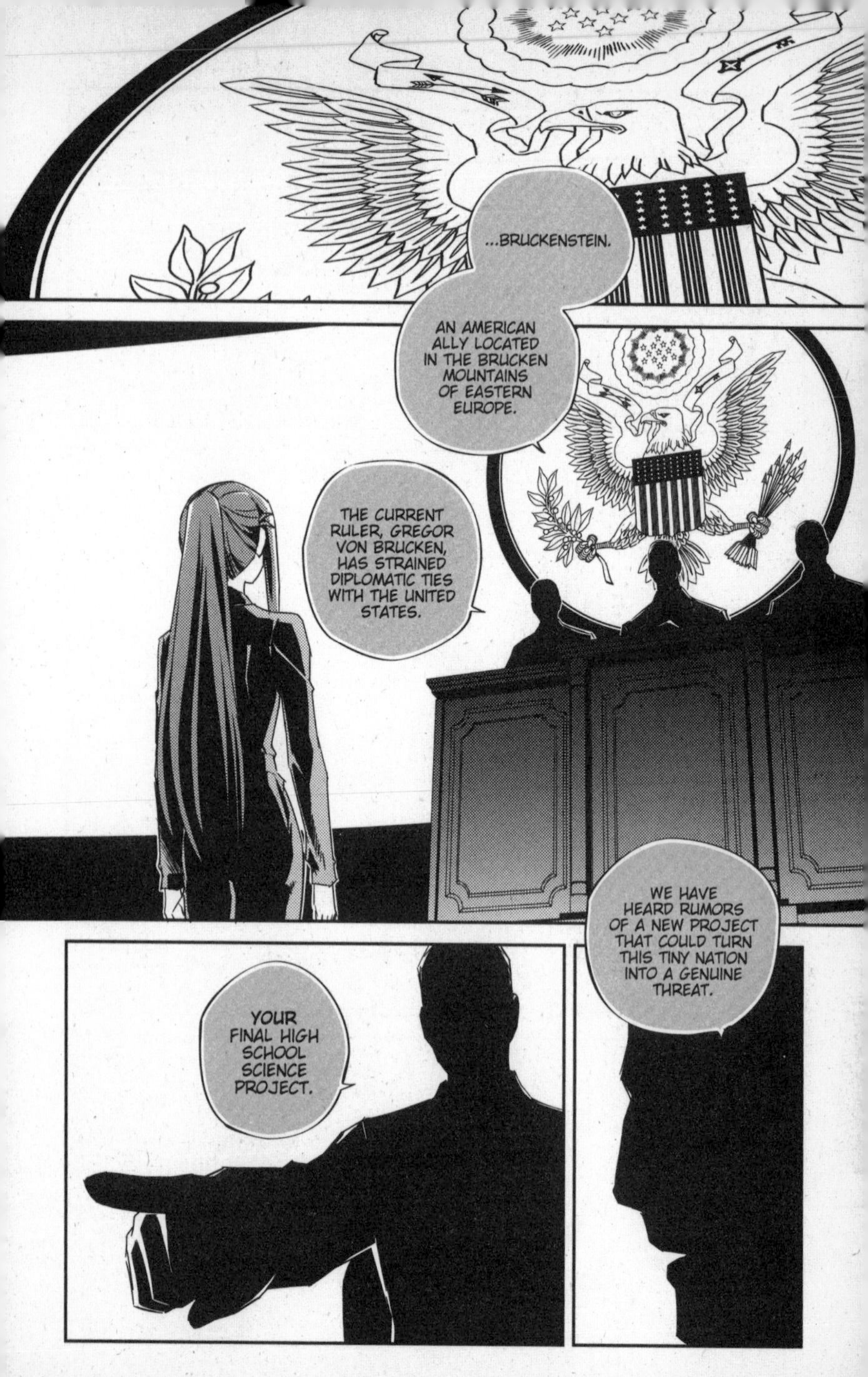
...BRUCKENSTEIN.
AN AMERICAN ALLY LOCATED IN THE BRUCKEN MOUNTAINS OF EASTERN EUROPE.
THE CURRENT RULER, GREGOR VON BRUCKEN, HAS STRAINED DIPLOMATIC TIES WITH THE UNITED STATES.
WE HAVE HEARD RUMORS OF A NEW PROJECT THAT COULD TURN THIS TINY NATION INTO A GENUINE THREAT.
YOUR FINAL HIGH SCHOOL SCIENCE PROJECT.

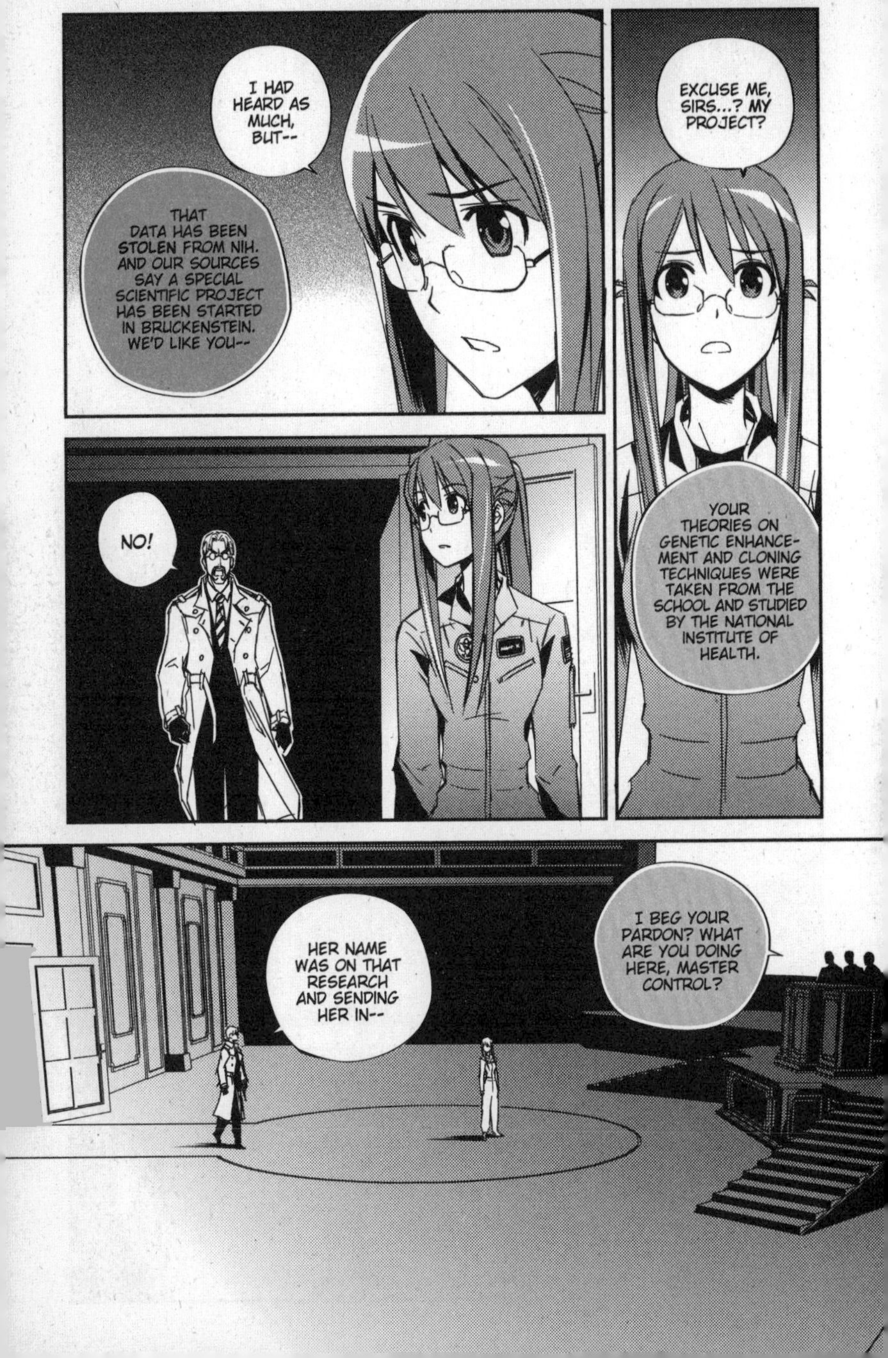
EXCUSE ME, SIRS...? MY PROJECT?
YOUR THEORIES ON GENETIC ENHANCE-MENT AND CLONING TECHNIQUES WERE TAKEN FROM THE SCHOOL AND STUDIED BY THE NATIONAL INSTITUTE OF HEALTH.
I HAD HEARD AS MUCH, BUT--
THAT DATA HAS BEEN STOLEN FROM NIH. AND OUR SOURCES SAY A SPECIAL SCIENTIFIC PROJECT HAS BEEN STARTED IN BRUCKENSTEIN. WE'D LIKE YOU--
NO!
I BEG YOUR PARDON? WHAT ARE YOU DOING HERE, MASTER CONTROL?
HER NAME WAS ON THAT RESEARCH AND SENDING HER IN--

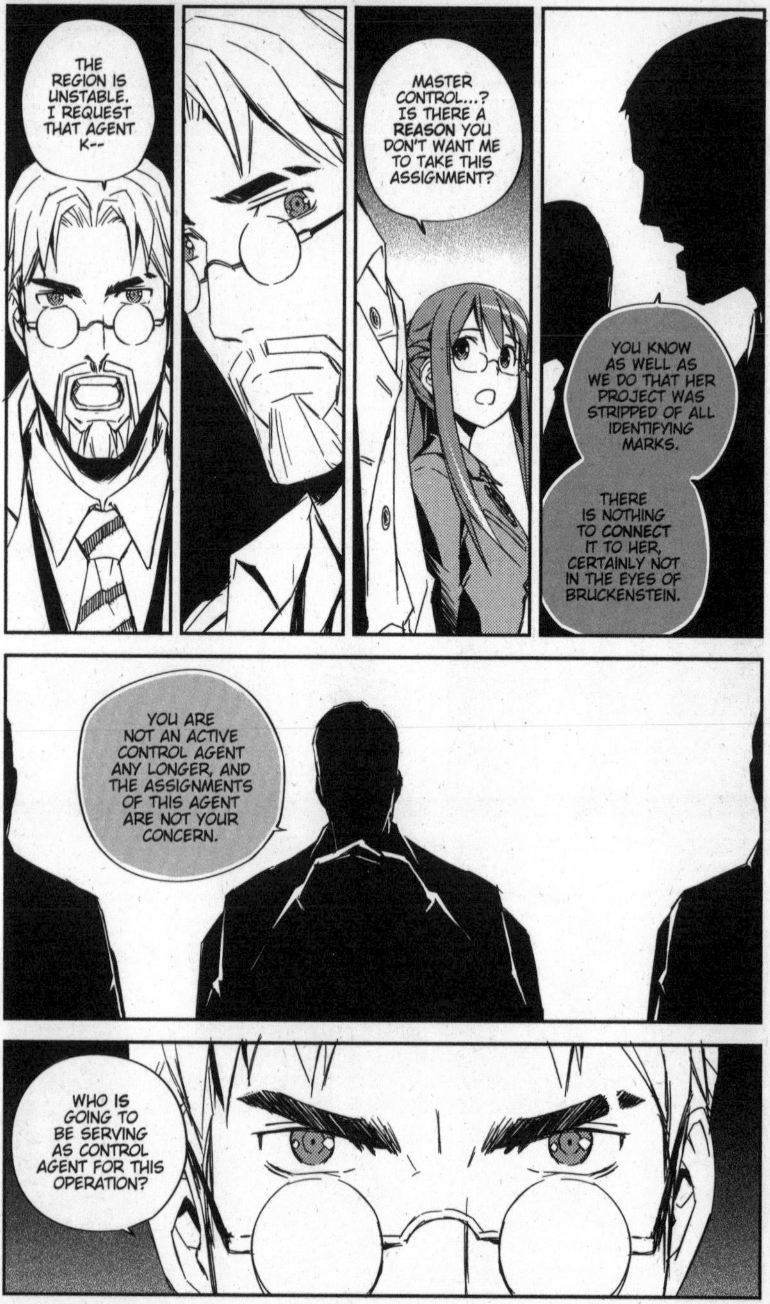
THE REGION IS UNSTABLE. I REQUEST THAT AGENT K--
MASTER CONTROL...? IS THERE A REASON YOU DON'T WANT ME TO TAKE THIS ASSIGNMENT?
YOU KNOW AS WELL AS WE DO THAT HER PROJECT WAS STRIPPED OF ALL IDENTIFYING MARKS.
THERE IS NOTHING TO CONNECT IT TO HER, CERTAINLY NOT IN THE EYES OF BRUCKENSTEIN.
YOU ARE NOT AN ACTIVE CONTROL AGENT ANY LONGER, AND THE ASSIGNMENTS OF THIS AGENT ARE NOT YOUR CONCERN.
WHO IS GOING TO BE SERVING AS CONTROL AGENT FOR THIS OPERATION?

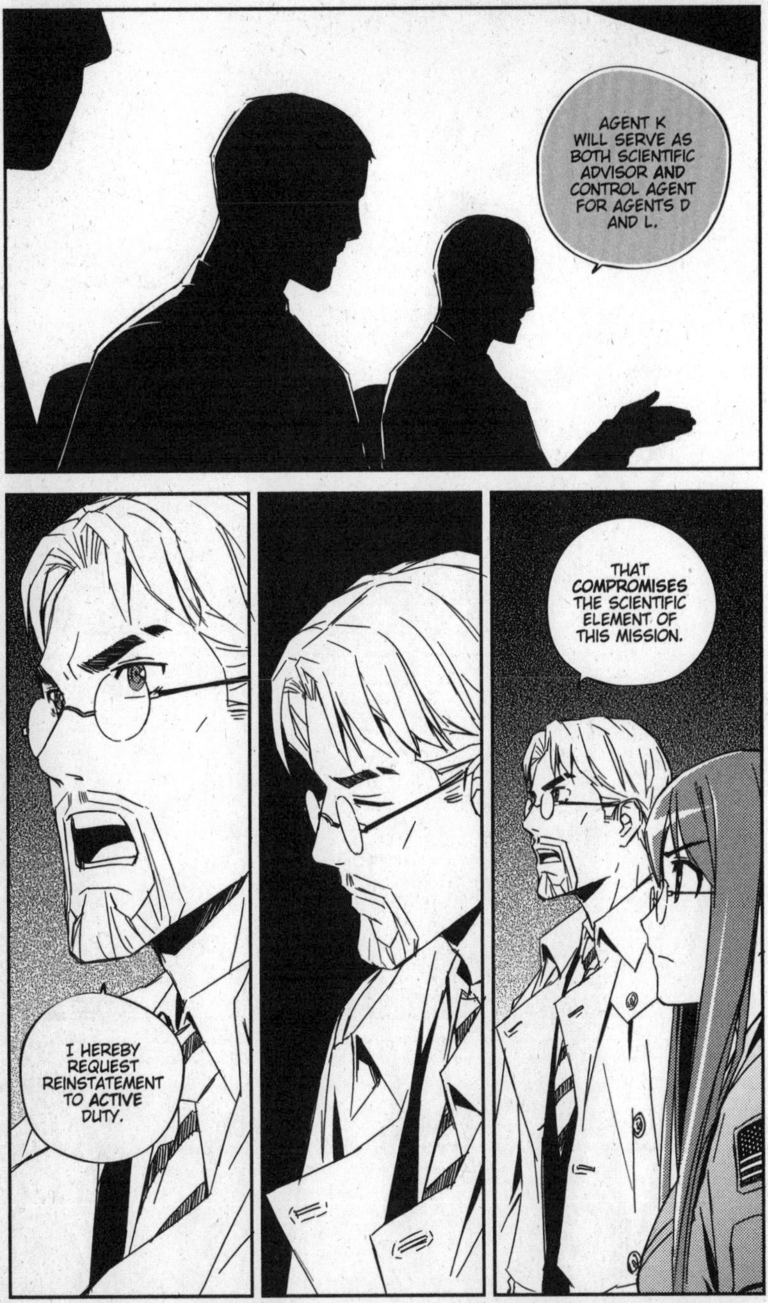
AGENT K WILL SERVE AS BOTH SCIENTIFIC ADVISOR AND CONTROL AGENT FOR AGENTS D AND L.
THAT COMPROMISES THE SCIENTIFIC ELEMENT OF THIS MISSION.
I HEREBY REQUEST REINSTATEMENT TO ACTIVE DUTY.

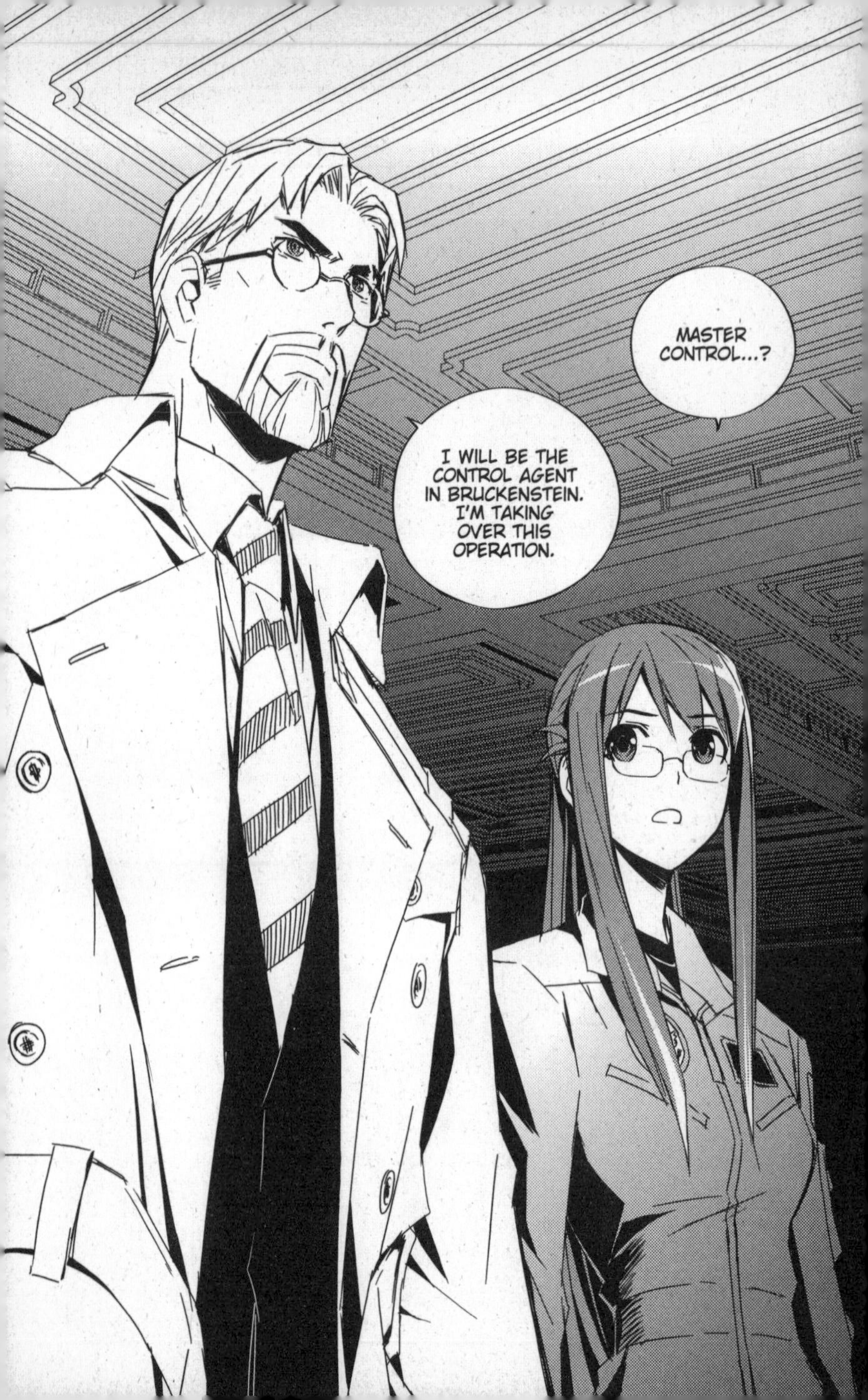
MASTER CONTROL...?
I WILL BE THE CONTROL AGENT IN BRUCKENSTEIN. I'M TAKING OVER THIS OPERATION.

FILE 5:
BEAUTIFUL BRUCKENSTEIN

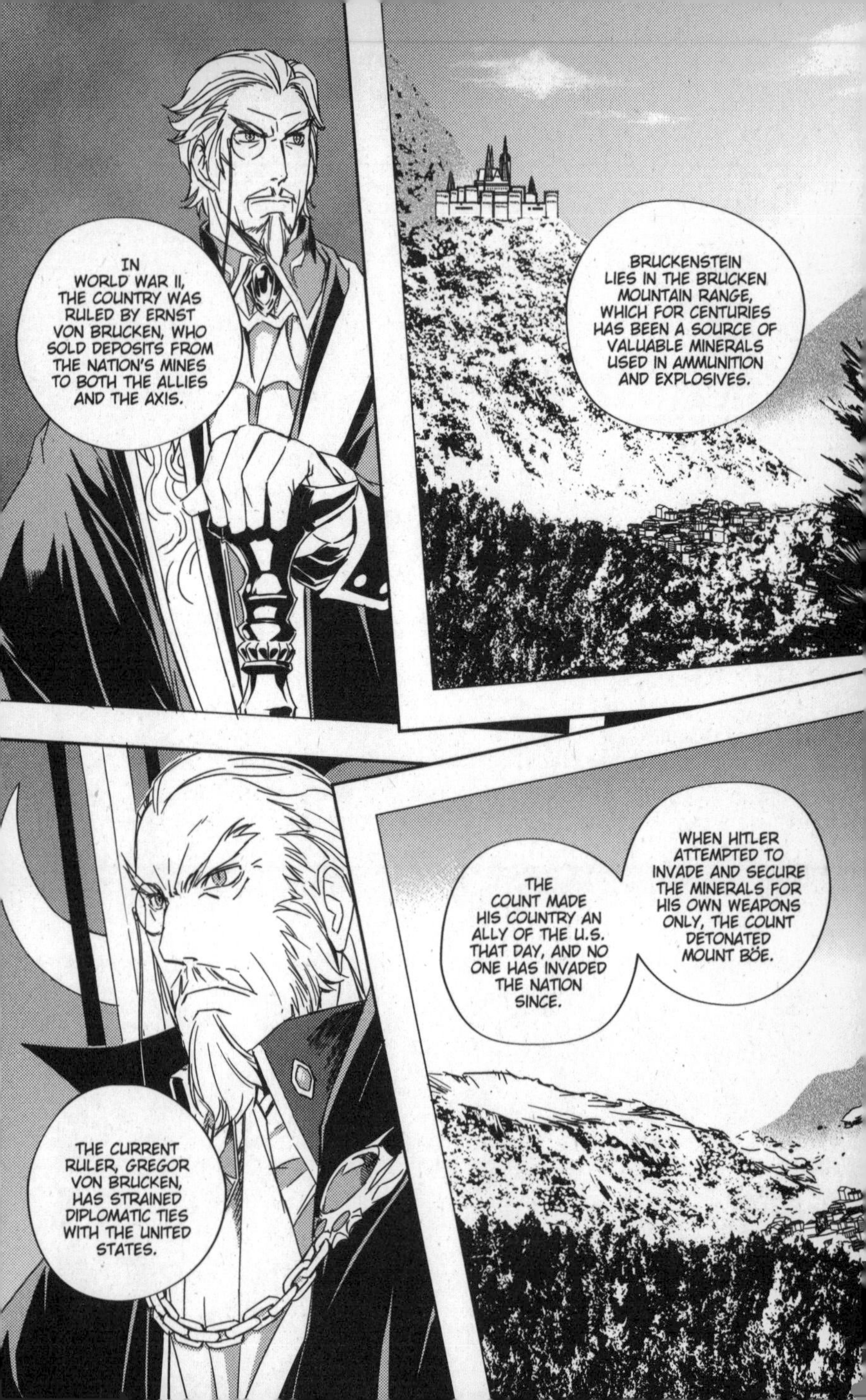
BRUCKENSTEIN LIES IN THE BRUCKEN MOUNTAIN RANGE, WHICH FOR CENTURIES HAS BEEN A SOURCE OF VALUABLE MINERALS USED IN AMMUNITION AND EXPLOSIVES.
IN WORLD WAR II, THE COUNTRY WAS RULED BY ERNST VON BRUCKEN, WHO SOLD DEPOSITS FROM THE NATION'S MINES TO BOTH THE ALLIES AND THE AXIS.
WHEN HITLER ATTEMPTED TO INVADE AND SECURE THE MINERALS FOR HIS OWN WEAPONS ONLY, THE COUNT DETONATED MOUNT BÖE.
THE COUNT MADE HIS COUNTRY AN ALLY OF THE U.S. THAT DAY, AND NO ONE HAS INVADED THE NATION SINCE.
THE CURRENT RULER, GREGOR VON BRUCKEN, HAS STRAINED DIPLOMATIC TIES WITH THE UNITED STATES.

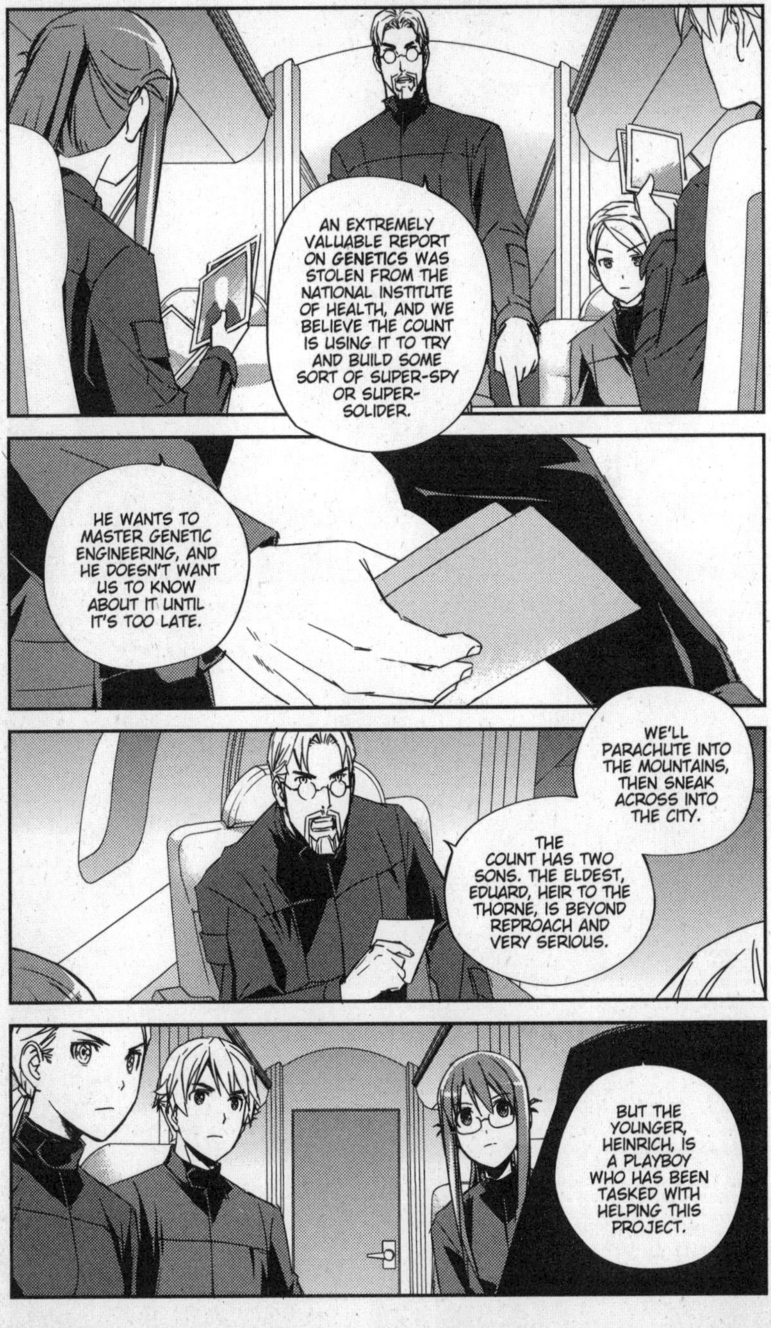
AN EXTREMELY VALUABLE REPORT ON GENETICS WAS STOLEN FROM THE NATIONAL INSTITUTE OF HEALTH, AND WE BELIEVE THE COUNT IS USING IT TO TRY AND BUILD SOME SORT OF SUPER-SPY OR SUPER-SOLIDER.
HE WANTS TO MASTER GENETIC ENGINEERING, AND HE DOESN'T WANT US TO KNOW ABOUT IT UNTIL IT'S TOO LATE.
WE'LL PARACHUTE INTO THE MOUNTAINS, THEN SNEAK ACROSS INTO THE CITY.
THE COUNT HAS TWO SONS. THE ELDEST, EDUARD, HEIR TO THE THORNE, IS BEYOND REPROACH AND VERY SERIOUS.
BUT THE YOUNGER, HEINRICH, IS A PLAYBOY WHO HAS BEEN TASKED WITH HELPING THIS PROJECT.

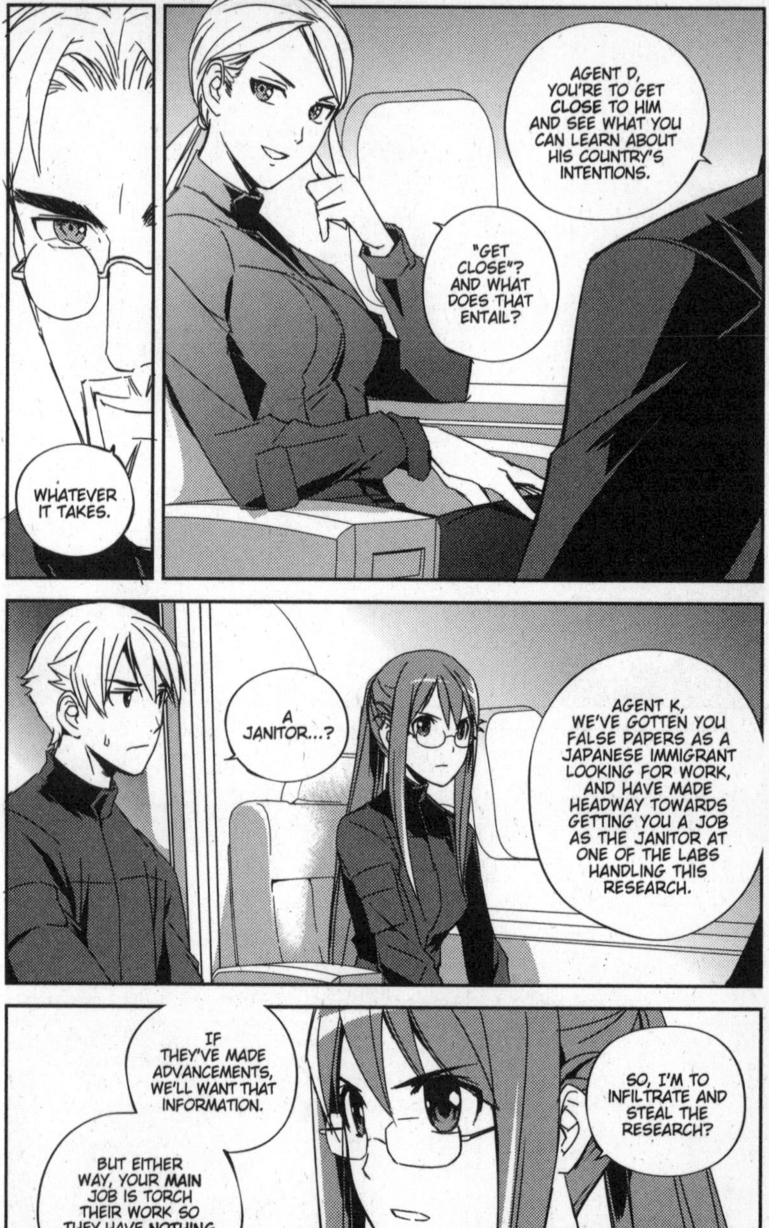
AGENT D, YOU'RE TO GET CLOSE TO HIM AND SEE WHAT YOU CAN LEARN ABOUT HIS COUNTRY'S INTENTIONS.
"GET CLOSE"? AND WHAT DOES THAT ENTAIL?
WHATEVER IT TAKES.
AGENT K, WE'VE GOTTEN YOU FALSE PAPERS AS A JAPANESE IMMIGRANT LOOKING FOR WORK, AND HAVE MADE HEADWAY TOWARDS GETTING YOU A JOB AS THE JANITOR AT ONE OF THE LABS HANDLING THIS RESEARCH.
A JANITOR...?
SO, I'M TO INFILTRATE AND STEAL THE RESEARCH?
IF THEY'VE MADE ADVANCEMENTS, WE'LL WANT THAT INFORMATION.
BUT EITHER WAY, YOUR MAIN JOB IS TORCH THEIR WORK SO THEY HAVE NOTHING LEFT WHEN WE LEAVE.

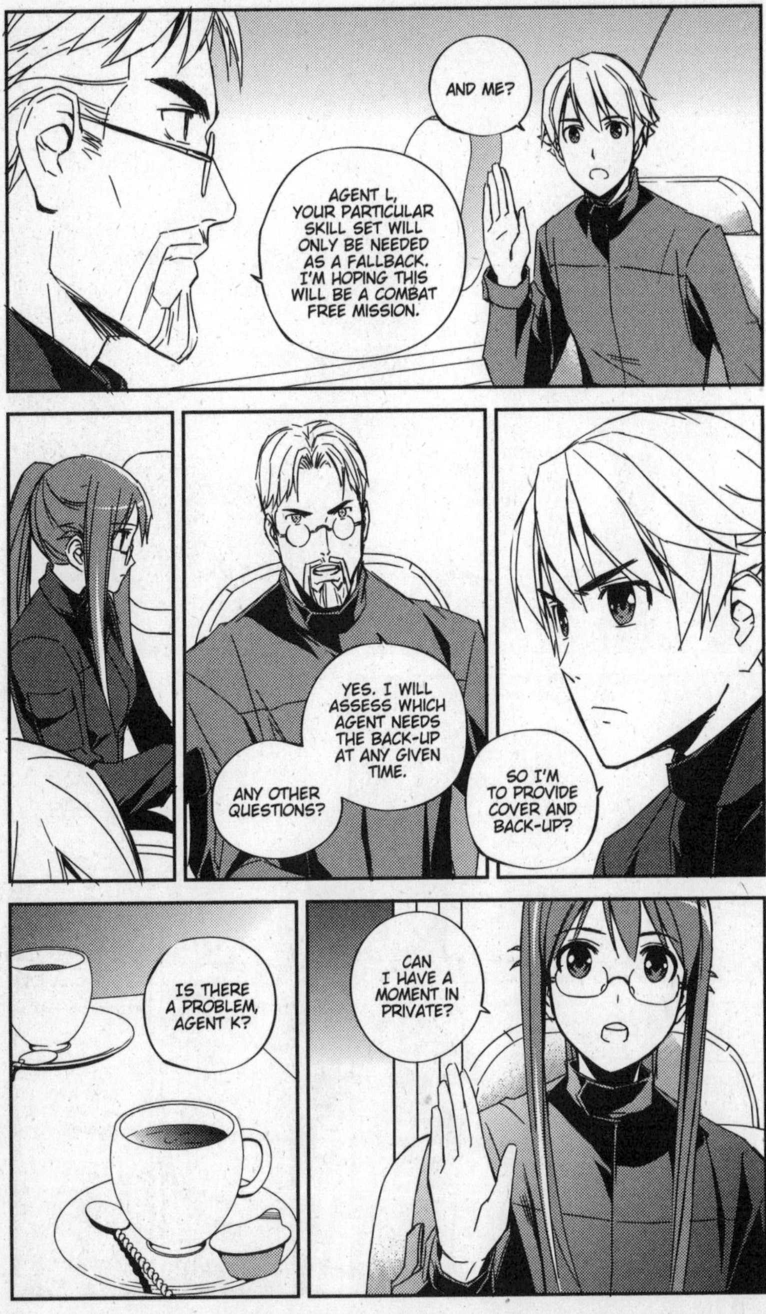
AND ME?
AGENT L, YOUR PARTICULAR SKILL SET WILL ONLY BE NEEDED AS A FALLBACK. I'M HOPING THIS WILL BE A COMBAT FREE MISSION.
SO I'M TO PROVIDE COVER AND BACK-UP?
YES. I WILL ASSESS WHICH AGENT NEEDS THE BACK-UP AT ANY GIVEN TIME.
ANY OTHER QUESTIONS?
CAN I HAVE A MOMENT IN PRIVATE?
IS THERE A PROBLEM, AGENT K?

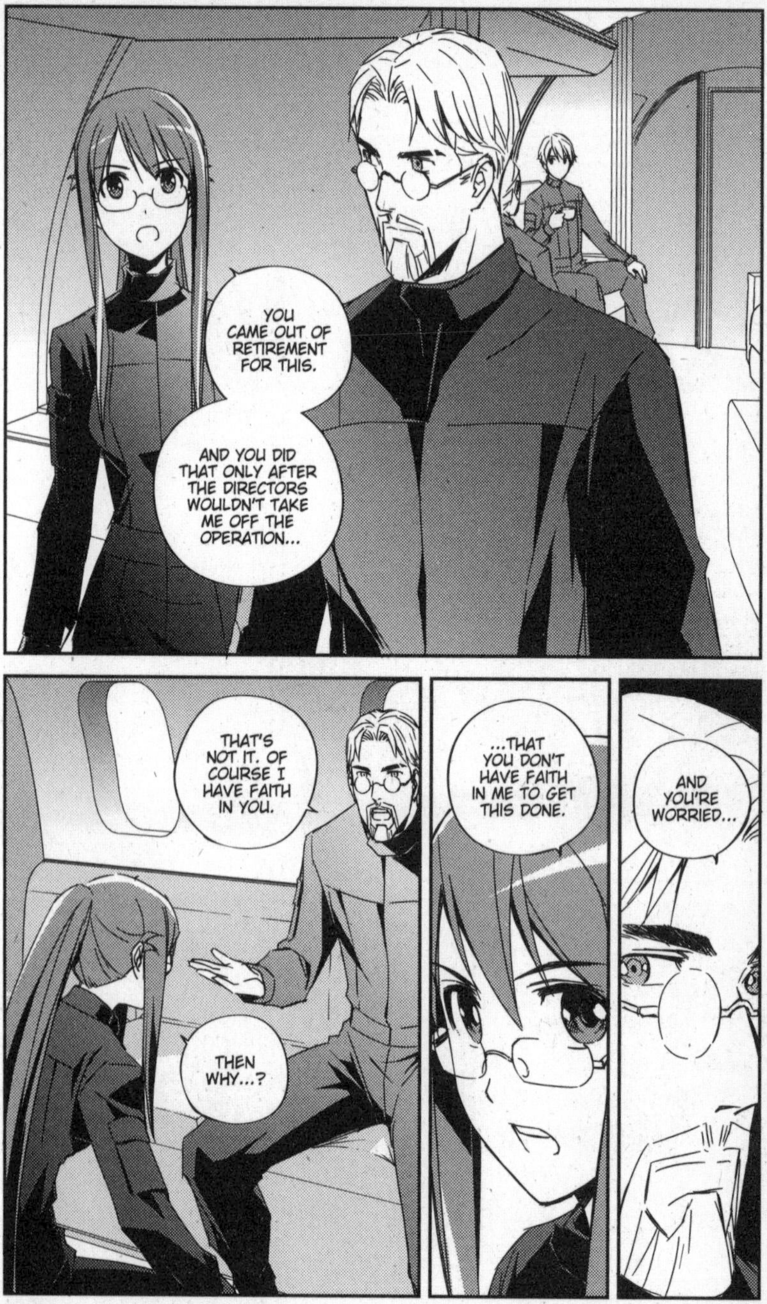
YOU CAME OUT OF RETIREMENT FOR THIS.
AND YOU DID THAT ONLY AFTER THE DIRECTORS WOULDN'T TAKE ME OFF THE OPERATION...
AND YOU'RE WORRIED...
...THAT YOU DON'T HAVE FAITH IN ME TO GET THIS DONE.
THAT'S NOT IT. OF COURSE I HAVE FAITH IN YOU.
THEN WHY...?

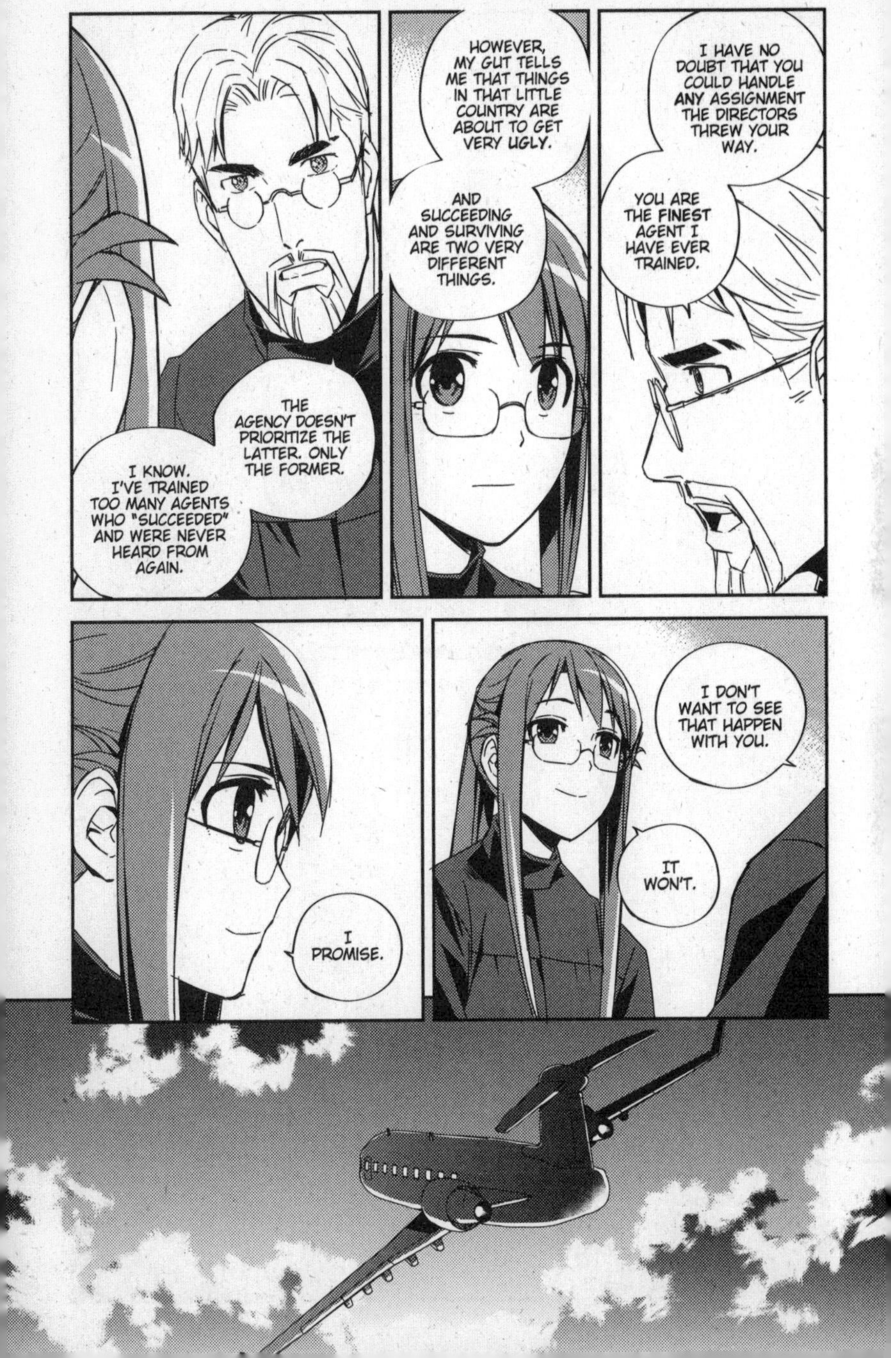
I HAVE NO DOUBT THAT YOU COULD HANDLE ANY ASSIGNMENT THE DIRECTORS THREW YOUR WAY.
YOU ARE THE FINEST AGENT I HAVE EVER TRAINED.
HOWEVER, MY GUT TELLS ME THAT THINGS IN THAT LITTLE COUNTRY ARE ABOUT TO GET VERY UGLY.
AND SUCCEEDING AND SURVIVING ARE TWO VERY DIFFERENT THINGS.
THE AGENCY DOESN'T PRIORITIZE THE LATTER. ONLY THE FORMER.
I KNOW. I'VE TRAINED TOO MANY AGENTS WHO "SUCCEEDED" AND WERE NEVER HEARD FROM AGAIN.
I DON'T WANT TO SEE THAT HAPPEN WITH YOU.
IT WON'T.
I PROMISE.

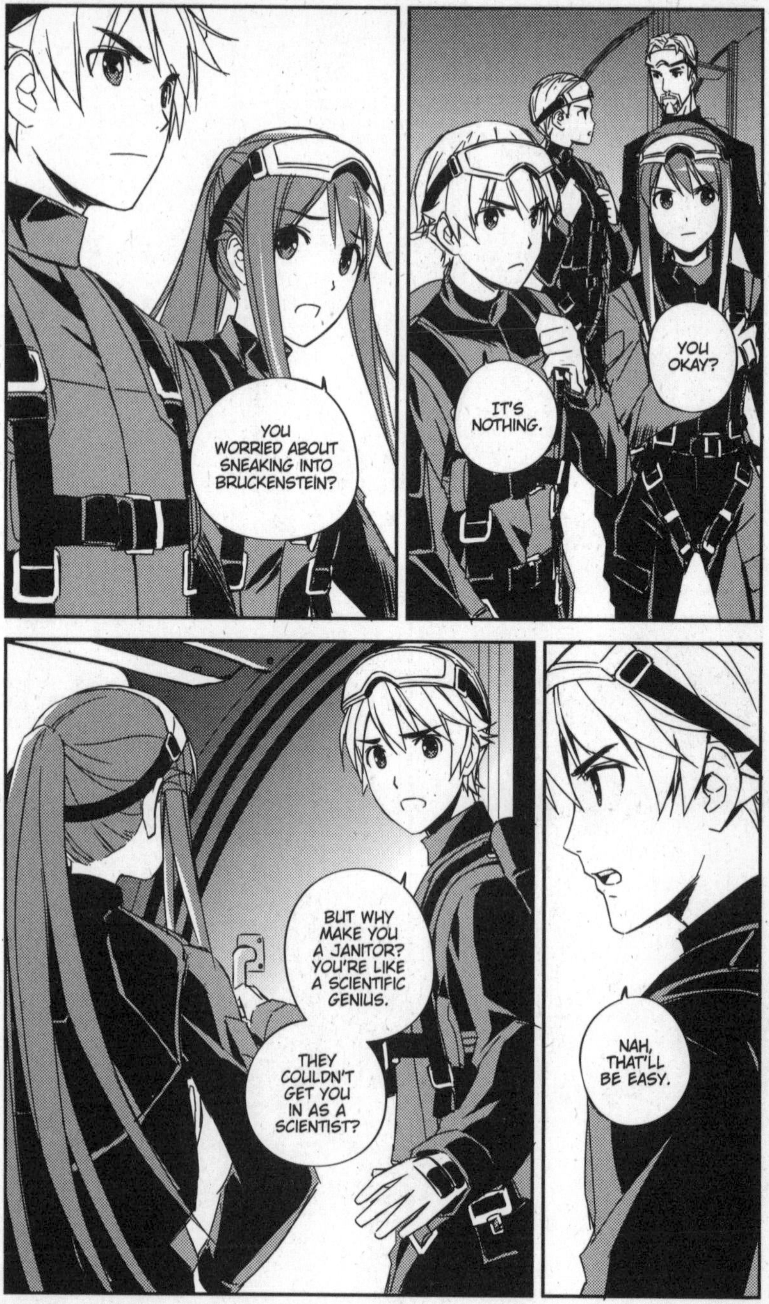
YOU OKAY?
IT'S NOTHING.
YOU WORRIED ABOUT SNEAKING INTO BRUCKENSTEIN?
NAH, THAT'LL BE EASY.
BUT WHY MAKE YOU A JANITOR? YOU'RE LIKE A SCIENTIFIC GENIUS.
THEY COULDN'T GET YOU IN AS A SCIENTIST?

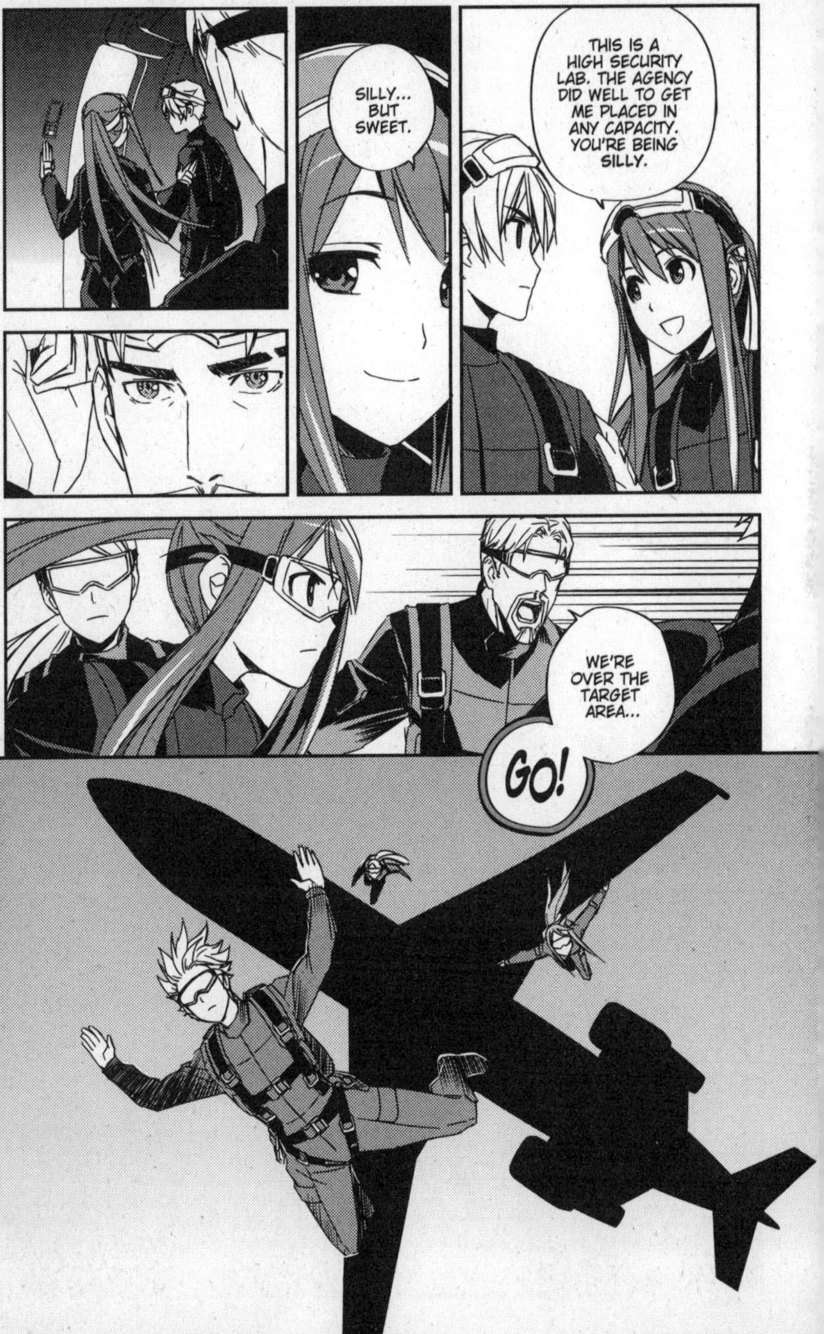
THIS IS A HIGH SECURITY LAB. THE AGENCY DID WELL TO GET ME PLACED IN ANY CAPACITY. YOU'RE BEING SILLY.
SILLY... BUT SWEET.
WE'RE OVER THE TARGET AREA...
GO!

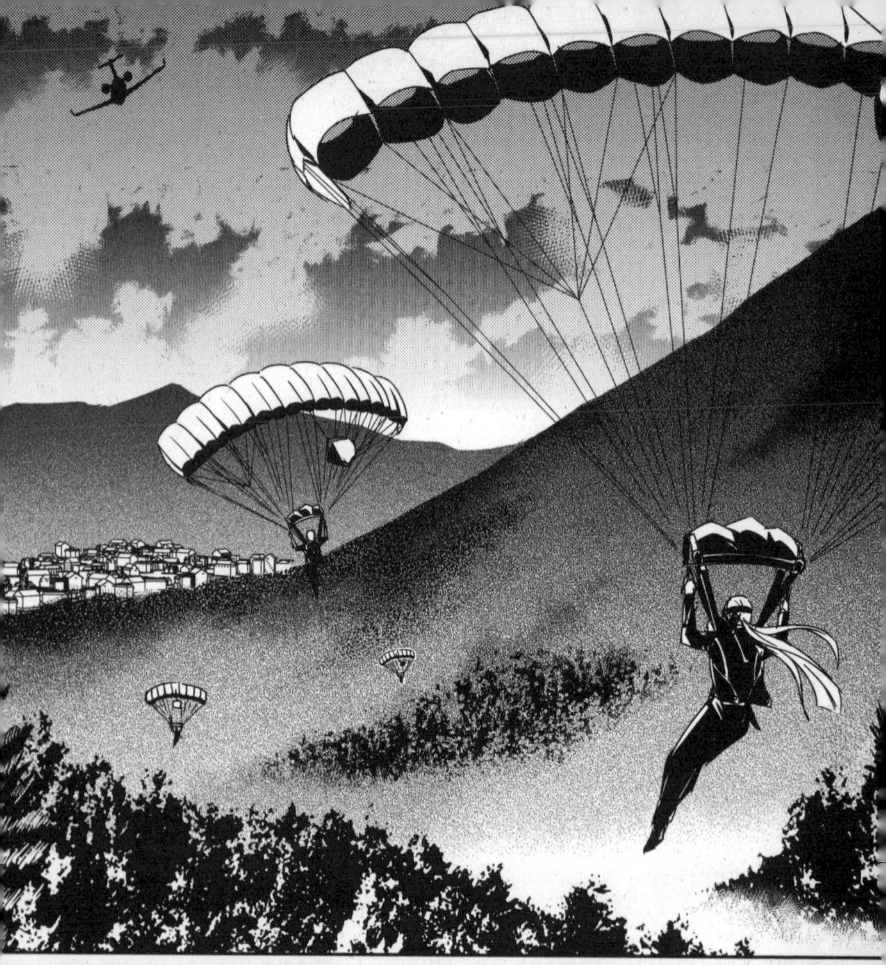
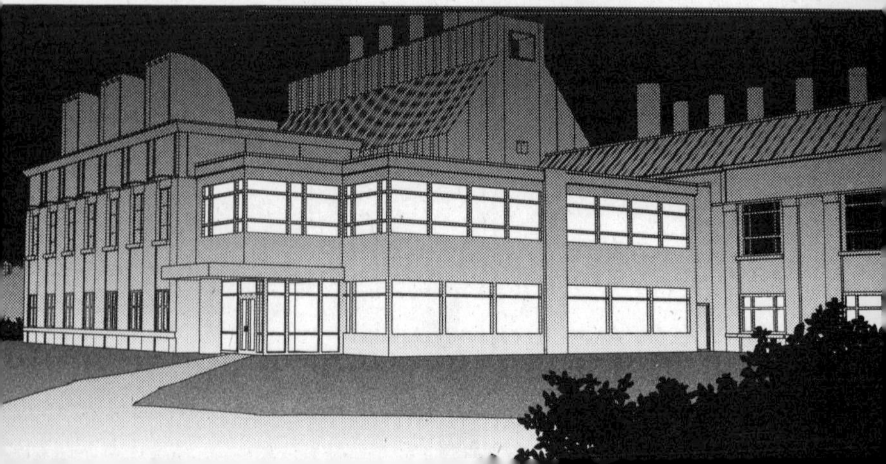

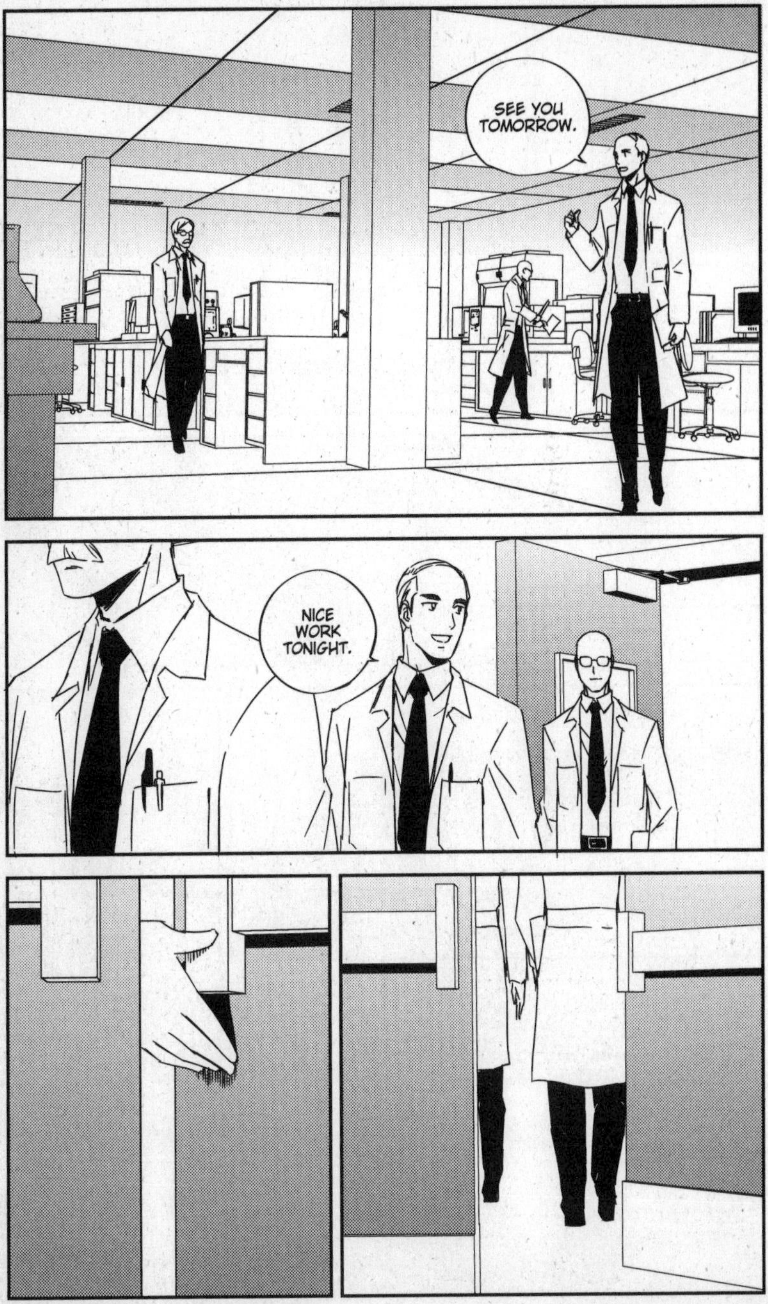
SEE YOU TOMORROW.
NICE WORK TONIGHT.

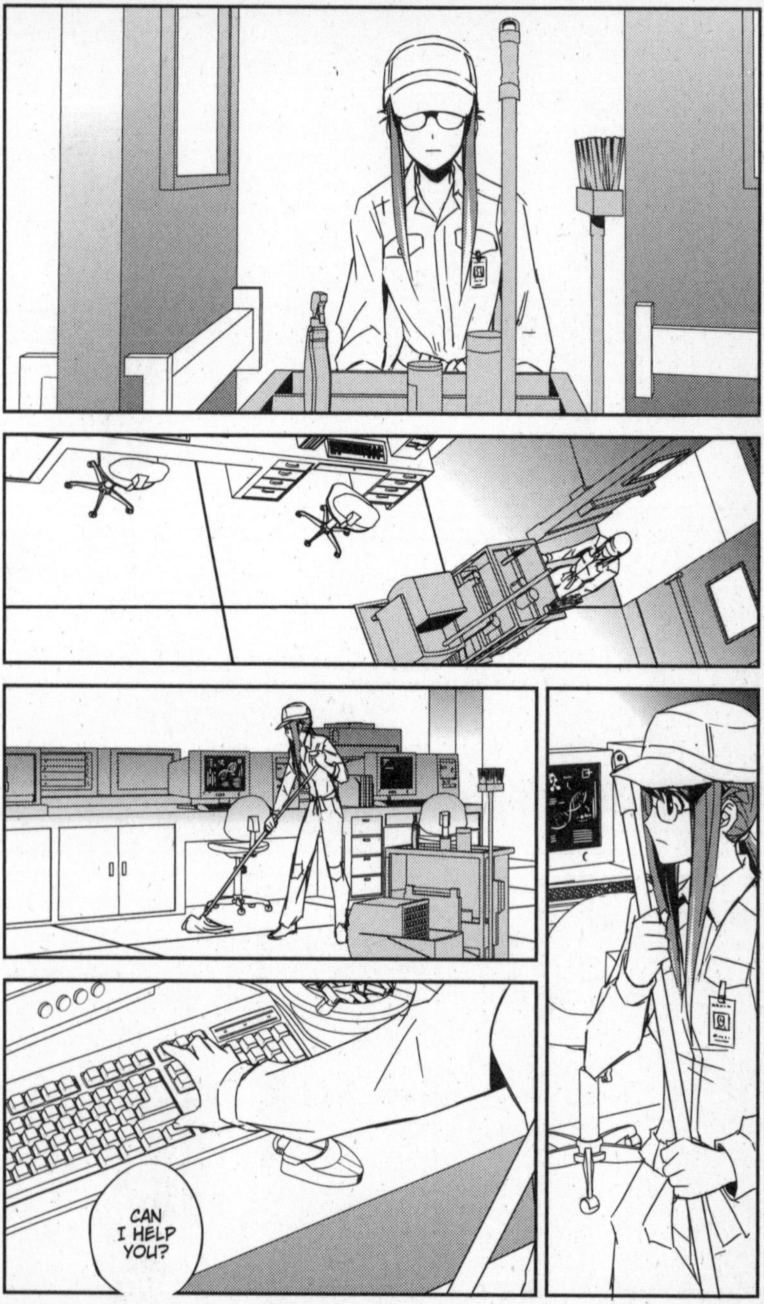
CAN I HELP YOU?

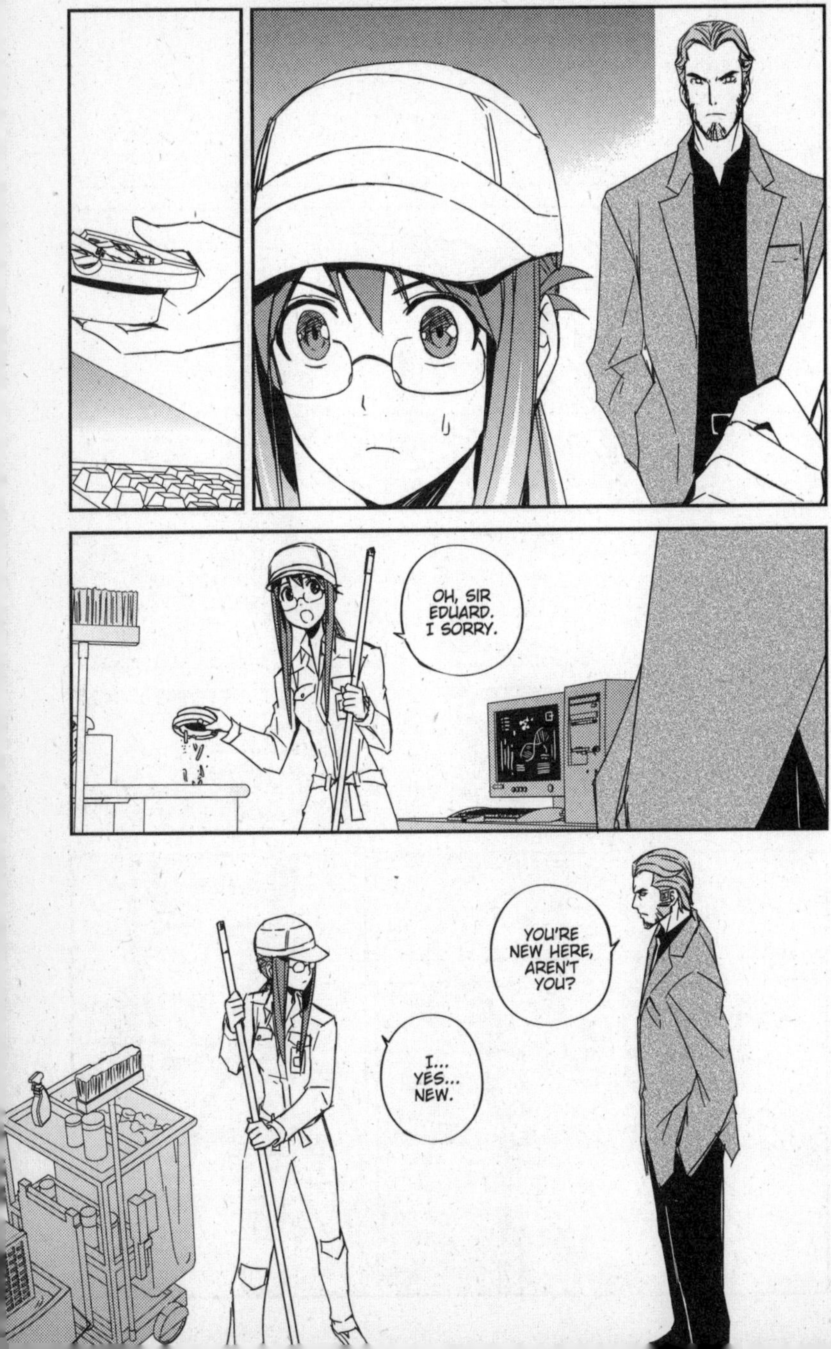
OH, SIR EDUARD. I SORRY.
YOU'RE NEW HERE, AREN'T YOU?
I... YES... NEW.

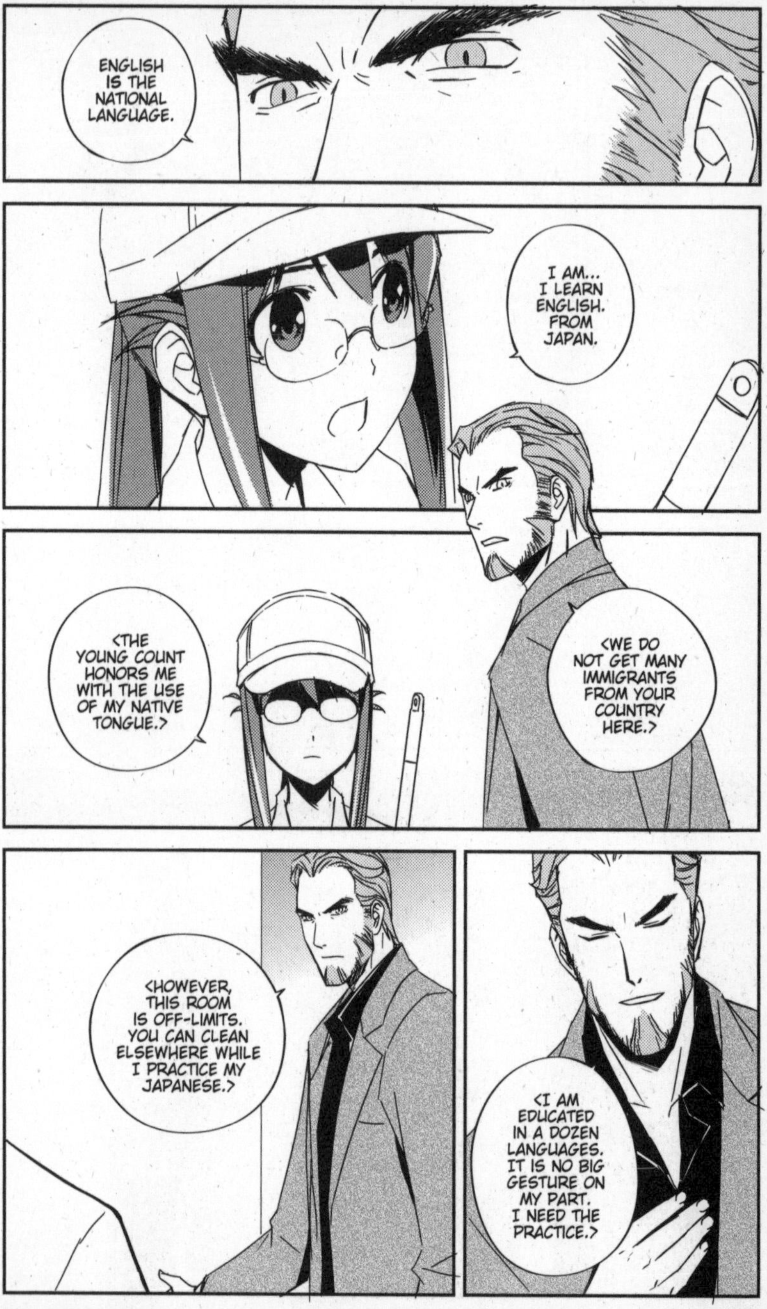
ENGLISH IS THE NATIONAL LANGUAGE.
I AM... I LEARN ENGLISH. FROM JAPAN.
<WE DO NOT GET MANY IMMIGRANTS FROM YOUR COUNTRY HERE.>
<THE YOUNG COUNT HONORS ME WITH THE USE OF MY NATIVE TONGUE.>
<I AM EDUCATED IN A DOZEN LANGUAGES. IT IS NO BIG GESTURE ON MY PART. I NEED THE PRACTICE.>
<HOWEVER, THIS ROOM IS OFF-LIMITS. YOU CAN CLEAN ELSEWHERE WHILE I PRACTICE MY JAPANESE.>

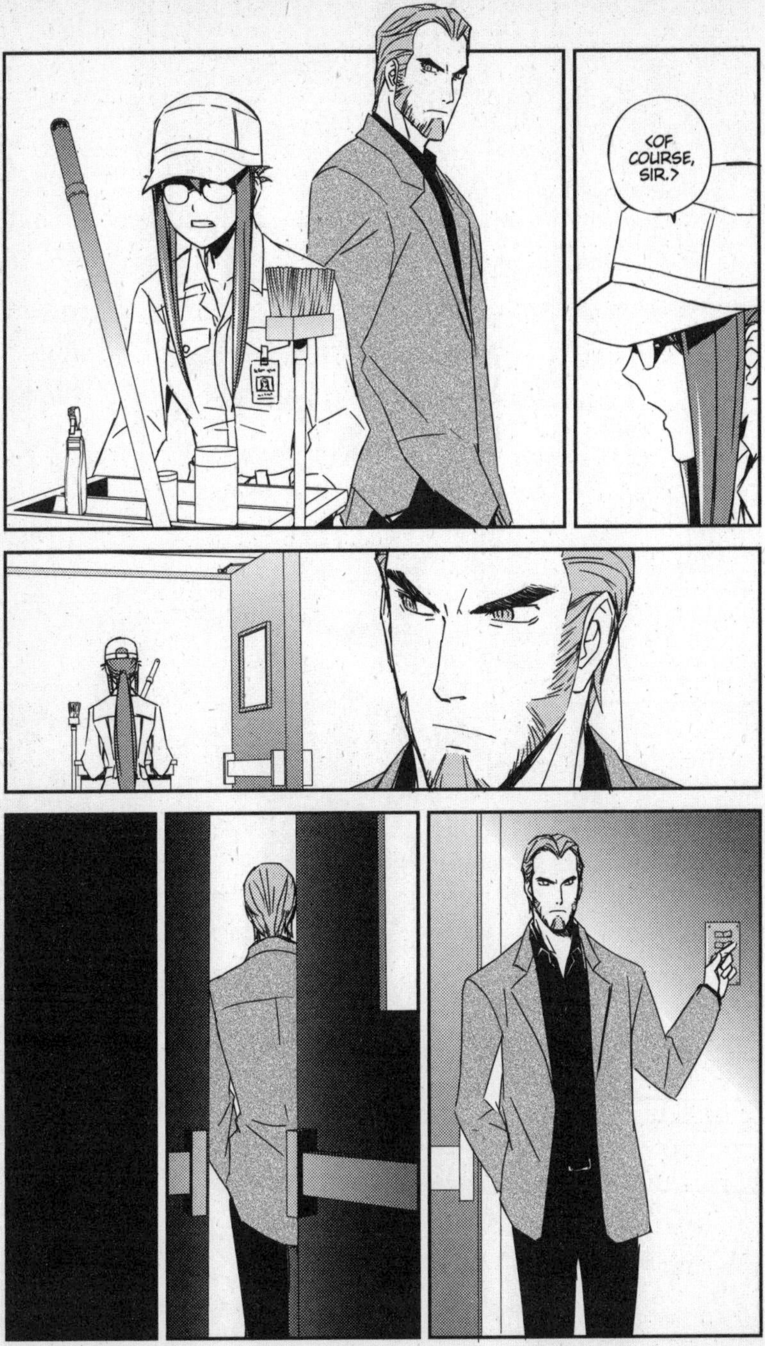
<OF COURSE, SIR.>

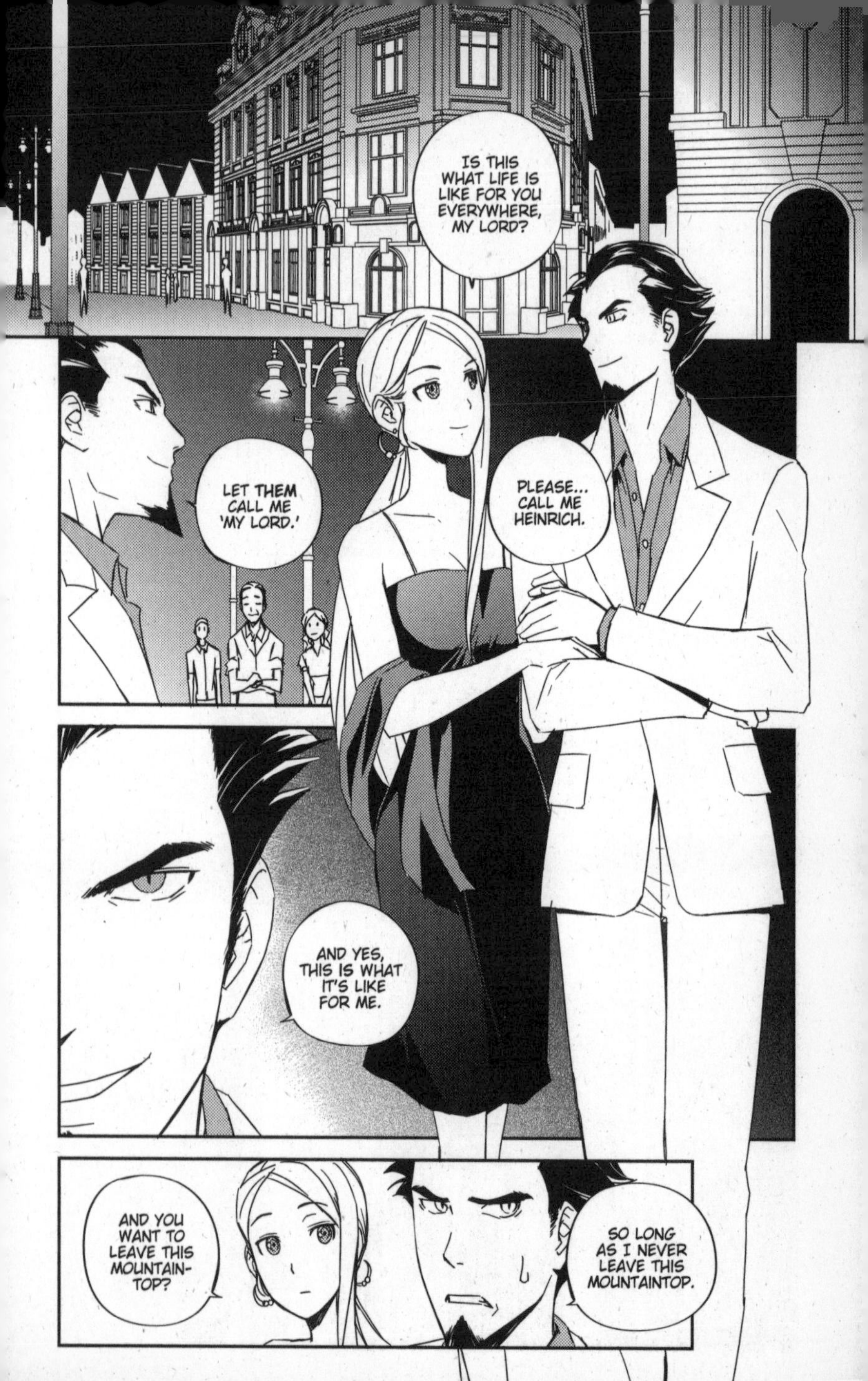
IS THIS WHAT LIFE IS LIKE FOR YOU EVERYWHERE, MY LORD?
PLEASE... CALL ME HEINRICH.
LET THEM CALL ME 'MY LORD.'
AND YES, THIS IS WHAT IT'S LIKE FOR ME.
SO LONG AS I NEVER LEAVE THIS MOUNTAINTOP.
AND YOU WANT TO LEAVE THIS MOUNTAIN-TOP?

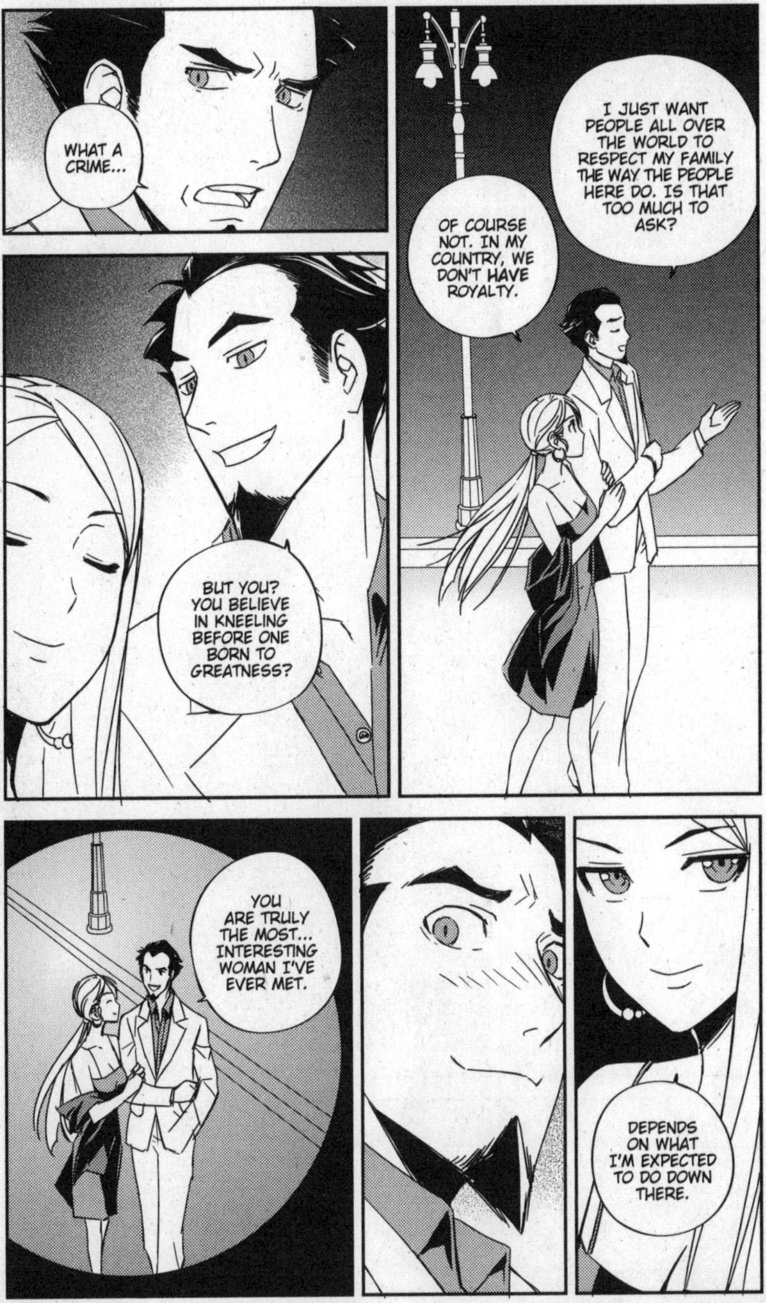
I JUST WANT PEOPLE ALL OVER THE WORLD TO RESPECT MY FAMILY THE WAY THE PEOPLE HERE DO. IS THAT TOO MUCH TO ASK?
OF COURSE NOT. IN MY COUNTRY, WE DON'T HAVE ROYALTY.
WHAT A CRIME...
BUT YOU? YOU BELIEVE IN KNEELING BEFORE ONE BORN TO GREATNESS?
DEPENDS ON WHAT I'M EXPECTED TO DO DOWN THERE.
YOU ARE TRULY THE MOST... INTERESTING WOMAN I'VE EVER MET.

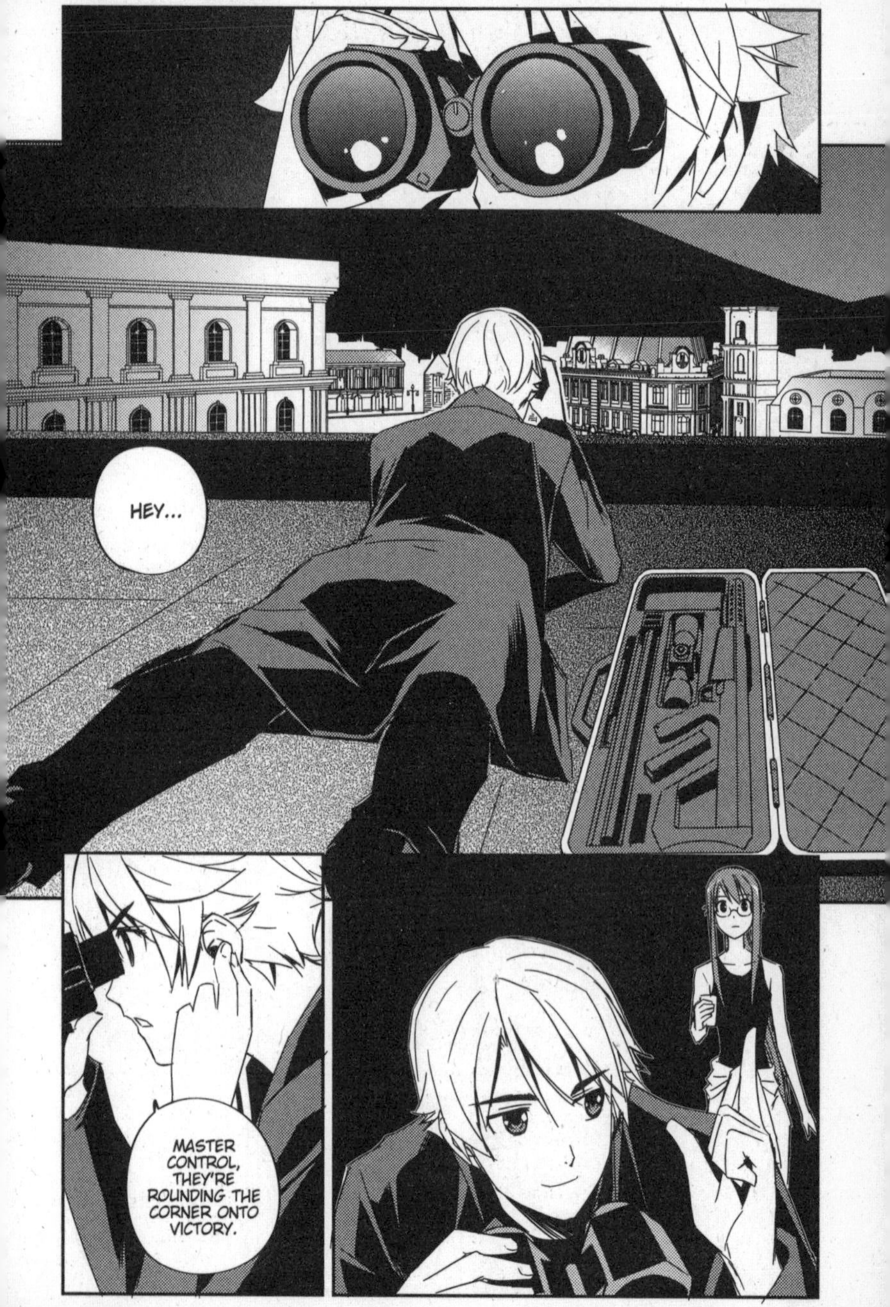
HEY...
MASTER CONTROL, THEY'RE ROUNDING THE CORNER ONTO VICTORY.

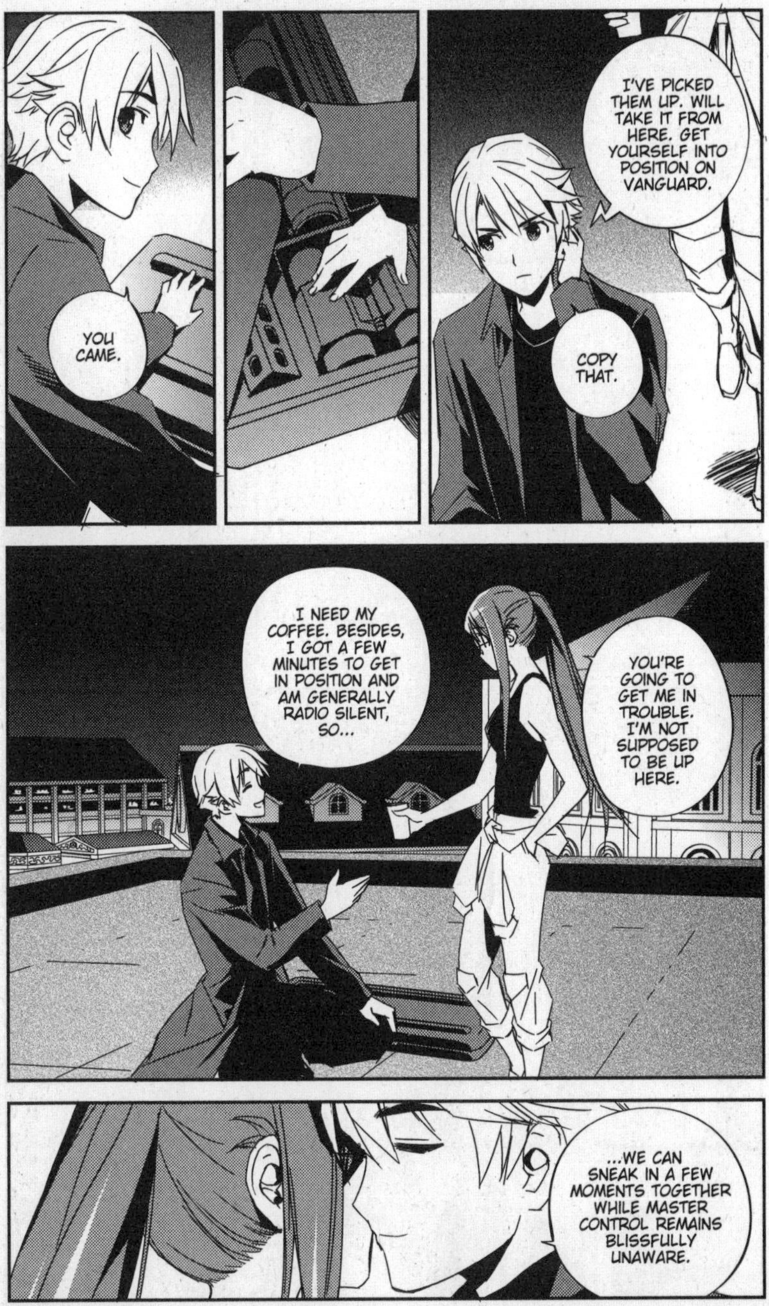
I'VE PICKED THEM UP. WILL TAKE IT FROM HERE. GET YOURSELF INTO POSITION ON VANGUARD.
COPY THAT.
YOU CAME.
YOU'RE GOING TO GET ME IN TROUBLE. I'M NOT SUPPOSED TO BE UP HERE.
I NEED MY COFFEE. BESIDES, I GOT A FEW MINUTES TO GET IN POSITION AND AM GENERALLY RADIO SILENT, SO...
...WE CAN SNEAK IN A FEW MOMENTS TOGETHER WHILE MASTER CONTROL REMAINS BLISSFULLY UNAWARE.

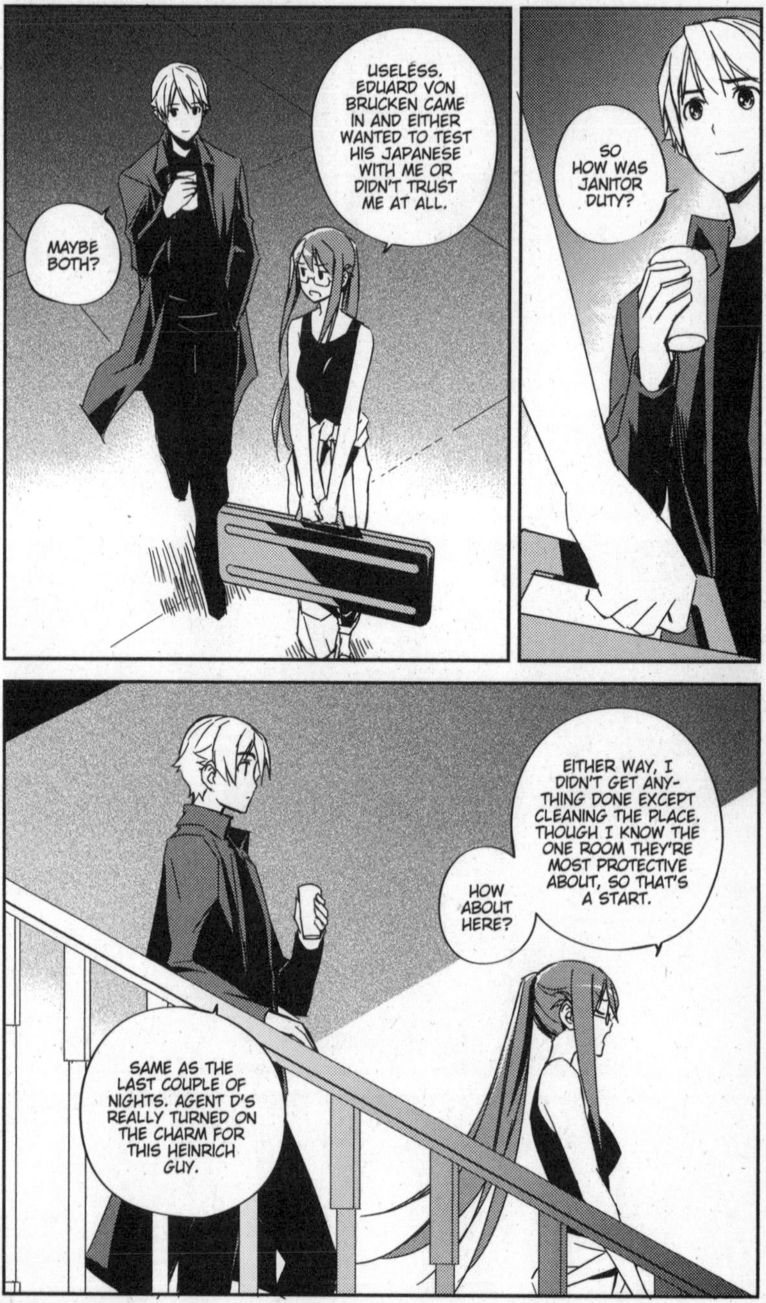
SO HOW WAS JANITOR DUTY?
USELESS. EDUARD VON BRUCKEN CAME IN AND EITHER WANTED TO TEST HIS JAPANESE WITH ME OR DIDN'T TRUST ME AT ALL.
MAYBE BOTH?
EITHER WAY, I DIDN'T GET ANY-THING DONE EXCEPT CLEANING THE PLACE. THOUGH I KNOW THE ONE ROOM THEY'RE MOST PROTECTIVE ABOUT, SO THAT'S A START.
HOW ABOUT HERE?
SAME AS THE LAST COUPLE OF NIGHTS. AGENT D'S REALLY TURNED ON THE CHARM FOR THIS HEINRICH GUY.

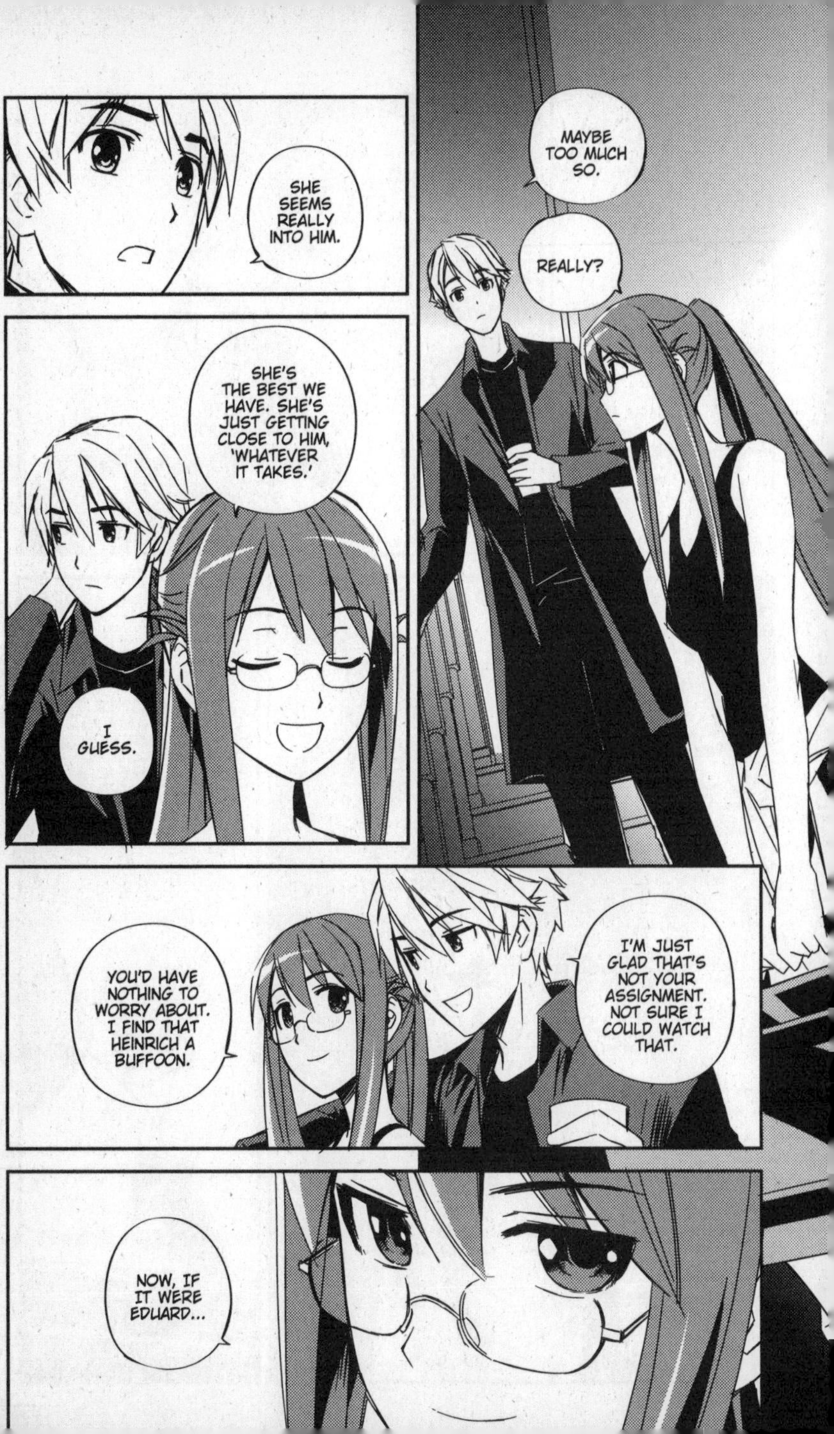
MAYBE TOO MUCH SO.
REALLY?
SHE SEEMS REALLY INTO HIM.
SHE'S THE BEST WE HAVE. SHE'S JUST GETTING CLOSE TO HIM, 'WHATEVER IT TAKES.'
I GUESS.
I'M JUST GLAD THAT'S NOT YOUR ASSIGNMENT. NOT SURE I COULD WATCH THAT.
YOU'D HAVE NOTHING TO WORRY ABOUT. I FIND THAT HEINRICH A BUFFOON.
NOW, IF IT WERE EDUARD...

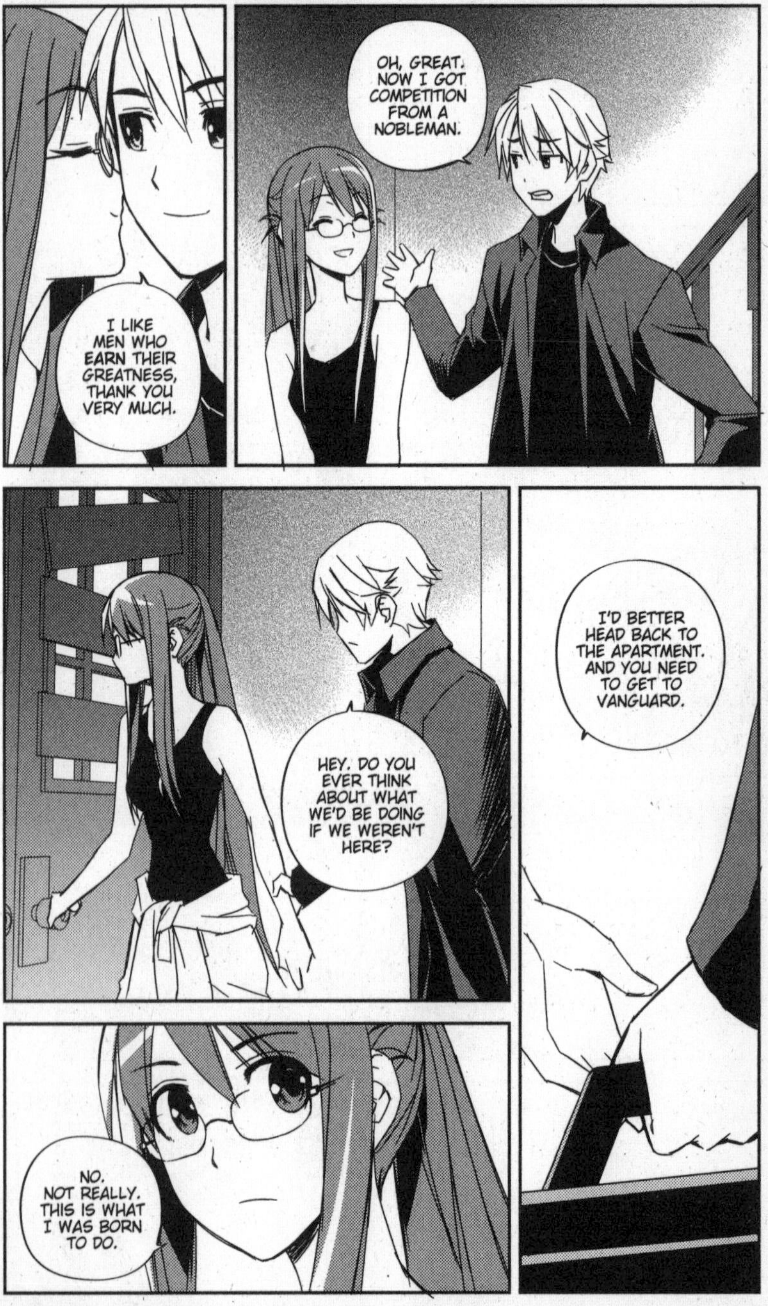
OH, GREAT. NOW I GOT COMPETITION FROM A NOBLEMAN.
I LIKE MEN WHO EARN THEIR GREATNESS, THANK YOU VERY MUCH.
I'D BETTER HEAD BACK TO THE APARTMENT. AND YOU NEED TO GET TO VANGUARD.
HEY. DO YOU EVER THINK ABOUT WHAT WE'D BE DOING IF WE WEREN'T HERE?
NO. NOT REALLY. THIS IS WHAT I WAS BORN TO DO.

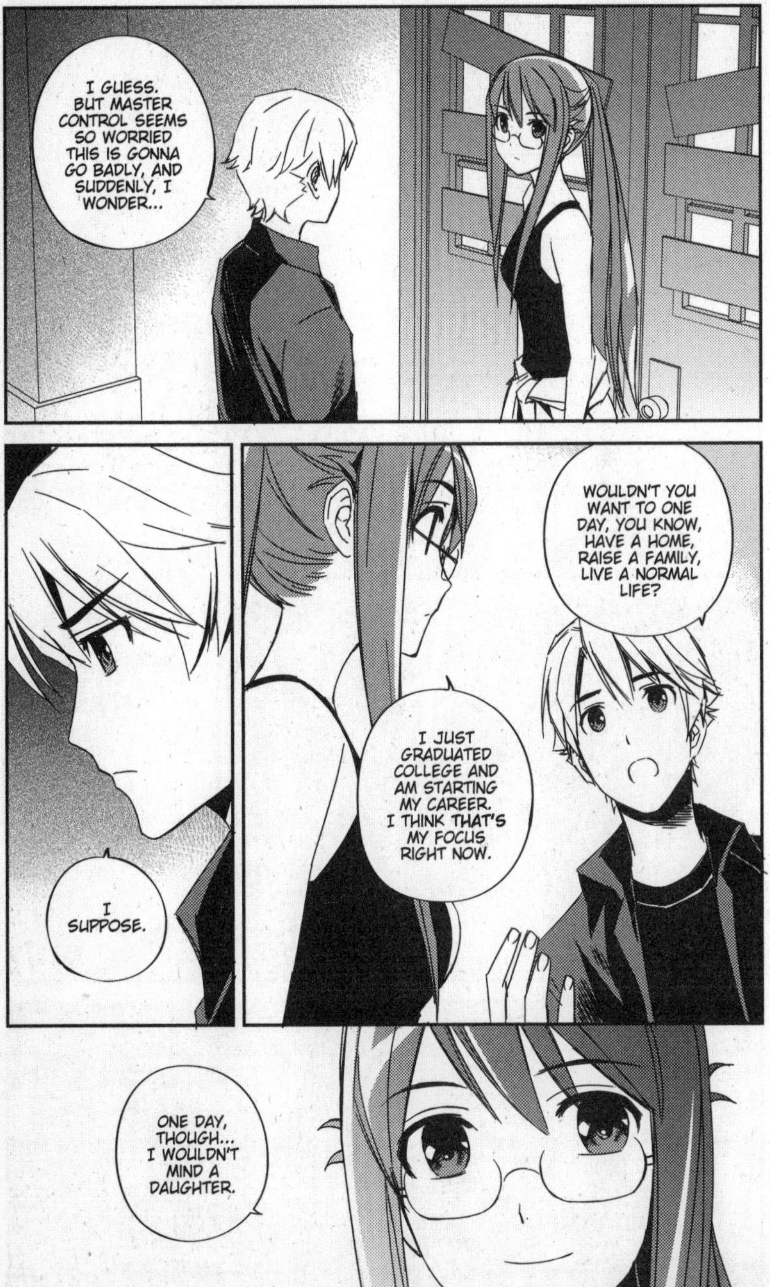
I GUESS. BUT MASTER CONTROL SEEMS SO WORRIED THIS IS GONNA GO BADLY, AND SUDDENLY, I WONDER...
WOULDN'T YOU WANT TO ONE DAY, YOU KNOW, HAVE A HOME, RAISE A FAMILY, LIVE A NORMAL LIFE?
I JUST GRADUATED COLLEGE AND AM STARTING MY CAREER. I THINK THAT'S MY FOCUS RIGHT NOW.
I SUPPOSE.
ONE DAY, THOUGH... I WOULDN'T MIND A DAUGHTER.

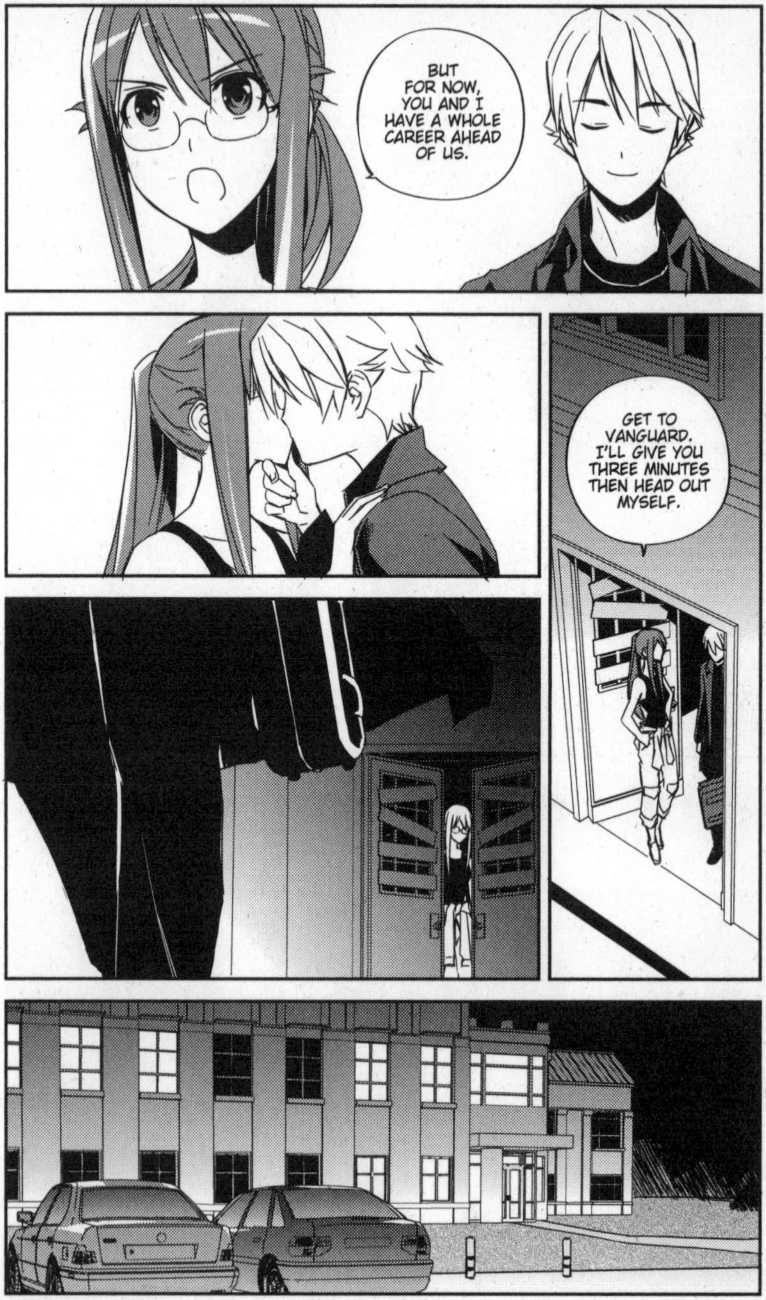
BUT FOR NOW, YOU AND I HAVE A WHOLE CAREER AHEAD OF US.
GET TO VANGUARD. I'LL GIVE YOU THREE MINUTES THEN HEAD OUT MYSELF.

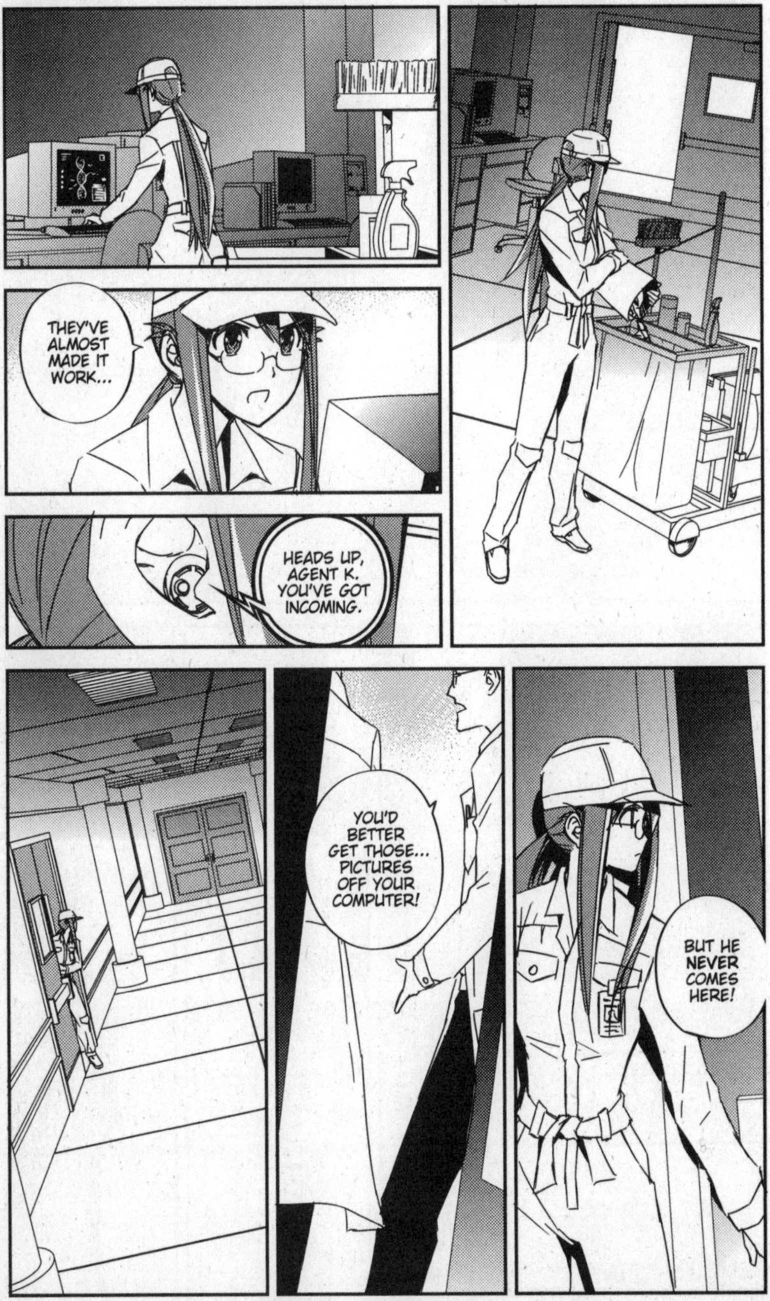
THEY'VE ALMOST MADE IT WORK...
HEADS UP, AGENT K. YOU'VE GOT INCOMING.
YOU'D BETTER GET THOSE... PICTURES OFF YOUR COMPUTER!
BUT HE NEVER COMES HERE!

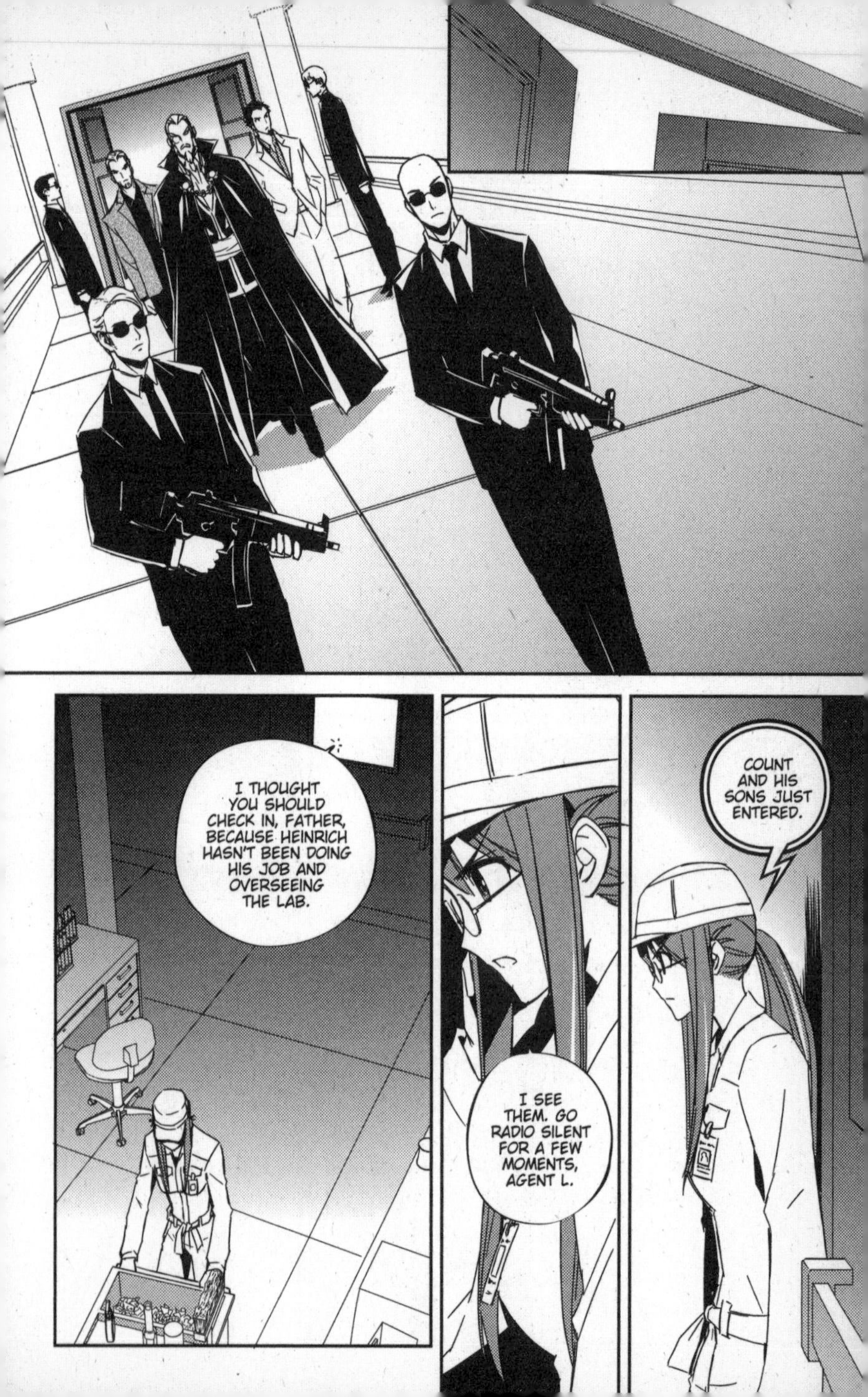
COUNT AND HIS SONS JUST ENTERED.
I SEE THEM. GO RADIO SILENT FOR A FEW MOMENTS, AGENT L.
I THOUGHT YOU SHOULD CHECK IN, FATHER, BECAUSE HEINRICH HASN'T BEEN DOING HIS JOB AND OVERSEEING THE LAB.

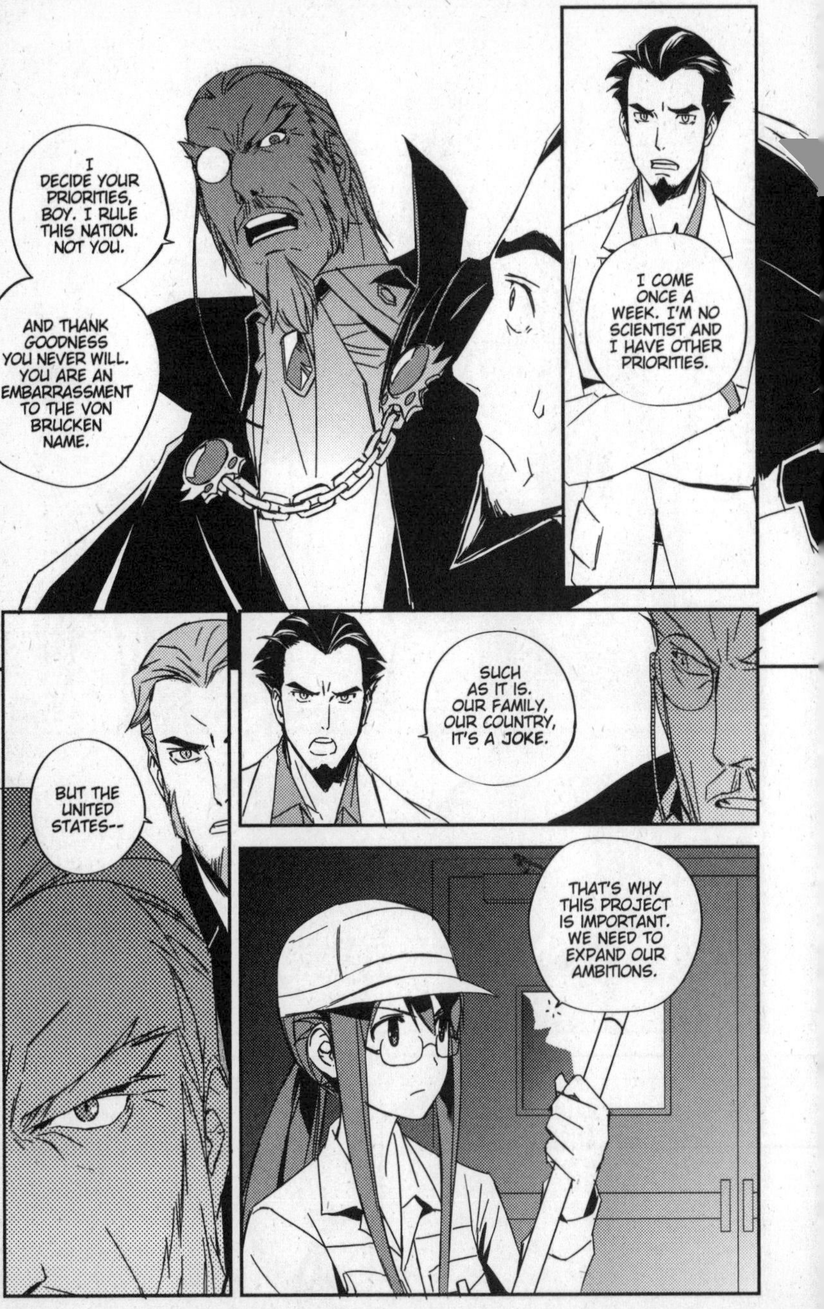
I COME ONCE A WEEK. I'M NO SCIENTIST AND I HAVE OTHER PRIORITIES.
I DECIDE YOUR PRIORITIES, BOY. I RULE THIS NATION. NOT YOU.
AND THANK GOODNESS YOU NEVER WILL. YOU ARE AN EMBARRASSMENT TO THE VON BRUCKEN NAME.
SUCH AS IT IS. OUR FAMILY, OUR COUNTRY, IT'S A JOKE.
BUT THE UNITED STATES--
THAT'S WHY THIS PROJECT IS IMPORTANT. WE NEED TO EXPAND OUR AMBITIONS.

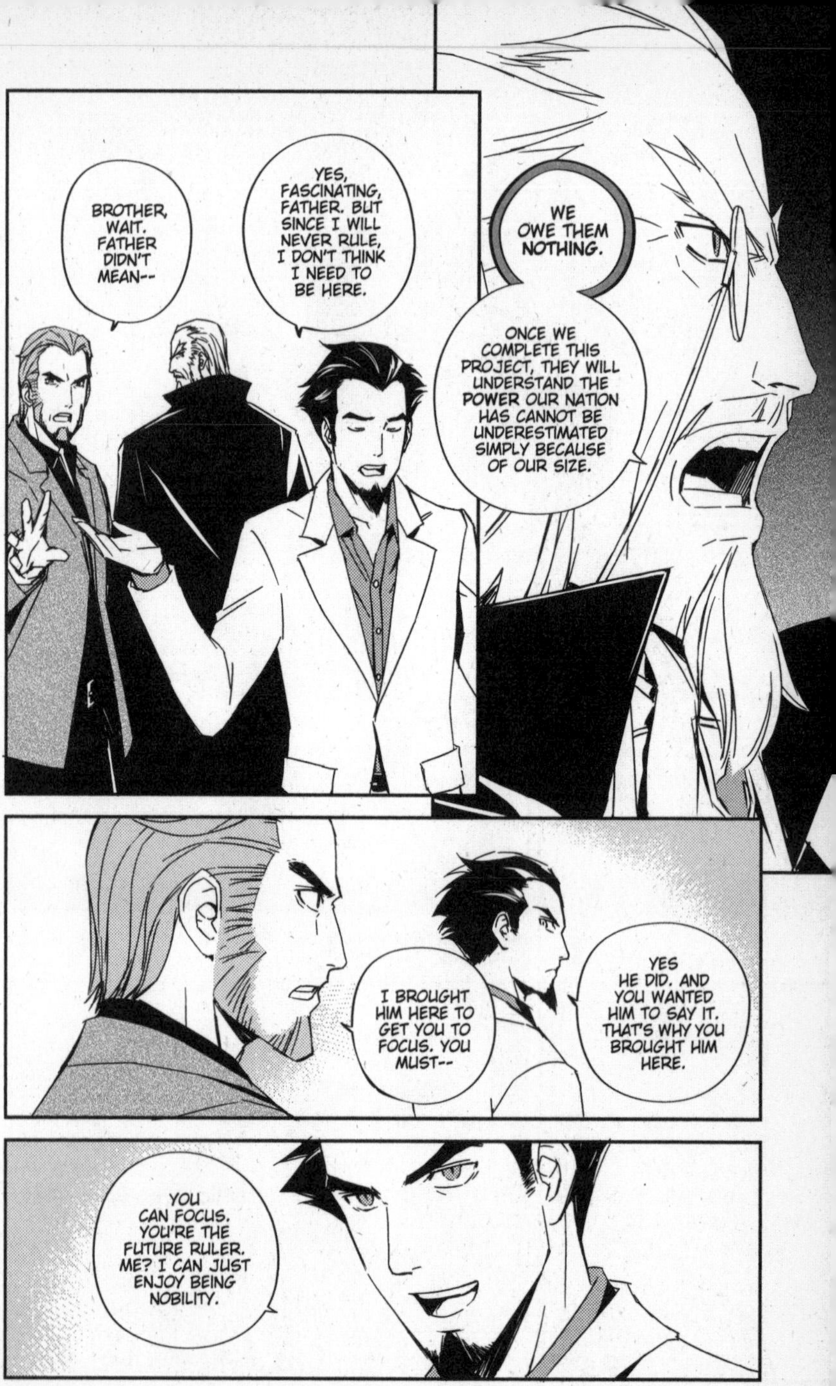
WE OWE THEM NOTHING.
ONCE WE COMPLETE THIS PROJECT, THEY WILL UNDERSTAND THE POWER OUR NATION HAS CANNOT BE UNDERESTIMATED SIMPLY BECAUSE OF OUR SIZE.
YES, FASCINATING, FATHER. BUT SINCE I WILL NEVER RULE, I DON'T THINK I NEED TO BE HERE.
BROTHER, WAIT. FATHER DIDN'T MEAN--
YES HE DID. AND YOU WANTED HIM TO SAY IT. THAT'S WHY YOU BROUGHT HIM HERE.
I BROUGHT HIM HERE TO GET YOU TO FOCUS. YOU MUST--
YOU CAN FOCUS. YOU'RE THE FUTURE RULER. ME? I CAN JUST ENJOY BEING NOBILITY.

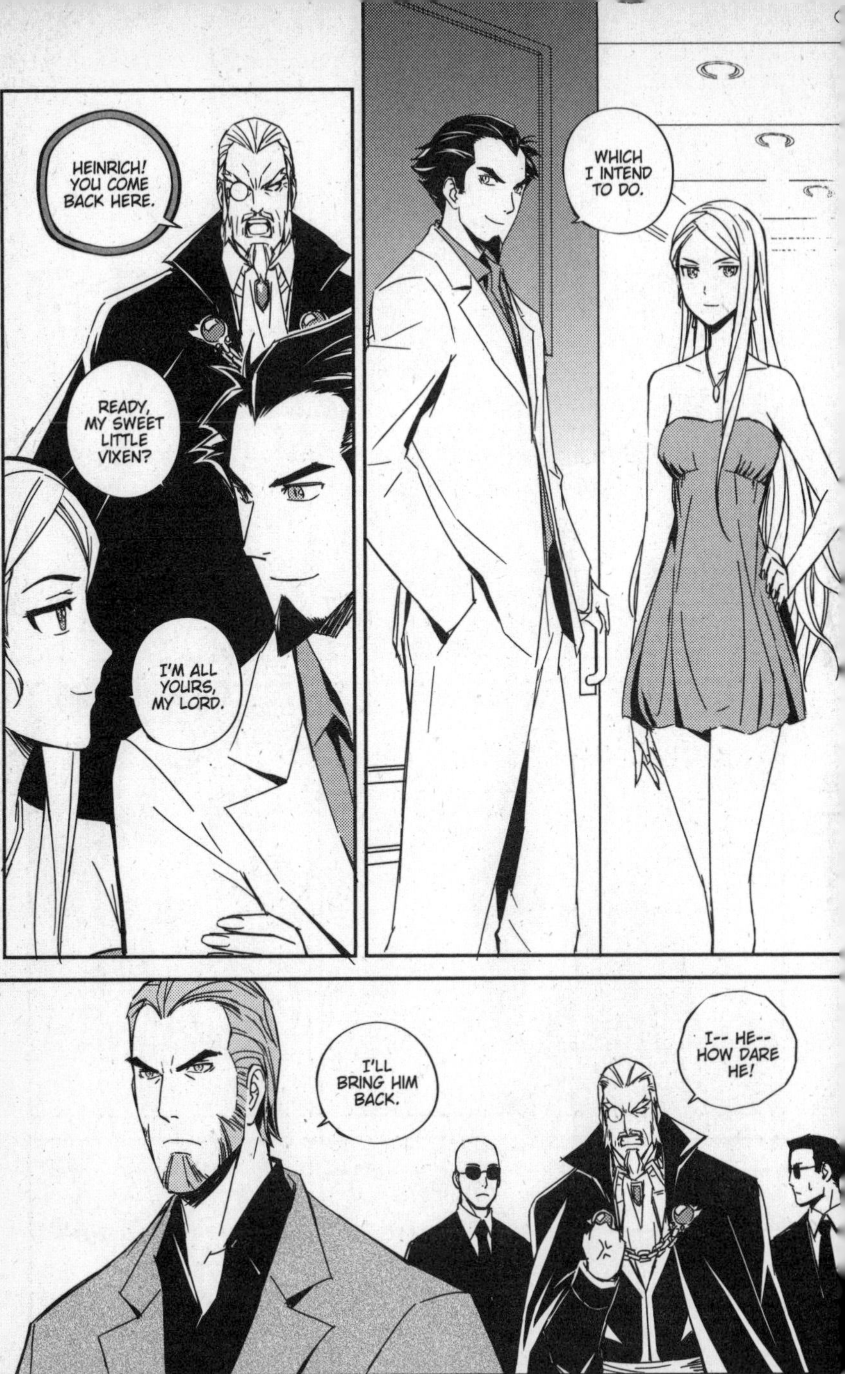
WHICH I INTEND TO DO.
HEINRICH! YOU COME BACK HERE.
READY, MY SWEET LITTLE VIXEN?
I'M ALL YOURS, MY LORD.
I-- HE-- HOW DARE HE!
I'LL BRING HIM BACK.

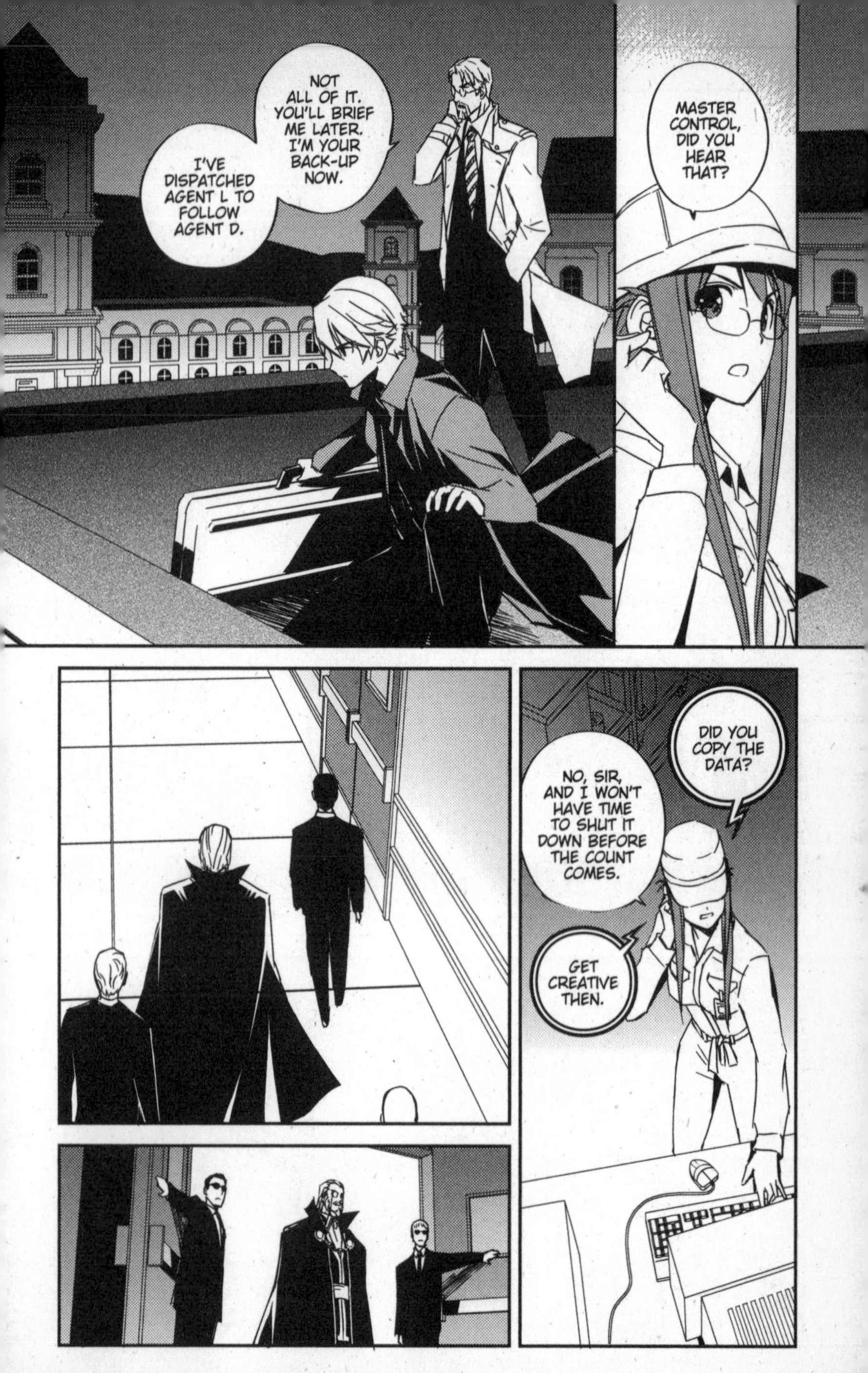
MASTER CONTROL, DID YOU HEAR THAT?
NOT ALL OF IT. YOU'LL BRIEF ME LATER. I'M YOUR BACK-UP NOW.
I'VE DISPATCHED AGENT L TO FOLLOW AGENT D.
DID YOU COPY THE DATA?
NO, SIR, AND I WON'T HAVE TIME TO SHUT IT DOWN BEFORE THE COUNT COMES.
GET CREATIVE THEN.

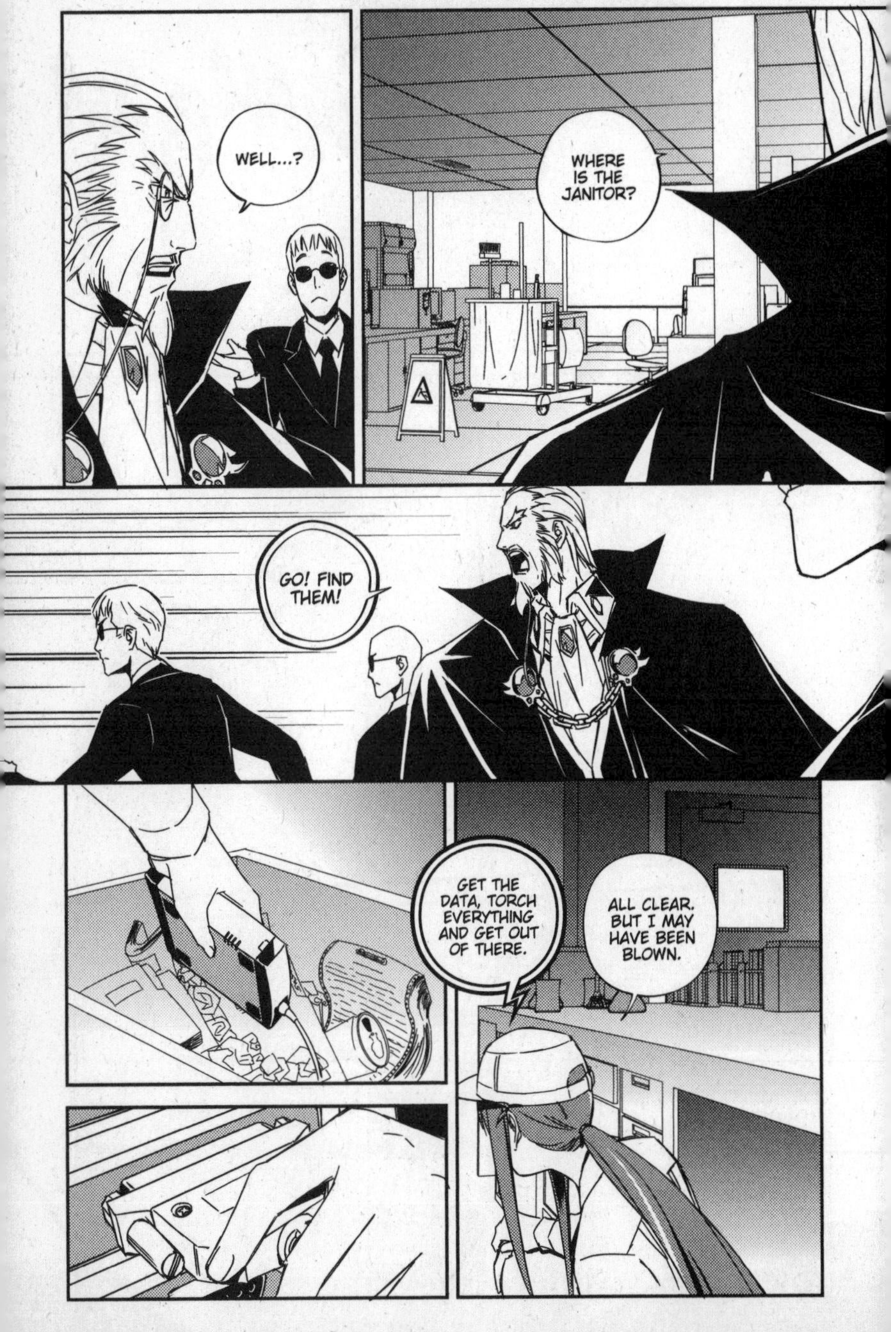
WHERE IS THE JANITOR?
WELL...?
GO! FIND THEM!
ALL CLEAR. BUT I MAY HAVE BEEN BLOWN.
GET THE DATA, TORCH EVERYTHING AND GET OUT OF THERE.

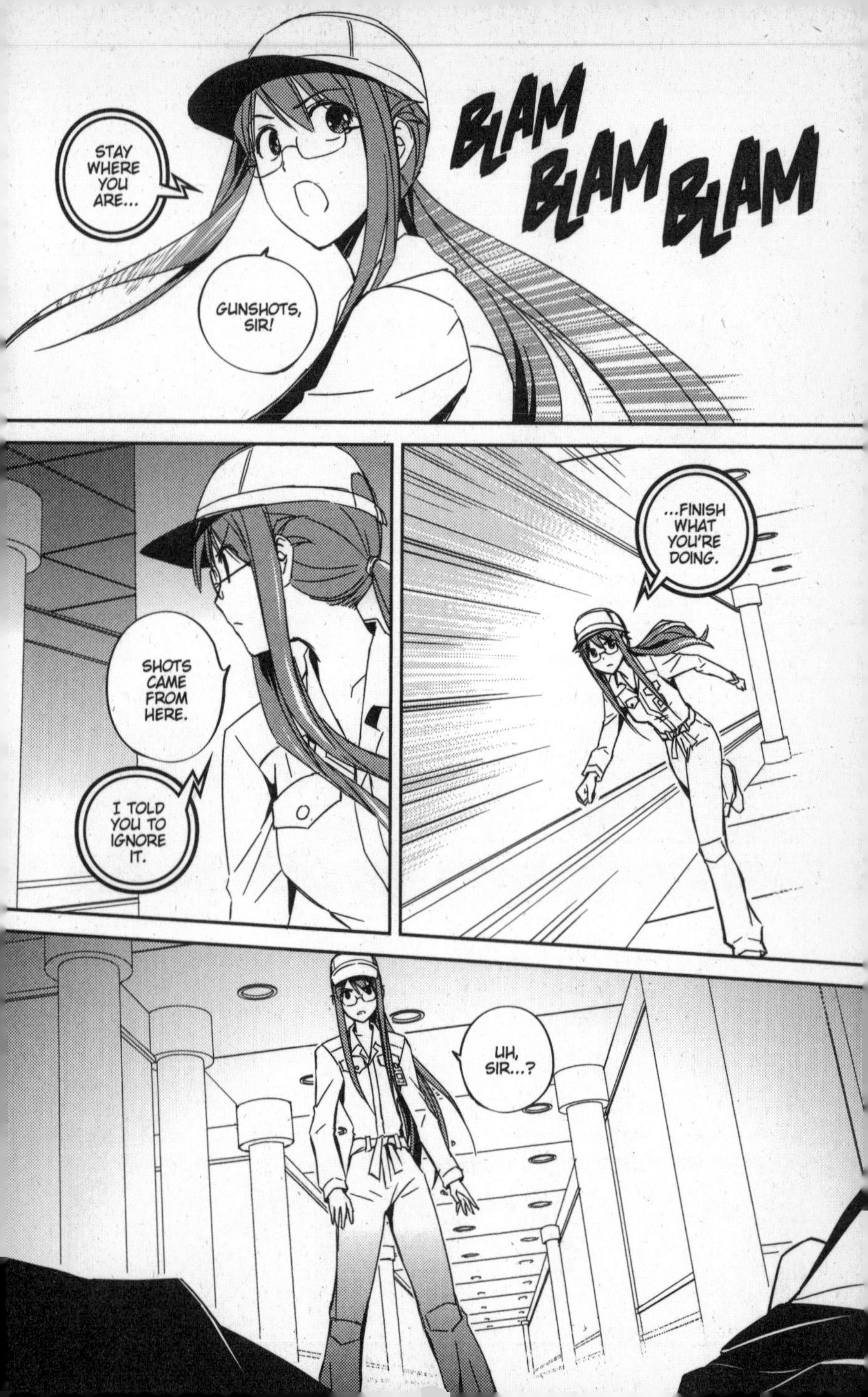
BLAM BLAM BLAM
GUNSHOTS, SIR!
STAY WHERE YOU ARE...
...FINISH WHAT YOU'RE DOING.
SHOTS CAME FROM HERE.
I TOLD YOU TO IGNORE IT.
UH, SIR...?

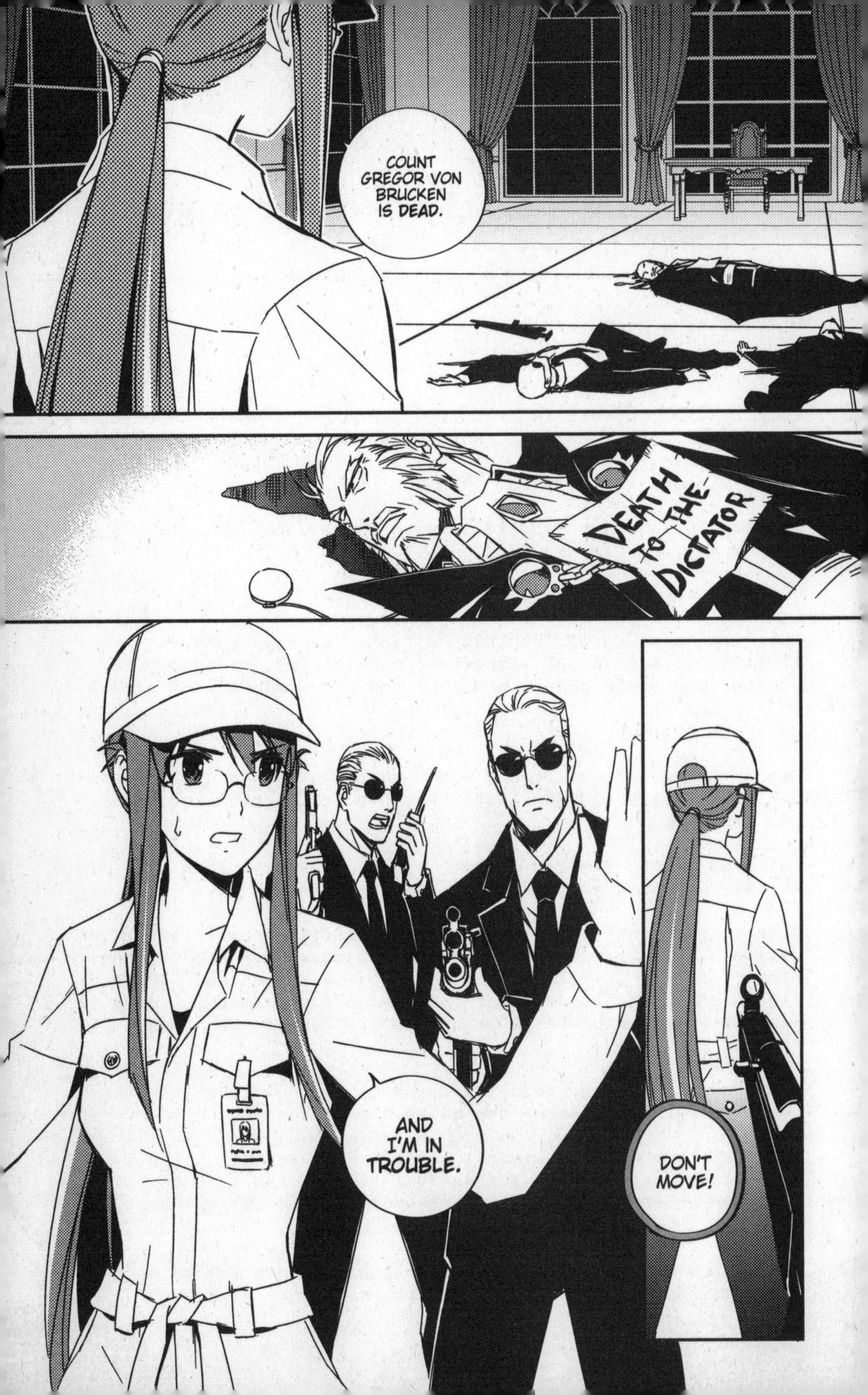
COUNT GREGOR VON BRUCKEN IS DEAD.
DEATH TO THE DICTATOR
DON'T MOVE!
AND I'M IN TROUBLE.

MEMORANDUM

TO: OUR READERS
FROM: NUNZIO DEFILIPPIS AND CHRISTINA WEIR
RE: AMAZING AGENT *JENNIFER*

Welcome to a brand new story.

Sort of.

For those of you who read Amazing Agent Luna, we're sure you're asking... Agent *Jennifer*? Not a new Luna volume? And art not done by Shiei? To you we say... take a look inside. The art, by Kriss Sisson, is wonderful. And the story? See below.

And for those of you who've never read a volume of Luna, we simply say... welcome.

To both groups, we say this:

This is the story of Jennifer Kajiwara. One day, she will be a Control Agent in an all-important mission for The Agency, a shadowy espionage group that even the CIA doesn't know exists. But at the start of this story, she is simply a teenager about to start college.

She is an exceptional young woman whose parents don't know just how great she could be if they would only let her figure out her own life.

But even if she figures it out, even *she* doesn't know what lies ahead.

This is a coming of age story that will take a brilliant young girl and turn her into a seriously hardcore government agent. Along the way, she'll have friendships start and end, she'll find first love, she'll learn the dangers of espionage, she'll face betrayal, and she'll learn she's stronger than anyone thought possible.

For those of you who read Luna, you'll see how Luna's "mother" got her start and became the woman she is today.

For those who don't... meet Jennifer. She started out as a supporting cast member. But she quickly morphed into a fully realized character not just worthy of her own story, but practically demanding it.

And as you may or may not already know, you don't mess with Jennifer. So we're excited to share that story with you.

AGENCY PERSONNEL INVESTIGATION DOSSIERS

AGENCY PERSONNEL INVESTIGATION DOSSIERS

EYES ONLY

[CLASSIFIED TOP SECRET]

DOSSIER # A12879

REPORT PRODUCED AT	DATE PRODUCED	FILE PROCESSED BY	NATURE OF REPORT	FILE NO.
CHQ A-3			EYES ONLY CLASSIFIED TOP SECRET	

Code Name: **Master Control**
Real Name: [redacted]
Age: **42**

Proficiencies:
Tactical Expert; Hand to Hand Combat Specialist proficient in seven martial arts; Basic understanding of tactically useful sciences; Military Free Fall techniques (including HALO and HAHO).

Assignment:
A former Control Agent, Master Control now oversees new recruit training at the [redacted] training facility.

History:
Master Control trained as a Control Agent, a role he assumed upon completion of his training in [redacted] He served as Control Agent in key operations in Bruckenstein, Russia, Saudi Arabia, China, and New Zealand (operation numbers and details withheld) as well as hundreds of minor operations in these and other locales. His operational success rate was sustained at 100%, making him the most successful Control Agent in Agency history.

However, mission success did not always coincide with the safe return of all field operatives to the U.S. In his fifteen years as Control Agent, Master Control lost exactly 13 field agents, a return rate greater than any Control Agent in Agency history, yet one that did not meet Master Control's standards. With the deaths of [redacted] in Saudi Arabia and [redacted] in China on back-to-back missions, Master Control turned in his resignation as an acting Control Agent six years ago. He was assigned to train new recruits, and given the title Master Control.

Since his assumption of control over the [redacted] training facility, the number of recruits to actually graduate from the four year training program has decreased by 25%, but the success rate of those agents in the field has increased by 12% and the survival rate by 32%, thus proving his exacting training standards have merit.

DOSSIER # A12879

REPORT PRODUCED AT	DATE PRODUCED	FILE PROCESSED BY	NATURE OF REPORT	FILE NO.
CHQ D-6			EYES ONLY CLASSIFIED TOP SECRET	

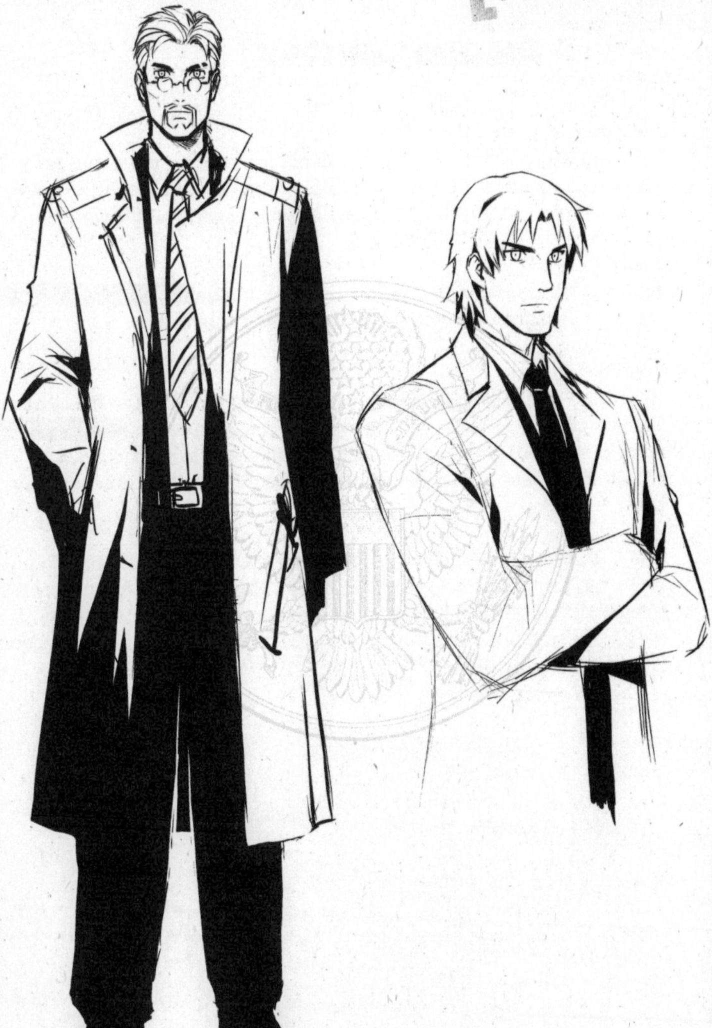

DOSSIER # D821001

REPORT PRODUCED AT	DATE PRODUCED	FILE PROCESSED BY	NATURE OF REPORT	FILE NO.
CHQ A-3				

EYES ONLY
CLASSIFIED
TOP SECRET

Code Name: **Agent D**
Real Name: [redacted]
Age: 21

Proficiencies:
Hand to Hand Combat Specialist proficient in three martial arts; Proficient gymnast; Skilled in social skills required for undercover field operative, including seduction, persuasion, and disguise.

Assignment:
Agent D has just completed her training at the [redacted] training facility and awaits her first field assignment.

History:
Recruited from [redacted] University, Agent D is the daughter of a prominent politician who resigned from his post as [redacted] after a scandal. Her family lost its wealth and prominence, and she would have been unable to afford the school's tuition had she not been recruited.

She is the only member of her training group to successfully complete the program this year, and her skills at seduction and social interaction, combined with above average gymnastics and stealth skills, make her a promising field agent for either physical or social infiltration operations.

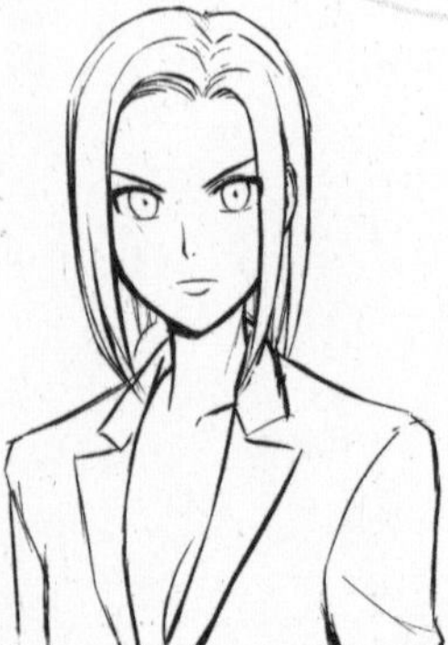

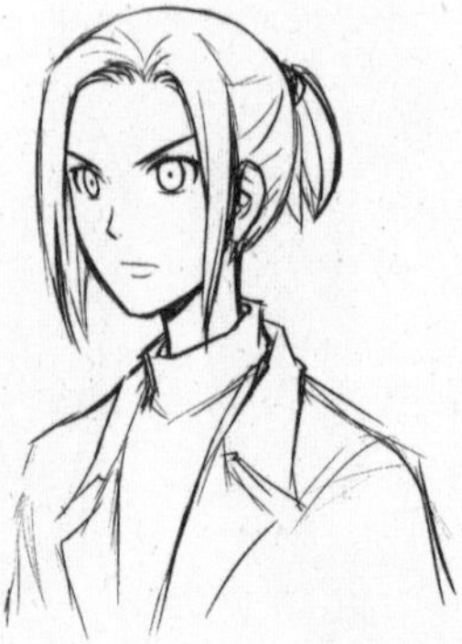

DOSSIER # D821001

FILE NO.

REPORT PRODUCED AT	DATE PRODUCED	FILE PROCESSED BY	NATURE OF REPORT
CHQ D-6			

EYES ONLY
CLASSIFIED
TOP SECRET

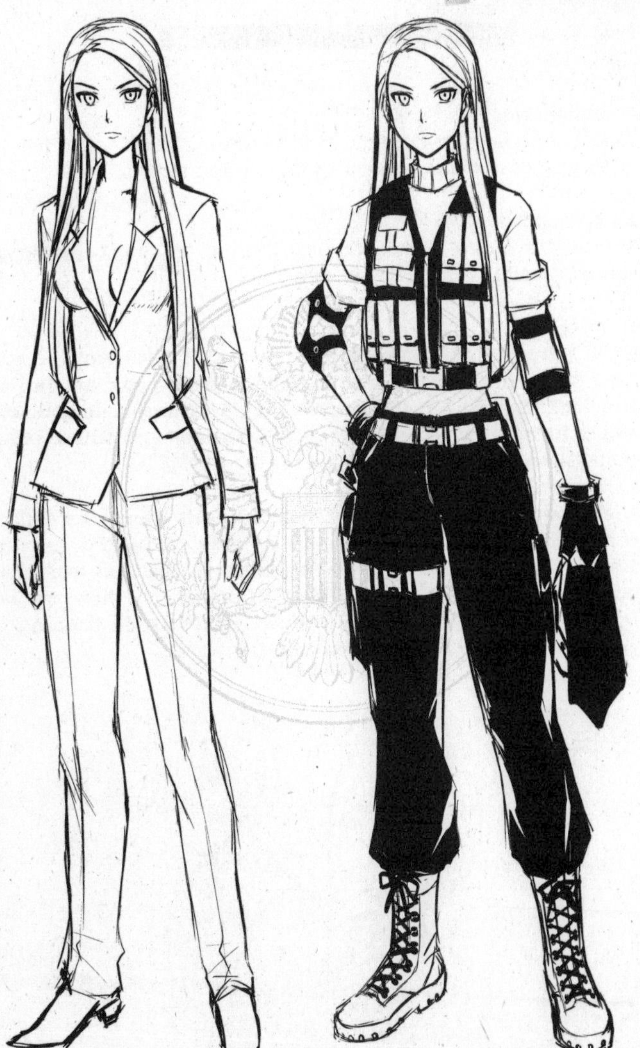

DOSSIER # L562123

REPORT PRODUCED AT	DATE PRODUCED	FILE PROCESSED BY	NATURE OF REPORT	FILE NO.
CHQ A-3			EYES ONLY CLASSIFIED TOP SECRET	

Code Name: **Trainee L**
Real Name: [redacted]
Age: 18

Proficiencies:
Rigorous physical training in high school athletics, including wrestling; Skilled marksman with rifles and pistols.

Assignment:
Trainee L is a new recruit who is beginning training at [redacted] training facility under Master Control.

History:
Having grown up in [redacted] in a working class family, Trainee L came to the program in order to avoid incurring student loan debt. His family is exceedingly patriotic, though Trainee L's social activities in high school indicate his interests were more athletic and social than patriotic or political.

His physical prowess and, most especially, his marksman skills, combined with a stubborn desire to exceed expectations, have led Master Control to mark his file as one worth watching from the current batch of new recruits. Master Control does, however, have concerns about how seriously Trainee L will take the training process, and worries he will become distracted.

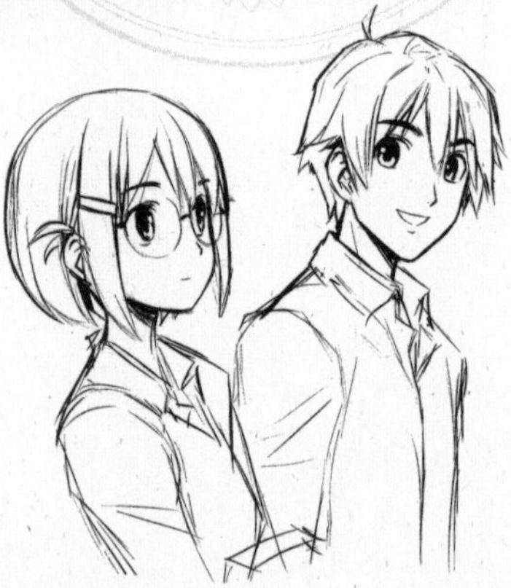

DOSSIER # L562123

FILE NO.

EYES ONLY
CLASSIFIED
TOP SECRET

REPORT PRODUCED AT	DATE PRODUCED	FILE PROCESSED BY	NATURE OF REPORT
CHQ D-6			

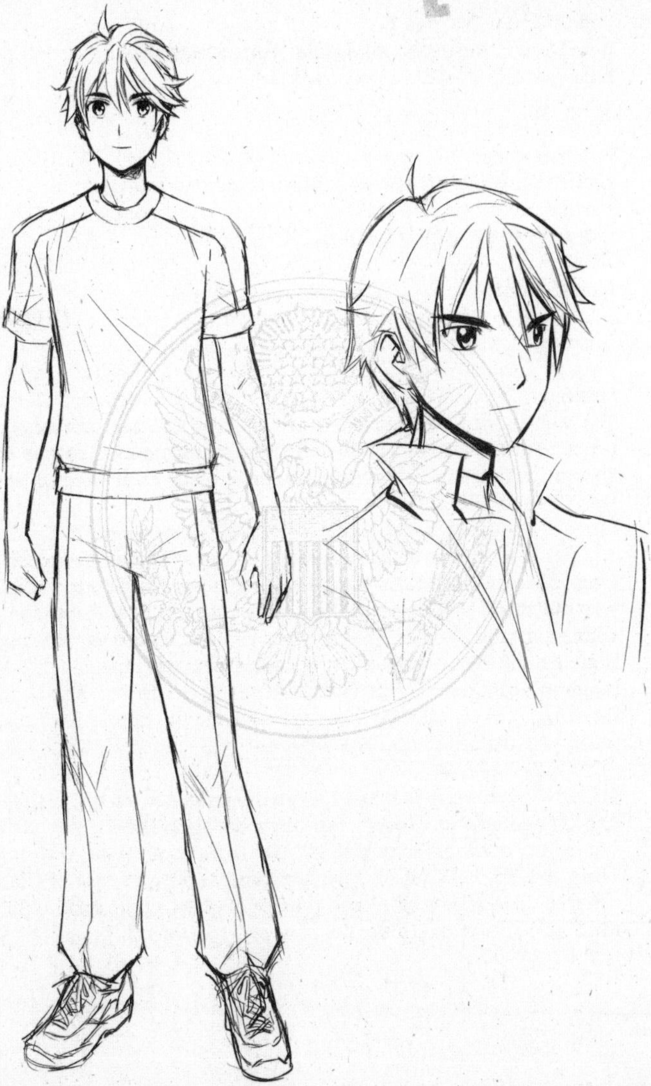

REPORT PRODUCED AT	DATE PRODUCED	FILE PROCESSED BY	NATURE OF REPORT
CHQ A-3			

FILE NO.

EYES ONLY
CLASSIFIED
TOP SECRET

Code Name: **Trainee K**
Real Name: **Jennifer Kajiwara** (redact after using file to perform
background check on personal contacts)
Age: 17

Proficiencies:
Scientific scholar of national merit; Olympic level gymnast and
swimmer; Instinctive ability in hand to hand combat; Acting training; Horseback riding training

Assignment:
Trainee K is a new recruit who is beginning training at ▮▮▮▮▮
training facility under Master Control.

History:
The daughter of **Benjiro Kajiwara** (**REDACT after investigation**), a
prominent investment banker in **Philadelphia, PA**, Trainee K has
shown proficiency in every endeavor she has attempted, despite a
lack of encouragement from her parents.

Trainee K's need to follow her own instincts in her education and
training has created the window of opportunity through which she
was recruited by Master Control. Recruitment of this trainee was
deemed vital when her Science Fair project, in her senior year of
high school, restructured what was considered possible in the field
of genetic engineering. If Trainee K is to pursue this line of scientific
inquiry, it is vital she do it for the Agency. In the meantime, her
work is being studied at the National Institute of Health.

Master Control has marked her as the most promising trainee he
has ever selected or seen in all his years with the Agency. However,
her family conflicts may prevent her from completing training.
Thus, a full investigation into her family and personal life has been
ordered (see attached non-Agency dossiers, to be **REDACTED**
after inquiry is complete).

DOSSIER # K173239

REPORT PRODUCED AT	DATE PRODUCED	FILE PROCESSED BY	NATURE OF REPORT
CHQ D-6			

FILE NO.

EYES ONLY
CLASSIFIED
TOP SECRET

DOSSIER # K173239-A

REPORT PRODUCED AT	DATE PRODUCED	FILE PROCESSED BY	NATURE OF REPORT	FILE NO.
CHQ A-3				

EYES ONLY
CLASSIFIED
TOP SECRET

Inquiry Pertains To: **Trainee K Background Check**
Subject: **Benjiro Kajiwara**
Age: **44**

Professional Information:
Benjiro Kajiwara is an investment banker with his own firm, Lauren Investment Group, located in Philadelphia, PA.

Personal History:
Born in Nagoya, Japan, Benjiro Kajiwara came to the United States to attend business school at Yale University, where he received an MBA before taking a job at the Lauren Investment Group in Philadelphia, a position he'd heard about through classmate (and daughter of the firm's founder) **Emily Lauren (now Emily Kajiwara)**. Within two years, he'd married Lauren and become Vice President at the firm. When his father-in-law retired, the firm became his, as his wife has not taken part in the business. The couple has only one daughter, **Jennifer Kajiwara**, who has been recruited by The Agency as Trainee K.

Observing Agent's Notes:

- Kajiwara is regarded as very intelligent, but displays a lack of flexibility which sometimes hinders his ability to take big chances in business.
- Very traditional.
- Skilled at bowling, which is his major recreational hobby.
- Currently unaware that his daughter has dropped all her business classes.

DOSSIER # K173239-A

REPORT PRODUCED AT	DATE PRODUCED	FILE PROCESSED BY	NATURE OF REPORT	FILE NO.
CHQ D-6			EYES ONLY CLASSIFIED TOP SECRET	

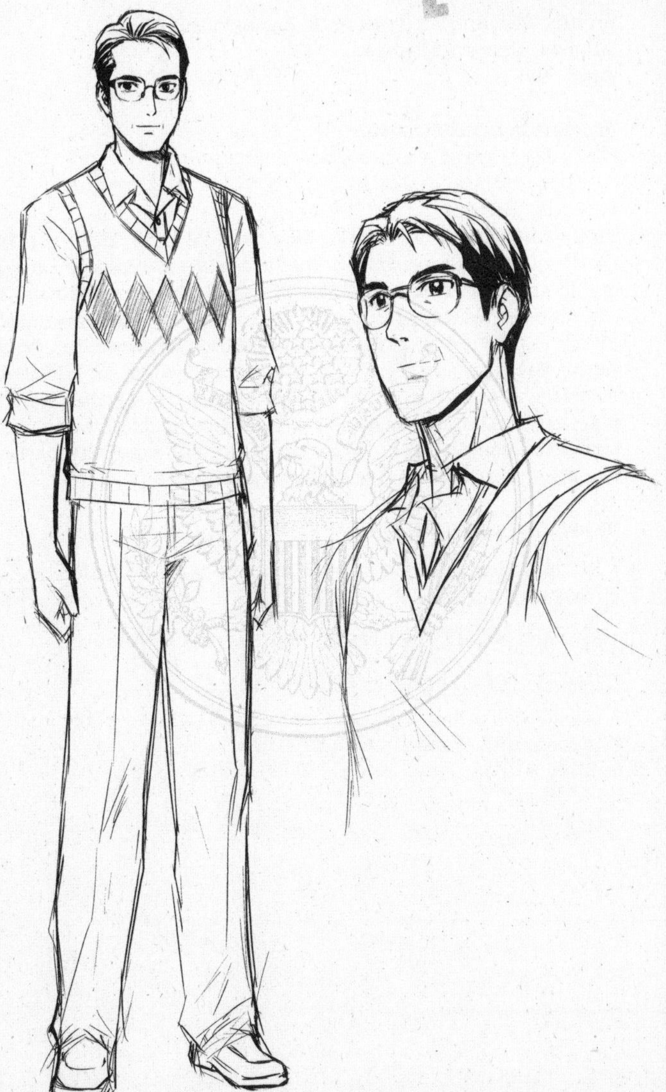

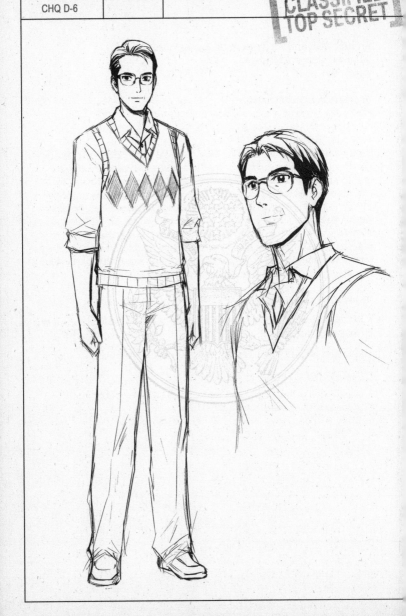

DOSSIER # K173239-B

REPORT PRODUCED AT	DATE PRODUCED	FILE PROCESSED BY	NATURE OF REPORT	FILE NO.
CHQ A-3				

EYES ONLY
CLASSIFIED
TOP SECRET

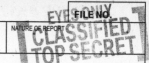

Inquiry Pertains To: **Trainee K Background Check**
Subject: **Emily Kajiwara**
Age: **42**

Professional Information:
Emily Kajiwara is a housewife.

Personal History:
Emily Lauren was born in Philadelphia, PA. Her father ran the Lauren Investment Group, one of the largest investment houses outside of New York or London. She studied drama at Yale University, but her primary goal at the school was to find a promising husband. She did so when she met Benjiro Kajiwara during her junior year (he was a graduate student, pursuing an MBA). She got Kajiwara a job at her father's firm, and soon after, the two were married. Emily Kajiwara has managed her husband's social life ever since. The couple has only one daughter, **Jennifer Kajiwara**, who has been recruited by The Agency as Trainee K.

Observing Agent's Notes:

- Emily Kajiwara is considered the belle of the Philadelphia upper class social scene.
- Member of the Daughters of the American Revolution.
- Has not acted since college.
- Considered a fine cook, and will not let the household staff prepare any of the family's meals.

AGENCY PERSONNEL INVESTIGATION DOSSIERS

DOSSIER # K173239-B

EYES ONLY
CLASSIFIED
TOP SECRET

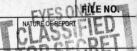

REPORT PRODUCED AT	DATE PRODUCED	FILE PROCESSED BY	NATURE OF REPORT	FILE NO.
CHQ D-6				

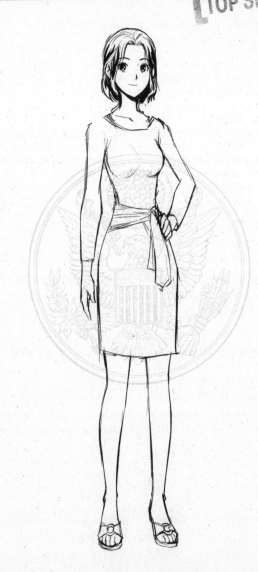

DOSSIER # K173239-C

REPORT PRODUCED AT	DATE PRODUCED	FILE PROCESSED BY	NATURE OF REPORT	FILE NO.
CHQ A-3				

EYES ONLY
CLASSIFIED
TOP SECRET

Inquiry Pertains To: **Trainee K Background Check**
Subject: **Kimberly (Kim) Donovan**
Age: **17**

Professional Information:
Kim Donovan is a college freshman.

Personal History:
Born to an upper-class family in Manhattan Beach, California, Kim Donovan has been in private schools her whole life. Captain of the cheer squad in high school, she has never excelled academically, but has always been popular among classmates. She was voted homecoming queen of her high school.

Observing Agent's Notes:
- Skilled surfer.
- Loves dancing.
- She's very pretty.
- Makes a cute sound when she laughs, almost like a hiccup.

[Control Agent's notes: field agent in charge of observing subject seems to have lost focus. Will send in a different agent.]

Second Observing Agent's Notes:
- Needs help in most academic subjects, but seems aware of this and is willing to seek tutoring.
- Pays very close attention when tutored. Stares, even.
- Has amazing grey eyes.

[Control Agent's notes: nothing to report, but if subsequent investigation needed, will send a female agent next time.]

DOSSIER # K173239-C

REPORT PRODUCED AT	DATE PRODUCED	FILE PROCESSED BY		FILE NO.
CHQ D-6			NATURE OF REPORT	

IF YOU ENJOYED READING ABOUT MY ADVENTURES IN *AMAZING AGENT JENNIFER*, THEN BE SURE TO CHECK OUT NUNZIO AND CHRISTINA'S NEWEST SERIES...

Dracula
EVERLASTING

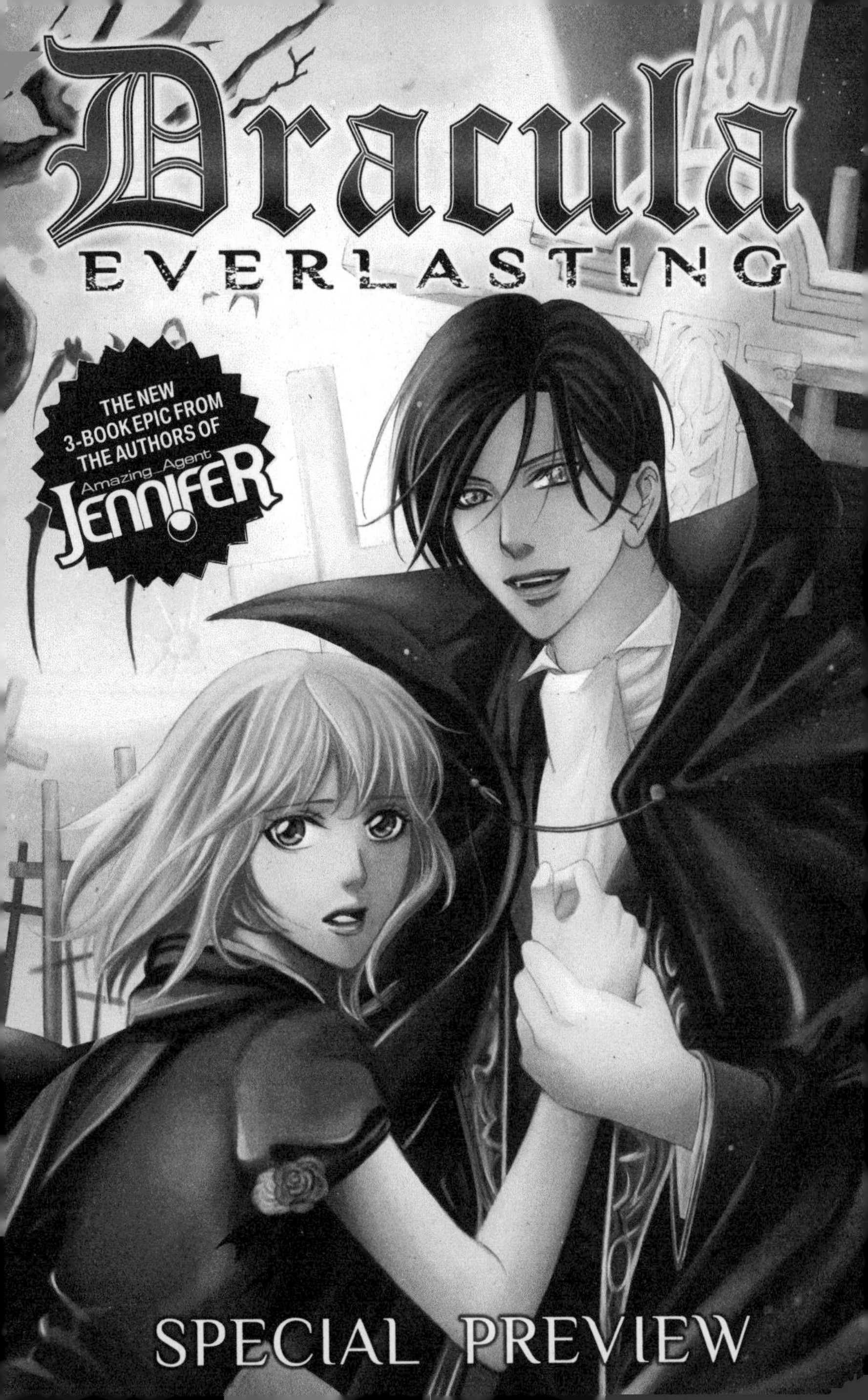
Dracula
EVERLASTING
THE NEW 3-BOOK EPIC FROM THE AUTHORS OF
Amazing Agent JENNIFER
SPECIAL PREVIEW

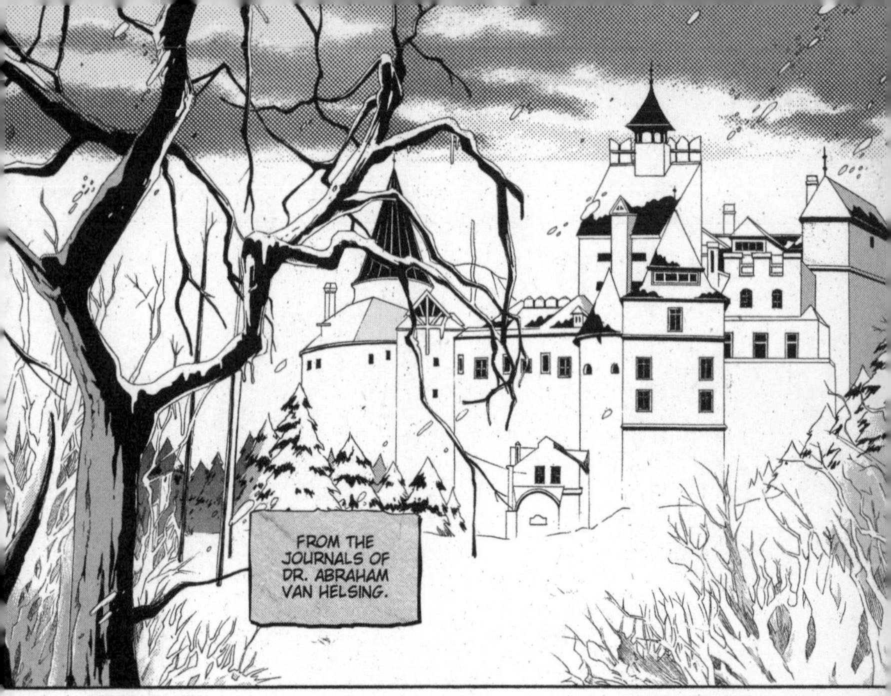
FROM THE JOURNALS OF DR. ABRAHAM VAN HELSING.

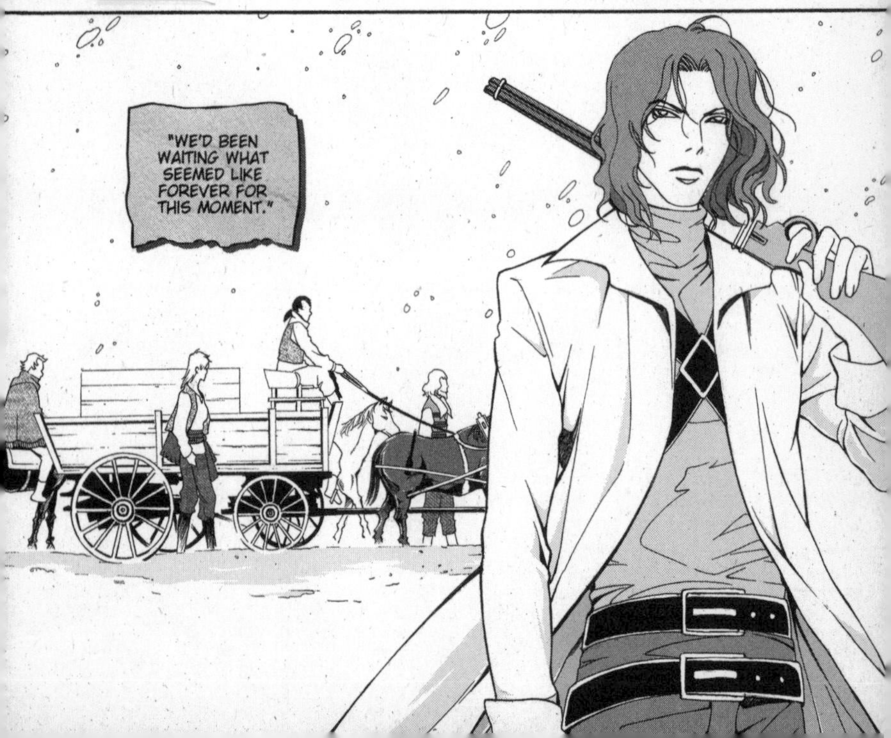
"WE'D BEEN WAITING WHAT SEEMED LIKE FOREVER FOR THIS MOMENT."

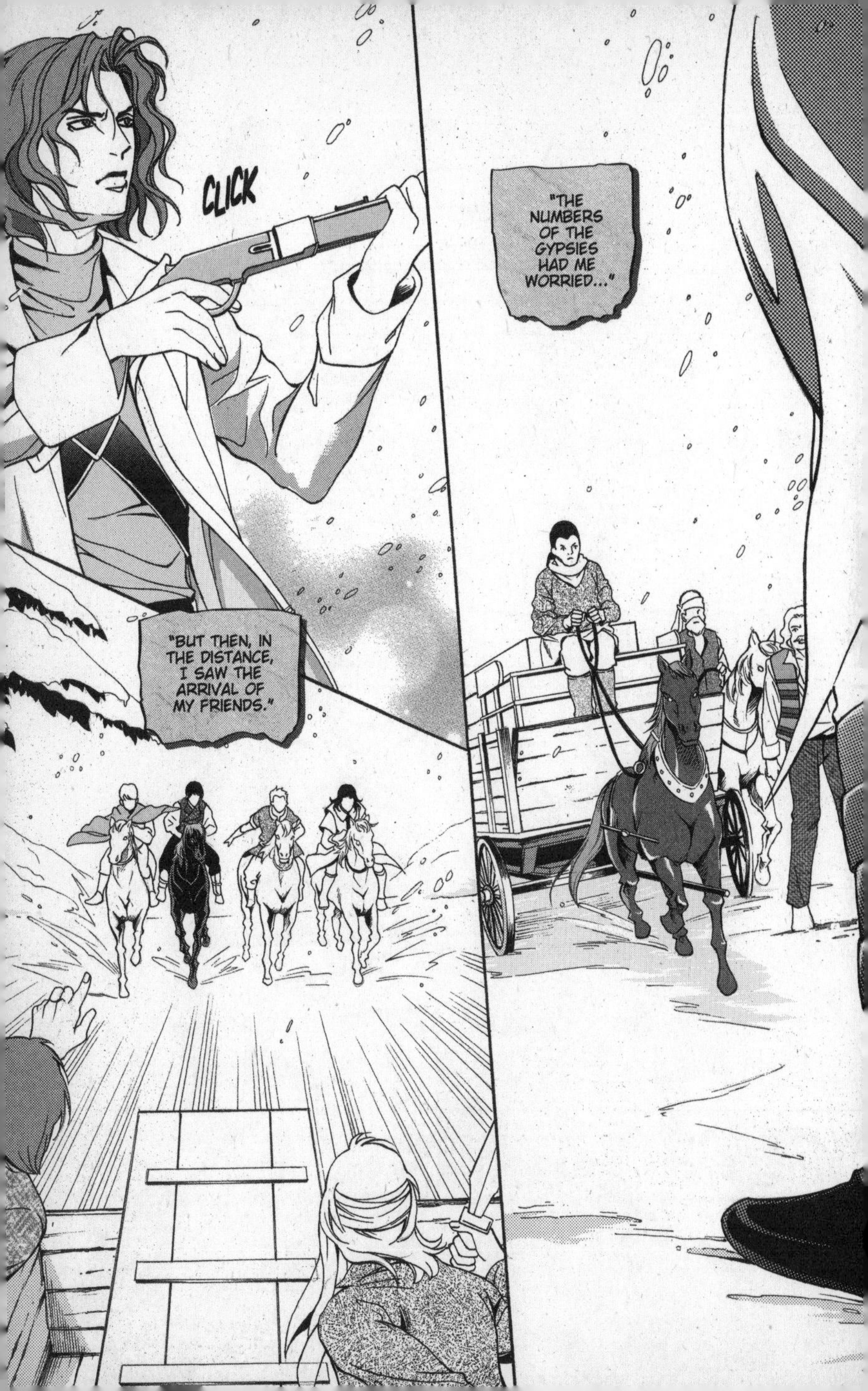
"THE NUMBERS OF THE GYPSIES HAD ME WORRIED..."
CLICK
"BUT THEN, IN THE DISTANCE, I SAW THE ARRIVAL OF MY FRIENDS."

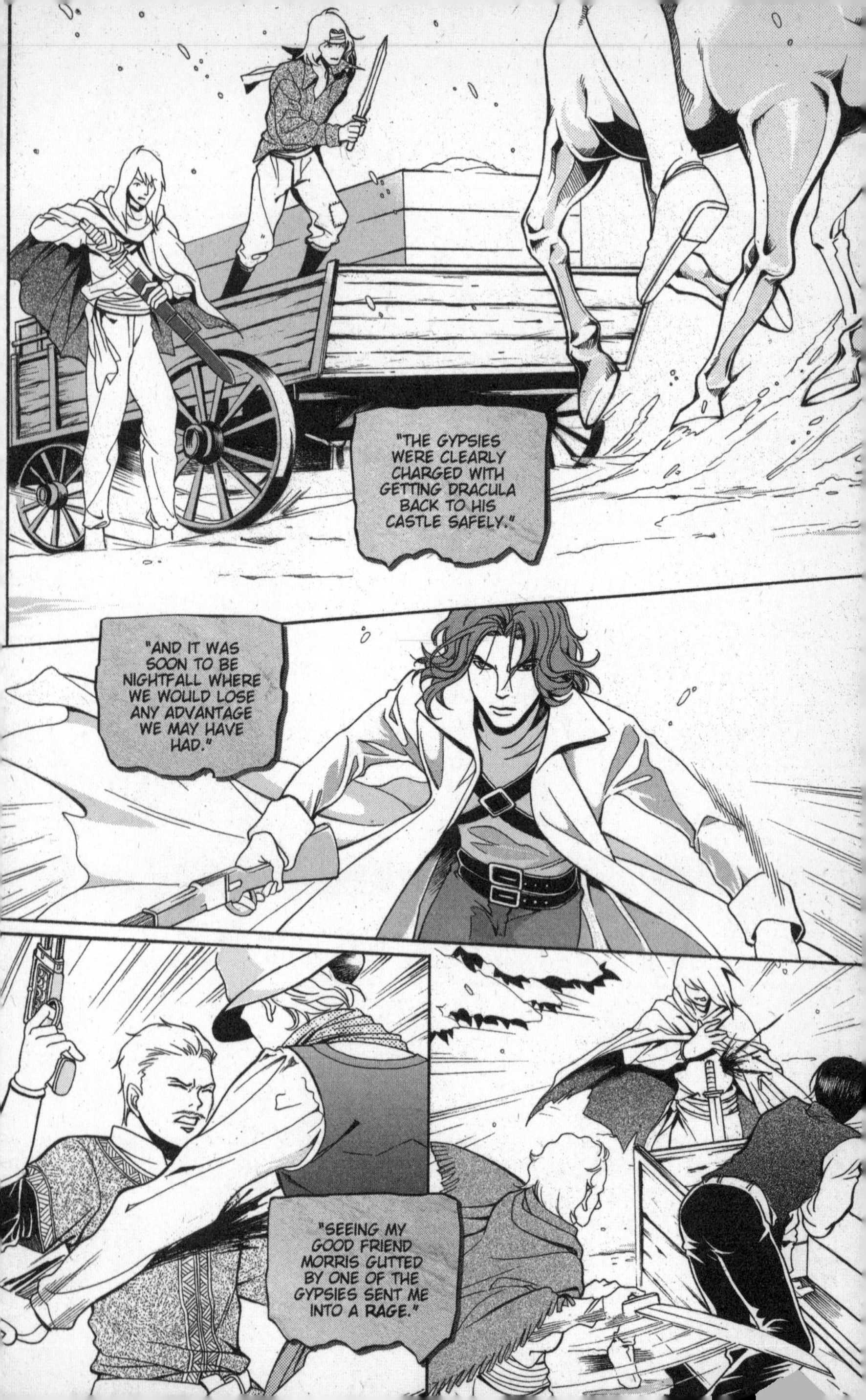
"THE GYPSIES WERE CLEARLY CHARGED WITH GETTING DRACULA BACK TO HIS CASTLE SAFELY."
"AND IT WAS SOON TO BE NIGHTFALL WHERE WE WOULD LOSE ANY ADVANTAGE WE MAY HAVE HAD."
"SEEING MY GOOD FRIEND MORRIS GUTTED BY ONE OF THE GYPSIES SENT ME INTO A RAGE."

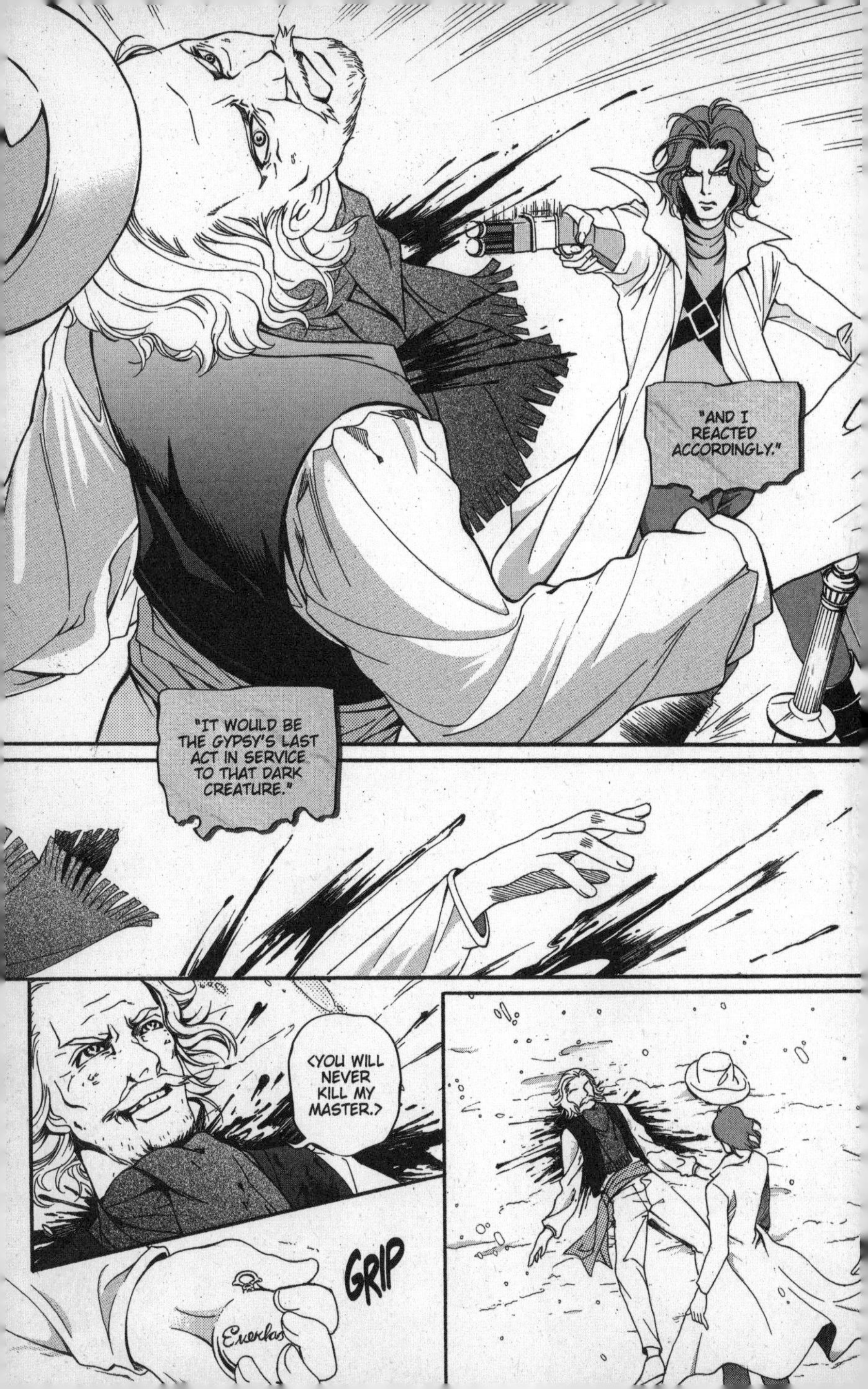
"AND I REACTED ACCORDINGLY."
"IT WOULD BE THE GYPSY'S LAST ACT IN SERVICE TO THAT DARK CREATURE."
<YOU WILL NEVER KILL MY MASTER.>
GRIP

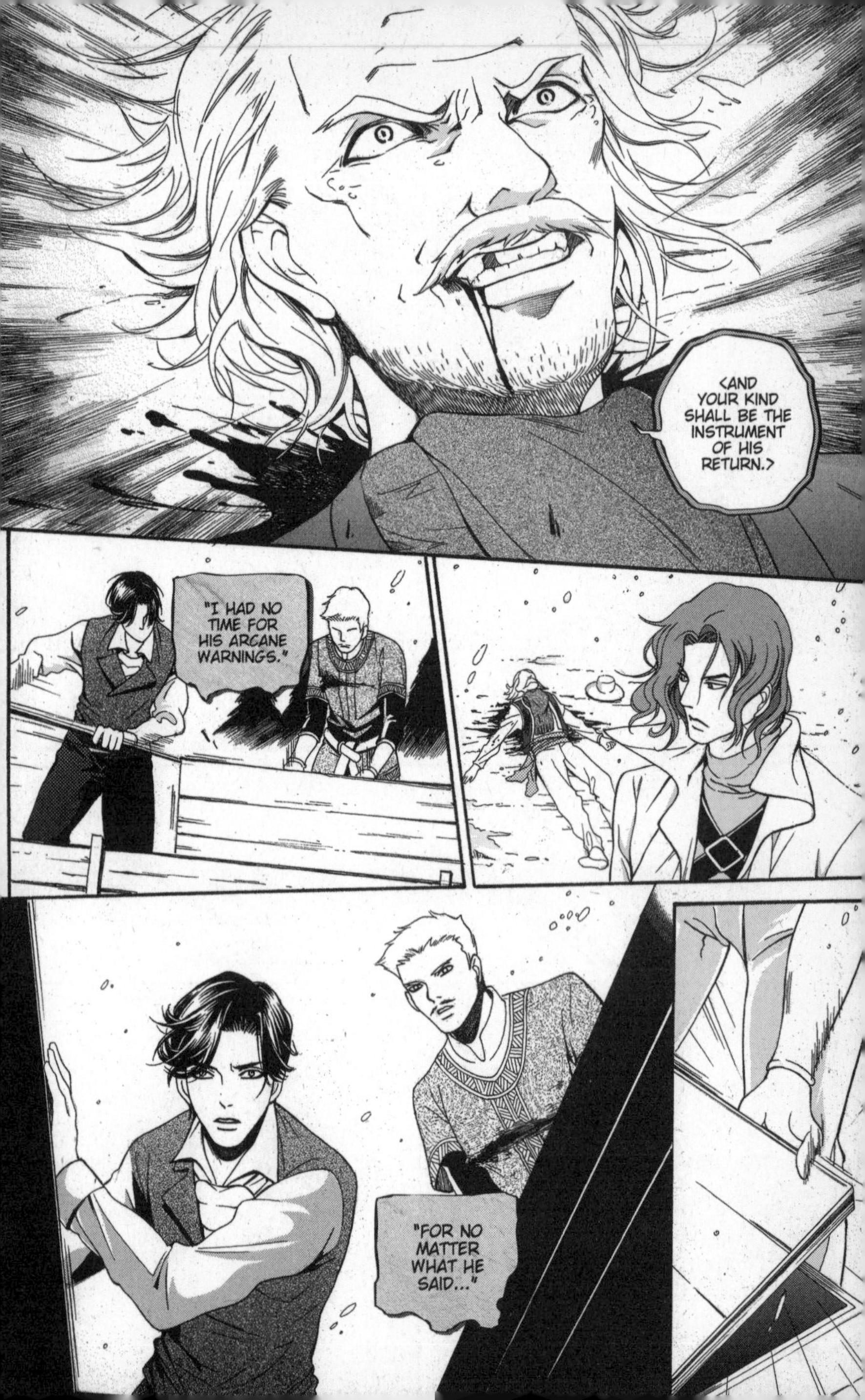
<AND YOUR KIND SHALL BE THE INSTRUMENT OF HIS RETURN.>
"I HAD NO TIME FOR HIS ARCANE WARNINGS."
"FOR NO MATTER WHAT HE SAID..."

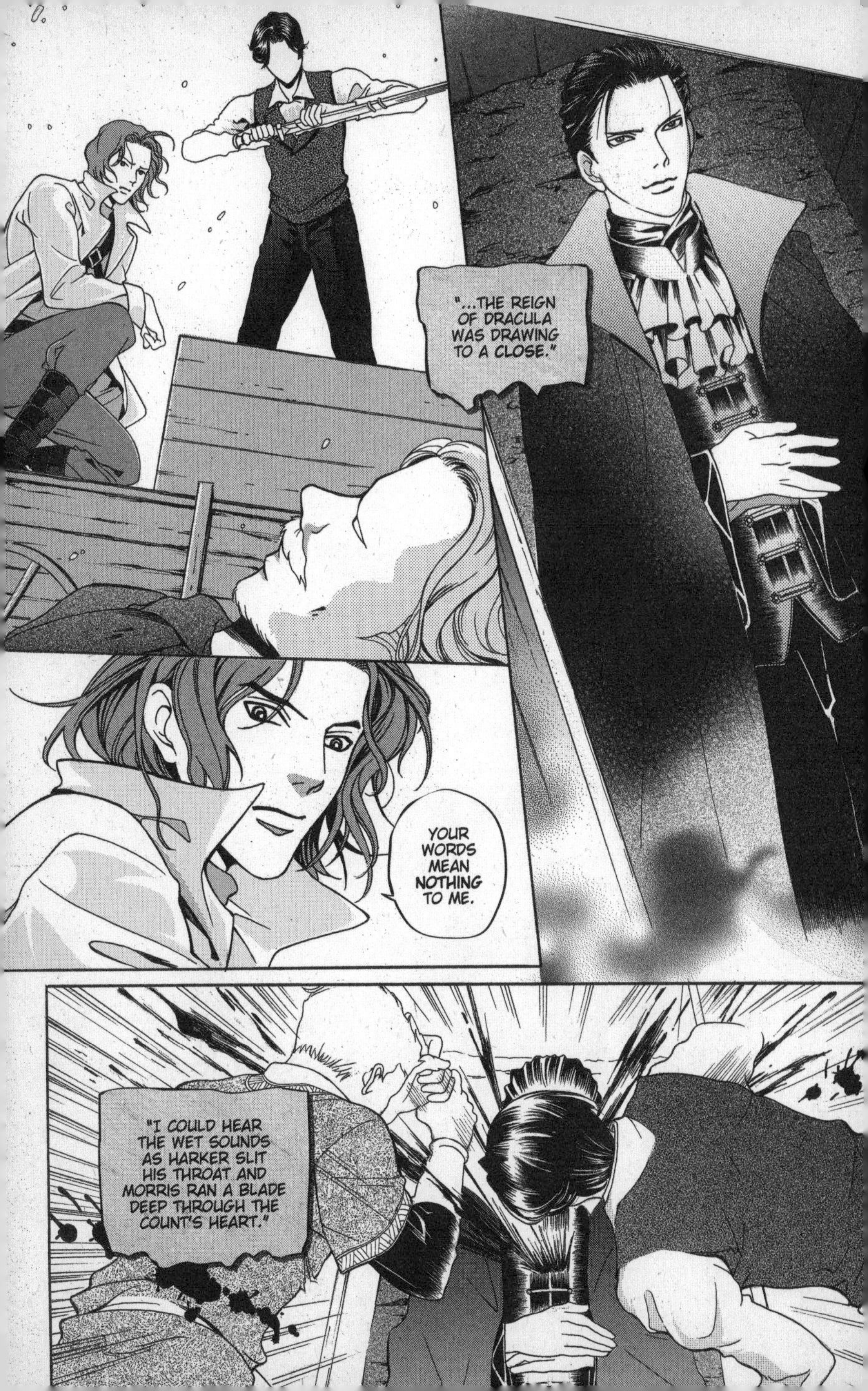
"...THE REIGN OF DRACULA WAS DRAWING TO A CLOSE."
YOUR WORDS MEAN NOTHING TO ME.
"I COULD HEAR THE WET SOUNDS AS HARKER SLIT HIS THROAT AND MORRIS RAN A BLADE DEEP THROUGH THE COUNT'S HEART."

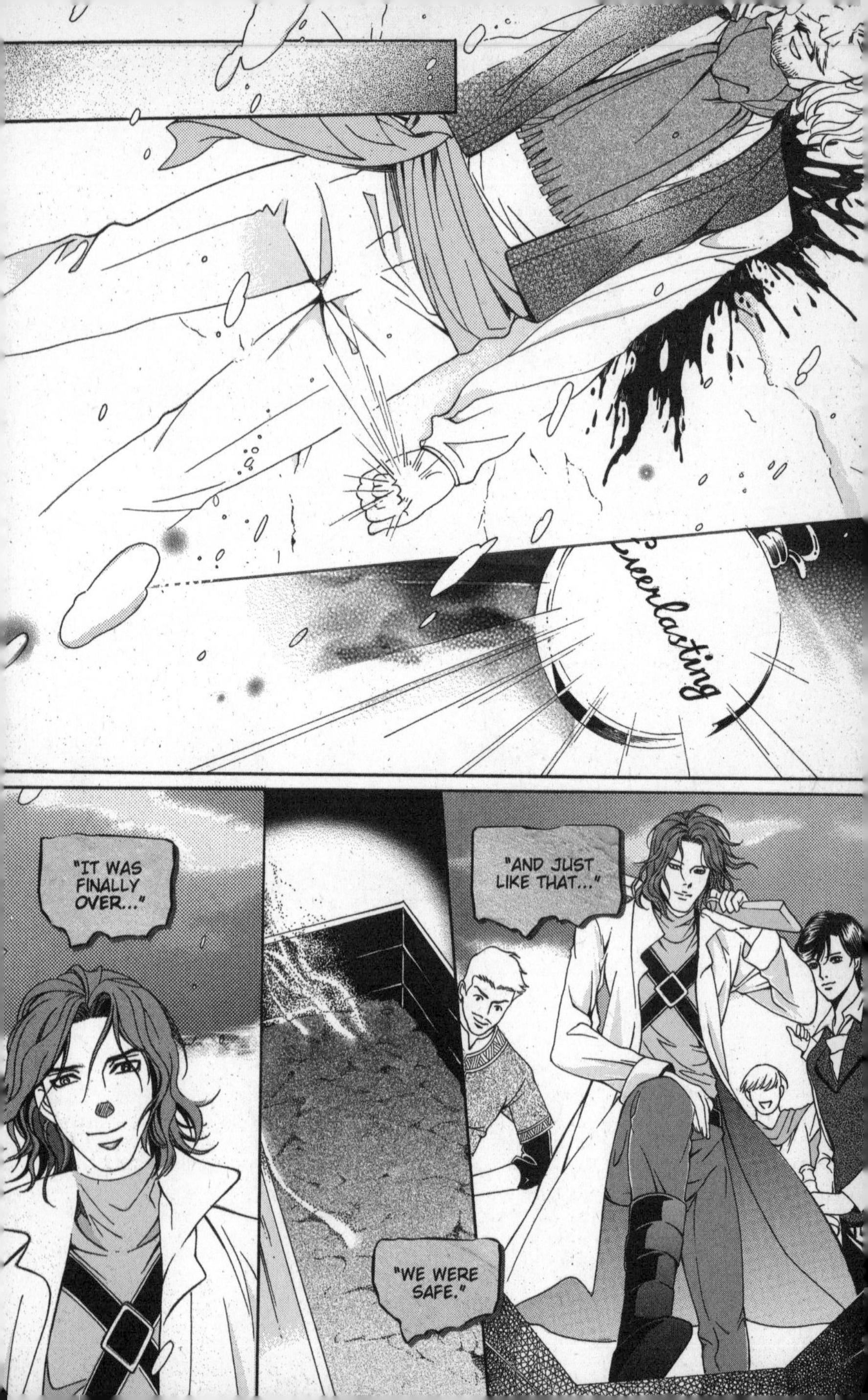
Everlasting
"IT WAS FINALLY OVER..."
"AND JUST LIKE THAT..."
"WE WERE SAFE."

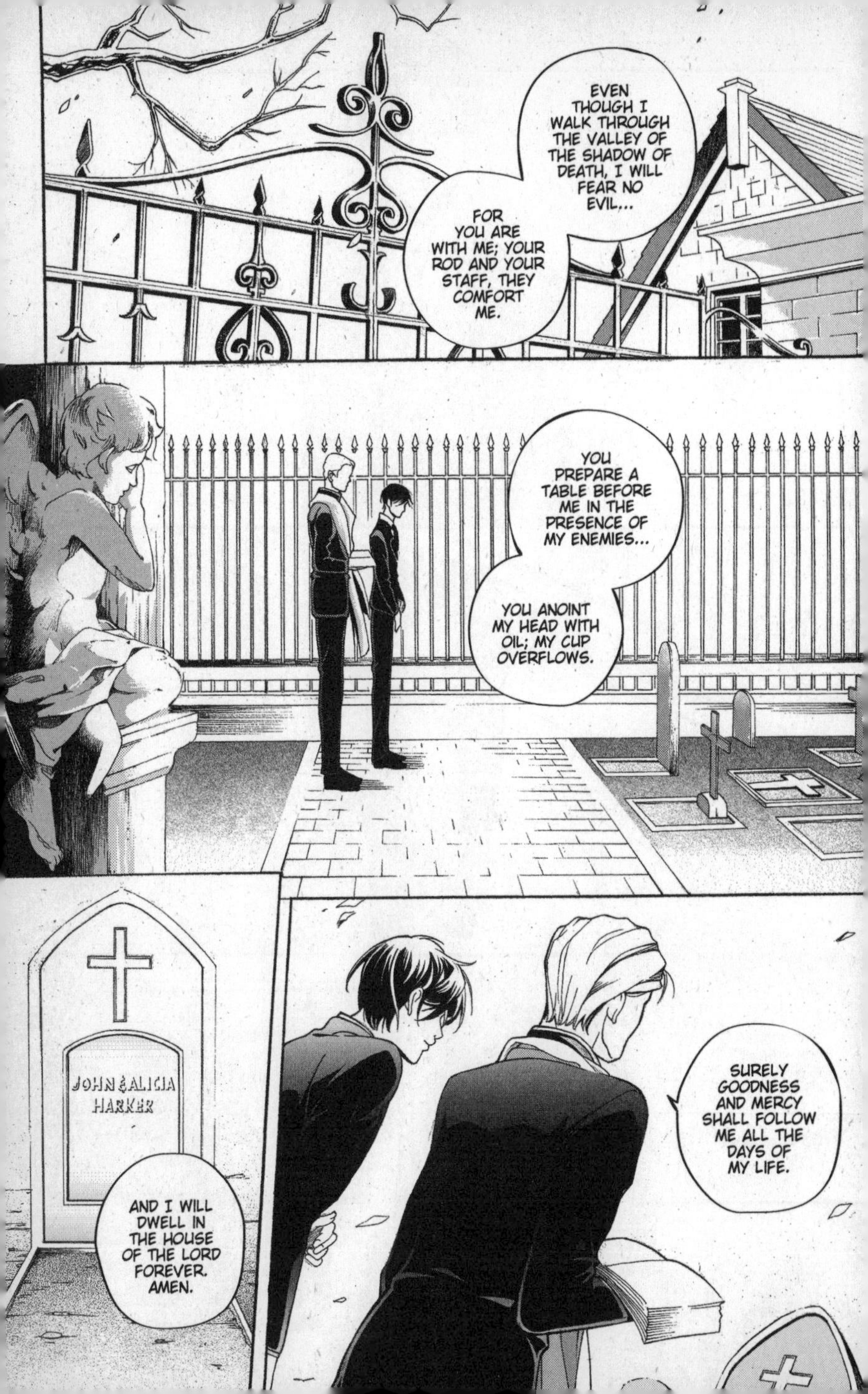
EVEN THOUGH I WALK THROUGH THE VALLEY OF THE SHADOW OF DEATH, I WILL FEAR NO EVIL...
FOR YOU ARE WITH ME; YOUR ROD AND YOUR STAFF, THEY COMFORT ME.
YOU PREPARE A TABLE BEFORE ME IN THE PRESENCE OF MY ENEMIES...
YOU ANOINT MY HEAD WITH OIL; MY CUP OVERFLOWS.
SURELY GOODNESS AND MERCY SHALL FOLLOW ME ALL THE DAYS OF MY LIFE.
JOHN & ALICIA HARKER
AND I WILL DWELL IN THE HOUSE OF THE LORD FOREVER. AMEN.

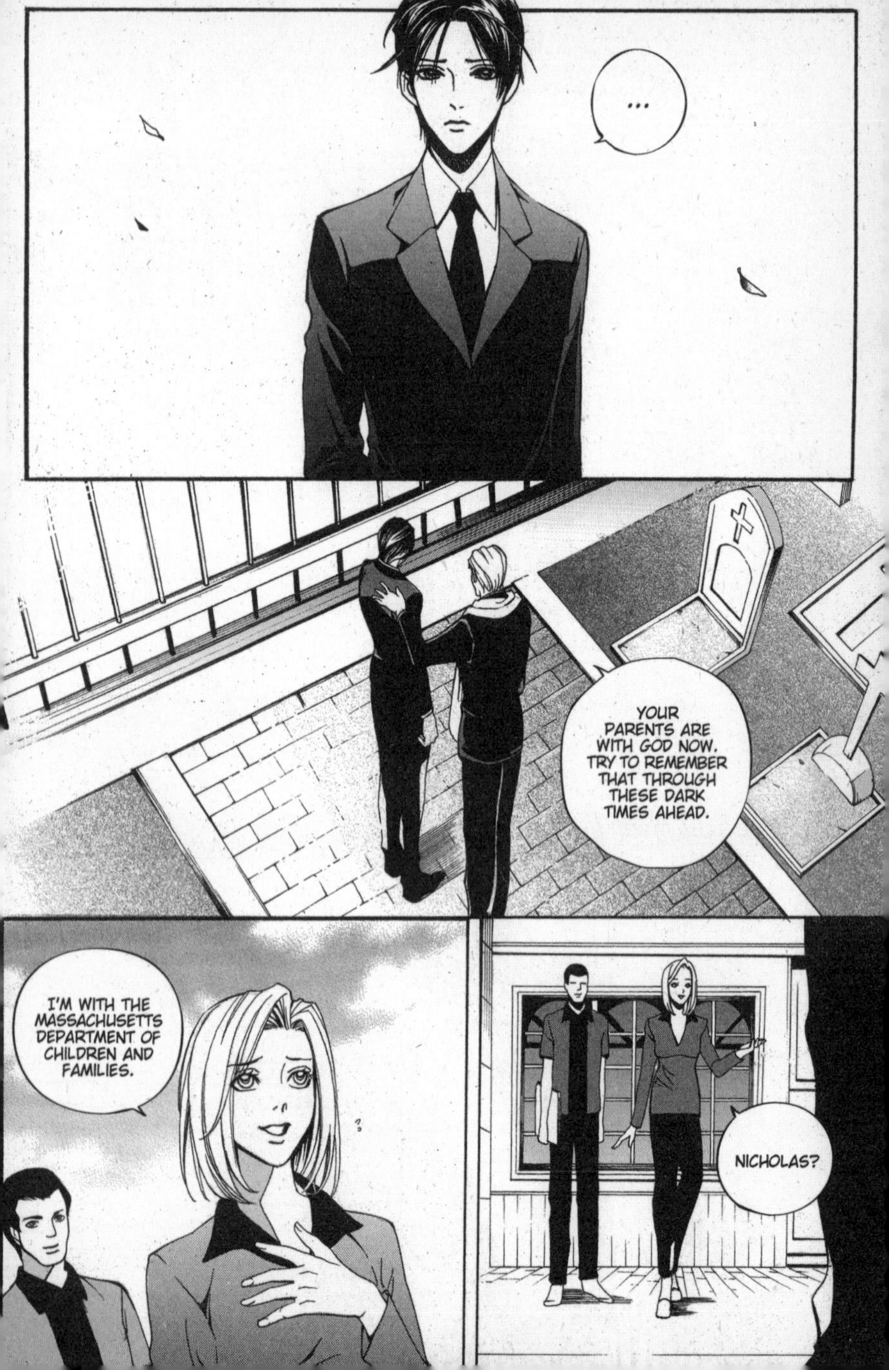
...
YOUR PARENTS ARE WITH GOD NOW. TRY TO REMEMBER THAT THROUGH THESE DARK TIMES AHEAD.
NICHOLAS?
I'M WITH THE MASSACHUSETTS DEPARTMENT OF CHILDREN AND FAMILIES.

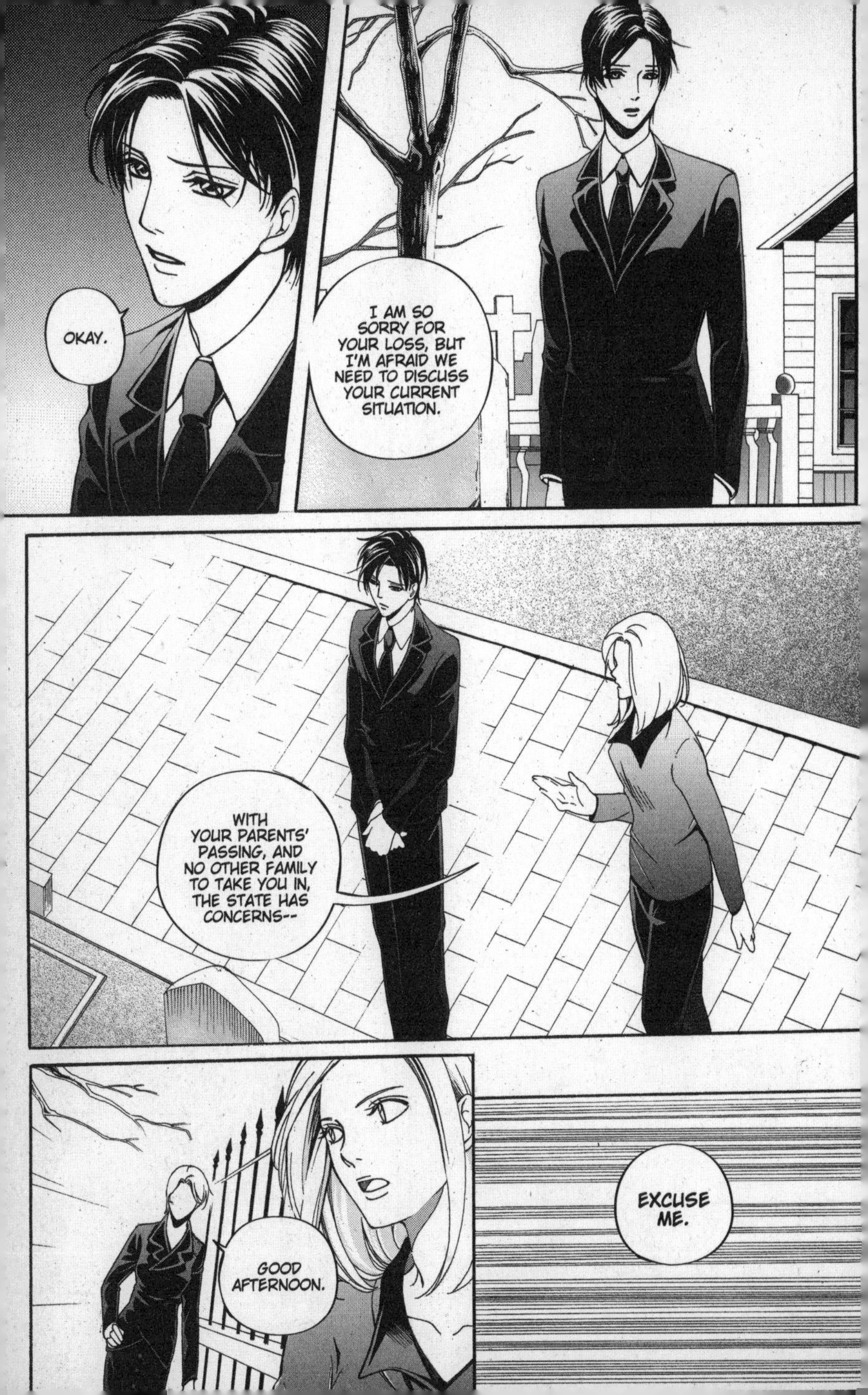
I AM SO SORRY FOR YOUR LOSS, BUT I'M AFRAID WE NEED TO DISCUSS YOUR CURRENT SITUATION.
OKAY.
WITH YOUR PARENTS' PASSING, AND NO OTHER FAMILY TO TAKE YOU IN, THE STATE HAS CONCERNS--
EXCUSE ME.
GOOD AFTERNOON.

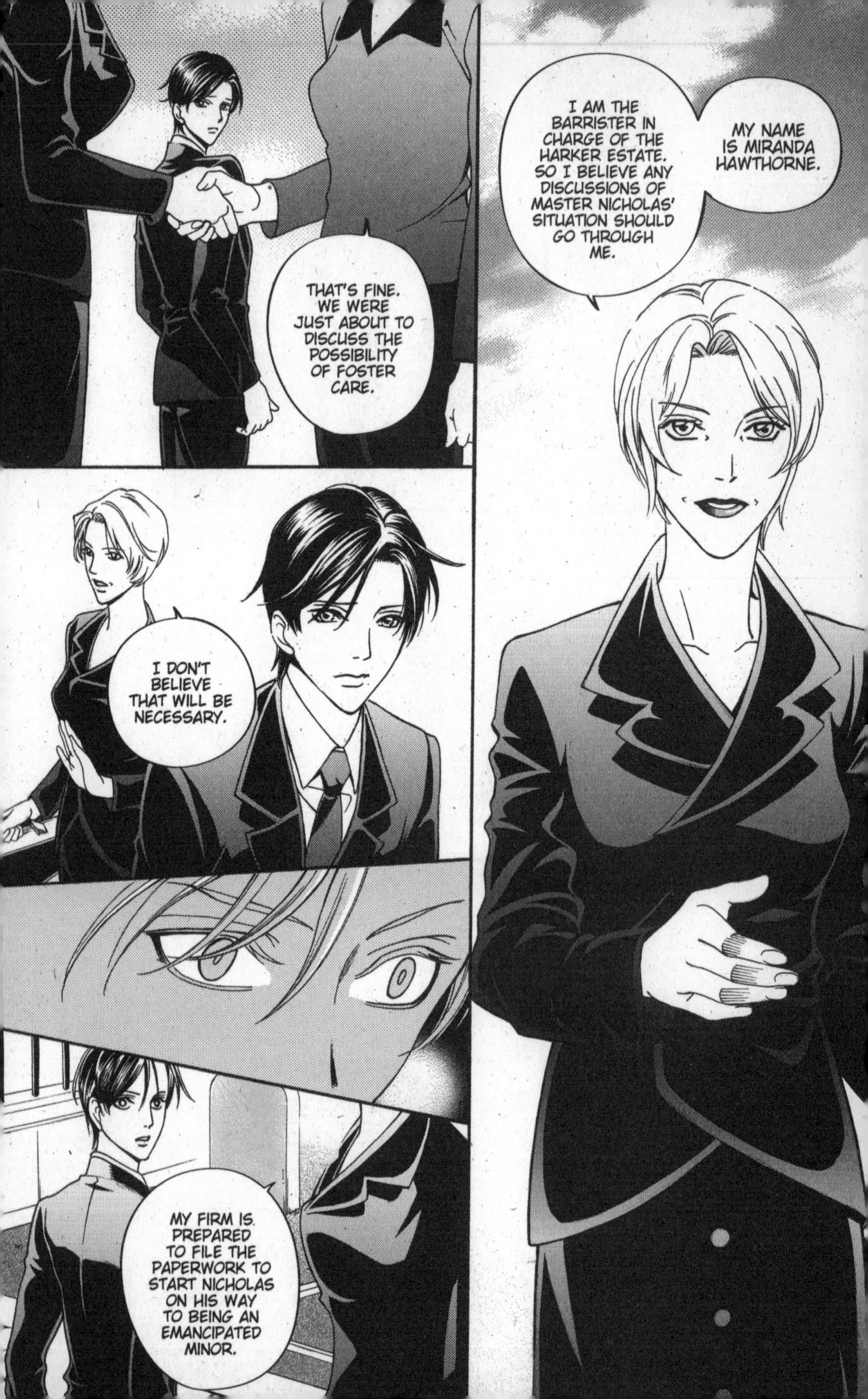
MY NAME IS MIRANDA HAWTHORNE.
I AM THE BARRISTER IN CHARGE OF THE HARKER ESTATE. SO I BELIEVE ANY DISCUSSIONS OF MASTER NICHOLAS' SITUATION SHOULD GO THROUGH ME.
THAT'S FINE. WE WERE JUST ABOUT TO DISCUSS THE POSSIBILITY OF FOSTER CARE.
I DON'T BELIEVE THAT WILL BE NECESSARY.
MY FIRM IS PREPARED TO FILE THE PAPERWORK TO START NICHOLAS ON HIS WAY TO BEING AN EMANCIPATED MINOR.

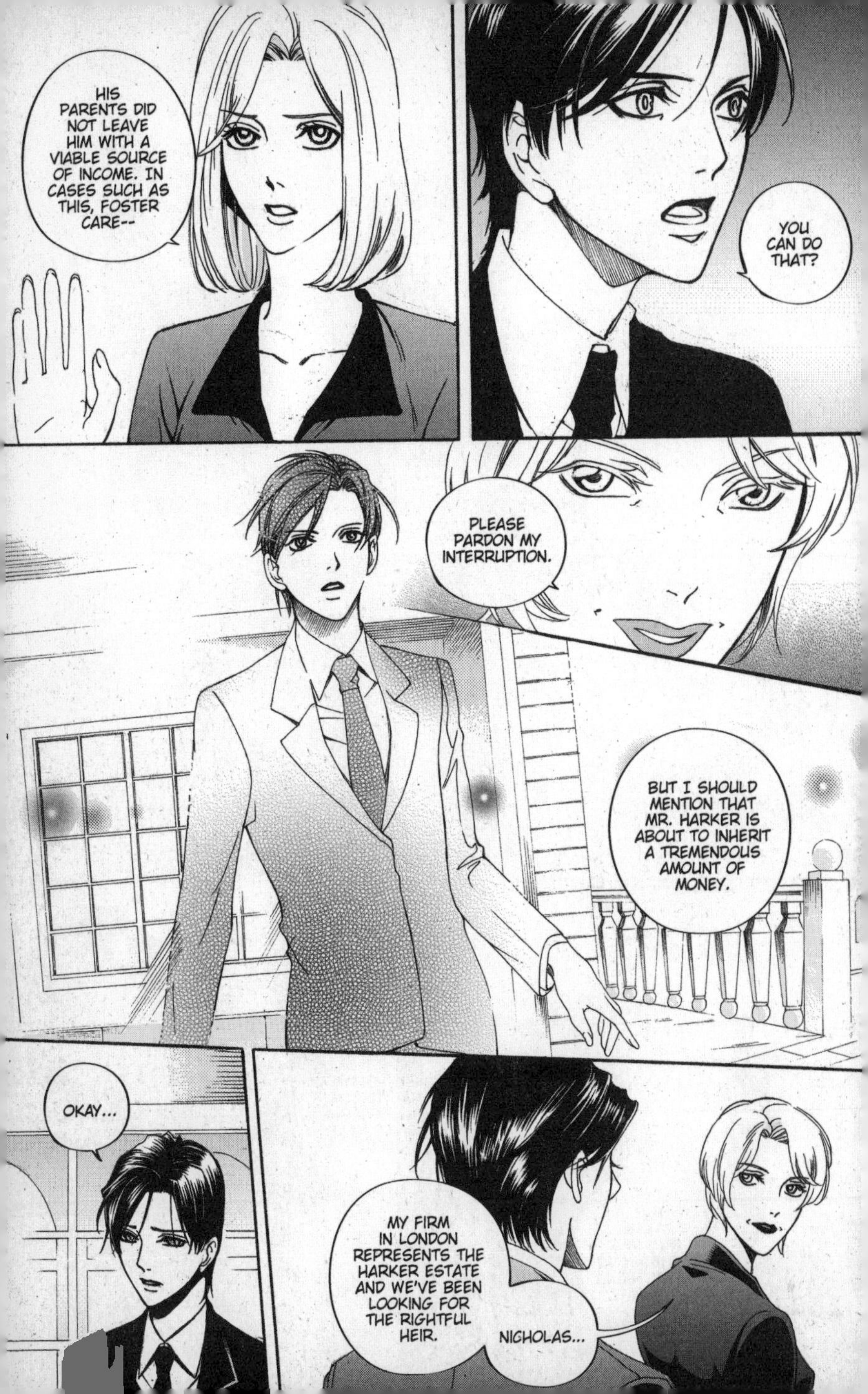
HIS PARENTS DID NOT LEAVE HIM WITH A VIABLE SOURCE OF INCOME. IN CASES SUCH AS THIS, FOSTER CARE--
YOU CAN DO THAT?
PLEASE PARDON MY INTERRUPTION.
BUT I SHOULD MENTION THAT MR. HARKER IS ABOUT TO INHERIT A TREMENDOUS AMOUNT OF MONEY.
OKAY...
MY FIRM IN LONDON REPRESENTS THE HARKER ESTATE AND WE'VE BEEN LOOKING FOR THE RIGHTFUL HEIR.
NICHOLAS...

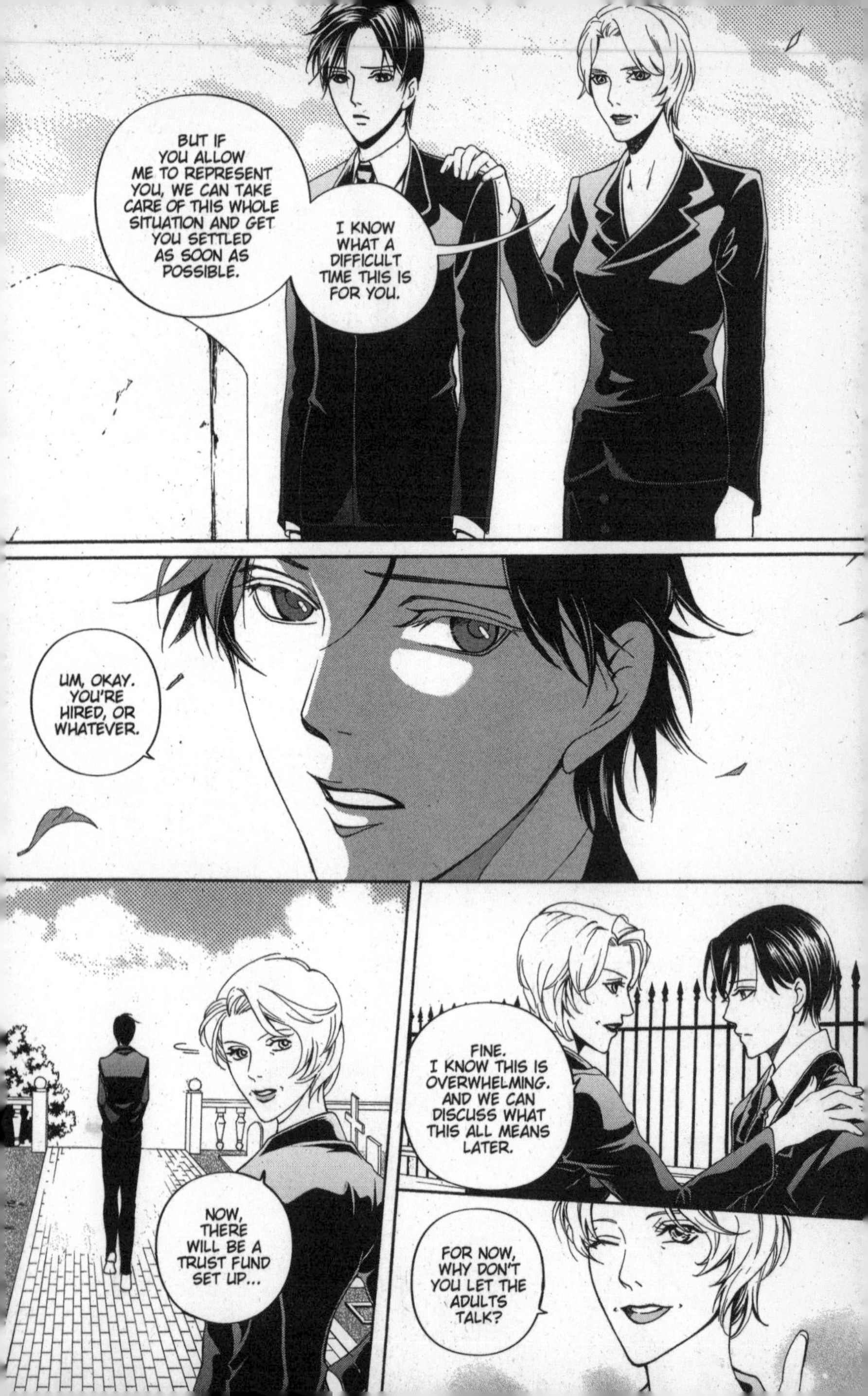
I KNOW WHAT A DIFFICULT TIME THIS IS FOR YOU.
BUT IF YOU ALLOW ME TO REPRESENT YOU, WE CAN TAKE CARE OF THIS WHOLE SITUATION AND GET YOU SETTLED AS SOON AS POSSIBLE.
UM, OKAY. YOU'RE HIRED, OR WHATEVER.
FINE. I KNOW THIS IS OVERWHELMING. AND WE CAN DISCUSS WHAT THIS ALL MEANS LATER.
FOR NOW, WHY DON'T YOU LET THE ADULTS TALK?
NOW, THERE WILL BE A TRUST FUND SET UP...

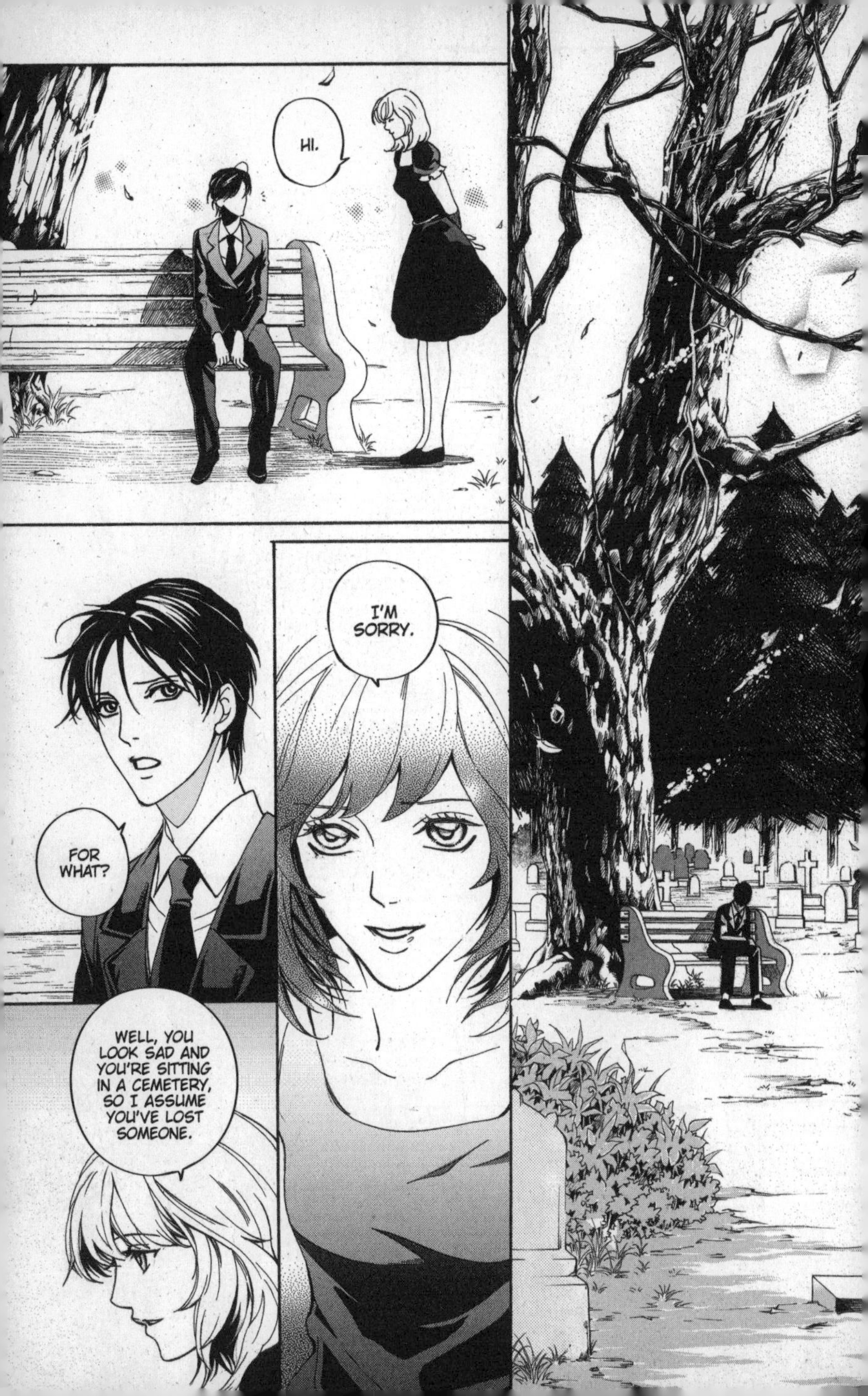
HI.
I'M SORRY.
FOR WHAT?
WELL, YOU LOOK SAD AND YOU'RE SITTING IN A CEMETERY, SO I ASSUME YOU'VE LOST SOMEONE.

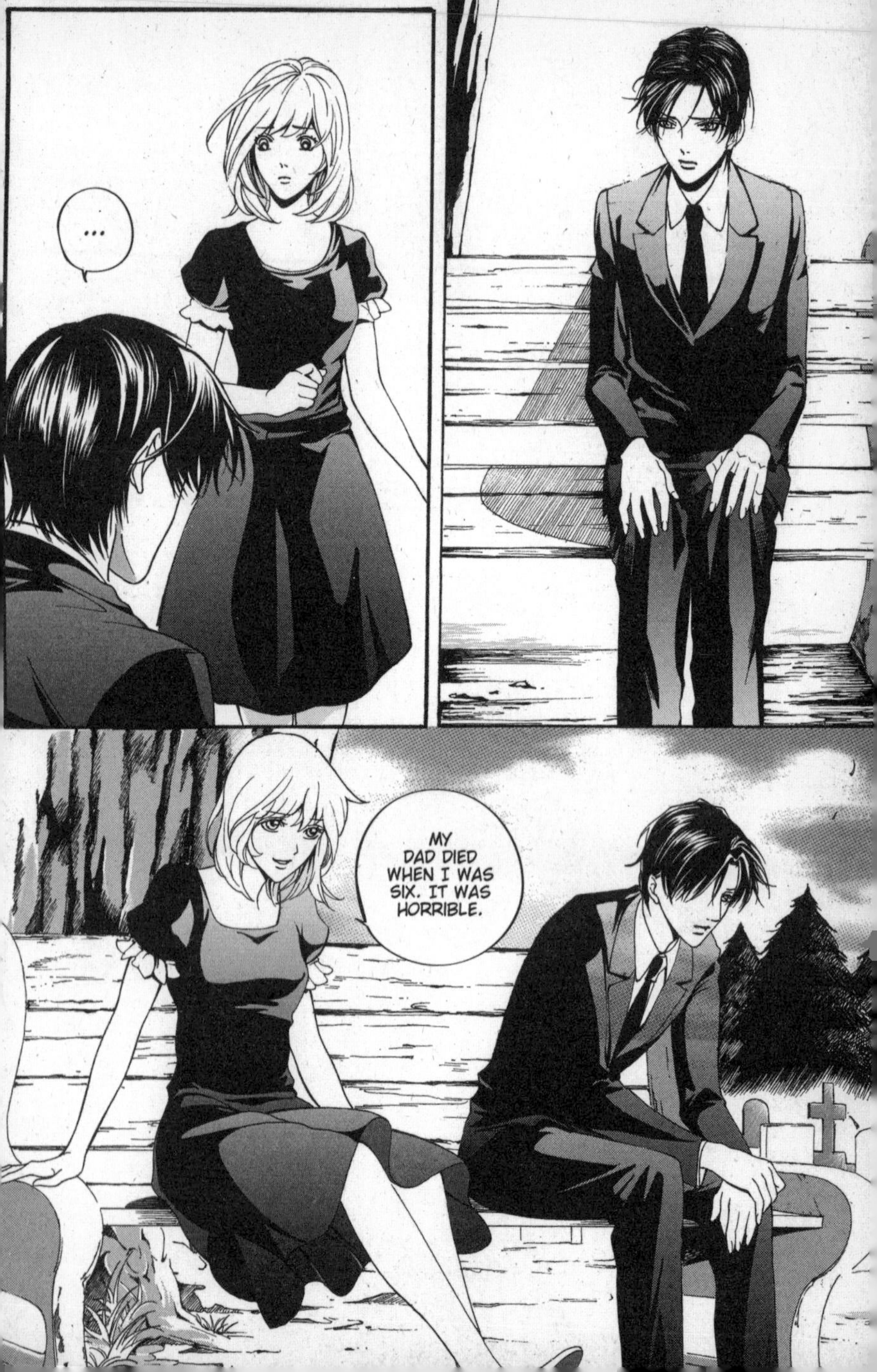
...
MY DAD DIED WHEN I WAS SIX. IT WAS HORRIBLE.

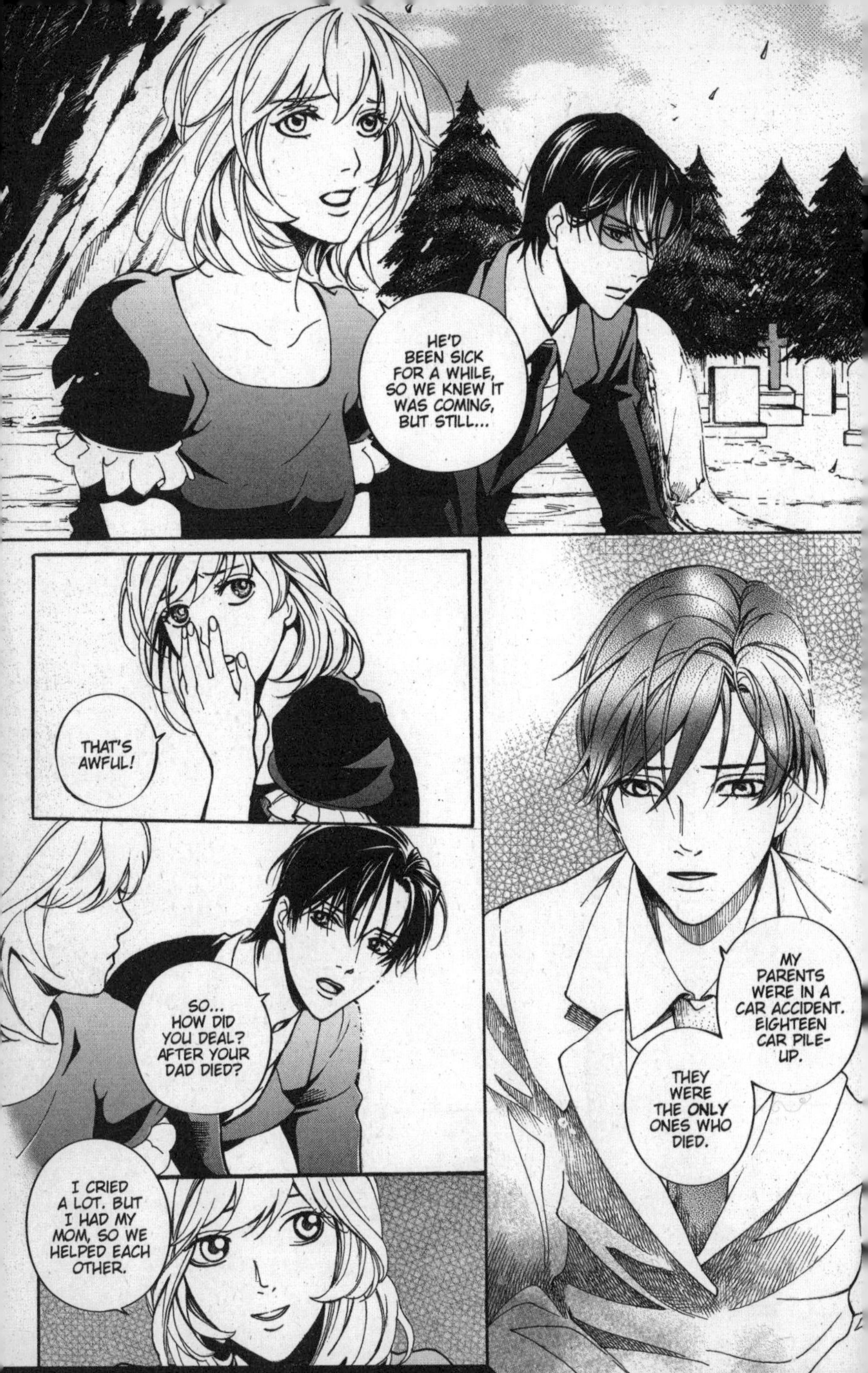
HE'D BEEN SICK FOR A WHILE, SO WE KNEW IT WAS COMING, BUT STILL...
THAT'S AWFUL!
SO... HOW DID YOU DEAL? AFTER YOUR DAD DIED?
I CRIED A LOT. BUT I HAD MY MOM, SO WE HELPED EACH OTHER.
MY PARENTS WERE IN A CAR ACCIDENT. EIGHTEEN CAR PILE-UP.
THEY WERE THE ONLY ONES WHO DIED.

Continued in Dracula Everlasting Vol. 1